Published by the Abertay Historical Society in association with
the University of Dundee Museum Services, 2015

ISBN: 978-0-900019-56-2

Text © Matthew Jarron

The Abertay Historical Society was founded in May 1947 and exists to promote
interest in local history. For membership forms and further information, please
visit our website at **www.abertay.org.uk**

Frontispiece: Invitation by John Duncan and Richard D Winter, 1891
(courtesy of the family archives of the Henry Taylor Wyse estate).

Fonts;
Paragraphs, Bodoni 10pt
Paragraph Headers, Bodoni Old Style 15pt

Printed by W&G Baird

Stock: Bright White 130gsm

Contents

Acknowledgements   3

Introduction – The Florence of Scotland?   4

Chapter One – Public Display of Private Wealth   8

Chapter Two – Collections & Commissions   32

Chapter Three – Decorative Art & the Celtic Revival   48

Chapter Four – Artists at Work   92

Chapter Five – Art & Journalism   125

Chapter Six – Art & Education   142

Chapter Seven – Art & Science   160

Chapter Eight – Artists Together   172

Chapter Nine – The New Art Patrons   192

Endnotes   208

Index   225

Acknowledgements

As the publishers are all too aware, this book has been many years in the making, and to give individual thanks here to everyone who has aided me in its completion would be impossible. Most of them have been given acknowledgement at various points in the endnotes, but a few individuals and organisations deserve special mention here. The first is former curator of art at what is now The McManus: Dundee's Art Gallery & Museum, Clara Young. In 2004 she allowed me to co-curate the exhibition *The Artist & the Thinker: John Duncan & Patrick Geddes in Dundee*, which was really the start of this project – the exhibition gave rise to a conference on Art in Dundee c.1900 and the conference gave rise to a publication proposal, which ultimately became this book. Among the speakers at the conference was the art curator and historian Bill Hardie, who in 1968 became the museum's first specialist keeper of art. He did much to raise awareness of several of the city's artists from the turn of the century, most notably George Dutch Davidson, and his work deserves recognition here.

In helping me with my own research, I must thank first and foremost the staff at Dundee Central Library's Local History Centre, without whose extraordinary collections this story could not be told. I would also like to thank the staff at Dundee's Art Galleries & Museums, Dundee City Archives, the University of Dundee Archive Services, the Royal Scottish Academy and the National Galleries of Scotland, as well as the committee of Dundee Art Society. Many individuals were also particularly helpful in providing both information and encouragement, among them Jim Barnes, Elizabeth Cumming, Nicola Ireland, Susan Keracher, Lesley Lindsay, Ann Prescott, Claire Robinson and Helen Smailes. Particular thanks are due to Kenneth Baxter, Anna Robertson and Sarah Easterby-Smith for reading some or all of the text and providing invaluable feedback on it.

Many organisations provided images for the book, but I would especially like to thank those who generously agreed to waive all reproduction and image supply fees: DC Thomson & Co Ltd, Dundee Art Society, Dundee City Archives, Dundee Heritage Trust, University of Dundee Archive Services, University of Dundee Museum Services, Aberdeen Art Gallery, University of Aberdeen Museums, Angus Council Museums, the Black Watch Museum, Calton Gallery, the Art Institute of Chicago, Christ's Hospital Foundation, Dumfries & Galloway Museums, Lyon & Turnbull, Paisley Museum, Paisley Art Institute, Special Collections at the University of St Andrews Library, the Museum of the University of St Andrews, Sotheby's, University of Strathclyde Library Department of Archives & Special Collections and various private collections.

Lastly, I give particular thanks to Andy Rice for his excellent layout and design work, and the DC Thomson Charitable Trust, the PF Charitable Trust, the R J Larg Family Trust, the Alexander Moncur Trust and the Tay Charitable Trust who generously provided grants to assist the publication costs.

INTRODUCTION
The Florence of Scotland?

"Well-nigh a generation ago there began to
arise a not inconsiderable art movement in
Dundee. To a Public Library and Museum
was added a Picture Gallery, which by and
by had to be enlarged; and their capable and
enthusiastic organiser… greatly daring, began
a series of picture exhibitions. This was the
golden age; with new factories and new big
houses going up everywhere, and more space
and ease even in a good many older ones;
so the pictures sold well; new ones came in
accordingly, and went off in their turn, till the
sales and shows were second to none out of
London itself."
Patrick Geddes, 1907[1]

Writing here for the *Dundee Advertiser*, Patrick Geddes
was describing the extraordinary artistic renaissance that
Dundee had undergone in the late 19th century. Geddes
had come to the city in 1888 to take up the Chair of Botany
at University College, but quickly extended his interests into
helping to foster Dundee's burgeoning art culture. His chief
artistic protégé was the painter John Duncan, who also spoke
about this artistic development in the city. At an address given
in 1911, he claimed that by the last decade of the previous
century,

"Dundee had had a run of fine Exhibitions
that were equal to anything outside London.
The most distinguished works by the most
distinguished artists had been ours to love and
live with. The best artists of the country were
coming and going amongst us, the guests of
our merchant princes; and the fame of Dundee
as an art centre was spread far and wide".[2]

This fame was certainly apparent in the wider art world –
in 1890, when the Dundee Graphic Arts Association (GAA)
was founded, many of Scotland's most notable artists wrote
to express their opinions in the most enthusiastic terms. John
Pettie claimed that "Dundee has been and is one of the art
centres of the North". William Hole described the "energy,
enterprise and artistic appreciation of Dundee," and William
Darling McKay concluded that Dundee was "perhaps the most
vital centre of art appreciation in Scotland."[3]

This was no fleeting interest – thirty years later, similar
claims were still being made. The Scottish Colourist G
L Hunter wrote in 1923: "After France, Scotland for
appreciation of painting, but indeed to talk modern art one has
to go from Glasgow to Dundee which seems to become what
Florence was to Rome."[4]

Here in the early 21st century, the city has once again
established a reputation for the vibrancy of its art and design
culture, but there is a tendency to assume that this is all a
recent development. The aim of this book is to chart Dundee's
first artistic golden age, which remains relatively unknown and
under-appreciated. Little attention has been paid to Dundee in
the standard histories of Scottish art, and at the same time most
histories of Dundee pay little attention to art.[5]

The starting point for this period is clear – while many
wealthy Dundonians began building up notable art collections
in the 1850s, it was the British Association exhibition of 1867
that provided the first public showing of that hitherto private
passion, and acted as the most important catalyst in the cultural
development of the town.

Over the next few decades, three factors in particular
combined to provide a unique stimulus to Dundee's artistic
creativity. Firstly a growing business and commercial
class eager to express its cultural awareness through the
appreciation of art, along with a sizeable artisan class inspired
by the contemporary Arts & Crafts ideals of art and decoration
for all. Secondly an impressive new museum and art gallery
hosting major exhibitions featuring some of the finest art to be
seen anywhere in Britain. And thirdly, the ready availability of
art education for students of all classes, with various bursaries
available for those who had hitherto been unable to afford such
education.

It should be no surprise then that the number of
professional artists recorded as working in the city rocketed,
from four in 1875 to 23 by 1895.[6] For the first time artists
were able to organise themselves collectively, the Dundee Art
Club being formed in 1880, replaced a decade later by the
more professional GAA. This gave artists the clout to organise
their own exhibitions, life classes and fund-raising events,
set up an Art Union and even create shared studio facilities
of the sort that would seem revolutionary when re-invented
in Dundee eight decades later.[7] Many of these artists were
unexceptional, but several were outstanding. David Foggie
painted portraits of working men and women with unrivalled
clarity and humanity; W B Lamond made vigorous landscapes
and seascapes that beautifully captured the blustery Angus
coastline; and Frank Laing was an etcher of great sensitivity
and Whistlerian freedom of line.

In particular, Dundee established for the first time an
artistic style of its own thanks in part to the influence of Geddes
on a number of artists who embraced his ideas of a Celtic
Revival in art and design. John Duncan, Stewart Carmichael,
Alec Grieve and George Dutch Davidson were the leaders of
this movement, creating richly decorated historical, mythical
or symbolic scenes, while Celtic motifs quickly found their way
into the rapidly growing field of applied art.

Dundee's reputation as an art centre, however, was not
necessarily reflected on these and other artists attempting
to make their living in the city, who often had to face harsh
criticism from their public. One writer to the *Piper o' Dundee*
magazine complained that "the little people of the Graphic Arts
cliques take themselves too seriously. After all, the majority
are merely dilettantes, and their affairs ought only to be
treated as the efforts of amateurs."[8] The local press was always
happy to support those artists working along conventional
lines, but showed far less enthusiasm for those whose work
demonstrated what one critic called "a tinge of precocity".[9]
However much success Dundee's artists enjoyed at exhibitions
in Glasgow, Edinburgh, London or Paris, the home crowd was

always their toughest audience. It was no doubt from bitter experience that Stewart Carmichael, in lecturing to the GAA on 'The Relation of the Artist to the Public', "considered the public lacking in the proper support and appreciation of the true artist" and concluded (perhaps more pragmatically than idealistically) that "the artist untrammelled by public taste and public opinion, and left free to express himself in his own manner, was the artist who created the noblest works."[10]

Frank Laing, one of those whose work certainly enjoyed an international reputation, recognised the unusual situation in which Dundee's art culture existed: "at once an incurable and in the enjoyment of rude and robust health", and he described the relationship between the city's artists and its art world as being like "strange spectators gazing through the window of a baker's shop."[11] Carmichael later recalled that at the major Fine Art Exhibitions held in the Albert Institute, "Dundee artists were treated tolerably as a whole, sometimes generously to encourage us. The promoters of these Big Exhibitions were genuinely interested in paintings and purchased largely from outside artists. Seldom did a sale stir the heart however of the Dundee boys."[12]

Choosing an end point for this book was less straight-forward than for its beginning. By the 1890s art had become a significant part of the cultural life of Dundee, but the initial run of Fine Art Exhibitions ended in 1895 and many of the collectors who had organised them were dead by the end of the century. The tragic death of Dutch Davidson in 1901 at the age of just 21 also had a major impact on the city's artistic community, so there is an argument for claiming that this first golden age ended as the new century began. But a new generation of collectors soon emerged, as did new artists, and the Dundee Art Society (as the GAA was renamed in 1904) soon had more members than ever before. A new collective, the Tayport Artists' Circle, was formed, and art education was given a boost by the opening of a new and larger School of Art in the city, while a major bequest from James Duncan of Jordanstone in 1909 promised even greater things for the future. The Fine Art Exhibitions were revived and continued (with wartime interruptions) into the 1920s. The most impressive of these later shows was in 1924, and I have chosen that as a somewhat arbitrary end point, though one

1. Martin Anderson, 'A Modern Art Patron' from *The Wizard of the North*, 1883 *(Libraries, Leisure & Culture Dundee)*.

2. Charles S Mills, *Dundee from Tayport*, oil on canvas *(Dundee City Council: Dundee's Art Galleries & Museums)*

3. Edwin J Smith, Dundee Art Society Exhibition promotional design, 1906 *(Dundee City Archives)*.

The Council have decided to hold the Corporation Concerts in the Art Galleries.—We can foresee happenings.

Mrs Birse : " Impident hussy !
*I never was in here afore—
And ne'er again I'll cross the door.*"

4. George Dutch Davidson, *Celtic Illumination*, watercolour on vellum, 1899 *(Dundee City Council: Dundee's Art Galleries & Museums)*.

5. Joseph Lee, 'Impident Hussy!' from *The City Echo*, 1908. Even an ardent socialist like Lee was happy to mock the working class's attitudes to art *(University of Dundee Archive Services)*.

6. Opposite page: H G Low, 'An Artist's Dream' from *The Piper o' Dundee*, 1906. Pasted by Stewart Carmichael into his scrapbook, the main figure in this cartoon seems to be modelled on him *(Dundee City Archives)*.

could certainly argue that art culture in the 1930s was just as strong as in the previous decade – despite Stewart Carmichael boldly declaring to the press in 1934 that "Art appreciation in Dundee is dead."[13]

A recurring obsession that runs throughout the activities described here is money. As far as the city's professional artists were concerned, they never saw enough of it, and the success of their exhibitions was rarely expressed in terms of sales. They did, however, take every opportunity of grumbling about the lack of "practical encouragement given to the Artists"[14] and often made a point of mentioning sales figures in an attempt to embarrass their audience: "Sales only amounted to £25 9s, surely a miserable figure to represent the disbursement of Art Patrons in an exhibition such as was provided."[15]

By contrast, the large-scale Fine Art Exhibitions were repeatedly judged according to the total value of art sold – the larger the figure, the more important the exhibition (the peak being an extraordinary £8,605 in 1883). Despite lofty claims by the organisers about the improving value of art upon society, if the pictures on display weren't being bought by wealthy clients, the show was deemed a failure, regardless of the thousands of visitors that flocked to it. To a large extent, the art market in Dundee was determined by the fluctuating health of the jute industry, and most of the town's largest private collections were eventually sold off as the fortunes of their owners dwindled.

The big collectors could normally afford such losses, but for struggling artists it was another matter. In 1886 Dundee's leading portrait painter, Hugh Collins, wrote a begging letter to one of his patrons: "Artists are in a very trying position just now for want of money owing to the depressed times, and I am feeling it as much as anyone... Artists are <u>obliged</u> to solicit their patrons and friends just now, and to send pictures to Sale-rooms just now is no use."[16]

A similar pecuniary obsession was evident in the running of the city's cultural amenities, on which the Town Council were proud to boast about how little money they spent. In 1903, for example, they claimed that Dundee was the only city in Britain to run its libraries, museums and art galleries at a tax rate of just one penny (by that time in England the legal minimum was 1½ pence).[17] They also repeatedly informed citizens that the city's growing permanent art collection had been built up entirely though private donations and had cost the tax payer nothing. When the Albert Institute celebrated its golden jubilee in 1917, the curator A H Millar again expressed the quality of the art on display in financial terms: "The permanent collection now numbers over 350 pictures, which are valued at £37,420, while pictures on loan ... are insured for £3,875, making a total of £41,295."[18]

This book is not intended as a work of art criticism. I describe some of the art produced during the period but do not attempt to analyse it in depth. Rather this is an attempt to map the whole of the city's art culture at the time, from private collectors to public commissions and from newspaper cartoonists to symbolist painters.

Chapter one looks at the private collectors who kick-started the appreciation of art in Dundee. While the jute industry and its associated businesses made them wealthy, many came from

lower class backgrounds and had a passion for sharing their artistic interests with the public at large. To this end they organised the series of Fine Art Exhibitions mentioned above – the largest of their kind outside London. This chapter also looks at the businesses that grew up as a result of this success – art dealers, framers and private galleries.

The second chapter chronicles the development of Dundee's permanent collection of art at the Albert Institute – now The McManus: Dundee's Art Gallery & Museum, where many of the paintings acquired in these early years are still much-loved favourites in the galleries. Less often seen today is an art-form that was then wildly popular, the presentation portrait – money was raised by public subscription to capture the great and the good of Dundee on canvas, for subsequent display in the galleries. The chapter concludes by discussing the various statues erected in the town, most of which proved highly controversial at the time.

In chapter three we turn our attention to Dundee's most notable artistic movement, a combination of decorative art, symbolism and the Celtic Revival. The careers of Duncan, Carmichael, Grieve and Davidson will be covered in detail, along with a wider overview of decorative and Celtic art in the city. The political interests of the artists will also be addressed – many were outspoken about their socialist, nationalist or suffragist beliefs, though only some found means of expressing this in their art.

Chapter four covers the more conventional (though in many cases no less talented) artists working in Dundee at this time – portrait painters and sculptors; landscape and topographical artists. For the latter there were significant opportunities to

record the changing face of the town, especially for those artists commissioned by antiquarian A C Lamb for his monumental book *Dundee – Its Quaint and Historic Buildings* (1895). The chapter ends with a detailed look at the career of Dundee's most important realist painter, David Foggie.

In the late 19th century, Dundee was rapidly establishing itself as a major centre for journalism, thanks to the newspaper empires of Leng and Thomson. Long before *The Beano* and *The Dandy* Dundee led the way in hiring artists to illustrate its papers. John Duncan began his career this way, as did the celebrated cartoonist Cynicus. Others, like Joseph Lee, would spend their entire careers in journalism. Chapter five looks at their contribution to commercial art in Dundee, and their exceptional success in London and further afield.

The growth of professional art in Dundee could not have occurred without a parallel development in art education. Chapter six tells the story of Dundee's first School of Art, based at the High School. It describes some of the many smaller art schools that sprang up as a result of that success, and charts the early development of what is now Duncan of Jordanstone College of Art & Design.

Although it only briefly taught art, University College, Dundee (now the University of Dundee) boasted a number of talented professors in its early years who combined an interest in science and art, most notably D'Arcy Thompson and Patrick Geddes. Chapter seven will look at their interdisciplinary interests, and the influence that their work had in some unexpected places.

It was only through working collectively that Dundee's artists could maximise their impact. Chapter eight examines their various attempts at grouping together in formal or informal organisations – the Dundee Art Club, the Tayport Artists' Circle and most notably the GAA. Every major Dundee artist (along with numerous minor ones) belonged to one or more of these bodies, but did not always agree about what they should be doing.

The final chapter concludes the story of art collecting and exhibiting begun in the first two. In the early 20th century a new generation of art patrons emerged in Dundee, who set their artistic sights further afield than before. As a result, the city's painters were now showing their work alongside that of Van Gogh and Matisse, while concerted efforts were made to revive the Fine Art Exhibitions of the previous century.

Dundee's story was not unique – similar developments took place in other industrial and commercial cities such as Leeds and Liverpool, and to a lesser extent in Scottish manufacturing towns such as Paisley and Kirkcaldy. But for its relative size, Dundee (then as now) punched well above its weight where art was concerned. More research is still needed in order to explore fully the extraordinary richness of this artistic culture, and I hope this book can act as a starting point for future investigation by others.

7. The Albert Institute before its various extensions, c.1867. Photograph by James Valentine *(Libraries, Leisure & Culture Dundee)*.

"There seems, then, little doubt that, to the community at large, a pictorial exhibition would be hailed as a very great boon... In pictures, the commonest mind can find a great deal to amuse and entertain, and a good share of instruction. There is much refined enjoyment in tracing on the canvas the pleasing play of the painters' fancy as expressed in the attitudes of his figures, and the expression of his faces. The eye drinks in with delighted rapture the glow of sportive colour, and the mellow tints of a heavenly sun-set. For hours an imaginative mind may revel in a picture gallery. Here it may enjoy a banquet graced by smiling beauty; there a touching scene of emotion. This picture may move our hearts to gladness, that one to sadness. In one frame we may find a pleasant companion; in another, a mentor, who, in deep and serious tones, tells us a lesson pregnant with profound wisdom. A picture, it has been well said, is sometimes religion, sometimes philosophy, sometimes history, sometimes poetry. It is great by virtue of its humanity; it is noble, because it ennobles whatever it touches; it is part of our civilisation, because it embodies those heroic deeds which make up the greatness of the times in which we glory."
Dundee Courier & Argus 26/5/1864

Chapter One
Public Display of Private Wealth

"I like the memory of those early days when the 'picture people' as we were called, lived in a kind of brotherhood, visiting each other's houses and spending our evenings looking at pictures and talking about art and artists. In the course of time other men took to looking at pictures, got infected with the love of them and soon a goodly number of Dundonians became picture buyers."
T S Robertson, 1906[1]

At the start of the 19th century, the population of Dundee was around 23,000. It had a rapidly growing linen industry and a busy and profitable harbour. Some fine buildings had been erected in recent decades and there seems to have been a genuine sense of civic pride throughout the town. Intellectual debate and cultural ambition were both in evidence, and in 1824 the Watt Institution was founded to promote education in science and the arts. It opened a museum in 1838 and held what were probably Dundee's first regular public art exhibitions in the 1840s.[2] There were a few 'old masters' lent by the local aristocracy – particularly Lord Kinnaird and the Earl of Camperdown – but most of the works were portraits lent by their well-to-do subjects, many of whom were doctors and surgeons at the new Infirmary. The subjects of the pictures were evidently considered more important than the artists, whose names were often not listed in the catalogues. Of those that were given, a few represented local talent, such as Henry Harwood and John Stewart (see chapter four). Some were born in Dundee but had long since left, such as John Zephaniah Bell, whose portrait of surgeon John Crichton was shown in the 1843 exhibition and is now in the city's collection.

Before the 1850s art collecting was something that only a small number of wealthy individuals in Dundee pursued, and they were generally just adding to collections built up by their families over generations. Perhaps the most significant was that of local MP David Hunter of Blackness, whose collection boasted works by Giotto, Raphael, Titian, Brueghel, Rubens, Velasquez, Van Dyck and Rembrandt. To these Hunter added more recent works by Henry Raeburn, Alexander Nasmyth and John Phillip. A talented amateur painter himself, Hunter made the acquaintance of a number of artists, David Roberts in particular being a frequent visitor to Blackness House. In 1867 a published catalogue of his collection ran to two volumes.[3]

By 1851 the population of Dundee had more than tripled from half a century before and in the following 30 years would almost double again to reach 140,000 in 1881. Following a slump in the price of linen in 1836, the town's mill-owners had looked to a cheaper fibre and found it in jute. Existing mills were converted, new and bigger ones were built, and by the time the industry peaked some 40,000 people were employed in 125 mills. While the majority toiled in deplorable conditions for meagre wages, those who rose to the top became exceptionally wealthy – it was said there were more millionaires per square foot living in neighbouring Broughty Ferry than anywhere else in the world. And one of the principal ways for these men to spend their money was in purchasing works of art. This might seem surprising given that most of the so-called 'jute barons' were self-made men who had had little formal education and whose formative years must have been largely deprived of the kind of cultural experiences enjoyed by the likes of David Hunter. In 1895 the local magazine *The Wizard of the North* claimed that it was the result of "what seems to be a natural law... [M]en began, apparently in obedience to this irresistible impulse characteristic of prosperous civic life, to lay some of their unwonted wealth on the shrine of Art."[4] The more cynical commentators suggested that for these men buying art was merely a quick way to social respectability, involving little genuine appreciation. The artist W G Burn-Murdoch claimed in 1894 that the typical wealthy Dundonian "has no taste; he is a business man, and taste has not been in his line. This he admits without the least shame, so he goes to the picture dealer and the artistic upholsterer who keep art in stock. These have neither taste nor conscience... They dangle the clever things in gold frames from exhibitions over the walls".[5] But there is no doubt that many of these early collectors were sufficiently engaged with the art world to cultivate close relationships with some of the country's most significant artists, and some were quick to recognise the wider social and economic values of art. William Robertson, for example, claimed that "In a purely manufacturing town like Dundee it is of vital importance that love for and a knowledge of Art should be widely diffused, especially among the working classes... it is mainly on account of the want of this that foreign competition has been felt so keenly in recent years."[6]

It was precisely this belief that had led Prince Albert to hold the Great Exhibition of 1851, the profits of which were used to found the South Kensington Museum and a network of government-funded art schools around the country – of which Dundee School of Art was one (see chapter five). When Albert died in 1861, Dundee like many other places looked for a way to pay tribute. Its leading citizens, determined to demonstrate the town's increasing self-confidence and civic pride, aimed at nothing less than the largest Albert Memorial outside London. In 1862 a limited company was formed to raise funds for the erection of the Albert Institute of Art, Science & Literature. Designed by Britain's foremost Gothic Revival architect, Sir George Gilbert Scott, work on the building began in 1865. The main part (including the spectacular Albert Hall) was ready for use when the British Association for the Advancement of Science (BA) held its annual meeting in Dundee in 1867 (figure 7).

The development of the building, and the BA's forthcoming visit, provided the necessary fuel for those in Dundee who felt that art was being woefully neglected in the town. In 1864, the *Dundee Courier* published a lengthy exhortation on the benefits of displaying art exhibitions, using the 1843 Watt Institution exhibition as a model and carefully noting its economic benefits as well as its cultural ones:

"Day after day, and night after night, the Exhibition was crowded, and a very handsome pecuniary result was evolved from the enterprise… [T]he revival of such an

8. British Association organising committee, 1867. Photograph by Thomas Rodger. Standing left-right: T S Robertson, William Ritchie, J C Bell, Alexander Scott, James Henderson, J G Orchar, Lord Kinnaird. Sitting left-right: William Small, Patrick Anderson, Bishop Forbes, John Leng, G B Simpson, P G Walker *(Libraries, Leisure & Culture Dundee).*

exhibition would reap an even greater amount of public favour than was awarded to the one of 1843… Many of our most successful citizens have no doubt possessed themselves of many fine specimens of modern art, and would hardly refuse to lend them for a time, in order to contribute to the refined culture of their less affluent townsmen".[7]

As part of the BA event, therefore, it was decided that "an Exhibition of Art and Industry, on a scale larger than had been previously attempted in the town, should be undertaken."[8] Since the Albert Institute did not yet have galleries suitable to host it, the newly constructed Volunteer Drill Hall was used as the venue. In total the exhibition comprised 572 works of art along with a further 132 miscellaneous items such as furniture, natural history specimens and samples of local industry.[9] During the relatively brief period that the show was open (less than a month) it was seen by an astonishing 36,710 people. A report published after the event noted:

"Picture Galleries and Museums, Schools of Art and marbles and fine paintings are no substitutes for good government, but they go some way to prepare the way for good government by educating the taste of the people, by refining their manners and above all things, by increasing their self-respect, which in nations and individuals is such an important constituent element of progress and success."[10]

Before exploring the early exhibition of art in Dundee, it is worth looking in more detail at the men who made it all happen, for without them there would be no story to tell here. It was their shared interest in art, coupled with a competitive desire to increase their social status by showing off what they had purchased, which allowed these exhibitions to happen. Six of them formed the art committee for the BA exhibition – G B Simpson (convenor), William Ritchie, J C Bell, J G Orchar, A B Spence and P G Walker (see figure 8). The first two were business partners, and possible rivals when it came to collecting art. George Buchan Simpson was born in 1820 and William Ritchie in c.1818. Simpson went straight into the manufacturing business as a young apprentice at Dens works, while Ritchie (whose father was an army officer and therefore of rather higher social standing) began his career in a commercial house in London. He came to Dundee to work at William Boyack's mill in Ward Road, with such success that he bought the works from Boyack and entered into a partnership with Simpson which also took in works on Nelson Street and Lower Pleasance.[11] Although these mills were relatively small, their profits were huge, and both men took advantage of this to move into luxurious new homes and start buying art to decorate them.

At Seafield House in Broughty Ferry (the present site of Grove Academy), Simpson began on safe ground with old masters such as Holbein, Rubens, Bruegel and even a supposed Leonardo (*St Catherine*), but his interest turned increasingly to contemporary art. Not content simply to buy from exhibitions, Simpson communicated directly with many of the leading Scottish painters of the day, and much of their correspondence survives in a remarkable collection of 964 letters from the 1860s and 1870s held in the National Library of Scotland.[12] Of the various artists whose letters feature in the collection, the best represented are George Paul Chalmers, William McTaggart, Alexander Fraser the younger and William Fettes Douglas. As well as referring to their own works, the artists

9. Alexander Fraser, *A Glade in Cadzow Forest*, oil on canvas, 1862-3, owned by G B Simpson *(Scottish National Gallery)*.

10. Below: William Fettes Douglas, *The Spell*, oil on canvas, 1864, owned by G B Simpson *(Scottish National Gallery)*.

often give Simpson their opinions on each others'. The same day that McTaggart wrote to suggest that *Castles in the Sand* (aka *Enoch Arden*) "will turn out to be the best thing I have done by a long way", Chalmers also wrote to say that he had studied the painting twice and "I was delighted with it. I do believe it is the best thing he has done."[13] He even enclosed his own sketch of the composition, and under the weight of this two-pronged attack, Simpson bought the painting.

Dealing with Simpson could be a difficult business – he was eager to be part of the creative process, making detailed suggestions about composition which probably infuriated his artists. Concerning Simpson's commission *A Glade in Cadzow Forest* (figure 9), Alexander Fraser wrote as tactfully as he could:

"Your criticism I think on the whole correct … [but] about showing the stool of the cut tree, you must remember that they are cut quite flat with the ground and unless close under the eye are not observable, besides in a place carefully looked after like Cadzow forest the place a tree is cut from is carefully covered over with turf to hide all marks of the axe. Still if it will or would improve the picture the stump or rather stool should be shown and I shall do so yet if on second sights it seems advisable. I painted the whole picture as carefully as I could under fear of criticism".[14]

Nevertheless, Simpson enjoyed strong friendships with many of his artists, and seems to have had a particularly close relationship with G P Chalmers, whose apparently self-destructive mental illness drove many of his clients to abandon him. Helen Smailes claims that Simpson "showed a visionary forbearance towards Chalmers, acting as confidant, counsellor and father figure from the very beginning of their acquaintance".[15] He even seems to have begun work on a memoir of the artist.[16] Sadly, many of Simpson's attempts to commission Chalmers came to nothing, prompting him to resort to verse to express his frustration: "I've tried him with love, I've tried him with Money, I've tried him with 'Ginger', I've tried him with 'Honey', but all to no purpose, he'll have his own way".[17]

The results of Simpson's (and his artists') efforts was a collection of exceptional quality. "If things of beauty be joys for ever," said the *Dundee Advertiser*, "there are enough and to spare at Seafield to make all the art critics of Britain happy for the rest of their days."[18] After lending selected works to the Royal Scottish Academy (RSA), the BA exhibition represented Simpson's first chance to show off his acquisitions en masse. His 26 loans (more than any other collector), included McTaggart's *Enoch Arden* and the pair *Spring* (now National Gallery of Scotland) and *Autumn*; Fettes Douglas's masterpiece *The Spell* (figure 10) and *Dante Arranging his Friends in Inferno*; as well as works by Fraser, Chalmers, W Q Orchardson, Sam Bough and James Cassie.

William Ritchie, meanwhile, purchased the villa Elmslea on Perth Road to house his growing collection – to visit it "was in many respects a liberal education in the fine arts. From time to time it sheltered under its roof many of the most distinguished artists of the time"[19] Ritchie's tastes were very similar to those of Simpson – indeed at times he was clearly trying to match his rival. The year after Simpson had commissioned McTaggart to paint *Spring* and *Autumn*, Ritchie commissioned his own pair of childhood scenes, *A Day's Fishing: Morning* (figure 11) and *A Day's Fishing: Evening* (both now in the Fleming Collection). As well as several other McTaggarts, he also acquired works by Fraser and Fettes Douglas along with James Cassie, W F Vallance, E T Crawford, James Archer, David Farquharson, John Smart, John Cairns and many others. If the resulting collection was never quite as large and impressive as Simpson's, it certainly came close.

The partnership of Ritchie, Simpson & Co was dissolved in 1877. Simpson took over the Nelson Street and Lower Pleasance mills but struggled make them pay. Ritchie, like many in Dundee, began backing business ventures in America, but his investments proved disastrous. Both men had to give up their collecting activities, and it soon became apparent that the only way to cover their losses was to start selling. Simpson went first – in 1880 Chapman & Son in Edinburgh sold his "Valuable Collection of Modern Pictures" (129 lots) followed by his "Collection of Art Treasures" (china, silver etc – 877 lots). This was followed by a sale of his rare books in 1882 and two sales of his exceptional collection of coins and medals in 1882 and 1885. Simpson evidently found it impossible to live without some of his art treasures, and these later sales helped him to raise enough money to buy back some of the paintings he had been forced to sell, including *A Glade in Cadzow Forest* and *The Spell*. Their return was short-lived, however – further failed business ventures meant a second sale of "Valuable Objects of Art" at Dowell's in Edinburgh in 1886 – 734 lots of which 106 were paintings.[20] Although prices were good, Simpson was simply paying off his debts, and when he died in 1892 his entire assets were said to comprise ten shares in the Ferryport-on-Craig Gas Company, valued at £4/10.

Ritchie fared only marginally better. His collection was sold at Dowell's in 1885. The *Advertiser* reported: "There was a large attendance of bidders, and in many cases there was spirited competition. The collection was much admired, and notwithstanding the present depression of trade the bulk of the better class of pictures were competed for, and fair prices were realised. The minor pictures did not sell so well."[21] Significantly, many other Dundee collectors were present, and "contributed largely to the success of the sale." The McTaggarts fetched by far the highest prices, including £115/10 each for the *Day's Fishing* pair and £120/15 for *The Murmur of the Shell* (the latter bought by John Simpson of Tayport). Although the bulk of his collection was gone (and for less money than he might have hoped), Ritchie managed to retain most of his books and antiques and continued to be an active member of the organising committee of the Dundee Fine Art Exhibitions – indeed the *Advertiser* claimed that "of all the members of the Committee it was he who came most into contact with the prominent painters and sculptors who

11. William McTaggart, *A Day's Fishing: Morning*, oil on canvas, 1865, owned by William Ritchie (© *The Fleming Wyfold Art Foundation / Bridgman Images*).

12. Opposite page: George Paul Chalmers, *John Charles Bell*, oil on canvas, 1875 (*Dundee City Council: Dundee's Art Galleries & Museums*).

sent their works to the city."[22] Following his death in 1902, the remains of his collection of art, antiques and books was sold at the Dundee Auction Rooms, but there were few paintings left to sell.[23]

In turning their interests towards art, Ritchie and Simpson followed the lead of John Charles Bell. As the *Wizard of the North* recognised, "If not absolutely the earliest of these devotees [of art], Mr Bell was the first conspicuous one – he certainly was the first discriminating worshipper who added knowledge to zeal."[24] Bell was born in 1816 in Berwick-upon-Tweed, moving to Ferryport-on-Craig (now Tayport) with his father in 1831. He earned success as a merchant and auctioneer, but "never indulged in the modern habit of luxurious and ostentatious living, and so, spending little on himself, had relatively speaking much to bestow upon art... To him art was a divine mistress, and the ardent love he gave her in early youth increased in fervour and constancy throughout a life which all but attained fourscore years."[25] Bell began collecting around 1850, shortly before the significant flourishing of Scottish art that came through the success (largely in London) of artists such as John Pettie, James Archer, W Q Orchardson, Hugh Cameron and Noel Paton. As the *Wizard* noted: "Mr Bell was among the first in Scotland to realise the full importance of this new manifestation, he became one of its most liberal patrons, and the warm friend of most of its talented members... [H]e was so warmly liked as a friend that artists strove to give him the very cream of their works."[26]

Certainly Bell seems to have been an easier patron for most artists to deal with than Simpson, and they often let the latter know it! "Bell seemed very pleased with our show this year" wrote Alexander Fraser after Simpson had complained that he was concentrating too much on landscapes for the RSA exhibition instead of working on the interior scene Simpson had commissioned. "And Bell let me tell you between ourselves *knows what's what*".[27] Plain speaking was evidently one of Bell's qualities: "He was not fluent of speech, and so never glibly talked that art jargon which repels possible admirers."[28]

To decorate the walls of his new home at 4 Douglas Terrace in Broughty Ferry, Bell commissioned many works from the same artists as Simpson and Ritchie, but also took up the

next generation of Scottish painters with similar enthusiasm, including J L Wingate, W D McKay, Joseph and David Farquharson and Charles Mackie. He was also one of the first collectors in Scotland to buy modern Dutch art, including G A Mollinger, James Maris and Jozef Israels.[29]

To paint his own portrait, Bell turned to G P Chalmers, with whom (like Simpson) he had already had several frustrating encounters, and had written to William McTaggart: "Do you know after this I am going to put no trust in getting anything from our friend Chalmers".[30] Luckily he persisted, and after an 1867 study (acquired by J G Orchar), the final 1875 version (figure 12) was hailed as a masterpiece: "Chalmers... loving the man he depicted, put forth the full strength of his fine genius, and produced what is esteemed to be one of the greatest portraits ever painted in Scotland."[31] The architect and art lover T S Robertson later claimed that "Sir Noel Paton said of this portrait that it was the greatest of the century, and Bell used to suggest the many sittings that he had to undergo for it by saying that these cost him a pair of boots."[32] Bell initially intended to leave the painting to the National Gallery of Scotland, but according to Robertson, the Albert Institute's curator John Maclauchlan persuaded him to bequeath it to Dundee's permanent collection. Evidently keen to stress the magnanimity of this gift, Bell wrote in his will: "As the Portrait is considered one of the distinguished artist's finest productions I think on that account it is more incumbent on me to leave it to Dundee although I have many request[s to] place it otherwise."[33] The art critic Edward Pinnington (Chalmers' biographer), later claimed that "no public gallery has its equal... It is like an Old Master suffused with the spirit of modernity."[34]

Bell was the first of the Dundee buyers to sell part of his collection, at Dowell's in Edinburgh in 1877. According to the *Wizard*, this sale "marked the extreme high water mark of the commercial value of Scottish Art. Never was so much enthusiasm seen at a sale, the successive presentation of so many choice examples came upon the spectators like a revelation, and the result was a total of £7,500 – never before reached, or attained to since, at an art sale in Scotland."[35] Among the top sellers were Erskine Nicol's *Out for the Day* (350 guineas), McTaggart's *Willie Baird* (330 guineas) and Alexander Fraser's *Loch Achray* (250 guineas). Many paintings went for five or even ten times the price Bell had paid for them. "The audience was carried away by enthusiasm, partly caused by their admiration for the splendid works submitted and partly by regard for Mr Bell, for many of the purchasers were his personal friends."[36]

Having made such lucrative profits from this sale, Bell's collecting continued unabated. Like Ritchie and Simpson, however, he fell victim to some unsuccessful investments and was forced to hold a second sale in 1890. This time the works realised the smaller sum of £3,500, but it was enough to allow him to continue purchasing until his death in 1897. Initially, it was believed that "Mr Bell has bequeathed his splendid works of art to the Permanent Collection of the Albert Institute" but sadly (with the exception of his portrait) this proved not to be the case.[37] The remaining collection (including works by McTaggart, Fraser, Nicol and Bough) was sold at Dowell's on 27 November and raised £474/12 (with a Wingate being sold separately for £94/10). His total personal estate in Britain was valued at £2,076/1/7. In opening its 1895 feature on him, the *Wizard of the North* had written: "When, as is sure to be the case some day, a local chronicler endeavours to tell the interesting story of the formation of the famous private Art Collections of Dundee during the second half of the century now hurrying to its close, the first name which must stand prominently out in his pages will certainly be that of Mr John Charles Bell."

In fact, the name best remembered today is that of James Guthrie Orchar. The reason is simple – Bell left just one painting to the city's permanent collection, Ritchie and Simpson none.[38] Orchar not only gave numerous donations to the city's collections, but on his death bequeathed his entire art collection (over 300 works) to the people of Broughty Ferry, eventually to be displayed in the Orchar Gallery.

Orchar was born in Craigie outside Dundee in 1825. His father was a joiner and the young James initially followed him into this profession before joining the engineering firm Kinmond, Hutton & Steele, based at the Wallace Foundry. This work took him to England for some years but he returned to Dundee in the 1850s and with William Robertson set up his own manufacturing company in 1856, taking over and expanding the Wallace Foundry to make textile machinery. With the linen and jute industries massively expanding (and mechanising), their business was a huge success, with orders not just from around Britain but also Germany, France and Belgium. They were soon designing new machinery and took out several patents on their inventions.[39]

From an early age Orchar had begun collecting small works of art and tried his hand at painting himself. According to his obituary in the *Dundee Advertiser*: "With advancing years his taste widened and became more elevated, and increased prosperity enabled him to gradually acquire a large and almost

13. William McTaggart, *Through Wind and Rain*, oil on canvas, 1875, owned by J G Orchar *(Dundee City Council: Dundee's Art Galleries & Museums)*.

14. Opposite page: Unknown artist, Portrait of A B Spence from *The Piper o' Dundee*, 1895 *(Libraries, Leisure & Culture Dundee)*.

faultless collection. It might almost be said to be perfect – containing the best works of the best men within his range, for his taste was exacting, highly critical, almost fastidious."[40] Like his fellow Dundee collectors, Orchar made many close personal contacts within the art world – it was said that "To artists struggling at the outset of their career... and to those laid aside by age or illness, he was a generous benefactor." These artists included many familiar names such as McTaggart, Cameron, Pettie, Orchardson and Chalmers. "Most of these artists were his warm personal friends and frequent guests... the supremest happiness which came to his life was in the hours spent in their refined and invigorating society."[41] Orchar also purchased works by noted English artists such as Turner, Millais and Leighton, and took a special interest in James McNeill Whistler, buying several oils and a substantial (and today very significant) collection of his etchings. But his favourite artist (as with so many of his contemporaries) was McTaggart; over the years Orchar acquired no fewer than 22 of his works, including his more 'impressionist' later paintings which were often attacked by the critics. Having bought *Through Wind and Rain* (figure 13) from McTaggart before its showing at the 1875 RSA exhibition, Orchar later wrote to the artist: "The *Advertiser* critic says [the painting] is sketchy, but it would not be a fair sample of the artist were it otherwise'(put that in your pipe and smoke it). Give my regards to Mrs McTaggart. I must tell her the next time I am over... to hide or burn all your big brushes."[42]

Orchar became a close friend of McTaggart's and in 1882 they travelled the Continent together, visiting Paris, Vienna, Munich, Prague, Dresden, Amsterdam and the Hague. Orchar commissioned McTaggart to paint his wife's portrait in 1886, but it was to another friend, John Pettie, that he turned for his own portrait (of which there are two versions – one for himself and one for William Robertson). By that time Orchar had retired and was able to devote more of his time to public life. He took a leading role in the Fine Art Exhibitions (regularly hosting large banquets for the visiting artists at the opening of each exhibition) and later became Convenor of the Free Library Committee which managed the city's museum and art gallery. As we shall see in chapter two, it was also Orchar who led the way in donating works to the permanent collection. In 1885 a banquet was held at the Queen's Hotel in his honour – 129 guests attended, and he was presented with a gold snuffbox inscribed "In grateful recognition of his valuable services to the Cause of Art, and munificent gifts to the Picture Gallery."[43]

In 1886 Orchar was elected Chief Magistrate (later Provost) of Broughty Ferry; in this role he laid out public parks and established a trust fund for the widows and children of fishermen drowned at sea. As well as his love of art, he also collected rare books and owned two Stradivarius violins. He was described by one obituarist as "eminently social... few living men had a larger collection of racy old Scotch stories, and his telling of them was superb."[44] In 1897, Orchar started work on a book of such stories, to be illustrated by McTaggart, but the latter's ill health postponed the project and Orchar himself died the following year. The *Piper o' Dundee* described him as "the most liberal patron of the fine arts that Dundee has ever seen", while according to the *Advertiser*, "There were few public men in whom the citizens of Dundee took greater pride".[45] Orchar claimed that his work in the cause of art "had been the special desire of his life... he keenly appreciated the refined pleasures and elevating influences of art, conscious that it has elevated his own life and purified his tastes."[46]

Although his collection was smaller than those described thus far, Dr Alexander B Spence (figure 14) seems to have been the first from this generation to invest his money in art. Born in Edinburgh in 1814, he practised medicine for some years

before joining his father's dental practice. He came to Dundee in the late 1830s to establish a branch of the business, and soon boasted one of the town's largest practices. "Of an exceedingly ardent, social disposition," said the *Piper o' Dundee*, "he took a leading part in various society matters, and was at once an amateur actor and an art patron and critic."[47] Spence began collecting in the 1840s, and first publicly displayed his acquisitions at the 1847 Watt Institution exhibition (including a supposed Sebastiano del Piombo and copies of Annibale Carracci and Van Dyke). Like his fellow collectors he made personal friendships with leading Scottish painters, and among the highlights of his collection were *Morning of the Fiesta* by Robert Herdman, *The Laird o' Cockpen* by Gourlay Steell and works by Horatio McCulloch, Erskine Nicol, E T Crawford and J C Wintour. He owned several works by G Ogilvy Reid, who also painted his portrait – though unusually this remained in the artist's possession rather than the subject's, and was presented to the city's collection by Reid in 1906. T S Robertson rather dismissively recalled that Spence "had some knowledge of art, but he was not one of our set."[48] Nevertheless, Spence played an active role on the Fine Art Exhibitions committee, and was jointly responsible with Orchar for the hanging arrangement of the oils. For a time, "no sale or exhibition of pictures could be said to be complete without him", though he gradually lost interest in local affairs "as the comrades of his youth and early manhood dropped away".[49] He died in 1895 and bulk of his collection was sold in Dundee by John C Crabbe. Despite "a fairly large attendance of interested parties" and "keen competition" for some pictures, the highest reported price was just £20 for Ogilvy Reid's *The Village Blacksmith*.[50]

The youngest member of the original 1867 exhibition committee was Peter G Walker, senior partner in the Balgay Jute Works. Born in Dundee in 1832, he entered into a long-established family business and would go on to hold various local offices including President of the Chamber of Commerce and a director of the High School.[51] Art seems to have been of passing interest only – he owned works by Crawford, Nicol, McTaggart and John MacWhirter. He died in 1896.

There were others who played a part in organising the BA exhibition but who were not officially listed as members of the committee. The most significant of these was undoubtedly the architect Thomas S Robertson, who would go on to serve with Orchar as joint convenor of the Hanging Committee for the Fine Art Exhibitions. Born in Blairgowrie in 1835, Robertson served his apprenticeship in Dundee under Charles Edward, with whom he later formed a partnership after practising for a while in Edinburgh and south of the border.[52] Although only 32 when the BA exhibition was held, he had earned enough money from his architectural work (possibly supplemented by some judicious property investment) to have built up a collection including work by Alexander Fraser, John Phillip and David Roberts.

Like Orchar, Robertson was an amateur painter himself (both of them exhibited with the Dundee Art Club in the 1880s), and he often went sketching with William McTaggart, to whom he had been introduced by G B Simpson. The two formed a close friendship, and Robertson later wrote of the fascinating tuition in painting he had received from McTaggart: "'You will,' he said, 'see many things in Nature which are not

in your drawing. Put in one of these; don't be in a hurry, only one at a time. Look again, put in another and another, until you find that there is nothing outside that is not in your drawing.' That was the greatest lesson which I ever got in painting from Nature."[53]

Robertson enjoyed close connections with many artists, and wrote a lengthy series of articles for the *Courier* in 1904 under the heading "Famous Scottish Artists", many of which drew on his personal reminiscences. Although his work as an architect saw him designing many well-known buildings (including Carbet Castle, Rosebank Parish Church and St Stephen's Church), his practice gradually diminished and with it his income. He down-sized his property and seems to have given up collecting art, but continued to play a leading role in the Fine Art Exhibitions, right up to their resurrection in 1920. In his later years, Robertson turned more to writing, most notably an acclaimed book on *The Progress of Art in English Church Architecture*. Unable to buy art himself, he acted as an advisor to Orchar, who made him one of the trustees of his will and appointed him as the architect of the gallery which he hoped would house his collection – it wasn't to be, however, and Robertson died in 1923.

One of the most frequent lenders to the Fine Art Exhibitions (and a long-serving committee member) was Sir William Ogilvy Dalgleish (figure 294). Born in 1832, Dalgleish studied at Edinburgh University before starting work at Baxter Brothers in 1854. Marrying Sir David Baxter's niece no doubt helped his rise to the top, and he became chairman of the company after Baxter's death in 1872. A notable philanthropist, he gave generous gifts to Dundee Royal Infirmary, University College, Dundee (UCD) and the Technical Institute.[54] His collection was rich in paintings by Alexander Nasmyth, including *Glencoe* and *Railway Bridge at Linlithgow*, but probably his best known works were Millais' *Puss in Boots* (1877, shown in the 1889 Fine Art Exhibition – see figure 44) and Peter Graham's

Moorland and Mist (1893, included in the 1895 show); both were left to the city's collection after his death.

One other person involved in the Fine Art Exhibitions from the start was Orchar's business partner William Robertson. Born on a small croft in Aberdeenshire in 1825, Robertson was truly a self-made man, perhaps explaining his firmly held beliefs in the improving power of art for the working classes. He came to Dundee as a boy hoping to improve his prospects and began work at Baxter Brothers' mills at the earliest age allowed. He worked his way up to become apprentice engineer then manager of the mechanical and engineering departments. In 1856 he and Orchar entered into partnership together. He joined the Town Council in 1869 and rose to become Provost in 1875. The Fine Art Exhibitions committee was just one of numerous boards Robertson served on, including the High School, the Royal Infirmary, the Mars training ship and UCD.

Although Robertson was never quite as devoted to the cause of art as Orchar, he took over from Simpson as chairman of the Fine Art Exhibitions committee for the 1877 exhibition (continuing until 1886), and became the first chairman of the Dundee Art Union, founded the same year. He lent 21 pictures to the BA exhibition (including works by Bough, MacWhirter and several English artists) but rarely after that – his only other substantial showing was in 1881 with works by Pettie, Chalmers and Cameron. In 1879 he commissioned Pettie to paint his portrait, possibly inspiring Orchar to do likewise. Although they were the same age, Robertson continued to run the business after Orchar's retiral, dying a year after his former partner in 1899.

With all of these men sharing similar artistic tastes, it's hardly surprising that for the artists they patronised, Dundee soon came to be seen as a significant cultural centre. John MacWhirter later wrote: "The men of Dundee are an example to other towns in their love of art, and the vigorous way in which they show it."[55] MacWhirter was one of five artists who clubbed together to take nine of their Dundee patrons to a dinner at Carnoustie in 1867, the year of the BA exhibition. William McTaggart chaired the event and the other artists present were G P Chalmers, George Hay and W F Vallance. The guests of honour were Bell, Ritchie, Simpson, Orchar, T S Robertson, P G Walker and some lesser (or at least more private) collectors, Thomas Cargill, Henry Macdonald and (probably) Thomas Smieton.[56] The full extent of their three collections is unknown – they only occasionally lent works to exhibitions in Dundee, though all three showed paintings at the RSA.[57] However, according to T S Robertson:

> "The most enthusiastic of these [early collectors] in art matters, and the one who lived most under its influence, was Thomas Cargill… I have seen [him] standing for hours all alone looking at a picture. His own collection was not in any sense furniture. Its purpose was to give pleasure from an art point of view, and on that account the pictures on the walls of his house were hung higgledy-piggledy, without any regard to their sizes. The only law observed by him in hanging was to have the centre of each picture on the level of his own eyes. There was only one row of them all round a room; and with so many pictures, they had to be placed close up to one another, an arrangement which would shock people who care more for furniture than art."[58]

Unfortunately, Cargill's fortunes fluctuated even more severely than the others', and (not for the first time) he was declared bankrupt in 1868 and forced to sell off his property, including his mill at Lower Pleasance.

The BA exhibition was a tremendous success – it was said that "the collection of paintings commanded the admiration of connoisseurs from every country and every school of art."[59] Some 2,000 visitors had been present on the closing night, when the principal patron of the exhibition, Lord Kinnaird, called for the establishment of a permanent art collection for Dundee – a call that would soon be answered. The total costs of the art committee had been £858/9/1 and the whole enterprise made a profit of £1665/7/9, of which £300 was set aside for further use of the Volunteer Hall as a picture gallery. This was not just a money-making exercise, however, and almost a third of all visitors to the exhibition had been allowed free entry – including inmates of the Poor Houses, the Orphan Institution, the Industrial Schools and the Deaf & Dumb Institution.

A permanent collection would require a permanent home, and in 1871 plans were drawn up by local architect David Mackenzie to add an east wing to the Albert Institute, in line with George Gilbert Scott's original ideas. Only half of this plan was actually carried out, but it provided much-needed space for a museum and art gallery (the original part of the building being used for the library). The opening in 1873 was marked with another large-scale exhibition of art and industry. This was an altogether grander affair than the BA show – spread over five galleries were 368 oil paintings, 203 watercolours, 30 pieces of sculpture and 65 prints and photographs (figure 15). A miscellany of decorative art was displayed in cases in the library, with separate displays representing local industries and a loan collection of casts and other items from South Kensington. Three galleries were set aside for the museum collections, the nucleus of which had been transferred from the now-defunct museum of the Watt Institution.

G B Simpson again chaired the Art Committee, and drew on his own expanding collection as well as those of Ritchie, Bell, Orchar *et al*. Once again he encouraged the local aristocracy to lend, particularly Lord Kinnaird, whose family portraits included work by Reynolds, Romney, Lely and Sir Francis Grant. Simpson also arranged to borrow seventeen works from the collection of Patrick Allan-Fraser at Hospitalfield, Arbroath. The Earl of Dalhousie, as Lord-Lieutenant for the county, opened the building and the exhibition at a special ceremony on 1 November 1873.

While most of the collectors showed off their latest purchases of contemporary Scottish art, Simpson's loans concentrated on his old masters, including Bruegel's *St Jerome in the Desert*, a *Holy Family* by Rubens and Holbein's *Portrait of Erasmus*. One of his most impressive loans was an early

work by Frederic Leighton, *The Star of Bethlehem*, to which the artist contributed a written statement to be reproduced in the catalogue. Along with Simpson, the most well-represented contributor was Orchar, who lent numerous works by Bough, Cameron, Robert Herdman and many more.

There were several new names appearing in the list of lenders. Some were only minor collectors (such as Henry Macdonald and James F Low) but at least one would go on to play a significant part in the Fine Art Exhibitions. Isaac Julius Weinberg was unique among the Dundee collectors in having come from a Jewish family in Germany, though he later became a naturalised British subject (figure 16). Born in Hamburg in 1833, it is not clear why he left his native country, but having begun work as a clerk, he "displayed marked individuality for commerce".[60] By 1855 he was in business in Belfast as joint owner of a firm buying linen, yarn and jute for export. This led him naturally to Dundee, where he relocated around 1862.[61] By that time he had already begun collecting art – according to art critic A H Millar: "Having a very refined taste, and a keen eye for the unobtrusive artistic merits of a picture, Mr Weinberg purchased solely for his personal gratification; but his aesthetic temperament led him to choose pictures by men as yet of unrecognised genius, and he has thus become the possessor of works that have greatly increased in value since he acquired them."[62]

Weinberg's collection reflected his international interests – he had connections in Germany, France, Italy and South America as well as a particular interest in Spain, becoming Spanish Vice Consul in Dundee. One of the highlights of his collection of Spanish art was Garrido's *The Rape of the Sabines*, later donated to the city's collection by his widow (figure 17). Painted when the artist was still in his teens, it was one of several examples of early works by notable artists. Inevitably, the Spanish-influenced Scottish painter John Phillip was also much admired by Weinberg, who owned several of his paintings including *A Mountain Daisy*, *A Highland Home* and *The Music Lesson*. Other Continental paintings included Meissonier's *Connoisseurs*, Focosi's *Torquato Tasso in Prison* and various German, Italian and Dutch landscapes. At the same time, Weinberg embraced the Scottish painters beloved of his fellow collectors in Dundee, and boasted fine works by Bough, Fraser, MacWhirter and McTaggart.

Weinberg displayed his collection on the walls of his mansion Fernbrae on Perth Road (now a private hospital). In 1898, A H Millar wrote an article on Weinberg's collection for *The Art Journal*, and described his visit to the house:

> "[T]he Weinberg Collection overflows in every part of the mansion. You find pictures decorating the dining-room; hallowing the billiard-room; making every bedroom pleasing to the eye; and relieving the lofty bareness of corridors and staircases. There is, therefore, an artistic tone throughout the mansion which exercises an influence such as could never be obtained, were all the works of art brought together in one saloon or picture gallery."[63]

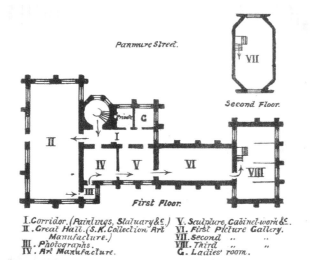

A. *Entrance*.
B. *Sticks &c receiving door*.
C. *Ticket Office*.
D. *Gentlemen's room (under stair)*

E. *Exit doors*.
F. *Sticks &c delivering door*.
IX. *Fourth Picture Gallery*.

I. *Corridor. (Paintings, Statuary &c.)*
II. *Great Hall. (S.K. Collection Art Manufacture.)*
III. *Photographs*.
IV. *Art Manufacture*.

V. *Sculpture, Cabinet-work &c.*
VI. *First Picture Gallery*.
VII. *Second " "*
VIII. *Third " "*
G. *Ladies' room*.

15. Dundee Fine Art Exhibition 1873, plan of the galleries *(Libraries, Leisure & Culture Dundee)*.

Weinberg became known as "one of Dundee's chief experts in trade."[64] He lectured on Commercial Education and served on numerous boards including the Chamber of Commerce, where he was elected President in 1876. He was an important benefactor to UCD, the Royal Infirmary, the Royal Victoria Hospital and numerous other organisations. He helped to establish Dundee's Day Nurseries and campaigned to abolish slum housing. A feature on Weinberg in the *Piper o' Dundee* described him as "an example of the best type of the modern man of business" but, after listing some of his many good works, concluded by saying: "Surely enough has been written to show that Mr Weinberg is a citizen of whom any community may justly be proud" – possibly suggesting that there were some in the community who felt otherwise. The article notably omits any reference to either Weinberg's German origins or Jewish faith, both of which could have proved a social barrier at the time. While noting the extensive influence of Weinberg and his family on the social and cultural life of Dundee, author William Blain (writing in the 1950s) claimed: "I do not feel, however, that this influence was of the highest kind. It was ostentatious and vulgar rather than a matter of good personal taste".[65]

The Jewish press, on the other hand, held him up as a model citizen, "greatly respected by Jew and Gentile alike... In local Jewish matters he has always closely interested himself. The present synagogue, which was opened by Mr Weinberg in 1897, is almost wholly his gift."[66] Weinberg's support for

the arts in Dundee was also never in doubt. He continued to lend to the Fine Art Exhibitions and those of the Dundee Art Society, and donated works by David Murray (figure 45) and J Herbert Snell to the permanent collection. He died in 1912, and his portrait by Orchardson was later gifted to the collection by his family.

The inaugural Fine Art Exhibition came to an end in January 1874 and was a phenomenal success, with 92,489 visitors over three months. In his opening speech, Lord Dalhousie had noted: "I trust this exhibition may be repeated, perhaps not year after year, but perhaps biennially or triennially, because I am sure the result will be most gratifying, not simply to the people of Dundee, but to the public of this great county and its neighbourhood."[67] In fact it would be over three years before another exhibition on the same scale was attempted, the jute and linen trade suffering severe decline in 1874-6. In the meantime, Dundee's permanent collection (to be described in chapter two) was officially opened to the public for the first time in May 1874. It was managed by John Maclauchlan, who had taken up his duties as the Albert Institute's first curator and librarian in January 1874. Born in Perth in 1838, he worked in Perth Library for fifteen years before coming to Dundee. The *Advertiser* later described him as "a connoisseur of discernment and technical skill" and much of the organisation of the Fine Art Exhibitions fell to him as secretary of the committee.

In March 1877 planning began for the second Fine Art

16. Isaac Julius Weinberg, from *The Piper o' Dundee*, 1901 *(Libraries, Leisure & Culture Dundee)*.

17. Eduardo Léon Garrido, *The Rape of the Sabines*, oil on canvas, 1874, owned by I J Weinberg *(Dundee City Council: Dundee's Art Galleries & Museums)*.

Exhibition, which this time would be mainly a selling show. Clara Young has described in detail the elaborate procedures that were put in place by the Executive Committee and its numerous sub-committees to ensure the success of the exhibition – these included personal visits to many of the most eminent artists of the day and the appointment of agents in Edinburgh, Glasgow and London to make the necessary arrangements.[68] The exhibition was opened by the Earl of Strathmore on 1 October 1877 and included 587 oil paintings and 455 watercolours and drawings (figure 18). "Some of the first painters in the world have sent masterpieces of their genius" said the *Dundee Advertiser*, and visitors evidently agreed, with total sales exceeding £6,000. Only a few loans were included, most notably Landseer's *The Studio of Sir Francis Chantrey*, courtesy of Her Majesty the Queen, but none from local lenders.

Consideration was now given to whether these exhibitions should become an annual event. The *Dundee Advertiser* questioned whether it would be possible to obtain as many paintings every year, and noted the high prices most works were sold at – "prices at which it is improbable many can procure purchases in Dundee, especially in the present unre-munerative condition of our staple trade".[69] In the end, it was agreed to hold the next one in two years' time, but before that an important change of ownership took place. Up to this point the Albert Institute building was still privately owned, but in 1879 the directors of the company arranged to sell it to the Town Council for £1,000 (£280 of which was later given back – a fraction of the £20,000 the building had originally cost).[70] The 1879 Fine Art Exhibition was therefore the first to be held in a publicly owned museum and art gallery, and was the most ambitious so far, with 1,335 works on show. Again it was a selling exhibition, but this time loans once again comprised a substantial part, with Simpson, Orchar and Weinberg all showing works from their collections (with a focus in all three cases on works by Sam Bough) along with many other lenders.

Two new names appeared in the catalogue, both of whom were amassing substantial collections. The first was John Mitchell Keiller (figure 19), taking the opportunity here of showing off four Bough paintings (and thus outstripping Simpson and Weinberg's three and Orchar's two). Aged only 28 at the time, Keiller was the youngest of the collectors from this period, and had enjoyed the quickest rise to the top. The family marmalade and confectionery business was already well established when he was born in 1851 and after being educated in Dundee, Edinburgh and on the continent, John was chosen (instead of his elder brother James) to become a partner in the business in 1872. His work in managing the firm's accounts was clearly appreciated, and on the death of his father in 1877, John assumed control of the company.[71]

Keiller generally avoided public duty, though he was a director of Dundee Royal Infirmary and donated £2,000 to the hospital. However, it was as a patron of the fine arts that he was best known: "No one was more earnest and zealous than he in promoting local exhibitions and in cultivating talent wherever found," claimed his obituary in the *Dundee Advertiser*. "His own collection of paintings has attained a wide and well-deserved celebrity, and includes valuable works by Constable, Turner, Raeburn, Phillip, Millais, Orchardson

and others."[72] Keiller was unusual in collecting early 19th century paintings as well as more recent examples (Constable's *View in Helmingdale Park* being a particular treasure), and he was always pleased to show off his collection to anyone visiting his Perth Road mansion, Binrock House. A feature in the *Art Journal* revealed that many of the highlights were shown in the billiard room: "made extremely high in the roof and top-lit, [it] shows his best pictures in an equable light."[73]

Orchardson was particularly well represented in Keiller's collection – he owned *The Queen of Swords* (shown at the 1883 Fine Art Exhibition), *Napoleon at St Helena* (shown at the 1895 exhibition, now in National Museums Liverpool) and the celebrated sequel *Mariage de Convenance – After* (shown at the 1886 exhibition, Keiller having bought it from the Royal Academy show the previous year; figure 20). Keiller also made various donations to the permanent collection, including W E Lockhart's *The Swineherd*.

In 1893 Keiller & Son became a limited company and John ceased to take an active interest. He had already moved to London (where Keiller's production had been based since 1879) and spent most of his time either there or at his Aberdeenshire estate, Morven, which he had acquired in 1886. Although his charitable interests turned more towards the east end of London, he continued to support the work of the Albert Institute, for example through donations of books to the Free Library.[74] A frequent traveller, he died at sea in 1899 aged just 48.[75]

The other collector whose name first appeared in the 1879 exhibition catalogue was the dental surgeon Dr John Stewart (figure 21). Born in Friockheim in 1849, he served his apprenticeship in Perth before coming to Dundee to work for the practice of Messrs Lothian and Chatham. Within a few years he had bought out the business and was expanding it rapidly. In 1889 the business paper *The Mercantile Age* recognised Stewart's surgery as the "largest and best appointed to be found north of the Tweed".[76] According to a feature in the *Wizard of the North*:

18. Dundee Fine Art Exhibition 1877, conversazione programme cover
(Libraries, Leisure & Culture Dundee, licensor www.scran.ac.uk).

19. David Clark, Portrait of John Mitchell Keiller from *The Piper o' Dundee*, 1887 *(Libraries, Leisure & Culture Dundee)*.

21. Unknown artist, Portrait of Dr John Stewart from *The Piper o' Dundee*, 1892 *(Libraries, Leisure & Culture Dundee)*.

20. Above: William Quiller Orchardson, *Mariage de Convenance – After*, oil on canvas, 1886, owned by J M Keiller *(Aberdeen Art Gallery & Museums Collections)*.

22. Opposite page: David Farquharson, *Dundee from Harecraigs*, oil on canvas, 1879, owned by John Stewart *(Dundee City Council: Dundee's Art Galleries & Museums)*.

"No dentist has made for himself a more enviable reputation in the science of dentistry. He has obtained first-class certificates of merit, and gold medals from various International and Industrial Exhibitions, including London, 1886, Paris, 1887, Philadelphia, 1887, and Dundee, 1888… As an author he takes an important position. His work 'The Teeth, and how to preserve them,' was a pronounced success".[77]

In his leisure time, like Dr Spence before him, Stewart turned his attention from teeth to art. He began to build up a private art gallery in 1872, focusing almost exclusively on Scottish artists. Among the many works he purchased were Fraser's *Queen Mary's Bedroom* and *At Loch Long*, Cameron's *A Cup of Tea* and *The Mother's Kiss* and Phillip's *A Village Beauty* and *The Rustic Well*. His collection numbered many hundreds, and sometimes included multiple views of the same scene – for example he owned at least three paintings of Kilchurn Castle on Loch Awe, two by Fraser and one by McCulloch.[78] Although a regular lender to the Fine Art

Exhibitions, he never served on the committee or took any other notable part in civic life. However, the *Piper o' Dundee* noted after his early death in 1892 that "his genial and kindly manner had won for him crowds of friends in the city and surrounding districts."[79]

Stewart donated only one painting to the permanent collection, *Dundee from Harecraigs* by David Farquharson (figure 22). In his will, he left his household belongings to his wife but instructed his trustees to sell his "pictures [and] ornaments".[80] His *Lady of the Lea* by Patrick W Adam was acquired by another dentist-collector, John Robertson (see chapter nine), who gifted it to the city.

From 1879 until 1886 the Fine Art Exhibitions were annual events. T S Robertson later recalled how the exhibitions were hung:

"At several of the earlier exhibitions the hanging committee was large, although only six members of it were supposed to be active. Some of these consulted together about the merits of pictures and the places they should occupy on the walls. Others did nothing of the kind, but took each his own way, and hung the pictures he liked most in the best places. In consequence of this the committee was divided into several parties, each working in its own way at different parts of the galleries. Such an arrangement was impracticable, and had gradually to undergo alterations till the number of the active hanging Committee was reduced to three. These were Orchar, and Dr Spence, who hung the oils; the water colours were left to me. When the oil hangers differed I was consulted."[81]

Such differences seem always to have been settled amicably. Robertson recalled one amusing example:

"I took Orchar's place one day for a time as he had to attend to important business, and during his absence had difficulty in restraining the doctor from hanging pictures by his many friends in some of the best places – for which there were plenty of better pictures. Orchar on his return asked me – 'Where is the doctor?' and I had just jokingly replied that 'he had gone to look for a friend to fill this vacant place' – when the doctor appeared with a picture by one of his greatest friends in his hand, and it so exactly fitted that it was put in and allowed to remain."[82]

The Fine Art Exhibitions quickly became one of the cultural lodestones of Dundee. They attracted notable guest speakers for their opening events – not just artists (such as Daniel Macnee in 1879 and Fettes Douglas in 1882, both President of the RSA at the time) but also members of the aristocracy, eminent judges and politicians (William Gladstone in 1890

being a particular coup – see figure 23). During the run of each exhibition there was also a series of Conversaziones to which season ticket holders were admitted, featuring music recitals and lectures, and sometimes poetry readings and tableaux vivants (figure 24). Various other public lectures on art were held in the galleries, again featuring an impressive array of speakers. All of these were widely promoted in the local press, which also published detailed reviews of each exhibition and continually exhorted the local public to support them. The magazines *Wizard* and *Piper* featured regular cartoons about the exhibitions as well as lithographic sketches of many of the paintings (figure 25). For several years one local cartoonist produced a series of short illustrated publications entitled *Our Special Artist at the Dundee Fine Art Exhibition* (see chapter five). The galleries stayed open in the evenings to encourage a wider attendance and on Saturdays "the rates of admission are specially arranged so as to meet the purses of the working classes" (3d instead of 6d).[83] Children were also admitted half price and there were many free group visits from schools and the local orphanage. The *Wizard of the North* also noted that the exhibition was popular with another type of visitor, namely "the young couples who make the galleries a convenient promenade for a little mild flirtation".[84]

One notable bi-product of the Fine Art Exhibitions was the formation of the Dundee Art Union. The initial conception came from John Kennedy, who had recently retired as art master at the Dundee School of Art and who was on the organising committee of the 1877 exhibition. As chairman of the committee, Provost William Robertson took up the scheme and formed a separate committee (with most of the same members) to run the Union. The idea was that subscribers were entered into a prize draw, the money raised being divided up into a number of cash prizes which were used by the winners to purchase works from the exhibition. 1,049 tickets (costing 10/6 each) were sold in the first year, giving the committee £490 for prize money – enough for 50 prizes of between £5 and £50.[85]

Art Unions were already well established in other cities and (as a form of public lottery) had to be strictly regulated by the

Board of Trade. Dundee's differed from those elsewhere in that the winners were not allocated pre-chosen artworks as prizes but were allowed to choose their own – and to supplement the prize money with their own to acquire something of higher value if they chose. Thus the £490 of prize money yielded £868 in purchases, clearly vindicating the main purpose of the Union – that of helping to ensure the financial success of the Fine Art Exhibitions. Dundee also prided itself on the very low costs involved in running the Union – around 10% of the income, compared to longer-established ones elsewhere which charged much higher subscription rates and cost 40% or more.[86] As the *Courier* reported in 1880:

> "the Art Union contributes more than
> anything else to the success of the Dundee
> Fine Art Exhibition... Unless pictures are
> sold, artists cannot be expected to continue
> to send; and all, especially those who do not
> buy pictures directly, are afforded an easy and
> inexpensive mode of assisting the sales of the
> Exhibition by becoming subscribers to the Art
> Union."[87]

This was amply demonstrated later that year, when £470 worth of prizes yielded £1,627 in sales, only just short of that spent by winners of the Edinburgh Art Union, which boasted ten times the income. In the annual reports of the Art Union, frequent mention was made of the importance of instilling an appreciation of art among the working classes, and this was generally held to be one of the principal achievements of the Fine Art Exhibitions. As one local journalist put it:

> "An advance in a people's taste for the fine
> arts argues an increase in general refinement
> and mental culture – always of very high
> value, but specially so in a community
> whose daily avocations have more than an
> ordinary tendency to lower and materialise
> the workers. Amidst the monotonous din
> and dust of revolving wheels and shafts, and
> the manipulation of jute and flax, there is no
> reason why visions of beauty first beheld in
> the Art Exhibition should not be conjured up
> before the mind's eye, and joy be felt anew in
> the presence of green fields, mountain vistas,
> incidents of pathos in domestic life, and scenes
> of historic valour and renown, of noble deeds
> and daring high."[88]

There was little hope of these newly joyful workers taking part in the Art Union, however – the half guinea subscription was sixpence more than the weekly wage of the average jute spinner. Most of those who bought tickets were middle class, and the names of many of the Union's managers appeared regularly in the lists of winners, there being no rule against their participation. Almost right from the start the Union found itself accused of malpractice – in 1879 the draw had to be done twice after certain numbers were found to have been left out, and in 1885 the committee were obliged to publish detailed statistics to refute allegations concerning the method of drawing. From that year they also began to employ "two

young ladies from the Blind Institution" to make the draw.[89]

There was no doubting the financial success of the scheme, however – as subscriptions rose, so did the prize money and so did the total amount spent. A bumper year in 1882 saw 1,225 tickets sold providing £600 in prize money yielding £2,000 of sales (almost a third of the £6,785 total sales from that year's exhibition). The following year was even more remarkable – 1,267 tickets, £615 of prizes and £2,809 in sales ("an amount quite unprecedented in Scottish Art Unions"), the total sales for the exhibition amounting to a massive £8,605.[90] The *Advertiser* later claimed: "No Fine Art Exhibition in Great Britain has ever attained results like these, which exceed the amounts realised in all the largest provincial towns, excepting Liverpool, and relatively, of course, far outstripping that city."[91]

Board of Trade rules stipulated that all works purchased with the Union's prize money must be publicly exhibited, and this too became a popular regular attraction. The exhibition of winners' choices from the 1883 exhibition was arranged by A B Spence and G B Simpson, and was said to prove "that these annual Fine Art Exhibitions are slowly but surely elevating artistic taste in Dundee – and are thus fulfilling their purpose – for the prizes selected this year are immensely superior in all the higher elements of art to those selected seven years ago, when the Art Union held its first drawing."[92]

Dundee was now widely recognised as one of the best places outside London to sell art. There had been frequent picture sales held since before the days of the Fine Art Exhibitions – at that time many art dealers travelled the country, setting up temporary exhibitions for a week or so then moving on with whatever remained unsold. The first to meet with notable success in Dundee was P L Everard of London and Brussels. He undertook a Scottish tour in 1867, selling "a large collection of paintings, including works by some of the most celebrated modern French, Belgian, Dutch, and German artists", but his stay in Dundee proved so successful (sales of over £4,000) that he returned later in the year to sell more.[93] Many more dealers followed. In 1880, for example, the whole of Mr Wolfe Lesser of London's "Fine Collection of High-Class Modern Pictures of the English and Continental Schools" was put up for sale in Dundee by Harris & Fairweather, including works by

Arthur Harris at the age of 14 before becoming a partner in the business in 1884 and taking sole charge in 1898. In 1909 Curr's clerk William Dewar became a partner and the business survives under the name of Curr & Dewar to this day.[96] There were many other auctioneers selling art in Dundee in the late 19th century (including James A McLean, John C Crabbe and John M Beatts), but most collectors bought their pictures through specialist dealers such as Alex Fraser, James Ogilvie and Grindlay Liddle (figure 27). As well as selling art, most of these also served as artists' colourmen and as carvers and gilders (ie frame-makers). "In recent years the growth of this industry has been very rapid" noted the *People's Journal* in 1879, when Grindlay Liddle opened a large wholesale warehouse for German mouldings. Liddle had just returned from visiting Hamburg and Berlin bringing with him "a very extensive assortment of all the different kinds of framework... it is gratifying to note that Dundee is now taking a step in advance in this direction."[97]

23. Opposite page: Opening of the Dundee Fine Art Exhibition by W E Gladstone MP, 1890. Curator John Maclauchlan is seated front right, with J G Orchar standing top left *(Libraries, Leisure & Culture Dundee)*.

24. Above: Dundee Fine Art Exhibition 1882, conversazione invitation *(Libraries, Leisure & Culture Dundee, licensor www.scran.ac.uk)*.

25. Below: John Duncan, 'Dundee Fine Art Exhibition', cartoon from *The Wizard of the North*, 1881 *(Libraries, Leisure & Culture Dundee)*.

Constable and Frans Hals (figure 26). W Lawson Peacock of T Richardson & Co, London, had been holding annual sales of "high class pictures" in Lamb's Hotel and other venues since 1872. Their 1879 catalogue boasted "important and beautiful works by some of the most esteemed of modern English and Dutch Artists".[94] The sales grew in size each year – in 1885 they brought with them 335 works (including *Baby's Breakfast* by B J Blommers, bought by Provost McGrady). Finally in 1891 Peacock and Richardson dissolved their partnership and a final auction of their collection was held in Dundee by Harris & Curr.[95]

Formerly Harris & Fairweather, Harris & Curr was one of a number of businesses that boomed during this golden age of collecting and exhibiting. Robert Curr had started as a clerk to

Like many dealers, Liddle ran a small gallery to show off his wares. Some of these galleries became notable exhibition venues in their own right, and important cultural attractions in the town. Perhaps the first notable example was Mr William A Scott's Fine Art Repository. Scott began his business in 1867 (the year of the BA exhibition) and operated from 13 Shore Terrace before moving into the town centre in 1880 and opening a New Fine Art Gallery in 92 Commercial Street, offering "A Very Fine Selection of High-Class Pictures for Sale".[98] He sold artists' materials – according to the trade paper *The Mercantile Age*, "everything an artist requires is here obtainable" – and "as a carver, gilver, mirror and frame-maker, this gentleman holds an enviable position in Dundee". Scott also undertook painting restoration work,

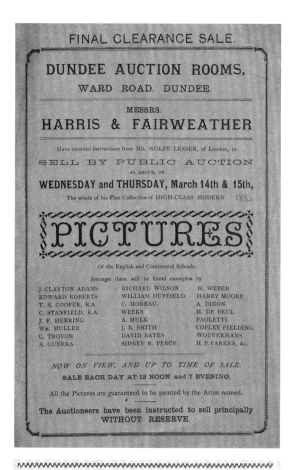

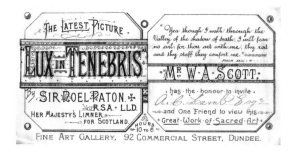

26. Sale notice for Wolfe Lesser's collection by Harris &
Fairweather, 1880 *(Libraries, Leisure & Culture Dundee,
licensor www.scran.ac.uk).*

27. Advertisement by Grindlay Liddle from the *King Street
Rocket*, 1885 *(Libraries, Leisure & Culture Dundee).*

28. Invitation for a viewing at William Scott's Fine Art Gallery,
1887 *(Libraries, Leisure & Culture Dundee, licensor www.
scran.ac.uk).*

sending his workmen to "gentlemen's mansions, far or near" to do
the work in situ.[99]

Scott dealt with the work of local artists (the *Mercantile Age*
feature in 1889 singled out Joseph Milne and Allan Ramsay for
special mention) but also became well-known for offering individual
viewings (for a small charge) of major paintings on loan, usually
large-scale religious or genre pictures (figure 28). In 1888 he
showed Goodwyn Lewis's *The Last Supper* ("as near an illustration
of the actual event as will ever be arrived at")[100] while in 1896 he
had a particular coup with R Caton Woodville's *The Charge of the
Light Brigade* ("The Great Military Picture"), straight from its
showing "by Royal Command" to Queen Victoria at Balmoral.[101]

By that time William Scott was in the unusual position of being
in competition with his own son. Robert Scott had served as an
apprentice under his father and was evidently eager to learn: "From
his earliest boyhood... [he] thoroughly mastered not only the
technique of a carver, gilder and picture-frame maker, but studied
closely all the best pictures, prints, engravings and etchings that
were within his reach."[102] To further his knowledge he travelled to
New York to study advanced print-making, and on his return he set
up his own business at 19 Albert Square in 1886. Initially called
the Queen Victoria Print & Picture Shop, by 1890 it had become
known simply as Robert Scott's Fine Art Gallery or Saloon (figure
29).

Like his father, Robert advertised special showings of major
paintings – in 1897 you could pay sixpence to see Noel Paton's *The
Choice* ("the Greatest and Most Impressive of all his Works").[103]
But his speciality was prints – by 1889 he was boasting the largest
selection in the north of Scotland.[104] Scott published a number
of prints himself, most notably James Douglas's *Dundee from the
Harbour* (see chapter four). Every year he held a large exhibition
of the latest etchings and engravings, including copies of old
masters and works by contemporary artists such as Whistler. The
exhibitions became important events in Dundee's artistic calendar,
particularly when the Fine Art Exhibitions became more sporadic.
Writing about Scott in 1905, the *Piper o' Dundee* was keen to
offer "a word of thanks to that gentleman for the opportunities he
so frequently affords Dundonians of learning what is going on the
world of art."[105] As the demand for large oil paintings declined, the
interest in etchings increased. Many collectors turned to prints as a
much cheaper way to buy contemporary art, and in 1900 Scott was
able to expand his gallery, taking over the shop next door (figure
30). The *Evening Telegraph* described the new premises:

> "The saloon is a beautifully compact one, its
> walls decorated in rich yet subdued crimsons;
> while by a simple expedient of awning the roof
> light is subdued to that radiation which... does
> not hinder a proper appreciation of delicacy.
> Art rugs contribute to the cultured atmosphere;
> sculpture... lends a chaste effect; Japanese
> bronzes [and] some Dutch brass work...
> contribute variety; ...Carved ivories, enamels,
> antique silver divide attention with portfolios of
> worth; and the mind and the eye of the visitor are
> thus equally engaged and refreshed... This is the
> chief point in Mr Scott's undertaking, and it seems
> to forecast an enlargement in Dundee's artistic
> knowledge and sympathies."[106]

29. Robert Scott's Fine Art Galleries, Albert Square, 1903. Photograph from the Wilson Collection (*Libraries, Leisure & Culture Dundee*).

30. Top: Unknown artist, Interior of Robert Scott's Fine Art Galleries, from the *Evening Telegraph*, 1900 *(used by kind permission of D C Thomson & Co Ltd)*.

31. Above: Thomas Murray & Son's Fine Art Saloon, Nethergate, c.1901. Photograph from the Wilson Collection *(Libraries, Leisure & Culture Dundee)*.

32. Top right: David Clark, Portrait of John Robertson of Elmslea from *The Piper o' Dundee*, 1888 *(Libraries, Leisure & Culture Dundee)*.

33. Opposite page: J Michael Brown, cover for the *Indiapolis* programme, 1888 *(Libraries, Leisure & Culture Dundee, licensor www.scran.ac.uk)*.

By the time of his 30th annual exhibition in 1916 he was noting "a wonderful increase in the number of print collectors", with demand frequently out-stripping supply.[107] In 1924, however, Scott fell seriously ill and was given only six months to live. He gave up the business but managed to make a miraculous recovery and started again with new premises in West Ferry. By the time he died in 1948, the art world in Dundee had changed dramatically.[108]

By far the longest running fine art business of the time was that of Thomas Murray & Son at 106 Nethergate (figure 31). It was originally begun at 64 Nethergate as a frame-making shop by James Fenwick in 1821, the same year that Thomas Murray

was born near Scone. Coming to Dundee as a boy, Murray became Fenwick's apprentice and worked his way up, taking over the business in 1859 from one of Fenwick's successors, Robert Stevens. By 1879 he was showing exhibitions, usually of work by local artists. After Murray's death in 1897, the business was acquired by James K Foggie (brother of painter David Foggie), who as a Bailie on the Town Council was also actively involved with the Albert Institute. It may have been more than mere coincidence, then, when Thomas Murray & Son earned a lucrative commission "to Clean and Restore a large number of the Old Paintings" from the permanent collection.[109] The business (still under Murray's name) continued until the 1940s.

The Fine Art Exhibitions had achieved extraordinary success in their first ten years, with sales unmatched almost anywhere else in Britain. The rapid rise in profits could not be maintained, however, and in 1884 the jute industry suffered another severe decline. "Even the most sanguine can hardly expect large purchases of pictures in these dull times" noted the *Courier*.[110] Still, 1,181 tickets were sold by the Art Union, though purchases were down significantly – the £545 prize money yielded £1,436 in sales, accounting for more than 40% of total sales at the exhibition. "Considering that this is perhaps the worst year Dundee has seen in the memory of man," said John Maclauchlan at the prize draw, "the result is considered highly satisfactory".[111]

It was the start of a downward trend, however – sales continued to be weak in 1885 and 1886, and there were increasing complaints about the poor state of the galleries, particularly the quality of the lighting. As Orchar himself admitted in 1885, "The rooms we currently possess are neither creditable to us nor fair to the artists who send us their works. In our present galleries we can place only about 150 pictures in a satisfactory position and a good light."[112] With the permanent collection also steadily growing, the need had therefore arisen for larger (and better lit) gallery space in the Albert Institute. In 1887 the annual exhibitions were put on hold while efforts began to raise money for a whole new suite of art galleries as a tribute to Queen Victoria in her jubilee year. A major stumbling block was the Albert Institute's existing debt of over £10,000. In an act of exceptional generosity, John Mitchell Keiller offered to cover this amount single-handed.

One of the leaders of the fund-raising efforts was the Vice-Chairman of the Fine Art Exhibition Committee, John Robertson of Elmslea – so-called after purchasing William Ritchie's house (figure 32). Although a less ostentatious collector than many of his contemporaries, he "took a deep interest in all matters pertaining to Art in Dundee... and was a liberal donor to the building fund."[113] The son of a Perthshire farmer, Robertson was born in 1831 and came to Dundee to find work at the age of 15. After gaining experience in various

INDIAPOLIS
OCTOBER · DVNDEE · 1888 ·

companies he became a partner in his uncle's successful jute business at Craigie Works. He joined the Town Council in 1872 and served for many years as Convenor of the Free Library Committee.[114] Robertson presented several works to the permanent collection, and died in 1906. Having no children, his collection was divided among his sisters in Norwood Crescent, his brother J C Robertson at Strathview and his nephew William R Kydd in Duntrune Terrace.[115]

The main focus of the fund-raising campaign for the new galleries was Indiapolis, an extravagant Indian Palace Bazaar held in the Drill Hall in October 1888 (figure 33). Since bazaars were held to be ladies' work, the Countess of Strathmore took charge aided by the wives of committee members and other local ladies. Several leading artists donated paintings for a special draw at the Bazaar by the Dundee Art Union, including McTaggart, Wingate and Cameron. 145 paintings with a value of over £9,000 were awarded to subscribers, but with only 806 tickets sold, just £412 was raised. Altogether, however, profits from the event (and from the accompanying souvenir publication) totalled over £4,000. £2,500 was given by the Town Council and further donations subscribed by members of the Fine Art Committee, the total costs ultimately coming to just under £15,000.[116]

There was considerable debate as to the design of the new galleries. The original designs by town architect William Alexander (a rather jumbled assembly of four rooms of various sizes with a new entrance on the east side) soon came in for criticism, and various alternatives were proposed. One published in the *Advertiser* included a large Continental-style covered courtyard, of the kind that the new Aberdeen Art Gallery (which had opened in 1885, following Dundee's lead)

would later create. T S Robertson published his own version, which was almost a separate building with just one connecting room on the first floor. There were even suggestions that the galleries be built on a different site entirely.[117] Ultimately, however, revised plans by Alexander (created in consultation with Orchar) were accepted and building began in February 1888 (figure 34).

Orchar's principal influence was in the unique design of the main Victoria Gallery, with its doubled-glazed roof and curved walls, the latter of particular benefit to the dense hanging arrangements of the time, angling the higher paintings down towards the viewer. Orchar had actually arranged for a full-size model of the gallery to be built in his Wallace foundry to test these features, and had invited William McTaggart among others to come and inspect it.

The other major innovation was the use of electric light. Galleries of the time were generally lit by gas, but the Albert Institute had pioneered the use of temporary electric lighting using portable generators for the Fine Art Exhibitions in the early 1880s and was keen to take this further. No less an authority than Lord Kelvin was approached to advise on the installation, and members of the committee visited the 1888 International Exhibition in Glasgow where electric light was used on a large scale. The electrical engineer for that exhibition, William Bryson, was employed as a consultant, and his idea of using both incandescent bulbs and large Phoenix arc lamps was put into practice. Half of the £2,000 needed to install the lights was donated by W O Dalgleish. Dundee thus became one of the first cities in Britain to have an electrically lit public art gallery (figure 35).

The Victoria Art Galleries were officially opened on 26 October 1889 by the Marquis of Lorne, Queen Victoria's son-in-law. Two days before, the Marquis had been granted the Freedom of the City, for Dundee was now officially a city, its status newly confirmed by a charter from the Queen.[118] Opinion on the architecture varied – the *Advertiser's* grudging praise claimed: "The Institute may not possess all the elements of the beautiful, but it is no longer deficient in mass and balance".[119] There was no doubt, however, that the 1889 Fine Art Exhibition (the first in three years) looked spectacular in its new setting – "apples of gold in a basket of silver" was how the exhibition catalogue put it. The electric lighting "enables the pictures to be seen in all their purity of tint, whilst it keeps the atmosphere cool and sweet – two very important conditions unattainable with gas light."[120] 1,270 works were included, yielding £6,446 in sales. £2,820 of this came from Art Union prizewinners – the organisation's best ever figure (the committee gleefully reported that the London Art Union had made only £2,000 that year).[121] Among the highlights on show were Landseer's *The Free Kirk* (from the Royal Collection), Orchardson's *Napoleon on board the Bellerophon* (lent by the Royal Academy, now in Tate Britain) and *The Farmer's Daughter* (lent by John Forbes White, now in Glasgow Museums), and a portrait of White by Sir George Reid (on loan from Aberdeen Art Gallery).

John Forbes White (figure 36) had recently moved to Dundee from his native Aberdeen, where he had inherited his father's flour mills and invested his money in building up a substantial art collection. Many art historians (particularly

34. One of a set of plans for the Victoria Galleries extension of the
Albert Institute, 1888 *(Dundee City Archives)*.

35. Dundee Fine Art Exhibition 1890, electrically lit in the new Victoria
Galleries *(Dundee City Council: Dundee's Art Galleries & Museums)*.

Jennifer Melville and John Morrison) have noted White's significance as a pioneering collector of modern Dutch and French art (including Mollinger, Israels and Corot), and the subsequent influence on Scottish artists from Chalmers and Reid through to the Glasgow Boys.[122] In contrast to most of his fellow collectors in Aberdeen or Dundee, White was also a great scholar of art who lectured regularly on the subject and published articles in the *Encyclopaedia Britannica*. He had already shown an interest in Dundee's growing art scene, lending two works to the 1873 Fine Art Exhibition and serving on the organising committee of the 1877 show. This was also a good business move, White having just opened the Dundee Flour Mills and no doubt wanting to develop closer relations with the town's leading businessmen. In 1883, "dictated by the inexorable necessitudes of modern competition", White closed his Aberdeen mills and relocated the rest of his business to Dundee.[123] Having made his home at Craigtay (now a hotel on Broughty Ferry Road), it was hoped by the *Piper o' Dundee* "that the city will share in his interest in art culture, and that our own important galleries and art life will receive all the help and assistance and experience which Dr White has brought from Aberdeen awa."[124] Unfortunately the move to Dundee had been caused by a major recession in the milling industry, and in 1888 White was forced to sell off most of his collection and began to suffer from severe depression. He served on a number of local organisations including the Chamber of Commerce, the UCD Council and the local Liberal Unionist Association, but was unable to do as much for the cause of art in Dundee as he had in Aberdeen. "From time to time he lectured on art subjects," the *Advertiser* reported after his death in 1904, "and always attracted large and appreciative audiences". The Dundee Art Society noted in its obituary that the city "has lost a well-known and greatly respected Art Patron and Connoisseur."[125]

The financial decline that affected White's flour mills was also felt in other industries. After the success of the 1889 Fine Art Exhibition, further shows were held in 1890 and 1891, but yet another slump in the jute trade had a notable effect on sales. Only £3,500 was raised by the 1891 show, and the decision was taken not to hold another until the local economy had revived. A cartoon in the *Piper o' Dundee* showed two men conversing outside the Victoria Galleries:

"Stranger to Dundonian:
'What building is that, please?'
Dundonian:
'That's the Picter Galleries.'
Stranger:
'Are they open to visitors?'
Dundonian:
'Na, na, no' th' noo. The jute trade's that
dull that they're shut doon, like some
o' the mills.'"[126]

Sales by commercial dealers continued to take place, but with diminishing returns. In 1897 the *Piper* noted: "The

number of art sales taking place in Dundee shows that both artists and collectors would rather finger the ready rhino than feast their eyes on the paintings... After inquiries, I found that the most of the sales are very flat, and that the best pictures are often withdrawn, there being no offers."[127] To some critics, it was as if everything the city had thus far achieved culturally counted for nothing: "We sincerely trust... that at some period Dundee may be an Art centre," said the *Wizard of the North*. "We fear, however, it is not in the near future."[128] Meanwhile in an editorial titled 'Culture Famine in Juteopolis', the *Piper o' Dundee* claimed: "In Art a select coterie has for too long represented artistic Dundee. All honour to those who have in the face of much discouragement gained and held for Dundee some reputation as an art loving centre; but to the crowd Art is an unknown quantity."[129]

The big exhibition of 1892 was therefore something quite different, and was guaranteed to appeal to the masses. 'Old Dundee' remains to this day the largest exhibition ever held of historical views of the town and its people (figure 37). It was prompted by the huge changes that had been taking place following the 1871 Improvement Act, which led to the

36. Unknown artist, Portrait of John Forbes White from *The Piper o' Dundee*, 1889 (*Libraries, Leisure & Culture Dundee*).

37. W H Donnelly, 'Old and Young Dundee' from *The Wizard of the North*, 1892 (*Libraries, Leisure & Culture Dundee*).

destruction of large parts of medieval Dundee. Narrow wynds of tightly packed houses were replaced by grand Victorian buildings along widely spaced boulevards. It is often suggested that few in Dundee mourned the passing of the old town, but the success of the Old Dundee exhibition clearly demonstrated a huge interest in remembering what had been.

The exhibition comprised over one thousand drawings, paintings, photographs and other artefacts, about a third of which came from the collection of one man. Alexander Crawford Lamb was born in Dundee in 1843 and began his career apprenticed to a bakery and restaurant business. Jobs in Manchester and Edinburgh followed before he returned to Dundee around 1866 to take charge of Lamb's Temperance Hotel, which had been established by his father on Reform Street. Having initially developed an interest in photography, Lamb (according to a feature in the *Wizard of the North*) "turned his attention to the higher arts, and it says much for his taste and knowledge of the subject that his cabinet of oil and water-colour paintings is one of the finest in the district".[130] It included works by Bough, Orchardson and Noel Paton as well as a fine collection of etchings, but Lamb's interest increasingly turned towards topographical views of his own town, along with portraits of local worthies and other documentary evidence of the cultural and business life of Dundee.

38. David Foggie, *Sir James Key Caird*, oil on canvas, c.1928-9 *(University of Dundee Museum Services, Tayside Medical History Museum)*.

Lamb was the guiding force behind the Old Dundee exhibition, serving as Convenor of the Special Organising Committee and, in John Maclauchlan's words, bearing "the burden and heat of the day". In his introduction to the exhibition catalogue, Maclauchlan claimed that its purpose was to "enable the citizens to realize better than before both the history of their fine old town, and the men of whom they have heard their fathers speak as 'The Makers' of Dundee."[131] Lamb was all too aware of the lack of appreciation of Dundee's long history, as he noted in his speech at the opening: "It is a curious fact that there is a very large number of our fellow-subjects who labour under the mistake that Dundee has sprung into existence about a century ago, and that it has no reasonable title to call itself 'Old Dundee'. To this objection a very complete answer is afforded by the exhibition itself."[132]

While's Lamb's collection was by far the largest on show, several hundred individuals and institutions also lent items for display. The largest private collection after Lamb's was that of James Falconer, who lent around 100 pieces to the exhibition. Falconer was a plumber and gas-fitter who had opened a shop in the Nethergate which became "one of the finest show rooms in the city for ironmongery work of all kinds".[133] His home in Miln's Buildings was said to be crammed full of pictures, books, plates, coins and other local antiquities. Along with over 300 views of Dundee and its surroundings, he also owned many other Scottish topographical scenes and also cartoons by local artists such as Martin Anderson and Max Cowper and other notable cartoonists including Phiz and Harry Furniss.[134] With superb timing, Falconer chose to sell his collection just days after the Old Dundee exhibition came to an end – the 992 lots were sold by James A McLean in Kinnaird Hall in May 1893.[135]

The Old Dundee exhibition was, unsurprisingly, a great popular success. Within a fortnight of its opening on 23 December, the catalogue had to be reprinted, and the *Piper o' Dundee* reported "Old Dundee has excelled all expectations as an attraction. Citizens and visitors from a distance have crowded to the Exhibition, and the holiday record of attendance beats all the former exhibition holiday records."[136] The show eventually closed in April 1893 having attracted some 50,000 visitors, but it had been expensive to organise and unlike the Fine Art Exhibitions it yielded no sales commissions and therefore no hope of making a profit – the one measure of success that counted among the Victorian businessmen that ran the city.[137]

When Lamb passed away in May 1897 the *Piper* was quick to report rumours that he had died intestate and that his collection was to be put up for sale.[138] Sure enough, Lamb's paintings, medals, china and literary treasures were sold at Dowell's in Edinburgh the following February, though according to the *Piper*, "the prices obtained for the paintings were not so high as might have been anticipated".[139] The biggest seller was Sam Bough's *Barges on the River Irwell* (for £157/10), but a watercolour of Broughty Castle by the same artist fetched just £3/3.[140] There was considerable fear that the Old Dundee collection would meet the same fate, but at the last minute the jute merchant Edward Cox of Cardean (son of ex-Provost Cox) stepped in and purchased the entire collection for the city "in the belief that future generations... will be interested in seeing how the Dundee of their ancestors looked and grew".[141] According

to John Maclauchlan, "It is undoubtedly the largest, finest, and highest-class Local Collection – historical, pictorial, and literary – possessed and preserved by any city in Great Britain".[142]

It was not until 1895 that another Fine Art Exhibition was attempted, this time held in conjunction with an exhibition of the Royal Scottish Society of Painters in Watercolour (RSW). The general opinion (according to the *Piper o' Dundee*) was that "it is the finest we have yet had the pleasure of looking upon in Dundee."[143] Orchar enrolled the help of RSA members Tom Graham and Robert Alexander to help with the hanging, which included as a centrepiece Whistler's portrait of Thomas Carlyle, on loan from Glasgow Corporation. A number of notable artists also gave lectures to accompany the exhibition (including W D McKay on 'Art of the Low Countries' and James Archer on 'Art Language in Painting'), but attendance was (in John Maclauchlan's words) "indifferent".[144] Even after reducing the admission fee, the public failed to show much interest, sparking a special feature in the *Piper o' Dundee* entitled 'Art and the Man':

> "The endeavour to interest the Dundee public at large in the Fine Arts Exhibition has not been rewarded as it should have been... This is all the more regrettable since we have been so frequently told that we are 'an artistic City.'... How can it [Dundee] become a centre of art unless the artistic tastes of the people are better manifested."[145]

Commercially too, the exhibition was deemed a failure. According to the *Courier*, "art has found only admiration, and has secured no patronage".[146] Although a number of buyers from outwith Dundee helped sales to top £5,000, the city's own collectors were more reluctant to part with their money. The Art Union also had its worst year, raising just £300 in prizes. John Maclauchlan blamed "the great and long depression in the staple trade of the town" but also noted a general trend away from the kind of large-scale picture buying that had once been so fashionable: "All over Europe there was not the same desire to acquire paintings – a generation had arisen which might talk about but did not purchase Art". It was finally decided "that the wisest course would be to suspend the annual Exhibitions until a time when a fresh interest in art, and a desire to acquire examples of it, should return, and a revived trade afford the means of purchase."[147]

It was certainly apparent that the super-rich collectors of the 1860s and 70s were a dying breed, but the less ambitious collecting of men like James Falconer showed that it was not just Dundee's wealthiest citizens who were interested in buying art. Another example worth noting of lower-middle class collecting was Jason Goodchild, a steeple-jack and electrician who had moved to Dundee from Oldham in the 1860s. His business was evidently a profitable one – at the time of his death he owned over 100 works of art, including paintings by John Pettie and a number of local artists such as Henry Harwood and John S Fraser. His end came swiftly in 1883 at the age of just 45 when he was accidentally pulled off a ladder at the Wellgrove Works in Lochee and fell over 60 feet to his death.[148] His extensive collection of art, books, china and antiques was sold by Harris & Fairweather at the Dundee Auction Rooms.[149]

At the other end of the social scale, many of Dundee's richest men were now choosing to spend their money in other ways, even those with direct artistic connections. A notable example is James K Caird (figure 38), who had inherited the Ashton Jute Works from his father and later bought Craigie Works as well. In 1873 Caird married Sophy Gray, whose sister Effie was married first to the writer and art critic John Ruskin and then to the Pre-Raphaelite painter John Everett Millais. As well as painting his own children, Millais also did at least one painting of the Cairds' daughter Beatrix, who died at the age of fourteen. Caird's marriage to Sophy seems not to have been a happy one – she died in 1882, possibly of self-starvation caused by her anorexia.[150] Caird continued to keep up his acquaintances in the art world – he was friends with Whistler, and invited him to stay with him in Dundee in 1894 (though there is no evidence that Whistler took up this invitation). Caird's sole art donation to the city's collection was an etching by Whistler. He was never involved in the Fine Art Exhibitions and if he had an art collection beyond a few pieces connected to the artists he knew, there is no surviving evidence of it. He made many generous donations to the city but usually preferred to spend his money in foreign travel and on expeditions – he was an important patron of the archaeologist Flinders Petrie and the polar explorer Ernest Shackleton, and later gifted both Egyptian and Antarctic material from them to the city's museum collections.[151]

Although the most intense period of art collecting in Dundee may have ended, its influence was strongly felt. Writing about J C Bell in 1897, the *Advertiser* noted: "The love of art for its own sake has spread widely in Dundee since Mr Bell set the example, and many collections have been formed, some of them more valuable than his. If less prosperous times have in the meantime dampened this ardour, the wider and higher influences of art have been abiding... [They] have very distinctly raised the taste of the whole community, and exercised a refining influence on all classes as beneficent as it is unconscious."[152] As we shall see in chapters three and four, one result was the fostering of a new generation of artists in Dundee. At the same time, the Dundee Art Union had helped to ensure that some £20,000's worth of art was purchased from the exhibitions by Dundee's citizens. In the next chapter we will look at the development of a permanent collection of art for the city and the increasing number of public art commissions that accompanied it.

Chapter Two
Collections & Commissions

39. George Paul Chalmers, *Old Letters*, oil on canvas,
donated by J G Orchar (*Paisley Museum, Renfrewshire Council*).

On 31 January 1874 the inaugural Fine Art Exhibition at the Albert Institute was formally closed with a large gathering in the Great Hall, chaired by Provost Cox. The great success of the exhibition was noted, along with the fact that the huge volume of ticket sales had yielded "a considerable surplus" which, it was proposed, should be put towards the acquisition of artworks "for the permanent gallery". The art committee, however, declined the responsibility of choosing what to acquire, suggesting "that this is a matter requiring the utmost care and the best advice, or probably that a small Committee might be named, with powers, to select from any public Exhibition, or otherwise, as opportunity might occur, such works of deceased or living artists as are really desirable for a public gallery."[1]

The local orator H B Fergusson then gave an address, noting that already, "a number of gentlemen had presented meritorious pictures to the institution, and among those was Mr Orchar, who had signalised himself by presenting a very beautiful picture, which was exhibited for the first time that evening." The painting referred to was *Old Letters* by George Paul Chalmers (figure 39), later described by James Webster (who wrote the first catalogue of the collection in 1899) as "a very charming little study on a simple and homely subject, full of a pretty sentiment, and, perhaps to some, of pathos also".[2] Speaking in 1911 about all the treasures in the permanent collection, the artist John Duncan described *Old Letters* as "perhaps the loveliest of all", recalling the "velvety shade of the background, the radiance of light on the still face."[3]

In years to come, *Old Letters* would come to be accepted as the first painting to enter the collection – the Free Library Committee, who ran the museum and art gallery along with the library, would later state categorically that "Orchar was the first to make a gift to the Collection".[4] Fergusson's statement makes it clear, however, that Orchar's was not the only donation made before the permanent gallery opened. The Report of the Free Library Committee to the Town Council in 1874 also noted gifts from T S Robertson (a landscape in oil by David Mackenzie) and C C Maxwell (two oils).[5] The Fine Art Exhibition catalogue (published in 1873) lists one of the latter works (*The Good Samaritan*, originally thought to be by Richard Wilson, later attributed to Jacob More and now re-attributed to Crone – figure 40) as "presented by Mr C C Maxwell" while all other works were lent. It seems, therefore, that Maxwell's gift came first, but was soon eclipsed by Orchar's.[6]

Surprisingly, given the Victorians' love of grand occasions, there was no formal opening event for the Free Library Museum & Picture Galleries, as the new permanent space was called. 1,540 people visited on the first day of opening (Saturday 9 May) and the *Courier* reported: "All appeared to enjoy their visit, and the utmost order and decorum prevailed throughout."[7] Unlike the Fine Art Exhibition, which charged for admission, the permanent galleries were free to everyone, which allowed Dundee's working men and women to visit in far greater numbers – something that clearly brought with it the threat (thankfully unrealised) of public disturbance. In reviewing the new displays, the *Courier* spent most of its time describing the artefacts and specimens in the Museum, before concluding: "The fine Picture Gallery contains some rather valuable works of art, although there is still plenty of space at the disposal of any wealthy philanthropist who has a love for the fine arts and a desire to place refining influences within the reach of all classes of the community."[8]

Three paintings clearly don't make a picture gallery, so the rest of the space was hung with loans from private collectors – essentially a miniature version of the Fine Art Exhibition. The *Courier* noted: "We hope the good example set by [the lenders] will be followed by our local art collectors, so that a succession of good paintings may be exhibited in the Gallery."[9] Unfortunately this did not help to encourage further donations to the collection – why give when you could merely lend? The Free Library Committee's reports for the next few years list numerous fascinating gifts to the museum, but mostly just loans to the picture gallery. Admittedly some were on a substantial scale – in 1882 it was reported that A B Spence had "withdrawn most of the sixty or so pictures lent by him last year, replacing them with fresh works."[10] When Dr John Stewart died in 1892 his widow wrote to ask for the return of "the sixty-five pictures belonging to him that have been lent to your permanent collection for the last fifteen years."[11]

Donations, however, were altogether rarer, and active purchasing was non-existent. There is no evidence that the suggestion of spending the profits from the first Fine Art Exhibition on acquisitions was ever taken up. Similarly, when the Dundee Art Union was set up in 1877, Board of Trade rules stipulated that 2.5% of its income must go into a reserve fund to buy works for the permanent collection. This led to the Free

40. Robert Crone (attributed), *The Good Samaritan*, oil on canvas, donated by C C Maxwell *(Dundee City Council: Dundee's Art Galleries & Museums)*.

41. Right: John Watson Gordon, *The Laird of Cockpen and Mistress Jean*, oil on board, from the Duncan Bequest *(Dundee City Council: Dundee's Art Galleries & Museums)*.

Library Committee reporting that "there are good grounds for hoping that Modern works of Art of Merit will now be permanently added to the gallery each year."[12] As it turned out, the money was simply carried over every year and by the time of the last draw in 1896 it had reached over £237 – no purchases had been made, and there is no evidence that they ever were. Instead, the Free Library Committee seems simply to have waited for donations. In an attempt to encourage collectors to give rather than lend, they were keen to point out the number of art students who were visiting the gallery to make copies – while this was possible with paintings belonging to the town, lenders "naturally enough... object to their pictures being copied."[13] This scarcely made for a convincing argument.

Nevertheless, shortly after the picture gallery opened they received their first bequest, from the late Thomas Weston Miln, a former flax merchant. Described by curator John Maclauchlan as "a number of interesting Pictures of cabinet size, principally of the Dutch School", the small collection included *The Expulsion of Hagar* by Gillis de Hondecoeter and *A Village Kermesse* ascribed to a follower of Salomon Rombouts.[14] In 1878, however, it was altogether eclipsed by the largest bequest the collection has yet received. It came from the late George Duncan, who had served as a Radical MP for Dundee from 1841-57. Born in 1791, Duncan had begun business as a haberdasher, beginning his political career on the Town Council in 1825. The first Scottish bailie to sit in

the House of Commons, he campaigned in favour of free trade, against monopolies, promoted reform in Scottish prisons and demanded an increase in government spending on education.[15] The last twenty years of his life were spent in comparative seclusion at The Vine, his house overlooking Magdalen Green. He was not involved in the Fine Art Exhibitions and rarely lent his works publicly, so his bequest of 38 paintings came completely out of the blue. According to A H Millar, "Mr Duncan had frequently visited the Continent at a time when the Napoleonic Wars had dispersed many valuable collections of pictures among the peasantry; and he was thus able to secure works of art at a very reasonable cost."[16] His gift to the permanent collection boasted old masters by van Berchem, Claesz, Melchior de Hondecoeter, Poussin-Dughet and

others, but most of the attributions given by Duncan have since been questioned and the collection is now largely catalogued as "follower of", "imitator of" or "studio of" the various artists.

Duncan's bequest also included a number of works by Scottish artists, including sketches attributed to David Wilkie and paintings by D O Hill and Sir John Watson Gordon. *The Laird of Cockpen* by Gordon (figure 41) was singled out for special praise by the artist John Duncan: "Is that not one of the most delightful pictures in the world? Who can look at it without smiling, and with no cynicism in the smile? The artist loved both the Laird and the Lady, and the shells on the mantelpiece, and he touched them with his brush with delicate distinction."[17] By contrast, James Webster called it "a small and unimportant sketch... of little interest". [18]

George Duncan made it a special condition of the bequest "that the pictures shall be exhibited to the public in the Art Gallery of Dundee. [They] shall not be sold or exchanged for other pictures, but shall be retained by the Magistrates for exhibition in all time coming".[19] J G Orchar, John Kennedy and J D Cox were tasked with arranging for the cleaning, labelling and hanging of the paintings. Duncan also left portraits of himself and his wife by Robert Scott Lauder to the Dundee Industrial Schools Society and divided his collection of engravings between the latter, Dundee Royal Infirmary, the Dundee Royal Orphan Institution and the art gallery.

Duncan's generosity seems to have acted as a catalyst to local collectors (many of whom were members of the Free Library committee, or one of its various sub-committees) and in January 1879 William Ogilvy Dalgleish wrote to offer John MacWhirter's magnificent landscape painting *The Falls of Tummel*, which he had had on loan to the gallery since 1875 (figure 42). Orchar thought the picture "one of the finest ever painted" and Councillor Henderson noted that "Mr Dalgleish

42. John MacWhirter, *The Falls of Tummel*, oil on canvas, c.1875, donated by W O Dalgleish *(Dundee City Council: Dundee's Art Galleries & Museums)*.

43. Right: John Pettie, *Disbanded*, oil on canvas, 1877, donated by J G Orchar *(Dundee City Council: Dundee's Art Galleries & Museums)*.

had the gratitude of the Committee in setting an example which he hoped would be extensively followed on the part of gentlemen who were lovers of art, and who wished to share with their fellow citizens some of the pleasures which the study of art was calculated to yield." [20]

In fact it would be 1881 before things really took off. In January the Convenor of the Free Library Committee, John Robertson (later of Elmslea), presented Alexander Fraser's *Bothwell Castle* ("a fine characteristic specimen of an artist at his best," according to the *Courier*), which he had acquired for 110 guineas from the sale of G B Simpson's collection the previous month.[21] In September, Orchar initiated another tradition by buying a work from the Fine Art Exhibition for donation, Hugh Cameron's *The Funeral of a Little Girl on the Riviera* – "unanimously declared to be not only the greatest work of the talented Artist, but one of the finest works painted in our time by any member of the RSA."[22] The Free Library Committee was so taken by Orchar's munificence that "a special Sub-Committee was appointed to draw up a minute suitably acknowledging the gift."[23] At the end of the year, Robertson made a second gift, presenting *The Port of Leith* by W F Vallance, which he had purchased from the RSA's annual exhibition. James Webster later dismissed it as "much too laboured and technical" but the Free Library Committee was delighted, noting "the progress that was being made in the formation of a representative collection of Scotch art". [24]

Orchar's gift of purchases from the Fine Art Exhibitions became an annual feature – he gave *The Gipsy* by Phil Morris in 1882; *A Message from the Sea* by McTaggart in 1883;

44. Dundee Fine Art Exhibition 1889. Many paintings from the exhibition later entered the permanent collection, including Millais' *Puss in Boots* (bottom right) *(Libraries, Leisure & Culture Dundee)*.

Disbanded by John Pettie in 1884; *The Lass that Baits the Line* by Colin Hunter in 1885 and *The Pass of Leny, Perthshire* by John Smart in 1886.[25] In accepting the McTaggart and noting Orchar's exceptional generosity in these repeated donations, the committee amusingly suggested that "if to the inscription to be placed on the frame were added the words 'Go thou and do likewise,' a very harvest of pictures might be confidently expected."[26]

Of all these gifts, *Disbanded* (figure 43) perhaps remains the most iconic today.[27] In 1899 Webster described it enthusiastically:

"The figure of the highlander… is graphically shown. His attitude bespeaks vigorous and impulsive action; the face is set in stern and unbending determination; the accessories of a bloody occupation, wrapped loosely together across the shoulders and painted with great fidelity, add to the dramatic fervour of the study. It is altogether a beautiful and vigorous piece of workmanship."[28]

John Duncan later recalled:

"The picture called 'Disbanded' by John Pettie, is one that I am sure we all thrilled to from the first. How vividly it realises the time. What can that sinewy Highlander want with the things he carries in the bundle on his back? The red Hanoverian coat that he never will wear, the sword he cannot handle, being used only to the broad-sword, the superfluous watch – has he not the shadows on the hills?"[29]

Further donations continued to arrive from other sources. In 1884 John Robertson gave *A Scene from "The Antiquary"* by Fettes Douglas and in 1886 he departed from the trend towards Scottish art by presenting English painter J E Hodgson's *Loot* and an old master, *The Sacrifice of Abraham*, originally attributed to Ribera and now to Battistello. Meanwhile that same year John Mitchell Keiller gave W E Lockhart's *The Swineherd* and a statue of Hamlet by Weizenberg; while I J Weinberg gave a "charming English landscape", *The Lock on the Colne River* by J Herbert Snell.[30]

By 1887 the permanent collection had grown to 71 works and "the time was rapidly approaching when the present Permanent Art Gallery might be too limited for [their] accommodation". Visitor numbers continued to increase, meanwhile, with the galleries "frequently crowded to inconvenience".[31] Speaking at a public meeting held in January to consider how best to mark the Queen's Jubilee, William Robertson explained the ever-increasing problem of holding the Fine Art Exhibitions in the same limited space:

"in order to hold their annual exhibitions, the permanent Picture Gallery had to be cleared out, and the whole of the loan and the permanent collections stored away in attics or in any other place capable of conveniently holding them, and the public of Dundee were excluded for five months out of the twelve from enjoying the free privilege of walking through the galleries, and of finding pleasure in looking at the pictures in the permanent collection."[32]

The result was the major fund-raising campaign already described to construct the Victoria Galleries as an extension to the Albert Institute, providing not just improved exhibition space but also a permanent home for the city's growing collection (figure 44). Rising to the occasion, several works were purchased for donation by local benefactors from the inaugural Fine Art Exhibition held in the new galleries in 1889-90. These included *Dewy Eve* by David Murray (donated by Weinberg, figure 45), *Kismet* by Tom Graham (donated by Orchar), marble busts of the Queen and Prince Albert by John Hutchison (donated by Hugh Ballingall) and the sculpture *Youth with Staghound* by Thomas Burnett (donated by W Brown Robertson). At the same time Orchar also donated *Holy Isle, Arran* by Sir George Harvey and an anonymous donor gave *The Funeral of the First Born* (aka *Her First Born, Horsham Churchyard*) by Frank Holl. Two important works by early Dundee artists were also donated at this time – the original version of the much-reproduced *The Executive* by Henry Harwood (given by Charles Lyell) and *The Opening of the Dundee and Arbroath Railway* by George McGillivray (given by the artist A S Edward).

The new permanent gallery opened on 8 March 1890, the Free Library Committee boasting that the collection "is now a very large and fine one, few provincial towns being so favoured". They also noted that "valuable as it is, it has been acquired *free of all cost* to the citizens."[33] This was something that the people of Dundee would be reminded of again and again, clearly suggesting that public subsidy of the city's art collection would not have gone down well with the ratepayers.

Not only did visitor numbers continue to increase year on year (over a quarter of a million visits were reported in 1893), but the fame of Dundee's collection was spreading far beyond the city. Loan requests were now a frequent occurrence – in 1893, for example, *Old Letters* was shown at the Society of Scottish Artists exhibition in Edinburgh, *Disbanded* at the Royal Academy in London and *The Swineherd* at the International Exhibition in Chicago. Donations also continued to arrive – in 1892 Dr John Stewart's widow gave *Dundee from*

45. David Murray, *Dewy Eve*, oil on canvas, c.1889, donated by I J Weinberg *(Dundee City Council: Dundee's Art Galleries & Museums)*.

Harecraigs by David Farquharson, while A J Buist gave Scott Lauder's *Christ and the Two Disciples on the Way to Emmaus*, followed three years later by Horatio McCulloch's *A Border Keep*. Edward Pinnington described Lauder's painting as "one of the most poetically conceived and masterly in style that ever left his easel... It is like an Old Master suffused with the spirit of modernity."[34] James Webster claimed that the McCulloch created impressions of "a certain rude dramatic force, of an excellently balanced composition, of nobility and simplicity in execution".[35]

In 1896 it was finally reported that the collection "has now overflowed the wall space of the large Permanent Gallery."[36] According to the Free Library Committee: "The rapid growth of the Collection of Paintings... is probably unique in the history of British provincial Art Galleries... It is one of the finest modern collections in Scotland, and is indeed a notable gift to the citizens."[37] In 1899, Dundee was chosen to feature in the first volume of an intended series of catalogues listing *The Art Treasures of Scotland*.[38] The publication listed an impressive 137 works of art, though this included paintings on loan.

One of the most notable ways by which the collection had grown so substantially was through the popularity of the 'presentation portrait'. Portraiture was something of an obsession among the Victorians, who were fascinated by the idea of finding clues to a person's character through their physiognomy. In Dundee, it also served as a mark of social status for the city's self-made businessmen. To have your portrait painted and hung in an art gallery was something previously only attainable by the aristocracy or others of exceptional wealth. As A H Millar explained:

> "In the course of time the work accomplished by some civic hero may be forgotten; but if his portrait has been painted by Millais or Orchardson, he will be remembered while the canvas endures... Hence, the Curator, for sake of the fame of the municipalist, as well as for the credit of his gallery, should encourage the development of this road to immortality. He will thus obtain portraits that may become worth a King's ransom, and will afford delight to future generations."[39]

From the outset, curator John Maclauchlan sought to follow this approach, and through the presentation portrait was able to achieve it at no cost to the collection. The money to commission each painting was raised through public subscription by the subject's fellow citizens (many of whom no doubt gave generously in the hope that they would one day be the recipient of the same honour), and the finished portrait was presented to the subject at a formal ceremony in the Albert Institute. It was then expected that the subject would gift the painting to the permanent collection, which most (but not all) did.

The Town Council had occasionally commissioned portraits in the days before the permanent collection began – as early as 1786, for example, they employed George Willison to paint his cousin, George Dempster MP. More recently, the Edinburgh-based painter Hugh Collins had been commissioned in 1871 to paint a posthumous portrait of former Town Clerk Christopher Kerr, who had died two years before. The success of this painting inspired a second commission the following

46. George Reid, *Ex-Provost Alexander Hay Moncur*, oil on canvas, 1886 *(Dundee City Council: Dundee's Art Galleries & Museums)*.

47. William Quiller Orchardson, *Henry Balfour Fergusson*, oil on canvas, 1896 *(Dundee City Council: Dundee's Art Galleries & Museums)*.

year, this time of the then-Provost James Yeaman. "The likeness is admirable," reported the *Courier*, "and the artist has succeeded remarkably in catching the true expression and working it out."[40] The cost of the commission was £120, the money being raised (and the portrait painted) in less than three months. The painting was presented to Provost Yeaman along with a "magnificent silver epergne" at a ceremony in the Town Hall on 26 September 1872. During his thank-you speech, the Provost declared that the portrait should "be presented to the town of Dundee", and it thus became the first presentation portrait to enter the permanent collection.

It would be another nine years, however, before the presentation portrait became a regular feature. On 9 September 1881 Dr John Boyd Baxter was presented with his portrait, painted by Sir Daniel Macnee, President of the RSA and "the foremost Scottish artist of the day".[41] Baxter was Procurator Fiscal for Forfarshire and as chairman of the Albert Institute Committee, he was primarily responsible for passing the building over to the Town Council. The *Courier* noted that "In handing over to the Doctor the admirable portrait, ex-Provost Robertson appropriately referred to the recipient's dignity and weight of character," while James Webster claimed: "It seems appropriate that the portrait of one who did so much to promote the best interests of these galleries should not be wanting from their walls."[42]

Macnee's portrait was shown at the Fine Art Exhibition that year, as was John Pettie's painting of ex-Baillie William Harris, the founding benefactor of Harris Academy, described by James Webster as "clever in its characterisation and vigorously painted".[43] This began a tradition of showing off the latest presentation portraits at the annual exhibition – it was followed by Robert Herdman's painting of ex-Provost George Rough in 1882 and a life-size portrait of the late Lord Kinnaird by James Archer in 1883. No presentations were made in 1884, but the year after Sir John Ogilvy was presented with his portrait by George Reid (soon to be Sir George, President of the RSA). Making the presentation, ex-Provost A H Moncur claimed that the painting "does eminent and full justice to the subject and infinite credit to the eminent artist." He also explained: "Although, by Sir John's request, individual subscriptions were limited to a comparatively small sum, money flowed in so abundantly that the Committee soon found themselves in possession of enough not only to get a portrait by a first-rate artist, but also a replica".[44] Robert Peyton Reid was commissioned to paint the replica, which was given to Dundee Royal Infirmary at Sir John's request.[45] The *Courier* described the original painting as "admirable... The features are clearly and finely worked out".[46] However James Webster concluded: "we are not able to regard it so favourably... the execution lacks firmness and distinction".[47]

Reid was commissioned again in 1886 to paint ex-Provost Moncur (figure 46), and the result was altogether more to Webster's taste: "an exceedingly well-intentioned and distinctively executed work... an altogether successful and truthful picture."[48] The presentation ceremony was masterminded by W O Dalgleish, who had led the fund-raising for the painting, and the various speeches (reported in full by the *Courier* on 22 January 1887) seemed to praise him more than Moncur – but it would be another 24 years before

Dalgleish had his own portrait presented (figure 294).

To coincide with the opening of the new Victoria Galleries in 1889, James Archer was again commissioned to undertake a posthumous portrait, this time of the 13th Earl of Dalhousie, who had died in 1887 aged just 40. Speaking at the unveiling, Provost Hunter noted:

"In our permanent collection within these walls there are many fine portraits of public men who have had connection with our city. Most of these portraits, however, are representations of men who had run the full race of human life. It is a sad feature in our recollections regarding the subject of the portrait just added to our permanent collection that Lord Dalhousie was taken so early in life… This portrait – excellent in execution, faithfully delineating the deceased nobleman – is one which the citizens of Dundee will always cherish and esteem".[49]

Despite the expansion of gallery space, there were no further presentation portraits of note until 1893, when nearly 200 citizens contributed towards W Q Orchardson's painting of Town Clerk Thomas Thornton. The Free Library Committee received it as "one of the most valuable gifts the Permanent Collection ever received... a work of art of great and permanent value, which future generations of our citizens will treasure".[50] According to the *Courier*, "The portrait is regarded as a very marked success, being not only a most characteristic likeness, but a magnificent work of art, possessing all the exquisite charm of painting and the subtle refinement always present in the pictures of the great artist entrusted with the commission."[51] James Webster claimed that "few men represented by Art on the walls of the Victoria Gallery are so deserving of a place thereon than as is Sir Thomas Thornton." Unfortunately he did not rate the painting so highly, noting "some indications of careless execution and of lack of finish, while the drawing is by no means irreproachable."[52]

In 1894 J G Orchar made a personal presentation of William McTaggart's portrait of the late Rev Archibald Watson, Minister of East Church, Dundee and Moderator of the General Assembly. Orchar had commissioned the painting especially for the collection, Watson having been an important member of the Free Library Committee for many years. The following year, the former MP George Armitstead gifted his portrait by the English painter A S Cope, which had just been shown at the Royal Academy in London. As a major benefactor to numerous Dundee institutions, a presentation portrait of Armitstead had been mooted some time before, but the subject declined to accept the honour – not his only such action as he was also said to have turned down the Freedom of Dundee and a peerage.[53]

Two of the strongest portraits in the collection were presented in 1896. Orchardson's painting of manufacturer Henry Balfour Fergusson (figure 47) was hailed by Webster as a "portrait of outstanding excellence, brilliant and incisive in technique".[54] Describing the city's portraits for the *Handbook* of the British Association's 1912 meeting, W H Blyth Martin

48. Hubert von Herkomer, *Ex-Lord Provost Henry McGrady*, oil on canvas, 1900 *(Dundee City Council: Dundee's Art Galleries & Museums)*.

49. C L Mitchell, *Sheriff John Campbell Smith*, oil on canvas, 1899 *(Dundee City Council: Dundee's Art Galleries & Museums)*.

claimed that "in the portrait of Mr Fergusson, which is probably the finest in the Galleries, and which has been many times exhibited in other cities, we have Orchardson impelled by his subject to the utmost charm of his power, resulting in one of the finest creations of this branch of art during the last half-century."[55]

Shortly after, Baillie Duncan Macdonald's portrait by McTaggart was presented, described by Edward Pinnington as "one of the treasures of the collection... It is doubtful if its equal can be found in any public collection".[56] James Webster, despite having misgivings about McTaggart's portraiture as a whole, found in this painting "a rugged fervour... not at all displeasing".[57]

As the century came to an end, the subscribers looked further afield to find suitable portrait painters for their commissions. Two portraits were commissioned from London's most fashionable painters – that of Dundee's most recent Lord Provost, Henry McGrady, by Hubert von Herkomer (figure 48), and of an earlier Provost, William Brownlee, by John Singer Sargent. Herkomer had already impressed Dundee's art loving public by giving one of the Armitstead Lectures in 1895 on the subject of Portrait Painting.[58] His picture was presented in 1900 while the Sargent was finally completed in 1902. Blyth Martin described the former as "an excellent example of Herkomer's art, full of strong and virile painting" though the poet Hugh MacDiarmid later dismissed it as "almost incredibly vulgar".[59] Sargent's painting was notably modern in its informality – as the *Advertiser* explained, "The Ex-Provost is in usual walking dress, with neither official robe nor uniform, but in the costume which is most familiar to those who encounter him daily."[60]

The Dundee Graphic Arts Association was disappointed, regretting the fact that "while there are several Scottish Artists of eminence still unrepresented publicly in Dundee, it should have been deemed necessary to go so far afield."[61] But at the same time, the city was also looking closer to home for its commissions. In 1899 the Association's President, C L Mitchell, was employed to paint a presentation portrait of Sheriff John Campbell Smith (figure 49).[62] This was altogether more satisfactory to the GAA: "nothing in recent Portraiture can give so much satisfaction to the members of the Graphic Arts Association compared with that newly acquired canvas... As an example of local talent this portrait takes its place in our gallery with a quiet confidence, and if this be the first of a series of local Celebrities by local Artists, we hail the occasion with hearty applause."[63] We shall look at Mitchell's career, as well as that of other Dundee portraitists, in chapter four.

Portrait painting was the most common type of artistic memorialisation in Dundee at this time. Sculpture was a more impressive medium, but the significantly greater cost, the complications of securing suitable sites and the unfortunate controversy which some of the results engendered meant that only a small number of public sculptural commissions were ever undertaken in Dundee.

The first major commission came in 1862 as a result of the gift by Sir David Baxter and his sisters Mary Ann and

50. John Steell, *Sir David Baxter*, marble, 1863 *(author's photograph)*.

51. Unknown artist, 'Opening of the People's Park, Dundee – The Procession Entering Baxter Park', engraving from *Illustrated London News*, 1863 *(private collection)*.

Ellen of the "People's Park" (soon renamed Baxter Park) as a "pleasure ground... where the labouring population of Dundee might breathe freely".[64] The value of this generous gift being estimated at some £50,000, a movement quickly sprang up to provide a lasting testimonial to the Baxter family. An initial meeting on 22 July 1862 led to the setting up of both a General Committee and a Special Committee to take the project forward, and within just a few weeks almost 17,000 of Dundee's grateful citizens had contributed to the fund. A proposal was put to the Baxters to erect a full-length marble statue of Sir David with accompanying marble busts of his two sisters. While the gentleman was agreeable, however, the ladies were not – though the Special Committee (whose members were clearly chosen for their skills in sycophancy) "could not but express their appreciation of the delicacy and excellent feeling with which their declinature was expressed"! This decision did not, however, dampen the committee's determination to make Sir David's statue a work of particular merit.

While various sculptors were discussed for the commission, Baxter's own choice was for the Edinburgh-based John Steell, already celebrated for his statues of Walter Scott and the Duke of Wellington in the capital. Although Steell had been born in Aberdeen, his family came from Dundee and he described it as "the place where the happiest of my early days were spent".[65] He had already sculpted a bust of Sir David, during the execution of which the two struck up "an intimate personal friendship".[66] Steell was thus the approved choice – not least because his familiarity with the subject made it more likely that he could complete the task in time for the park's opening the following year.

Steell quickly accepted the commission and promised to have it in place by 31 July 1863. Due to delays in having the site ready it eventually arrived on 3 September, and Steell personally supervised its erection (figure 50). The grand opening of the park proceeded on 9 September, featuring the usual mix of processions, speeches, band music and fireworks, and an estimated attendance of over 70,000 people (figure 51).[67] In all this the inauguration of the statue was just one brief item, featuring an address from John Leng, who had been chair and treasurer of the committee, and another from fellow committee member William Thoms to Steell, in which he noted:

> "A public statue is justly regarded as the highest tribute which can be paid to public worth, an honour only granted to those who have distinguished themselves in the eyes of their fellow-citizens. Allow me then to congratulate you on the successful completion of your task. In that statue you have not only embodied the form and features, but caught the spirit and expression of the original, while you have breathed into the marble the inspiration of your own genius, and stamped the whole as a masterpiece of art."[68]

52. John Steell, *George Kinloch*, bronze, 1872 (*Libraries, Leisure & Culture Dundee*).

53. John Hutchison, *James Carmichael*, bronze, 1876. Photograph from the Wilson Collection, 1895 (*Libraries, Leisure & Culture Dundee*).

The success of this enterprise gave an added impetus to a campaign which had been underway in Dundee for the past 30 years, with the intention of erecting a statue depicting the town's great Radical politician George Kinloch. Kinloch had been forced to flee the country after giving an inflammatory speech on Magdalen Green in 1819 condemning the Peterloo massacre in Manchester and advocating liberty and the rights of working men. When the Reform Act of 1832 changed the voting system, massively increasing the size of the Scottish electorate, Kinloch was returned as Dundee's first MP in the

THE ⁙ BURNS ⁙ STATUE ⁙ IN ⁙ DUNDEE.

54. Martin Anderson, 'The Burns Statue in Dundee', line drawing from a souvenir supplement to the *People's Journal*, 1880 *(used by kind permission of D C Thomson & Co Ltd)*.

55. Unveiling the Burns statue, 1880 *(Libraries, Leisure & Culture Dundee)*.

newly reformed Parliament. He did not have long to enjoy the position, however, dying the following year. His supporters had called for the erection of a monument in his honour ever since (a public meeting was first held to discuss the matter on 23 April 1833), and various plans were discussed over the years, including a large monument designed by architect James MacLaren to be placed close to where the Royal Arch was later erected; a drinking fountain on Magdalen Green; and even the suggestion that a proposed Free Library and Museum should be named in Kinloch's honour.[69] In 1863 it was decided that a monument would be erected in front of the Town House, but an interdict was served by the land owner preventing the scheme.[70]

Finally in February 1868 it was agreed that a statue could be placed in the grounds of the Albert Institute, by which time subscription money of around £500 had been raised. In March 1869 the Kinloch Committee (chaired by local builder James Sturrock) considered a proposal for a Redhall stone statue from Edinburgh sculptor William Brodie (who it had been hoped would sculpt the proposed busts of the Misses Baxter), but instead chose to go back to John Steell, who generously offered to undertake a bronze sculpture for considerably less than his normal £700 fee, in recognition of his connections to Dundee. Steell was supplied with various portraits of the subject to work from, chiefly a miniature by local artist Miss Margaret Saunders, whose father had been a close friend of Kinloch's. The sculptor set to work and it seemed that finally the long wait was over.

It was then that further troubles began. The Town Council had agreed a site for the sculpture with the Kinloch Committee and the sculptor, and a pedestal (designed by John Wright of Aberdeen) had been laid on that site in summer 1869. Steell had chosen to depict Kinloch in the act of making his celebrated address to the people on Magdalen Green, but disagreement broke out over which direction he should be facing to do so. The pedestal was placed so that the subject would be facing the street (to represent the people) but an opposing camp argued that since his address was an attack on the government, he should be facing the Post Office on Meadowside, which was the only government building in sight.[71] Without getting approval from the Town Council, the pedestal was shifted by an unknown power early one morning in September 1869 to face the Post Office. The Kinloch Committee also denied giving permission for this, though everyone knew that the workmen who carried it out were employees of James Sturrock! A public furore ensued with the press divided in their opinions, the *Advertiser* strongly supporting the move and the *Courier* opposing it.[72] Much of the argument centred around Town Councillor (and future Provost) William Brownlee, who had been tasked by the Council with staking out the site in consultation with the sculptor, but who had evidently chosen a different orientation for the pedestal than that preferred by the Kinloch Committee (or at least Sturrock). Considerable disagreement ensued as to whether Brownlee's remit extended as far as choosing the precise angle, or merely the area of ground on which the pedestal was to be placed. The *Advertiser* condemned Brownlee's "absurd crusade for angularity", referring to "the all but unanimous verdict of public opinion as to the propriety of keeping the Kinloch Monument as it is"

(ie in its revised position).[73] One anonymous correspondent wrote to the *Advertiser* suggesting that the pedestal should be placed "on a turnplate or casters, with a fixed centre [so that] competing parties could meet at any time and have a twist for it." [74] There were threats of legal action reported on both sides, but the Kinloch Committee were clearly unwilling to take the necessary steps to replace it. Brownlee's camp had a telegram from Steell confirming that he wanted the statue "parallel with the side of the Albert Institute, and square with the street" but when the Provost suggested asking Steell his opinion of the new position, they backed down, claiming it was of no use "as Mr Steell would come to no decision at all." [75] Meanwhile Steell was struggling with the commission due to frequent bouts of ill health, and it was not until the beginning of 1872 that the work was finally completed. Just a few days before its installation, the pedestal was finally returned to its original position, and the unveiling took place on 3 February (figure 52).

After all these difficulties, the inauguration event was a great success. The sun shone and huge crowds filled the streets, mostly working class men and women who had come straight from the factories to honour Kinloch's memory. According to the *Courier*, "The scene which the tremendous concourse presented was such as has never before been witnessed in the streets of Dundee." [76] A grand procession made its way from the Town Hall to Albert Square and there were speeches by Provost Yeaman, Kinloch's son and Lord Kinnaird, who had been one of the few members of the nobility to support Kinloch. On unveiling the statue, Kinnaird was heard to exclaim, "I fancy I see him before me". Kinloch's son claimed that "a more perfect statue I have never seen in Scotland" and congratulated the working men of Dundee for having finally accomplished "this great task". [77] Much of the press coverage (and many of the speeches) focused on the substantial increases in the rights, conditions and salaries of the working class throughout Britain that had been won as a result of Kinloch's campaigning.

By contrast to the protracted problems of the Kinloch statue, Dundee's next attempt at public memorialisation ran altogether more smoothly. On 17 July 1872, just five months after the previous unveiling, a meeting was held in the Town Hall with a view to commemorating in sculpture the late engineer James Carmichael of the Dundee ironworkers James Carmichael & Co. His invention of the fan blast had revolutionised the casting of iron, and he had offered the device to the industrial world free of charge, despite the fact that taking out a patent on it would have made him immensely rich. One of Carmichael's employees, George Hood, had first tried to raise interest in some form of memorial at the time of his death in 1853, but it was only when a paper was read by J G Orchar at the British Association meeting in 1867 that public and scientific interest in Carmichael's work was re-awakened. Because of the subject's national importance, fund-raising was carried out throughout Scotland, and by October 1873 the organising committee (chaired by John Sharp) were able to report £1,122 in subscriptions with more expected. [78] William Ritchie and J G Orchar were among those tasked with selecting the artist, and after holding an open competition, the design of another Edinburgh-based sculptor, John Hutchison,

was selected. Hutchison was no stranger to the area, having begun his career as a wood-carver at Hospitalfield and having already been commissioned to execute a bust of James Cox of Camperdown Works and a statue of the Earl of Dalhousie. He proposed a massive bronze sculpture at a cost of £1,500, which the *Scotsman* described in some detail:

> "In representing the old engineer, Mr Hutchison has aimed at being thoroughly realistic. He has not sought to invest the plain, homely Scotchman with any artificial graces of classical drapery, but has reproduced him in such attire as he was accustomed to go about in, and in connection with objects suggestive of his special claims to public recognition. The old man is supposed to have been taking a turn through his works, when, becoming suddenly possessed by some idea he has sat down to think it out." [79]

As a location for the statue, Hutchison requested the north side of Albert Square, at the opposite end from Kinloch. This was agreed in 1874 and by the following summer the model was complete and was sent to the foundry for casting. Shortly before its delivery to Dundee, one of Carmichael's former employees (possibly George Hood) visited Hutchison's studio to see the finished work. Styling himself "An Old Mechanic", he wrote to the *Courier* to say that upon seeing the statue he could not help but cry out, "That is my late master minus the breath." [80] The statue was erected on 16 June 1876 and unveiled the following day (figure 53). Pouring rain did not prevent over 10,000 people gathering to watch the proceedings, "the larger portion of whom consisted of the horny-handed sons of toil, factory girls, and mill operatives in their dusty garb." [81]

As well as his involvement with the Kinloch statue, James Sturrock was also one of the prime movers behind Dundee's next public art commission, a statue of the poet Robert Burns. The idea had arisen not in Dundee but in New York – in 1872 a committee of American Scots found that they had money to spare after commissioning John Steell to execute a statue of Sir Walter Scott for Central Park, the reason being that Steell had offered them the statue half price since it was a replica of the one created for the Scott Monument in Edinburgh. The committee decided to use the money to commission a new sculpture of Robert Burns, and wanted Scotland to reap the same benefit they enjoyed in having the chance to purchase a copy half price. Discussing the matter with Steell, Dundee was suggested in view of its many commercial transactions with New York and Steell's family connections with the town. Steell communicated this to Sturrock and ex-Bailie Drummond while the two were visiting his studio in February 1877, and the pair quickly called a public meeting and set to work raising the thousand guineas Steell was asking. [82] The following year a grand fund-raising bazaar was held, opened by the Earl of Strathmore, which included a display of original letters, manuscripts and other Burns relics loaned by local collectors such as A C Lamb. Along with concerts, individual subscriptions and a special donation from the Dundee Burns Club, a total of £1,400 was soon raised, covering the cost of the statue and its

twenty-ton pedestal made out of Peterhead granite by George Leslie-Jamieson of Aberdeen. The pedestal was erected in August 1879, and the decision was taken to include inside it a time capsule – two glass jars containing various local newspapers and publications, "so that future generations might learn from them what sort of town Dundee was in the nineteenth century."[83] The significance of art was evident from the inclusion of the two most recent Fine Art Exhibition catalogues and a copy of *Our Special Artist*.

This time there was no controversy beforehand about either the site of the statue (on the south-west corner of Albert Square) or its design (figure 54). Steell had chosen to depict Burns "in that rapt mood, when, on the anniversary of his Highland Mary's death, and when the day's hard toil over, he had gone out to meditate in the fields, the inspiration which produced the tender sweetness and pathos of 'Mary in Heaven' came upon him."[84] The *Advertiser* described Steell's sculpture as "the finest effort of his genius".[85] The *People's Journal* declared it to be "certainly the chef d'oevre of Sir John Steell's works; ...Dundee ought to be proud that the only realistic statue of Burns yet extant will be in Dundee."[86]

The unveiling of the statue was arranged for 16 October 1880, less than a fortnight after the original was inaugurated in New York. The Town Council declared the date to be a public holiday, and a crowd of at least 20,000 gathered on the day to watch the proceedings (figure 55). According to the editorial in the *Courier*:

"All along the way from Magdalen Green to Albert Square vast crowds gathered on the streets, in the house windows, on the house-tops, to witness the procession, while the great space at Albert Square presented one of the grandest of all sights – a throng of many thousands of people crowding every inch of standing room, filling up every window, and the roof of every house."[87]

The only disturbance to the proceedings came from Dundee's own bard, William McGonagall, who attempted to mount the platform dressed in Highland costume in order to perform his latest ode, 'The Burns Statue':

This Statue, I must confess,
is magnificent to see,

And I hope will long be appreciated
by the people of Dundee;

It has been beautifully made
by Sir John Steell

And I hope the pangs of hunger
he will never feel. [88]

Fortunately, the Poet and Tragedian never got this far, being swiftly moved on by the police. The Provost introduced Frank Henderson MP, who gave a lengthy address which concluded by entrusting the safety of the statue to "the protection it will find in the veneration and love which the name and memory of Burns can never fail to excite in the hearts of all true-hearted citizens of Dundee."[89]

It was only after the event that criticism of the statue started to grow. There was increasing complaint about the awkward pose of the limbs and the angle of the head (though the *Advertiser* claimed that herein lay its realism and its "entire freedom from conventionality").[90] Edward Pinnington later claimed that it was "the creation of a great artist's decline... It would be no loss to Dundee were it quietly consigned to the oblivion of the North Sea".[91] He claimed to have visited Steell while the work was under construction and found the artist stricken with self-doubt, fearing that "the commission may have come too late" (Steell was 76 by the time the work was completed). Whatever the truth of this, Steell made various alterations to the design when constructing two further versions of it for London and Dunedin.[92]

Encouraged by the success of the Burns statue, James Sturrock quickly proposed that a statue of Walter Scott should join it. He started a movement to commence fund-raising, but the idea never gained momentum, and Sturrock's death in 1882 put an end to the scheme. Attentions turned to the campaign for the Victoria Galleries, and it would be fifteen years before another piece of public sculpture was commissioned. In the meantime, smaller sculptural works were becoming more numerous in the permanent collection of the Albert Institute. Already the galleries boasted busts of Lord Kinnaird, David Livingstone and Prince Albert by William Brodie (the former gifted by the family, the latter two by Mary Ann Baxter), while the opening of the Victoria Galleries was marked by busts of the Queen and Prince Albert by John Hutchison being gifted to the collection by Provost Ballingall. Another Edinburgh-based sculptor, George Webster, was also a popular choice for commissions, undertaking busts for the galleries of Provost Thoms, Frank Henderson MP and the inventor James Bowman Lindsay (the latter donated by Lord Provost McGrady).

The addition of the Victoria Galleries allowed the museum displays of the Albert Institute to expand, and in 1890 the South Room was redesigned as an Art Museum to show casts of classical sculpture (figure 56). The suggestion had come from Principal Peterson of University College, Dundee, and a grant from the Science & Art department at South Kensington (see chapter six) covered half the £1000 cost. Curator John Maclauchlan was responsible for building up the collection from scratch (acting under the guidance of Prof Baldwin Brown of Edinburgh University, who had lectured in Dundee the previous year on 'The Uses of an Art Museum'), and within eighteen months it was being hailed as "the finest in Great Britain out of London."[93] The new gallery was opened on 8 March and contained "a large and very representative collection of casts from the most famous sculpture of classic and Renaissance times...; high class photographs of the finest architecture in the world; ...electrotype reproductions of

56. The Sculpture Court, Albert Institute, 1906. Photograph from the Wilson Collection *(Libraries, Leisure & Culture Dundee)*.

renowned metalwork, &c."[94] Maclauchlan later claimed that the collection (which quickly expanded to include Scottish sculptural work such as Celtic crosses)[95] was "certainly the most representative and up-to-date collection of sculpture in Scotland" and acted as an important stimulus to other cities such as Aberdeen and Glasgow to improve their own collections.[96]

In 1911 the opening of the new Central Reading Rooms in Barrack Street (now the McManus Collections Unit) enabled new, larger galleries to be created there for the collection, which had grown to over 100 pieces. Speaking that year to members of the Dundee Art Society, John Duncan praised the "extravagantly rich" collection:

> "I tell you it means much for the crowds of shy children who steal awe struck through the rooms hand in hand, or huddled together in queer groups. Do not believe they are just strange, naked, stucco figures to them. They are half divine, powerful, and beautiful beings set free somehow from the cramping sordid troubles they themselves endure. They make it possible for the child to believe in ideals, to have faith in unseen powers, and in other possible worlds."[97]

By that time a fourth and final statue had appeared in the

Albert Institute grounds. In 1896 the city fathers began to consider how Dundee might mark the Queen's forthcoming Diamond Jubilee. The principal scheme envisaged was the building of a new hospital (the Royal Victoria) but the idea of a statue of Her Majesty quickly gained support – possibly inspired by the fact that Aberdeen had erected a bronze statue of the Queen three years before (replacing an earlier marble one). As with previous works of public art, the decision was taken to open up subscriptions to the city's working classes to allow them to show their support for the monarch. Such was the enthusiasm that the sum required (some £3,500) was apparently subscribed in just one day.[98] For the first time, the committee appointed to commission the work included several of Dundee's notable art collectors, including J G Orchar, I J Weinberg and John Robertson of Elmslea. In early February 1897 Orchar and Lord Provost McGrady travelled to London and Edinburgh to interview various artists about the commission. It soon became apparent that no artist would be able to have the statue ready in time for the Jubilee, with only two claiming they could complete the work in less than two years. These were both London sculptors, Harry Bates and William Thornycroft, and since Bates' fee roughly matched the amount raised through subscriptions, he was awarded the commission. A regular exhibitor at the Royal Academy, Bates' most notable works of monumental sculpture prior to this were statues of Lord Roberts and Lord Lansdowne in Calcutta.

57. Plaster version of the Queen's statue outside the High School, 1897. Photograph from the Wilson Collection *(Libraries, Leisure & Culture Dundee)*.

Almost immediately, two separate arguments began. The first concerned the bas-relief panels which Bates intended to include around the base of the sculpture, representing scenes from the Queen's long reign. While most of the committee were in favour of depicting great events such as the coronation, the Town Clerk Thomas Thornton wanted the panels to show only the Queen's private acts of goodness, such as visiting wounded soldiers from the Crimea – he claimed that Greek and Italian sculptors "had always displayed the cardinal virtues, and had ignored wretched historical incidents."[99] In the end, Bates sought to appease both camps by depicting two public and two private incidents (her marriage to Albert, her visit to Dundee, visiting wounded soldiers and reading the Bible at the bedside of a poor Highland woman).

A much more prolonged dispute concerned the site of the statue. On visiting Dundee in late February 1897, Bates was shown two sites – directly in front of the High School, and in front of the grand staircase entrance of the Albert Institute, where a large fountain was then sited. The former was dismissed as causing an interruption of the view of the High School from Reform Street, but no one was particularly keen on moving the fountain either. The latter was also very close to the Burns statue, and considerable protest erupted when the suggestion was made to move that as well. A third suggestion was made to site the statue in front of the Clydesdale Bank at the end of the High Street. This was then countered by claims that it would hold up the traffic. Further suggestions were made and all were found to have some objection against them.

Bates succeeded in having a plaster cast of the statue ready to be displayed on the day of the Jubilee celebrations in June, and it was erected in front of the High School (figure 57). This

prompted a further rash of letters in the local press about the site, including one from Bailie Ferrier suggesting the north side of the Albert Institute between the statues of Kinloch and Carmichael.[100] The *Piper o' Dundee* suggested placing it on top of the Law: "People would come from far and near to see it, and Dundee would again become as famous as it was in the early days of the Tay Bridge."[101] Many in the Town Council, however, continued to support the idea of moving the fountain and placing the statue in front of the stairs, despite widespread objection. The appearance of the plaster cast also led to renewed criticism of the design of the statue, not least from the *Piper*:

"It is called the Queen's Statue, but nobody can really make up their minds whether the artist who designed it and the authorities who lured him on to commit the fatal deed were striving after the ideal or the burlesque... It is no traditional object of the artist, least of all the sculptor, to idealise the failings of old age, as has been done in the present instance... The image of a very ordinary looking woman with a crown on her head, a branch in one hand, and a toy ship very much out of date in the other, is hardly what humanity have in their minds when they think of Queen Victoria".[102]

On 16 February 1899 the statue finally arrived in Dundee, but still the Council had not settled on where to put it (as well as the previous options, a new site outside the City Churches was also being considered). Her Majesty sat resplendent in a railway goods shed ("in a site dedicated to left luggage") while

58. Unveiling the Queen's statue, 1899. Photograph from the Wilson Collection *(Libraries, Leisure & Culture Dundee)*.

the arguments continued.[103] Finally on 2 March a site was fixed, the Town Council unanimously (for once) agreeing on Ferrier's suggested site on the north site of the Albert Institute. The *Piper o' Dundee* was not alone in agreeing that this was "for many reasons the best that could have been selected."[104] Just when it seemed that the matter was finally settled, a fresh argument erupted as to which way the Queen should be facing, Thomas Thornton wanting her to face the Institute while almost everyone else preferred the opposite direction, facing the Royal Exchange. There was some suggestion that Thornton's proposal was made "in a splenetic mood, as a retaliation on certain royal personages who had the audacity to refuse to come to Dundee to unveil our statue."[105] Whatever the cause, Thornton's idea found little favour and in July the statue was finally erected facing the Royal Exchange.

While the Prince of Wales (whom it can be safely assumed was the "certain royal personage") was unable to perform the unveiling, the Town Council were able to secure the Queen's third son, the Duke of Connaught, whose visit on 26 August 1899 was another landmark day in the history of the city (figure 58). The *Courier* expressed the political mood by noting that "within recent years democracy has gained in strength and volume, and this particularly in industrial towns like Dundee, but Dundee, like everywhere else, dearly loves a Prince. The Socialist stood cheek by jowl with the Constitutionalist in the greeting extended to His Royal Highness as he drove through the various streets."[106] In his speech, the Duke referred to the exceptional speed with which the money for the statue was raised, claiming: "It is doubtful whether any other city in the Empire could have surpassed what you have done in Dundee."[107] The only hiccup in an otherwise smooth event came during the unveiling itself – when the Duke pressed the

switch, an electrical device was meant to release the jute cloth covering the statue. Unfortunately the cloth got snagged on the masts of the ship which the Queen held in her left hand, and "the hand of man had to complete what it was thought electricity would satisfactorily accomplish."[108] The Graphic Arts Association reported that "the unaffected pleasure and delight manifested by the public in this work of Art is something to be remembered."[109] Sadly, the sculptor Harry Bates did not live to see the unveiling – he died in January 1899.

The end of the century also brought an end to this interest in public memorialisation through sculpture. There was an attempt made in 1897 to raise public support for a statue of Admiral Duncan, the hero of Camperdown, but it found little support.[110] By that time vandalism was already proving a problem – in 1894 a decision was taken to move the statue of Sir David Baxter out of the park and into the safety of the Albert Institute, "where it will be preserved from wind and weather and the attacks of young vandals."[111]

Dundee's own professional sculptors rarely received opportunities to showcase their work on such a scale – we shall return to examine their achievements in chapter four. Some of the most notable examples of mural painting in the city, however, were the work of Dundee artists, including John Duncan, Stewart Carmichael, David Foggie and Alec Grieve. Many of these had either political or nationalistic intent, as part of an increasing awareness of Scottish identity which manifested itself through the Celtic Revival movement, to be explored in the next chapter.

CHAPTER THREE
Decorative Art & the Celtic Revival

"Dundee occupies a unique place in relation to the Celtic movement. In the tartan of its humanity... a large part of the fabric is Highland."[1]

59. Etta Johnston, Portrait of Patrick Geddes from *The College*, 1889 *(University of Dundee Archive Services).*

60. Unknown artist (possibly George Salmond Peddie), Portrait of John Duncan from *The Wizard of the North*, 1911 *(Libraries, Leisure & Culture Dundee).*

In the late 19th and early 20th centuries, Dundee was one of the centres of a Celtic Revival movement in Scotland that was closely related to a growing interest across the country in Highland and Gaelic culture. Two leading figures in this revival were Patrick Geddes of University College, Dundee (figure 59), and the painter John Duncan, who was born in Dundee and would arguably become the city's most significant artist, certainly of this period (figure 60). Because their best-known collaborations took place in Edinburgh, the Celtic Revival is usually described as an Edinburgh-based movement; as we shall see Dundee not only provided the crucial catalyst in bringing Geddes and Duncan together, but the work of a close-knit group of artists based in the city gave Dundee critical recognition at the time as the principal centre of a new and distinctive style of Celtic art.

In 1888, Patrick Geddes had taken up a Chair of Botany at UCD that had been specially created for him and endowed by an important patron of the arts and sciences in Dundee, James Martin White. Born in 1857, White had started his career in the family textile business, J F White & Co, before inheriting the estate of Balruddery on the death of his father in 1884. A Fellow of the Royal Physical Society, White's scientific endeavours included lighting his house with electricity (the first person to do so in any country house in Scotland, according to the *Piper o' Dundee*).[2] He became actively involved in educational causes, and was a keen supporter of UCD, Harris Academy and the science and art classes at the Young Men's Christian Association (YMCA), as well as serving as President of the Dundee Technical Institute committee. His wife, Mary Macrae, was a painter and the couple were also art collectors, owning works by G F Watts and Gaston la Touche among others, as well as a notable collection of oriental art.[3] He would later become Honorary President of Dundee Art Society, his wife already being a professional member.

White was also an active member of the Dundee Naturalists' Society and would have known Geddes from his lectures to the Society (the first of which was in January 1881) if not earlier – one of Geddes's biographers describes them as boyhood friends.[4] Certainly as a youth Geddes attended science classes at the YMCA in Dundee and may have met White then. In 1884 Geddes had applied for the Chair of Biology at UCD but lost out to D'Arcy Thompson (see chapter seven).[5] White was evidently determined to bring Geddes to Dundee, and this part-time chair seemed the ideal way – Geddes was only required to be present for the summer term, leaving him free to pursue his many other interests during the rest of the year.

Geddes was three years older than White, and was born in Ballater in 1854. He grew up in Perth in a house on the lower slopes of Kinnoull Hill, the summit of which provided spectacular views of the River Tay and its surrounding landscape which were to prove a significant inspiration for him.

Although Geddes had trained as a biologist, he was already developing much wider political and sociological ideas by the time he took up the Dundee chair – his published papers by that time included 'An Analysis of the Principles of Economics', 'Conditions of the Progress of the Capitalist and of the Labourer' and 'Co-operation vs Socialism'.[6] He had also developed unusual abilities as a visual thinker, using sheets of folded paper to classify ideas into tables that he called "thinking machines" – a legacy from a period of temporary blindness that he suffered while in Mexico in 1879-80.

61. John Duncan, *Head of Christ after Holman Hunt*, pencil on paper, c.1881 *(Royal Scottish Academy collections).*

62. John Duncan, *The Councillors of Lucifera*, etching on paper, 1888 (*Dundee City Council: Dundee's Art Galleries & Museums*).

It is not surprising, therefore, that Geddes took a swift interest in the new Graphic Arts Association (GAA) in Dundee, becoming an Associate Member in 1891. In May that year he approached the society with a request to create a series of oil and watercolour paintings of plant life that he could show to his students (to be discussed further in chapter seven). One of the members who approved the scheme was John Duncan, so if he had not already met Geddes, he must surely have done so at the GAA meeting of 1 June 1891 which Geddes hosted at UCD.

John Duncan was born in Dundee on 17 July 1866 to a fairly prosperous but working-class family – his mother was a power loom weaver and his father and uncle ran a business as "meat salesmen, provision merchants and teamen".[7] They lived in Fletcher's Land, Ann Street, but moved various times during Duncan's childhood. By the time Duncan was ten his father had gone into business on his own as a butcher – firstly at 127 Hawkhill and then 26 Overgate, with the family living next door at 28. Duncan's humble background seems to have been something he tried to conceal later in life – when he got married in 1912 he entered his father's profession as "school teacher" on the marriage certificate.[8] Art was clearly his vocation from early on in life – at the age of about nine his class at school was asked to draw a map showing the travels of St Paul, and Duncan is said to have stunned his classmates with

the quality of his work, a story later related by the artist George Wilkie Gahan:

"It was as perfect as it could have come from the printing room of a Bartholomew or a Johnston. The topography was beautifully worked and shaded, the seas and islands were perfect, and the whole finished with absolutely spider-like lines denoting the latitude, longitude, &c. Finally, even the lettering was all that the most demanding could have wished."[9]

From the age of fourteen or fifteen, Duncan began publishing cartoons in the local magazine *Wizard of the North*, and around 1883 was head-hunted by Martin Anderson to become his assistant in the art department of the *Dundee Advertiser* (see chapter five). Studying at Dundee School of Art in the High School (see chapter six), he achieved the Art Class Teachers Certificate in 1887.

It was at the School of Art that Duncan's lifelong sense of sublime beauty became apparent through his exceptionally sensitive appreciation of the school's classical casts:

"The friends I made there are all life-long friends, the plaster casts, hardly less dear, are life-long friends too… [They] were centres of inspiration and joy to crude, inarticulate boys who could not justify the faith that was in them, but who felt themselves touched to an awe of loveliness, and to a sense of an imminent divine world that could even manifest itself through plaster of Paris images."[10]

It was this divine world that Duncan would constantly struggle to reach in his art:

"Sometimes it seems to me that I see with the inner eye of imagination forms more beautiful than any I see with the outer eye… Often the vision eludes me. Just peeps and no more. Melts as foam melts on the sea. The writing is effaced before it can be read."[11]

Duncan was also exhibiting work at the Fine Art Exhibitions from the age of fifteen. He showed three watercolour studies at the 1881 exhibition, which was notable for including one of the most celebrated examples of Pre-Raphaelite painting, Holman Hunt's depiction of the young Christ, *The Shadow of Death*. Completed in 1872, this was its first appearance in a public exhibition. It was billed as "One of the Greatest Works of this Century" and evidently made a powerful impact on Duncan as he made a charcoal copy of the head of Christ (figure 61).[12]

Duncan continued to exhibit regularly at the Fine Art Exhibitions, and with Dundee Art Club from 1884, mostly etchings that showed his early interest in supernatural and mythological subjects – they included *The Death of the Dryad and Walpurgisnacht* (in 1884); *Gretchen* and *The Car of Lucifera* (1885); and *A Fallen Angel* and *A Guardian Angel aka 'A Bogle'* (1886). Many of his early works are obsessively packed with minute details, and reveal a fondness for procession scenes that would recur many times in later paintings like his RSA Diploma Work, *Ivory Apes and Peacocks* (1923).

Duncan first came to the attention of the press in 1885, when the *Courier* highlighted his etchings in the Fine Art Exhibition. Noting the influence of illustrator George Cruickshank, the reviewer concluded: "Mr Duncan is not aiming sufficiently at independent conceptions. With the facility of drawing and beautiful touch he possesses, more originality is all he requires to take a high position."[13]

Two years later, the *Piper o' Dundee* paid special attention to him in its review of the 1887 Art Club exhibition: "Mr John T Duncan takes a first place amongst the exhibitors... In conception, treatment, and execution, [his] etchings will vie with the best work of the masters of to-day."[14] The *Courier* praised his "masterly etchings", describing *The Councillors of Lucifera* (figure 62 – presumably another version of the *Car of Lucifera)* as "an exquisite work of art symbolic of the passions."[15] Local printer Robert F Mackay published the etching in 1888. One of Duncan's last etchings, *Faust and Mephistopheles*, was shown at the Royal Academy in 1893, but by that time painting had become his principal medium.

63. John Duncan, *Title unknown*, ink on paper, c.1880s *(private collection)*.

64. John Duncan, Invitation card for the unveiling of his portrait of Mrs Hunter, 1890 *(Libraries, Leisure & Culture Dundee, licensor www.scran.ac.uk)*.

65. John Duncan, *William Winter*, oil on canvas, 1891. Winter's son Richard was Duncan's brother-in-law *(private collection)*.

Duncan first received critical praise for his painting in 1887. The *Piper* noted: "His oil painting *Prometheus* displays work which has astonished his friends. With his accustomed masterly draughtsmanship, this artist displays a command of colour which will win him fresh laurels."[16] The *Courier* also singled out this painting, "in which he has caught the style of some of the old masters to a degree that might almost prove deceptive to the casual glance."[17]

Most of Duncan's work thus far was drawn from classical mythology or Germanic subjects, but in 1888 he showed the oil painting *Phaedria*, a scene from Spencer's *The Faerie Queen*.[18] The *Courier* described it as "a perfect gem" while the *Piper o' Dundee* concluded: "Mr Duncan promises to become as facile with the brush as he has already become with the pencil and graver. He fairly revels where he is fancy free, and in 'Phaedria' he has painted a thing of beauty."[19]

Duncan joined the Art Club committee in 1885, continuing to serve on it (at least nominally) while he was based in London doing commercial work in 1887-8 (see chapter five). From London he moved to Antwerp to train at the Academy, where Van Gogh had studied just a few years before. As we shall see, this was to become something of a tradition for Dundee artists, though Duncan did not find the teaching of its director, Charles Verlat, particularly inspiring. He soon moved on to the Art Academy in Düsseldorf before returning to Dundee and taking a studio at 36 Victoria Road. He was back in the city in time to be present for the opening of the new Victoria Art Galleries in October 1889, where he showed two paintings in the Fine Art Exhibition.[20]

In January 1890 Duncan became one of the founding members of the GAA, serving as a member of council during its first year. In November, however, he left Dundee again to spend the winter on the Continent. He travelled first to Paris to study the paintings in the Palais du Luxembourg and the Louvre (Rubens' *Life of Queen Marie de Medici* paintings he described as the "loveliest feasts of colour" he had seen anywhere).[21] He also made a close study of the Panthéon murals by Puvis de Chavannes, which would prove to be an important inspiration for the mural series he would create for Geddes in Edinburgh (although he disliked some of the figures in them, describing one of them as "a little wishy-washy").[22] Accompanied by his sister and the sculptor Giuseppe Gonnella, Duncan then embarked on a tour of Italy which took him to Rome, Florence, Lucca, Bologna and Venice. He found the architecture of Rome and Bologna disappointing but the other destinations made up for it, particularly Venice. Of the art that he saw, he was especially impressed by the work of Vasari and Botticelli, but concluded that "Raphael is horribly disappointing, ... played out ... antiquated [and] not up to the times."[23] He was also disenchanted with the winter temperatures, writing home that he now "understands the secret of the blue Italian skies. They are blue with cold."[24]

Overall, his trip had given him much to think about regarding colour, composition and technique of painting. He concluded that the "best effect of colour is only to be got by splashing pure unmixed colours over or amongst other tints" – something that would become particularly apparent in his oil painting during the 1890s.[25]

66. John Duncan, cover illustration for *The Grammar Fairies*, 1892 (*Libraries, Leisure & Culture Dundee*).

By spring 1891 Duncan was back in Dundee and moved into a new studio at 3 Sea Wynd, off Nethergate (though he was still living with his family, who had now moved to Agrabank Cottage, Carnoustie). At the beginning of July that year the *Piper o' Dundee* reported:

"Mr Duncan has thrown his studio open during this week to give his many friends an opportunity of viewing the work he has been doing, and especially to show his Italian impressionist studies… Mr Duncan revelled in the lovely scenery of Italy, and his sketches shew his ability to transcribe nature in her ever varying moods."[26]

With such increasing acclaim and with so much colourful inspiration for his painting, it must have been frustrating for Duncan that the only commissions that came his way were for more conventional subjects, chiefly portraits. At the Fine Art Exhibition in October 1889 he had shown a portrait of jute merchant John L Luke and a female subject, *Annette*. These were followed in March 1890 with two life-size portraits of the daughters of Lord Dean of Guild (later Lord Provost) McGrady shown at Valentine's saloon on Reform Street. The paintings were favourably reviewed – the *Piper o' Dundee* thought them "undoubtedly the finest examples of the artist's portraiture... By these works Mr Duncan places himself in the front rank of portrait painters".[27]

In July, Duncan unveiled portraits of Mrs John C Scott of Fern Tower (shown at Methven & Simpson's) and Mrs Hunter of Hilton (at Murray & Son's), both subjects depicted in Court dress (figure 64). The latter was shown at the Dundee Fine Art

67. Detail from a group photograph of attendees at the Edinburgh Summer Meeting, 1893. Patrick Geddes is seated at the front, with John Duncan directly above him (*University of Strathclyde Library, Department of Archives & Special Collections*).

Perhaps Duncan's most interesting money-earner at this time was a return to the fantasy line-drawings of his earlier years. He was commissioned to illustrate *The Grammar Fairies*, a "cantata for juvenile performers" written by T M Davidson and J M Smieton which had been performed to great acclaim at the High School in February 1891 and was now being published by A M Holden of London. Duncan illustrated the cover of the book in colour (figure 66) and produced 22 charming black and white drawings and head pieces to adorn its pages. The book came out in December 1892, and in its review the *Courier* highlighted "the very clever and amusing way in which [Duncan] has illustrated the work. His etchings alone would make the work valuable."[30]

By that time Duncan had left Dundee to join Patrick Geddes in Edinburgh. Geddes had become convinced that the study of biological systems could help in understanding the evolution and complexities of city life. When not teaching at UCD, he was spending much of his time on social and urban renewal projects in Edinburgh's Old Town, the increasingly slum-ridden state of which he described as "an inexcusable scandal".[31] Geddes believed in the principle that "cities flourished or declined according to the people who lived in them" and as a first step towards practical regeneration of the area he left his comfortable New Town flat and moved into a dilapidated tenement in James Court in 1886, which he and his wife proceeded to renovate.[32] In 1887 he started hosting annual Summer Meetings in the Old Town, which brought together leading intellectuals from various countries "interested in the reconciliation of specialisms with synthesis of knowledge".[33] The programmes featured lectures, seminars and excursions, and embraced both science and the arts. Duncan is known to have attended from 1891 (figure 67) and would soon be asked by Geddes to take charge of the art content of the meetings, along with W G Burn-Murdoch (see chapter seven) and Charles Mackie.

Initially, Geddes channelled many of his ideas for renewal through the Edinburgh Social Union, which championed the idea of bringing art and decoration into the lives of working people. A key starting point for this was the Arts & Crafts movement and the ideas of William Morris, but Geddes believed that Morris had failed in his intentions to give art to the people, recognising that his products were too expensive for the average working man to afford.[34] By 1892, Geddes had distanced himself from the Arts & Crafts movement, believing it to be "essentially dominated by capitalistic consumption" and had also left the Edinburgh Social Union.[35] He would now pursue his own cultural agenda, the 'Celtic Renascence', with John Duncan as his principal ally.

Geddes had observed the social and cultural developments that had taken place in Ireland and Wales.[36] Although there had been some development in Scotland (particularly the popularity of the Kailyard school of literature), it had largely continued the trend begun during the Enlightenment and then made fashionable by Walter Scott of re-imagining Scotland as 'North Britain'. Geddes, who was generally opposed to Enlightenment thinking as symptomatic of the New Town rather than the Old, preferred to stress Scotland's pre-Union Celtic culture, which linked it internationally to Ireland and Continental Europe. He hoped that through remembering and

Exhibition later that year, while the former was reproduced as a double-page spread in the *Piper o' Dundee*, its reviewer praising "a marvellously artistic piece of painting," and noting that "Mr Duncan has reason to be proud of his latest achievement in the art of which he is so able an exponent."[28]

November saw a painting of the four-year-old son of Treasurer James Nicoll, and the following year saw another child portrait (of future newspaper artist Frank Coutts), and paintings of Rev James Graham and William Winter (figure 65). The last portrait known from this time (possibly dating to early 1892) was of a Mrs Sellar of Carnoustie, commissioned by her husband. After Duncan's death in 1945, the sitter's son reminisced about the painting:

"Mr Duncan was, I believe, much dissatisfied with the resultant portrait of my mother – he had had trouble with one of the arms – and wished to destroy it, but my father, quick to recognise it merits, would not allow this to be done. In 1931 I met Mr Duncan for the first time, in an Edinburgh studio, and when I told him who I was he pretended horror at the mention of the portrait, and said: 'Forty years ago, laddie, I fractured your mother's arm, and was never able to set it properly.'"[29]

celebrating the past, people's outlook for the future could be strengthened –"in some young soul here and there the spirit of the hero and the poet may awaken" – and it was this that he referred to as "our Scottish, our Celtic Renascence".[37]

Geddes found an ideal collaborator in John Duncan. Already interested in painting scenes from mythology and fairy tales, he was encouraged by Geddes to draw on traditional Celtic stories and songs, linking them visually with the unique and distinctive style of decoration that Duncan would already have known from the many Pictish stones in the countryside north of Dundee. In 1892, Duncan moved into Riddle's Court, a 16th-century mansion off the Royal Mile that Geddes had adapted into a hall of residence for students, part of his pioneering University Hall complex comprising the first self-governing student hostels in Britain.

The particular role that Geddes had in mind for Duncan was that of director of a new kind of art school. Originally conceived in 1892 as the University Hall School of Art, it was renamed the Old Edinburgh School of Art when it was more formally constituted the following year. Geddes intended it "to plant the sure and certain hope of the resuscitation of beauty possible before every eye... to bring beauty into the interior of every home".[38] Geddes was convinced that "if there is literal gilding within a building, it will free its occupants from the lust for further gold", so the school concentrated on the decorative (and symbolic) arts. From 1895 this included an elementary class in Celtic Ornament, taught by Duncan and an assistant, Helen Hay.

This was not Duncan's first attempt at teaching – in 1892 he was invited by Fra Newbery to run a series of six classes in press illustration at Glasgow School of Art, showing that his work was already well-known further west.[39] Duncan was not a natural teacher – Geddes would later claim that his lectures were delivered in a permanent state of "stage fright... his students had difficulty hearing him, particularly as he dropped his voice at the end of each sentence. He thought out his subject as he progressed and constantly changed his point of view, which perplexed his audience."[40]

Joining Duncan and Hay on the teaching staff in Edinburgh were regular Geddes collaborators Charles Mackie and W G Burn-Murdoch, among others. The work produced by artists and designers at the school was occasionally shown in public exhibitions, and included paintings, drawings, textile designs, metalwork, jewellery, leatherwork, wood carvings and furniture.[41]

The principal object of the Old Edinburgh School of Art was "public and educational usefulness" – Geddes and Duncan hoped to attract "students who have already acquired some preliminary training, workmen who have already mastered the essentials of handicrafts, painters and architects who have studied their profession" with the intention that they would "organise their efforts upon the City" along the lines of medieval art workshops.[42] Instead of capital being the artist's master it would be used in the artist's service, though as usual Geddes did not make it entirely clear how this would work in practice. Referring specifically to Duncan's class in Celtic Ornament, Geddes noted: "It is hoped that the members of the various crafts may themselves soon assist in preparing

68. John Duncan, *The Combat of Fionn and Swaran*, mural in Ramsay Garden, 1895-6 (© *Courtesy of RCAHMS, licensor www.rcahms.gov.uk*).

designs adapted to their special materials and requirements, which may thus become of use in the Industries of Edinburgh and of the Highlands."[43] Duncan himself was uncertain of his own abilities to teach such students, confessing to Geddes "I do not know sufficient about their trades to be of any great use to them".[44]

It is unclear to what extent designs produced by the school were taken up by industry, though Elizabeth Cumming has ascertained that the Dunfermline linen manufacturer Henry Beveridge did produce damasks to patterns created at the school.[45] However Geddes had a more local project in mind – a series of murals and other forms of decorative art for his Ramsay Garden complex by the Castle Esplanade, where the school was based.

Geddes had acquired Ramsay Lodge, the former home of the poet Allan Ramsay, in 1890, and (with the help of his wife's money) renovated it and built around it in an eclectic but organic Scots vernacular style to form a series of student and private flats. He also took over the neighbouring Short's Observatory and recreated it as the Outlook Tower, a combination of museum and sociological laboratory. The Ramsay Garden complex was to become not only Geddes's home (he took the best apartment for himself, moving there in 1893) but also the centre for all the various activities that made up his cultural renascence. To decorate its walls he planned an extraordinary series of murals that included "the vastest and most elaborate Celtic illumination in the modern world".[46]

Geddes later claimed that "no more sustained and magnificent scheme of design and colour, no more vital symbolism has been produced by modern art in Scotland, indeed few such anywhere".[47]

Duncan began his mural work for Ramsay Garden early in 1893, when he and Charles Mackie were commissioned by Geddes to decorate his flat. Duncan's subject was 'The Evolution of Pipe Music', perhaps inspired by the cover design he had created for Dundee magazine *The Piper o' Dundee* (figure 177). The mural does not survive, but elements from it exist as watercolour studies as well as line drawings in *The Evergreen* (see below).[48]

What do survive today are the magnificent series of murals that Duncan executed for the Common Room of Ramsay Garden's student halls. Six large panels were created in 1895-6. Two were drawn from pre-Christian Ossianic legend – *The Awakening of Cuchullin* and *The Combat of Fionn and Swaran* (aka *The Combat of Fingal*, figure 68);[49] one was from Arthurian legend – *The Taking of Excalibur*, a reminder of the Scottish connections to the story made explicit in neighbouring Arthur's Seat; and the remaining three depict characters from early Christian and medieval Scottish history – *The Journey of St Mungo, The Vision of Johannes Scotus Erigena* and *Michael Scot* (also spelt *Scott).* A further panel, *The Admirable Crichton*, was created in 1897-8. Two decades later, Geddes invited Duncan back to Ramsay Garden to bring the history up to date with panels showing John Napier, James Watt, Walter Scott, Charles Darwin and Joseph Lister, created in 1926-7.

The murals attracted considerable attention at the time, and have been much studied since.[50] It is therefore unnecessary to discuss them in further detail here, except to note that all of them contain underlying themes of renewal or renascence, showing the distinctiveness of Scottish cultural and intellectual tradition as well as its engagement with a wider European culture.

While Duncan painted the main designs, the decorative borders and linking panels featuring Celtic symbols and knotwork were created by Helen Hay and some of their students from the Old Edinburgh School of Art – most notably Nellie Baxter from Dundee. Born in 1874, Baxter studied at Harris Academy where she became female Dux in 1891. In the evenings she studied art and physiology at the Harris's Science & Art School,[51] and in 1890 she showed an oil still life at the Fine Art Exhibition.[52] In 1892 she became the first woman to win one of the art prizes offered annually by the Dundee Institute of Architecture, Science & Art.[53] Her academic success meant she was offered a free place on the LLA course at St Andrews University, but she chose instead to study under Duncan in Edinburgh.[54]

At the same time, two other artists, Mary Hill Burton and Anne Mackie, were working on other murals under Duncan's direction, but the money to keep them all in employment was not always forthcoming. In November 1895 Duncan wrote an anguished letter to Geddes:

"You assured me that there was abundance of work to be done, and exhorted me to make converts, telling me at the same time not to bother my head about financial matters as that was your business.

I need not remind you of the various efforts we as a body made to carry out these ideas. In one thing at least, amongst all my failures, I was successful, and that was in getting together four ladies able and willing to work sympathetically into my hands. I spared no effort in teaching those young ladies all I knew about ornament…

Then at the moment when I expected you to incorporate them into your School of Art and get them to work – you tell me you have no work for them to do!! Miss Mackie's offer of assistance is repulsed, Miss Mason, after getting one or two small jobs to do, is dismissed, and Miss Baxter is threatened with the same treatment.

What am I to think?"[55]

Although Geddes gave a suitably mollifying reply, it was becoming clear to Duncan that there was an increasing gap between Geddes's ideas and the funds to carry them out. It is notable that in the surviving minutes, Duncan is not recorded as being present at any of the School's committee meetings, despite nominally being its director – was he naively ignoring the realities of business here or did Geddes deliberately contrive to exclude him?[56]

Whatever the truth, Geddes was trying to find other work for Duncan. In 1895 Henry Beveridge commissioned him to create a mural triptych in watercolour of *Orpheus and Eurydice* for his home at Pitreavie Castle in Fife.[57] The same year, Geddes encouraged the Franco-Scottish Society (which he had helped to found) to commission a painting of Joan of Arc with her bodyguard of Scottish archers. The result was originally displayed in the University Hall residence of St Giles House and is now in the City of Edinburgh's collections. A line drawing of it was presented to the French branch of the society at its official opening at the Sorbonne in April 1896, and was subsequently published in *The Evergreen.*

The Evergreen (figure 69) was the other principal component of Geddes's Celtic Renascence with which Duncan was closely involved. In 1893 Geddes produced a small publication with contributions by various residents of his halls of residence, which he titled *The New Evergreen* in tribute to Allan Ramsay's book of Scots poems, *The Ever Green*. This gave him a taste for publishing and a meeting with author William Sharp led to the founding of Patrick Geddes & Colleagues Publishing Company, with Sharp as one of its managers. The company would produce various Celtic-inspired books including the anthology *Lyra Celtica* and an edition of Macpherson's *The Poems of Ossian*, as well as various popular works by Fiona Macleod (actually Sharp writing under

a pseudonym). But the project that best encapsulated Geddes's ideal of the synthesis of arts and sciences, and which acted as a manifesto for the Celtic Renascence, was *The Evergreen: a Northern Seasonal*, a quarterly publication of four issues, *The Book of Spring* (1895), *The Book of Autumn* (1895), *The Book of Summer* (1896) and *The Book of Winter* (1896-7). It had four sub-themes: the Season in Nature, the Season in Life, the Season in the World and the Season in the North (ie Scotland). The idea for a Celtic quarterly had been Sharp's, but Geddes made it his own, drawing on a wide range of contributors including biologists and social scientists. It was also truly international, featuring Scottish, Irish, English, American, French and Dutch contributors, but its heart was based firmly in the Old Town of Edinburgh.[58]

John Duncan (who had produced both art and verse for *The New Evergreen)* was the principal artistic contributor to *The Evergreen* (figure 70), with Nellie Baxter, Helen Hay and Anne Mackie creating various head and tail pieces under his direction. Charles Mackie designed the covers and contributed various illustrations, as well as securing a contribution from the French painter Paul Sérusier. Other artists involved included Robert Burns, James Cadenhead and E A Hornel. Duncan may already have known artists like Hornel having recently spent time in Kirkcudbright.

A significant influence on *The Evergreen* was the *Yellow Book*, which had commenced publication the year before. A scandalous London-based periodical, its use of yellow binding linked it to modern French novels, seen by many in Britain as "intrinsically immoral and depraved."[59] Its visual style was dominated by Aubrey Beardsley, the epitome of *fin-de-siècle* decadence. This, of course, was the very opposite of Geddes's intention, which was to celebrate life and renewal, and yet Duncan and his fellow artists were clearly impressed by the Art Nouveau graphic style of Beardsley's work. Some reviewers recognised Geddes's publication as a positive riposte to its rival – the *Sunday Times*, for example, described it as "the first serious attempt we have seen on the part of genius and enthusiasm hand-in-hand to combat avowedly and persistently the decadent spirit which we have felt to be over-aggressive of late".[60] But many others focused on the visual similarities – the *Glasgow Herald* noted that the illustrations "look as if they had been meant for the *Yellow Book*" and referred again to decadence, claiming "there is no mistaking the school to which Mr Duncan belongs."[61] Even one of the periodical's main contributors, William Sharp, took a strong dislike to the art. Writing to Geddes on receiving the first volume, he stated "there is not a drawing which is not crude in draughts-manship and design – or, in one or two instances, frankly meaningless!"[62] Over the years, Duncan would get used to what he described as "the criticism of vulgar persons who, having no desire towards a spiritual beauty of high kind, have no patience with the particular ugliness the artist falls into to

THE
EVERGREEN

A NORTHERN SEASONAL

THE BOOK OF WINTER

PUBLISHED
IN THE LAWNMARKET OF EDINBURGH
BY PATRICK GEDDES AND COLLEAGUES
IN LONDON BY T. FISHER UNWIN, AND IN
PHILADELPHIA BY J. B. LIPPINCOTT CO.
1896-7

69. John Duncan, Title page from *The Evergreen: The Book of Winter*, 1896-7 *(University of Dundee Archive Services)*.

70. John Duncan, decorative headpiece from *The Evergreen: The Book of Winter*, 1896-7 *(University of Dundee Archive Services)*.

71. Nellie Baxter, 'Almanac' from *The Evergreen: The Book of Winter*, 1896-7 *(University of Dundee Archive Services)*.

72. Top left: John Duncan, *The Admirable Crichton*, mural for Ramsay Garden, 1898 *(© Courtesy of RCAHMS, licensor www.rcahms.gov.uk)*.

73. Top right: John Duncan, *Titania and Puck*, oil on canvas, 1896 *(private collection)*.

74. Bottom left: John Duncan, *The Glaive of Light*, oil on canvas, 1897 *(University of Dundee Museum Services)*.

75. Bottom right: John Duncan, *A Sorceress*, oil on canvas, 1898 *(University of Dundee Museum Services)*.

achieve it". He believed that "a picture need not and ought not to stop at mere corporeal beauty but should on the contrary... be indifferent at times to bodily beauty if by that means a higher and more spiritual beauty is to be attained".[63]

Duncan's contributions to *The Evergreen* show his awareness of French symbolist painting as well as sources much further afield – Japanese and Egyptian art, for example. Robin Nicholson draws parallels between Duncan's graphic style and that of the artists contributing to German periodicals of the time such as *Pan* and *Jugend*, some of whom Duncan would have met during his studies in Düsseldorf.[64] Most striking to modern readers of *The Evergreen* are the head and tail pieces by Duncan and his students. "In these there are distinct Celtic overtones," notes Duncan Macmillan, "but the designs are quite startlingly bold and modern looking"[65] Some (in particular examples by Nellie Baxter – see figure 71) could be seen as anticipating the Art Deco style of a quarter of a century later.[66]

Despite his attempts to distance himself from William Morris and the Arts & Crafts movement, Geddes's publishing output had much in common with Morris's Kelmscott Press, founded in 1891. He also found himself guilty of the same pricing problem that he had attacked Morris for – in order to recover its production costs, even foregoing any profits *The Evergreen* had to be highly priced at 3/6, a fact not lost on reviewers.[67] The *Student* praised it as "a triumph of the art of artistic and luxurious bookmaking" but lamented, "one could wish that its price were not such as to somewhat restrict its circulation".[68] Geddes had hoped to continue publication with another "season-cycle" but it was clearly not going to be financially viable.

With the last issue of *The Evergreen* in circulation in early 1897, Duncan decided to return to Dundee. Although he remained devoted to Geddes, it was clear that money for further projects was drying up, and the Old Edinburgh School of Art could not be sustained.[69] Geddes had only one more commission for him at this time – the *Admirable Crichton* panel for Ramsay Lodge, which Duncan completed in his new Dundee studio in the Prudential Insurance Buildings, 31 Albert Square (figure 72). The *Piper o' Dundee* later reported that "a breakdown in health obliged Mr Duncan to return to Dundee" but this may simply have been a euphemism for lack of money![70]

Duncan certainly lost no time in rejoining the GAA – he was re-elected on 1 March 1897 and submitted nine works to the annual exhibition which opened less than three weeks later. Many of these were panels relating to his Ramsay Garden murals. The *Courier* noted: "The drawing is strong and true... All have an air of distinction about them, showing acute artistic conception and high executive skill."[71]

In December that year Duncan also contributed to the annual exhibition of etchings at Robert Scott's gallery, and began work on two paintings that he intended to submit to the RSA's annual exhibition in 1898. However, he confessed to having little hope of their acceptance: "They will find my pictures dafter than ever I fear. I can't help it. I must just drive ahead, and do things the way I think best myself.".[72] As it turned out, one was accepted – a panel entitled *Crimora*. Duncan

seems here to have been moving towards a more minimalist form of expression – he felt that the painting "realises my intention nearer than anything I have done for a long time. It is just a face looking out from a grey background. I have named it after one of Ossian's heroines, but that as you know is neither here nor there."[73]

At the same time Duncan showed another panel, *Ennui*, at the Glasgow Institute, and later that year he became one of the founder members of the Glasgow-based Scottish Society of Art Workers along with Fra Newbery, Phoebe Traquair, Robert Burns and others. His work may have been getting more widely seen, but his financial situation had not improved – in May 1898 he wrote to Geddes asking for an advance of 10 guineas for the *Crichton* panel, which he badly needed in order to pay the rent on his studio.[74] The finished work was shown at the GAA exhibition that year before being sent to Edinburgh. By now Duncan was a council member of the GAA and on the hanging committee for the exhibition, in which he showed seven works. These included some landscape paintings but, as the *Courier* noted, "it is to the emblematical and symbolical branch of art that Mr Duncan more especially devotes his attention, and he achieves a very distinguished success."[75]

Two notable oil paintings included in this exhibition were *The Glaive of Light* and *A Sorceress* (figures 74 & 75), both now in the University of Dundee's collections and beautifully enhanced by Celtic-inspired frames presumably also designed by Duncan. The works immediately stand out from Duncan's mural paintings (and his later work in tempera) in their thick, patchwork-style use of paint that almost gives them the appearance of tapestries. The *Advertiser* compared them to the work of E A Hornel, deciding that "In their own peculiar way Mr Duncan's curious mosaic pictures... are very meritorious."[76] *A Sorceress* in particular is an exceptionally rich and exotic decorative work, and Frances Fowle has drawn parallels between it and Gaughin's scenes of Polynesian mythology.[77]

The failure of the Old Edinburgh School of Art had not put Duncan off teaching, and in autumn 1898 he commenced a class in Celtic ornament at the Dundee YMCA (see chapter six). In a letter to Geddes, Duncan claimed to have "got together a very respectable class of architects, carpet designers, book binders, lithographers etc and [I] hope to do wonderful things."[78]

How successful the course was is unrecorded, but through the influence of Patrick Geddes, Duncan next commenced teaching at UCD. In January 1899 Geddes announced a "Class in Original Design applied to Home Arts – Embroidery, Woodcarving, and Metal Work, Illuminating, Wall Decoration, etc" to be taught by Duncan, with Geddes chairing the first meeting.[79] The venue was the Botanical Lecture Room at UCD and Geddes gave a talk on "The Arts and Crafts, Yesterday and To-morrow" before handing over to Duncan to give his first lecture (in a series of twenty, twice weekly) on "The Home Arts".[80] According to the advert, students "will receive individual guidance in the preparation to a simple but progressive series of designs in form, outline, colour, etc, adapted to the material and method of the particular art they desire to practise."[81]

The class seems to have been an entirely unofficial one – the copy of the advert held in the University Archives has written in pencil at the top of it (and thought to be in the handwriting of the Mathematics Professor J E A Steggall): "Issued without any consultations with professors". This of course was typical of Geddes, who probably thought the College wouldn't dare to cancel a course that had already been advertised.

Whether the rest of the course took place or not is uncertain, but either way, Duncan definitely did run an advanced course in "Figure Drawing and Composition" at Dundee Technical Institute from October 1899, which included a series of twenty lectures on art. The course outline given in the Institute's syllabus indicates the broad range of subjects Duncan covered:

"1. Beginning in an elementary way with a study of the drawings of simple people in Primitive Times – Barbaric – Grotesque – Touching on Mythologies and Early Religious belief – Gods, Demons, Heroes, Monsters – Conventions of the Egyptians, Assyrians, and Early Greeks.

2. Historical Times – Review of Medieval Christian Art – Christ, The Virgin, Angels, Saints, Knights, Ladies – Costumes, Armour – Methods of Medieval and Renaissance Painters.

3. Surface Forms of the Human Body – Expression in Figure and Face – Drapery – Modern Dress in Painting, in Design and in Sculpture – General Theory."[82]

For all this, Duncan was paid £20 by the Institute – most tutors only received £15.[83] Conventional teaching like this may have helped pay the bills, but Duncan still hoped that the workshop model of the Old Edinburgh School of Art could be made to succeed, and he had ambitions to set up a Studio of Design in Dundee, with Celtic ornament at its heart.

At this point it is worth pausing to look at the development of the Celtic Revival and decorative art in Dundee. Long before Geddes began his projects in Edinburgh, Dundee had

76. Top left: Celtic Bazaar programme cover, 1898 *(Libraries, Leisure & Culture Dundee, licensor www.scran.ac.uk)*.

77. Top right: Interior decoration of St Salvador's Church by G F Bodley, 1874 *(author's photograph)*.

78. Above: Window in St Stephen's Church by William Morris and Edward Burne-Jones, part of a series installed 1893-1915 *(author's photograph)*.

developed a strong interest in all things Celtic. Staunchly Jacobite during the 1715 uprising, a Highland Society was first formed in Dundee in 1814.[84] The society ran until 1868, while a separate Dundee Highland Association ran from 1855 until around 1869. There was also an Ancient Caledonian Society which existed briefly around 1834. Dundee also had a Gaelic Church and (after the Disruption) a Gaelic Free Church for worshippers in the Celtic language.

A revival of Highland interests took place in the latter half of the century, doubtless due in part to the large number of Highlanders moving to the city to find work in the jute mills. In 1871 a Dundee Celtic Club was begun, and its first AGM attracted a large audience:

"Mr Colin Treasurer, teacher, Invergowrie… read an able paper on 'The Celt,' for which he was frequently and warmly applauded. The same gentleman, having donned his Highland costume, admirably sustained the part of the Gael in the combat scene in the Lady of the Lake, Mr Smeaton, Broughty Ferry, sustaining the part of the Saxon."[85]

In 1880 the Dundee Association of True Highlanders was formed, which seems to have run in direct competition with the Dundee Celtic Club. Ultimately the latter was eclipsed by the overwhelming popularity of the Dundee Highland Society, a rebranding in 1898 of the Association of True Highlanders. Credited with its success was a new secretary, J Abrach Mackay, who (according to the society's first yearbook) provided "a constant prod to the Celtic soul, somnolent under the spell of Sassenach influence."[86] The early mission statement of the society claims as its principal interests: "preserving the Language, the Literature and the Music of the Highlands… encouraging the use of the National Dress, [and] to promote the welfare and watch over the interests of Highlanders in Dundee".[87] The emphasis is clearly on oral culture, something shared by the popular Dundee Gaelic Musical Association – indeed it was later claimed that "Nowhere in recent years has Gaelic music been more thoroughly studied and appreciated than in Dundee".[88] In 1902 the Highland Mod was held in Dundee, claimed as "the biggest success attained by An Comunn Gaidhealach [the organisers, to which the Dundee Highland Society were affiliated] since its inception."[89]

Visual culture, however, was less in evidence. Apart from the occasional talk on Pictish symbol stones at the Dundee Highland Society there seems to be little in its early activities to suggest a particular interest in the art and imagery of the Gaelhealtachd. But Celtic imagery was beginning to be seen in the city – most prominently in Dundee's coat of arms, featuring (at that time) two wyverns on either of side of the crest, their tails interwoven in a pattern clearly based on Celtic knotwork.[90] Celtic-style crosses start to appear in the Western cemetery in the 1860s, becoming more numerous and more elaborate in the 1880s. And in March 1898, a Grand Celtic Bazaar was held in the Victoria Galleries to raise funds for Clepington Parish Church (figure 76). A preliminary event in the Kinnaird Hall featured "a series of tableaux vivants of Scottish songs and scenes", while the main bazaar appears (from illustrations in the *Courier*) to have featured large painted backdrops of

Highland settings and a general profusion of tartan.

Dundee could also boast some exceptional examples of decorative art. Outstanding among these must be the interior design of St Salvador's Episcopal Church in the Hilltown (figure 77). Constructed between 1857 and 1874, the church was designed by George Frederick Bodley, brother-in-law and pupil of Sir George Gilbert Scott, who had recently designed St Paul's Episcopal Church (now Cathedral) in Dundee. Bodley was a member of the Medieval Society in London along with William Morris and several of the Pre-Raphaelites, and his magnificent design scheme for St Salvador's was inspired by 14th-century Gothic architecture. While the nave is beautifully coloured and features a variety of stencilled patterns based on medieval designs, "Bodley reserved his full polychromatic orchestration for the chancel, where reds, greens, pale blues and golds all react to produce a crescendo of visual harmony."[91]

79. Window from the Town House by William Morris and Edward Burne-Jones, 1888-9, depicting David, Earl of Huntingdon (*Dundee City Council: Dundee's Art Galleries & Museums*).

80. Programme for Dundee Exhibition of Industry, 1887 *(Libraries, Leisure & Culture Dundee, licensor www.scran.ac.uk)*.

The building opened in 1874, the *Courier* praising its "very magnificent appearance".[92]

Bodley's design undoubtedly influenced the redecoration of the sanctuary in St Andrew's Roman Catholic Chapel (now Cathedral) in the Nethergate, which was undertaken the following year. Local painter and decorator Alexander Drummond designed the decorative scheme in a richly coloured Gothic style which the *Courier* claimed was "one of the finest specimens of church decoration to be met with in Dundee."[93] Much of the execution of this design was carried out by Drummond's two apprentices, Allan Ramsay and James Watterston Herald, both of whom later became successful artists in their own right.

Born in Montrose, Drummond came to Dundee in 1863. As a Bailie on the Town Council he was actively involved in local politics and played a significant part in the erection of the Robert Burns statue. Drummond was responsible for one of the most prominent examples of secular design in Dundee, the interior of the saloon of Methven & Simpson, music sellers, which opened in the Nethergate in 1873.[94] This also featured medieval-style patterns, along with stained glass windows featuring figures representing Music and Poetry, and mural paintings of Mozart, Handel and Beethoven created by Allan Ramsay (see chapter four). Drummond died aged only 52 in 1882.[95]

By that time, decorative art in Dundee was beginning to come under the significant influence of the Arts & Crafts movement and the ideas of William Morris and John Ruskin. In 1884, St Luke's Free Church opened in Broughty Ferry with five stained glass windows by Morris and Edward Burne-Jones. To mark the occasion, the Rev W W Peyton invited Ruskin to Dundee to give a series of evening lectures from his pulpit.[96] Morris glass was also installed in Dundee Parish Church of St Mary (a large window depicting the twelve apostles along with two smaller windows), St Rule's Parish Church, Monifieth (a large two-part window) and St Stephen's Church, Broughty Ferry (a complete scheme installed over 22 years representing perhaps the largest single collection of Morris glass in Scotland – see figure 78).[97] Most notably, in 1886 the Town Council decided to install stained glass in the windows of the Council Chambers as part of Dundee's celebrations for the Queen's golden jubilee:

> "The Provost suggested that the designing of the windows should be entrusted to Mr E Burne-Jones, ARA, an artist of the highest ability… and that the staining and other technical matters should be executed by Mr William Morris, MA, one of the greatest poets of our age."[98]

Morris visited Dundee and studied the location, pronouncing it (unsurprisingly) "most suitable for the introduction of stained glass". He and Burne-Jones selected six figures from a list of significant historical figures "in scenes where our local and national history blended".[99] The chosen figures were David, Earl of Huntingdon (figure 79), William Wallace, Robert the Bruce, George Wishart, Provost James Haliburton and Mary, Queen of Scots. The cost was around 80 guineas each, paid for by Lord Provost Hunter, ex-Provost Ballingall and the families of four other former Provosts, and the windows were eventually installed in October 1889 in time for the visit to Dundee by the Marquis of Lorne.[100]

The fashion for stained glass in private houses was also beginning to take off at this time. In August 1883 the *Courier* reported that Messrs Lindsay & Scott, glaziers in Barrack Street, had just taken possession of two specially commissioned glass panes belonging to "the newest branch of decorative art".[101] Notably, the panes depicted Highland scenes – Killiecrankie with the Bridge of Garry and Rannoch with Schiehallion in the distance – and had been commissioned by an unnamed client for the cloakroom of his Dundee mansion, the views taken from photographs by Valentine. It was noted that "this is the first out of several orders for similar panes with which Messrs Lindsay & Scott have been favoured." At that time no Dundee craftsmen were apparently available to make the glass so the work was done in Birmingham.

An important impetus in the development of the decorative arts in Dundee was the opportunity to exhibit work afforded by the Albert Institute. In 1887, rather than hold the usual annual Fine Art Exhibition, it was decided to stage an Industrial Exhibition instead (figure 80). Although mostly concerned with engineering models and machinery, the exhibition included several examples of decorative work by local craftsmen and amateur workmen, such as carved furniture, picture frames, jewel cases and ivory work.[102]

81. James Eadie Reid and James Bremner, sculptural decoration on the Ward Road Gymnasium, 1891. Photograph from the Wilson Collection (*Libraries, Leisure & Culture Dundee*).

82. Allan Inglis, *Design for a Garden Seat*, reproduced in *The Studio*, 1899 (*Duncan of Jordanstone College of Art & Design*).

This was followed by a major exhibition of Home Industries held in the Victoria Art Galleries in 1891, organised by the Forfarshire branch of the Scottish Home Arts & Industries Association. This had recently been set up to "promote, improve, and develop home industries in Scotland, and to circulate information regarding them, to promote the sale of produce and to receive money to further their objects".[103] Although not formally part of the Arts & Crafts movement, it shared the aim of improving quality of life through well-made craftwork and decorative art. The exhibition had been two years in the planning and featured over 2,000 objects of "both useful and ornamental character."[104] A wide variety of local organisations were involved in creating models, embroidery, ceramics, metalwork and paintings including schools and orphanages, girls' clubs, the Institution for the Blind, Dundee & District Mill & Factory Operatives' Union, students at Dundee School of Art and of private art tutors such as C G L Phillips. The members of the GAA made notable contributions to the exhibition, which also featured numerous historic items on loan from local houses such as Glamis Castle. A considerable number of prizes were awarded as incentives to take part.[105]

It is worth looking at some of the city's most notable decorative artists in the years before the explosion of popularity that Duncan and the GAA helped to create in the late 1890s. William Norwell was a painter and decorator based at 36 Commercial Street, who was also actively involved in the local art scene, joining the Dundee Art Club and then the GAA. He exhibited frieze designs at the GAA's first annual exhibition and also lectured at the YMCA on "Decoration and its Relation to Architecture".[106] He worked with various local artists to realise his designs, including Martin Anderson (see chapter five). One of Norwell's most notable successes was the redecoration of St Joseph's Roman Catholic Church in 1889. Said the *Courier*: "The appearance of the church from an artistic point of view is now almost perfect, and reflects the highest credit on Mr Wm Norwell".[107] The *Piper o' Dundee* noted: "We have much to learn in Dundee in the art of church decoration, and a visit to St

Joseph's would be an education to many of the Philistines who are the arbiters in the matter of church decoration."[108] Other public commissions included the redecoration of Willison Free Church (1881), St Luke's Parish Church, Lochee (1897) and Longforgan Parish Church (1900), the latter featuring carving by sculptor Alexander Neilson and stained glass by Robert Burns, one of Patrick Geddes's Edinburgh protégés.

One of those who worked for Norwell was James Eadie Reid, a talented painter and designer who also worked briefly as a newspaper artist with Martin Anderson in 1884-5 before working at UCD, creating drawings and diagrams for the Professor of Biology, D'Arcy Thompson (see chapter seven). In 1886 he moved to Edinburgh but kept up his Dundee connections, showing three works at the Fine Art Exhibition of 1889, and continuing to do design work for Norwell. He then moved to London and studied under Sir William Blake Richmond, who then took him on as an assistant. He returned to Dundee in 1891 to design sculpture decoration for the front of the new Gymnasium on Ward Road, to be executed by James Bremner (figure 81). By this time he had been elected a member of the City of London Guild of Handicrafts. Reid's last known work in Dundee was a painting of the crucifixion to decorate St John the Baptist Episcopal Church in 1896. He later moved to Paris and continued to work both as a painter and in church decoration (including stained glass and mural designs).[109]

James Bremner was a woodcarver and sculptor with a workshop in Brook Street, Broughty Ferry. He trained under Angus artist James Christie and became well-known for his work in church decoration, including St John's Free Church on Perth Road and St Luke's, Broughty Ferry. He was one of several local designers to show decorative art work in the 1887 Industrial Exhibition (a chair carved from antique wood) and the 1891 Home Industries Exhibition (where he won first prize in woodcarving for two panels). He showed sculptures, decorative work and paintings at the Fine Art Exhibitions and

GAA exhibitions, and was the first President of the GAA, where he got to know John Duncan. It is not clear to what extent he embraced the Celtic Revival, though at the 1903 GAA exhibition he showed a Celtic tomb design. The *Celtic Annual* hailed him as "a true artist... In the carving of Gothic ornament – gargoyles, and other fantastic figures – he inherited the true mediaeval spirit."[110] Bremner taught wood carving (and later clay modelling) at Dundee Technical Institute from 1892-1901. Some time after 1905 he emigrated to Canada, where he died a decade or so later. His attempts at a new career there seem not to have succeeded – George Wilkie Gahan believed that "he was too tenderly and peculiarly Scottish to bear transplanting at the rather late age he ventured to undertake the journey."[111]

The work of the Technical Institute played an important part in developing interest and skills in decorative art (see also chapter six). The building opened in 1888 with a series of relief carvings on its façade depicting various craftsmen at work. In 1890 the Institute collaborated with UCD to bring to the city G Baldwin Brown, Professor of Fine Art at the University of Edinburgh, to give a "Popular Course of Lectures on the Decorative Arts".[112] Brown was an enthusiastic supporter of Geddes, who may have had a hand in bringing him to Dundee.[113] His lectures were delivered to day students at UCD and then to evening students at the Technical Institute.[114] The students were encouraged "to make sketches and notes from the examples used in illustrating the lectures".[115]

Later that year, local architect J Murray Robertson began a class "for instruction in the Principles of Design and in Colouring", though this was restricted to "operative painters and decorators who have a good knowledge of freehand drawing".[116] In January 1892, more public lectures were offered when the Technical Institute engaged Fra Newbery of Glasgow School of Art to give a course on 'Principles of Ornament and Decoration'. Newbery was a key supporter of the Arts & Crafts in Glasgow, organising a major exhibition in 1895 and helping to make Glasgow design internationally famous.

Under Thomas Delgaty Dunn, the art school at the Technical Institute expanded rapidly after 1892, and his students began to be noticed further afield. Among them was Allan Inglis, who later joined the teaching staff. In 1899 *The Studio* reproduced his innovative designs for a garden seat (figure 82), and two years later they noted: "Some of the best students go through a phase of imitative Celticism, if we may so describe it... The work of Allan Inglis (Dundee) promises to outlive these temporary influences and to show fine qualities of its own".[117]

While Delgaty Dunn lectured on historic ornament to his students, they were also drawing inspiration from the latest international fashion in design in the 1890s, Art Nouveau. Its influence was already starting to be seen in the graphic design of advertisements and other press illustrations (particularly in the work of Max Cowper – see chapter five). As with the designs by Duncan and his students in *The Evergreen*, Dundee's art students began to draw both on Celtic and Art Nouveau styles, with interesting results (see figures 83 & 84).

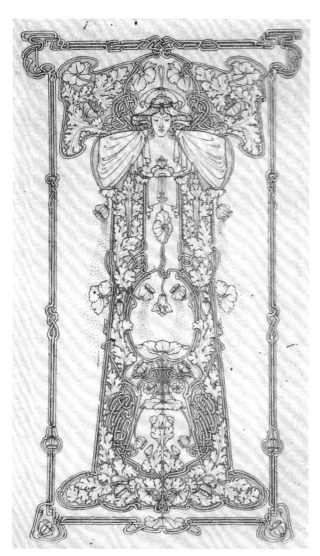

83. Top: Unknown art student, *Untitled Design*, c.1890s *(Duncan of Jordanstone College of Art & Design)*.

84. Right: James Wyse, *Design for Stencilled Hanging*, c.1890s *(Duncan of Jordanstone College of Art & Design)*.

85. Stewart Carmichael. Photograph from *The Scottish Patriot*, 1902 (*Dundee City Archives*).

86. Unknown artist, illustration of the Council Lodging House in Drury Lane, showing Stewart Carmichael's mural *Labour*, 1895 (*Dundee City Archives*).

To help inspire the city's art students, regular exhibitions of technical and decorative art were shown from 1894 at the Victoria Art Galleries, on loan from the South Kensington Museum (later the V&A). James Martin White was the prime mover in this initiative, personally selecting many of the exhibits. He also paid for an exhibition of textile design the same year, as well as gifting a collection of books on the subject to the Technical Institute library. The exhibitions were highly popular (the first loan collection attracted over 82,000 visitors in a year) and Delgaty Dunn later took over their organisation from Martin White.[118] Describing the 1895 selection, the *Courier* noted:

> "Architects and all engaged in the building trades, workers in metal – whether ornamental or useful – and in the plastic arts, artists and decorators, designers of textile patterns, cabinet-makers and marble workers, may all gain much profit and new inspiration from these splendid and suggestive works."[119]

It was to this increasingly receptive culture in Dundee that John Duncan returned in 1897. That a distinctive artistic school was already forming in the city had been apparent to Patrick Geddes when, the previous year, he gave the opening address at the GAA's annual exhibition, as reported by the *Courier*:

> "Here they had the beginning of a little local school, a centre of future possibilities. Beside possibilities, they already had some substantial performance… In this city they seemed to be very much where Glasgow was ten years ago, at the beginning of forming a local school. If they did not like the Glasgow school, all the better, the more opportunities there would be for getting interested in this one, which would be different."[120]

The artist that had led this development during Duncan's absence was Stewart Carmichael, arguably the most important champion of art that Dundee had for over half a century (figure 85). Although frustratingly little attention is usually paid to his work today, the poet and academic Alan Riach recently described him as "one of the first truly Modernist Scottish artists, a painter of real stature."[121]

Carmichael was a year younger than Duncan and their careers had thus far followed a similar path. He was born in Heathfield Place, Dundee on 8 February 1867, the son of a leather merchant, and his first art training was at Peter D Lauder's Central School of Art, one of the many small educational establishments that proliferated in Dundee at that time. In 1883, Carmichael began to train as an architect with James Hutton while taking evening art classes alongside Duncan at the Dundee School of Art. He was soon exhibiting his work at the Fine Art Exhibitions (from 1883) and the Dundee Art Club (from 1884). In 1885 he joined Duncan as a committee member of the Art Club.

Carmichael's early interest in symbolic and historical or mythological subjects is apparent from the elaborate titles of his early artworks, such as *Humanity led by Faith through the Snares and Temptations of Life* or *The Minstrel's Last Farewell to the Dryads of the Wood* (both 1885). His name started to be noticed by the critics – in 1887, for example, the *Piper o' Dundee* praised his work as "pleasingly pictorial".[122] That same year he decided to give up on his work as an architect and try his hand as an illustrator in London, where he managed to get employment at the publishers Alexander Strachan & Co.[123] Since we know Duncan was in London at the same time, it's likely that the two went there together.

In 1888 Carmichael travelled to Antwerp to study at the Academy under Verlat. Again this was probably with Duncan, but from there their paths diverged, Carmichael moving to Brussels to study under the more modern Lieven Herremans.[124] He was back in Dundee in time to become one of the first recorded members of the GAA in February 1890, and was soon working on the kind of striking symbolist paintings that both attracted and puzzled the critics:

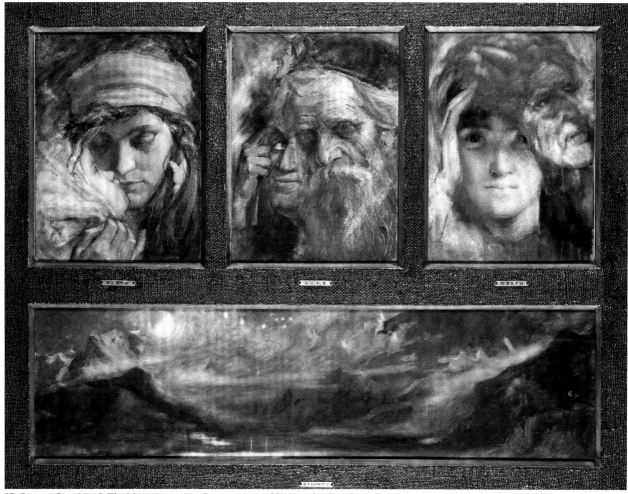

87. Stewart Carmichael, *The Mysteries*, watercolour on paper, 1891 *(Dundee City Council: Dundee's Art Galleries & Museums)*.

"In the large picture, 'The Bridal Party,' there is a reminiscence of a Tennysonian idyll in which a barge-borne bier takes the place of the bridal party. The colouring is brilliant, and the whole effect pleasing; but why doleful looks and the despondent attitude of the party? I'd like a little more joyousness on the occasion of my wedding, I know."[125]

In October Carmichael held his first solo exhibition – according to the *Piper o' Dundee*, "the exhibition was visited by many connoisseurs, and we hear that a number of the completed pictures were bought by patrons of art."[126] Shortly after this, Carmichael returned to London and from there embarked on a sketching tour of France and Italy (again the dates coincide with Duncan's tour, so they may have travelled together for at least some of the time), staging an exhibition at the Imperial Hotel on his return in March 1891. The critics particularly noted the impressionistic quality of his watercolours: "There is a freedom about them and an unconventionality in their treatment which takes them out of the category of the ordinary artist's sketch."[127] Strong colour was also noticed: "By a few clever touches the impression of a landscape is conveyed, a vineyard slope under grey troubled skies, or a picturesque campanile lifted its warm-hued sides high in the intense blue, which looks almost aggressively bright to Scottish eyes."[128]

Carmichael was still dividing his time between Dundee and London, and while his commercial work there never really took off, he did manage to secure a commission to paint a 30-foot-long mural entitled *Labour* for a council lodging house in Drury Lane (figure 86). It would eventually be completed in 1892, shortly before Duncan began his murals for Geddes. When the building was opened in January 1893, Carmichael's work was warmly commended:

"You enter, and you behold a sight wonderful enough to make the dead... start from their graves...Here we soar into the very empyrean of art... Just imagine a 'doss' house with a mural painting! I can promise you that the lodgers will admire the beauty of the industrial arts that Mr Carmichael has painted".[129]

Carmichael showed a colour study for the mural at the first GAA exhibition in 1893, where it received strong praise from the *Dundee Advertiser*:

"It represents a cycle of the industrial arts, indoor and outdoor, each figure full of force, admirably proportioned, graphic, and beautiful. The imaginative power exhibited in these works is of itself sufficient to make the painter's reputation. When we add to this the unique method by which he develops his effects, the strange tremulous play of colour on the canvas, the way the vibrations are managed, and the subtleties of his technique – all make out a claim for recognition which is too strong to be denied."[130]

88. Stewart Carmichael, *An Old Scotchwoman*, oil on canvas, 1895 *(Angus Council Museums)*.

Carmichael's symbolist works were more of an acquired taste. The *Advertiser* began its exhibition review by admitting:

"Beyond doubt the pictures which will first send the inquisitive visitor to his catalogue will be those of Stewart Carmichael, a painter who unites to the artistic temperament with something of the fire of the poet and the seer… I could quite well understand people being bored by such compositions as 'Birth' and 'A Dream,' as to some whatever is unintelligible is not worth looking at."[131]

Even Carmichael's fellow artists in Dundee were not always in sympathy. According to the *Piper o' Dundee*, "one set [of artists] upholds him as a coming man; the minority condemn the Carmichael and all his works."[132] Carmichael's introduction to French and Belgian symbolist painting clearly had a profound influence on him, perhaps even more so than on Duncan. In early 1891 he had painted a "decorative panel containing four heads representing Anarchy, Sorrow, Regret, and Mystery".[133] Later that year this idea was reworked into one of his most celebrated paintings, *The Mysteries*, featuring three portraits (Birth, Life and Death) in separate panels and a long landscape panel beneath them representing Eternity (figure 87). In 1903, this would become the first of his paintings to enter Dundee's permanent collection, after it was purchased from an exhibition of Carmichael's work held by the GAA in his honour in 1902. Carmichael had briefly summarised the meaning of the four panels when the work was first shown at the Fine Art Exhibition:

"*Birth* – The weakly mother, foreseeing the future, troubled for the spiritual and material welfare of her offspring; *Life* – Futility of effort – the everlasting conflict of Worker and Scoffer; *Death* – Not the hateful change, superstition of ages – but life in Death; *Eternity* – These human phases above transient – Sun, Moon, and Stars eternal."[134]

The *Courier* described it in more lyrical terms:

"The first panel, 'Birth,' wherein the tender clinging, yet withal inscrutable, quality in which it is bathed tells one of the emotion of human hopes and love; while the second panel, strong from the intellectual point, depicts life as a thing of strenuous strife, continually in jarring contact with folly and its jangling bells, and as a whole striking rather a pessimistic note. 'Death,' the third panel, is of emotional quality, showing that when the ugly mask is lifted it becomes a beautiful, loving reality. The pessimistic note is again struck in 'Eternity,' with its illimitable space and matter enveloped in shadowy mystery. The conception of the picture as a whole is virile, and shows the swelling of the emotional hope of the artist softening the pessimism."[135]

Carmichael continued his artistic connections with the Continent, and in 1896 was reputedly elected a member of the Brussels art society L'Areopage.[136] He also continued his

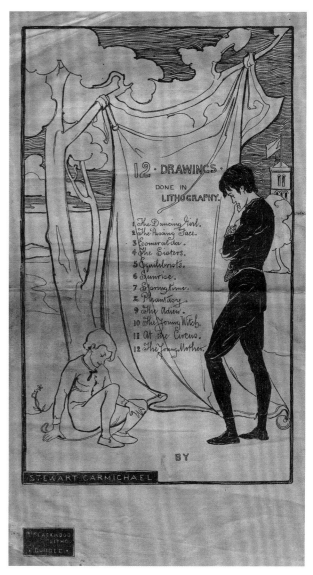

89. Stewart Carmichael, cover for a folio of lithographs, 1898 *(Libraries, Leisure & Culture Dundee, licensor www.scran.ac.uk).*

90. Opposite page: Stewart Carmichael, *Faith*, watercolour on paper, 1905 *(Dundee City Council: Dundee's Art Galleries & Museums).*

London connections, and in 1897 held a solo exhibition of oil paintings at Gray's Inn. A review in the *Star* described him as one of "the Dundee school … The Celtic feeling for the poetry of line is as perceptible in these bold and original pictures as is the demand for beauty of form and colour."[137]

Most of Carmichael's major works from this time were bluntly allegorical, such as *Truth's Martyr*, shown at the GAA exhibition in 1896, and depicting a dark figure with an axe leading a naked female to the execution block. However, Carmichael also painted more naturalistic subjects – usually portraits, such as *A Newspaper Reader* (1895) or *An Old Man in the Sunlight* (1896), many of which critics were still determined to view as symbolic. *An Old Scotchwoman* (also exhibited as *The Old Scots Woman*, figure 88) was reproduced in *The Studio* in 1897, the reviewer writing, "Being a Scot, and a patriotic Scot, nothing inspires his brush to such pathetic realism as a genuine native model… Subjects such as this are truly national in character, and full of that pathos which has its counterpart in the finer elements of modern Scottish literature."[138]

occasionally did he directly incorporate Celtic design elements into his work at this time, however – an example being the brooch seen in his watercolour *Faith* (figure 90).

The other Dundee artist pursuing a symbolist course in the years prior to Duncan's return was Alec Grieve (figure 91). Born in Park Entry off Temple Lane on 13 October 1864, Grieve was the son of a journeyman plumber and began his working life in a draper's.[141] A story was later told about his employer, who "finding him busy with a drawing, said, 'Alec, you'll need to make up your mind. Is it to be business or is it to be art?' To which the emphatic answer was – 'Art!'"[142] Grieve's early career was closely bound up with that of Duncan and Carmichael – he began his studies with them at the High School, exhibited with them at the Dundee Art Club, then moved to London at around the same time, working both as a commercial artist for various publishers and exhibiting at the Royal Academy, and went on to further study on the Continent (in Grieve's case at the Académie Colarossi in Paris). He returned to Dundee in 1890, showing at the Fine Art Exhibition that year and joining the GAA soon after.

In 1893 he held an exhibition from his Castle Street studio, at which landscape paintings were the most acclaimed. The *Piper o' Dundee* noted: "Not a few of the pictures portray in charming manner bright bits of local landscape... while one bit of woodland caught in misty mood is a masterpiece worthy of a place in the finest collection."[143] Grieve defined art in intellectual terms as

"the suggestion or the expression on canvas of an emotion or thought impressed on the soul, as seen by the contemplative intelligence. Art is therefore a language of suggestion, expressing what the soul seeks to convey. The soul has certain ultimate types by which it expresses itself; these we may call the 'Platonic Ideas,' the eternal, immortal essence of things. Art grasps these types and sets them forth so that all the world may contemplate them. Art thus becomes the spiritual, mental and moral food for all humanity".[144]

With this in mind, Grieve began painting symbolist or religious works such as *Death and the Miser* (1893), *Sancta Spirita* (1897) and *The Longing of Eve* (1898) that sought to express his intellectual ideals. The critics largely ignored these in favour of his landscapes, but when they did receive attention, opinion was decidedly mixed. The *Advertiser* referred to Grieve's "dangerous quality of imagination" and "original

Scottish literature was one of Carmichael's passions, particularly the Gaelic poets, and traditional Highland music was another love – for example, he would go on to serve as vice-president of the Dundee Gaelic Musical Association. He was noted for his recitations of poetry and for his singing – one of his obituarists said "To hear him... sing 'The Standard on the Braes o' Mar' accompanied by flashing eyes and telling gesture, was always a joy."[139] Carmichael's parents had come to Dundee from Aberfeldy and may have been Gaelic speakers – certainly Carmichael felt a strong Highland connection and studied with fascination the history of the Clan Carmichael and its significant role in the Jacobite rising.

It is no surprise, then, that Carmichael responded enthusiastically to Duncan's Celtic interests. It is notable that, prior to Duncan's return to Dundee, Carmichael had not directly embraced subjects from Scottish history and legend, but in 1897 he produced a series of drawings inspired by dramatic incidents in Dundee's history, including "scenes of bloodshed and the horrors of pestilence".[140] They were exhibited at Thomas Murray's gallery along with a decorative panel depicting *Wallace, the Maker of Scotland*. The following year Carmichael showed *Geillis Duncan, A Dundee Witch, 1591AD* at the GAA exhibition and would continue to draw on Scottish historical sources for the rest of his career. Only

ideas".[145] *The Longing of Eve* was damned with faint praise by the *Courier*, who merely reported that it "shows good figure drawing".[146] A writer in the *Evening Telegraph*, however, found it "simply horrible".[147] More serious attention was paid in December 1897, when Grieve held a solo exhibition in Thomas Murray's gallery. One reviewer singled out *The Soul of the Rose Entered my Blood*, "a Rossetti-ish face of a young woman, seen through a trellis of white roses, a bud pressed to her lips... The face is too square and sphinx-like for mere beauty, but there is a fascination about it, a sense of power which attracts the beholder."[148]

After this show, the critics seemed to react more positively to Grieve's work. *Finis* (1898) was widely praised, and after its debut at the GAA exhibition was shown at the Glasgow Institute and RSA (figure 92). The *Courier* was even more complimentary about *Lux Fiat* (1899), "a remarkable example of his best style in the painting of ideas and expression in symbolism."[149] By now, Grieve's work had been purchased by both Patrick Geddes (a *Nocturne*) and James Martin White (*Leda and the Swan*).

91. Stewart Carmichael, *Alec Grieve, Artist, Tayport*, lithograph on paper, 1903 *(Dundee City Council: Dundee's Art Galleries & Museums)*.

92. Alec Grieve, *Finis*, oil on canvas, 1896, reproduced in *The Meal-Poke*, 1903 *(University of Dundee Archive Services)*.

The most exceptional talent associated with Celtic, symbolist and decorative art in Dundee at this time was George Dutch Davidson, and it was Davidson who most came under the influence of John Duncan. Thirteen years younger than Duncan, Davidson was born on 12 August 1879 in Goole, Yorkshire, where his father was temporarily based as a marine engineer. A few weeks later they returned to the family home in Dundee, and Davidson's childhood was one of great promise, excelling in his studies at Harris Academy.[150] Davidson originally intended to follow his father in becoming an engineer, but a severe bout of flu in 1896 left him with a serious heart condition which prohibited him from working. His close friend David Foggie recalled the effects of this debilitating illness:

"through his whole life the effects of his malady were disturbing in the extreme, necessitating complete abstinence from strain or excitement, and worst of all, about every two months he endured a time of severe pain, prostrating him for eight or twelve days."[151]

The family moved to the village of Baldragon to aid his convalescence, and Davidson interested himself in botanical studies. Eager to keep his mind active, in 1897 he enrolled in Dundee School of Art (against the advice of his doctor), winning a Government Free Studentship and Second Prize for Art.[152] There he met and formed a close friendship with David Foggie, who introduced him to the members of the GAA.

93. Alec Grieve, *Title unknown*, etching on paper, c.1890s *(Libraries, Leisure & Culture Dundee)*.

Davidson's first significant completed work as an artist was the extraordinary symbolist watercolour *Envy* (figure 94 – now in Dundee Art Galleries & Museums, as are the other Davidson works described here), incorporating a loose form of Celtic knotwork in its composition, which he showed at the GAA exhibition in April 1898. David Foggie said that "its singleness of thought and its intensity are remarkable: it is a sonnet in colour."[153] Two studies for the work survive revealing that Davidson's original intention was to feature a human skull with glowing eye-sockets rather than the anguished green figure.

Also striking is Davidson's *Self Portrait*, which presumably dates from around this time (figure 95). An Edvard Munch-like psychological portrait of Freudian intensity, it is like little else in Scottish art of the time, save perhaps the work of The Four in Glasgow. William Hardie (who has done more than anyone to reawaken interest in Davidson's work) writes: "It appears to set the artist in an aerial view of the Tay estuary, suggesting inner and outer reality, conscious and unconscious, id and ego, in a highly original composition".[154]

Most breathtakingly modern today are Davidson's early abstract paintings, described by Foggie as "some half dozen drawings in water-colour, applied in flat wash and with great strength, the form being curved lines merely."[155] Davidson showed one of this series (under the title *Design*) at the GAA exhibition alongside *Envy*, and two are known to survive today, one with a plain background (figure 96) and one featuring stars suggesting some sort of cosmic manifestation. Although their composition still draws on Art Nouveau decoration, it is impossible to view them now without thinking of later work by artists like Kandinsky.

The critics ignored Davidson's work at the GAA exhibition (though one visitor wrote to the *Evening Telegraph* complaining about "that dreadful green face"), but he was encouraged by praise given at the opening by the Glasgow painter Macauley Stevenson.[156] His fellow GAA members certainly took note, Stewart Carmichael recalling that Davidson's work "made a very strong impression on the Society".[157] John Duncan evidently recognised his talents, and invited Davidson to share his studio in Albert Square.[158] Duncan's mentorship was of inestimable value to the young artist – David Foggie recalled that, under Duncan's influence, "his aim became clear, his expressions became ordered towards a well understood ideal. From that time he was rid, practically, of the swervings and errantry of thought which usually make up the years of a painter's beginning."[159] Duncan recalled: "He was the most ardent student, assimilated everything that came in his way, Celtic ornament, Persian ornament, Gothic Architecture, early Renaissance art, 17th Century tapestries, and wove very new influence into the tissue of his style."[160] Foggie particularly noted Davidson's embracing of Celtic decoration:

"Under John Duncan's teaching he became enthusiastic in the study of Celtic art, a style fascinating to him from its essential decorative character and its weird beauty; he liked to feel a personal relationship with it, and often associated his own imaginative gifts with the thought that his ancestors in some far back time were Highlandmen."[161]

This most clearly manifested itself in Davidson's *Celtic Illumination* (figure 4), richly painted on vellum in 1899, but Celtic elements mix with more exotic influences in many of his works, most famously a watercolour illustrating Fiona Macleod's verse, "And a strange song I have heard / By a shadowy stream / And the singing of a snow-white bird / On the hills of dream" (figure 97).[162] Davidson wrote to Duncan saying: "With no one do I feel so perfectly at home as with Fiona McLeod [sic]. Her 'Hills of Dream' I carry next my heart."[163] Lindsay Errington has written that the work of Duncan and Dutch Davidson represented "the only serious attempt to create a new Celtic art".[164]

Despite his ongoing health problems, in September 1899 Davidson embarked on a year-long tour of the Continent accompanied by his mother and (for part of the journey) David Foggie. Travelling first to London, they then moved on to Antwerp. Davidson originally intended to study at the Academy (as Foggie was doing) but John Duncan persuaded him otherwise. Davidson later wrote to him: "you can hardly

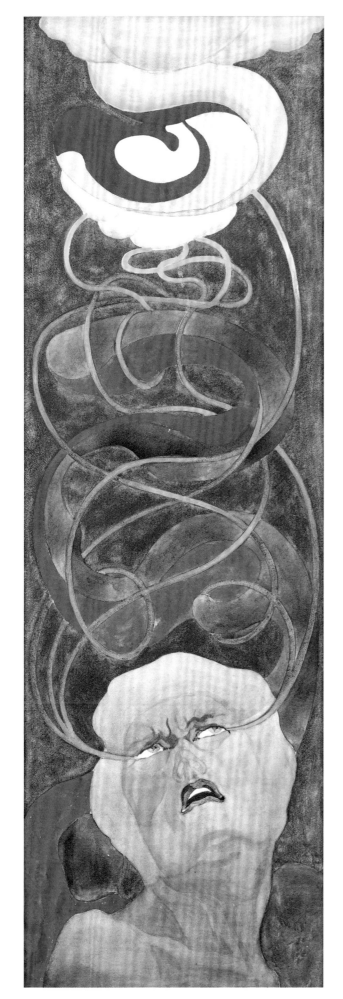

94. Left: George Dutch Davidson, *Envy*, watercolour on paper, 1898 *(Dundee City Council: Dundee's Art Galleries & Museums)*.

95. Top: George Dutch Davidson, *Self Portrait*, watercolour on paper, 1898 *(Dundee City Council: Dundee's Art Galleries & Museums)*.

96. Bottom: George Dutch Davidson, *Abstract Design*, watercolour on paper, 1898 *(Dundee City Council: Dundee's Art Galleries & Museums)*.

97. Opposite page: George Dutch Davidson, *The Hills of Dream*, watercolour on paper, 1899 *(Dundee City Council: Dundee's Art Galleries & Museums)*.

realize how grateful I am for your advice... [If] I had not come to Antwerp with the determination not to attend the Academy, I should have gone very far astray, and perhaps have never been able to enfranchise myself from the deep pit of Realism".[165] Instead, Davidson created some of his finest decorative works in Antwerp, including *The Hills of Dream*, *A Street Corner in Antwerp* and *The Tomb* (figure 261).

In February 1900 Davidson and his mother moved on to Florence, where above all the work of Cimabue and Fra Angelico inspired him. Surrounded by great masterpieces of art, he was encouraged rather than intimidated. "I feel there is a place for us yet –" he wrote to Duncan, "to decorate with beautiful pictures as finely and sympathetically drawn, but perfectly conscious of our limitations". He and Duncan began to discuss by letter plans to work together:

> "I am sure that our interests and aims are so much akin that such a combination is eminently possible. I know that most of what I have learned I learned while working with you, and that my latest work is the outcome of it. Besides if we wrought together it would be possible to accomplish much more than if we were plodding away apart, and so we might be able to make some impression".[166]

The development of Celtic and symbolist painting in Dundee did not meet with obvious approval from audiences or critics. In reviewing the 1898 GAA exhibition, the *Evening Telegraph*'s 'Here and There' columnist noted disparagingly the tendency of Dundee artists to be "mystic and misty in paint".[167] Public reaction was often far more hostile. A letter to the same paper signed "A Philistine" referred to the "horrors" of the GAA exhibition: "those extraordinary specimens of studies in impossible colour harmonies... As a revolt against mere prettiness these may serve their turn, but they are only too successful."[168] He (or she) goes on to describe some of the works (which include Dutch Davidson's *Envy* and Carmichael's *A Dundee Witch*), saying "don't they sound like fragments of a nightmare? and so they are. They *may* have an occult meaning; but if they have there is too much time – and imagination – wanted to find it out."

Referring to the 1899 GAA exhibition, the *Dundee Advertiser* noted that almost an entire gallery had been reserved for that "development of art which old-fashioned artists and art critics call 'eccentricity,' and which the new School of artistic connoisseurs denominate 'originality.'"[169] Although generally complimentary, the reviewer (almost certainly A H Millar) condemned John Duncan for following "the passing phase" and making "his drawing distorted and his colouring flat and almost repulsive. This craze will certainly not last".The newly established *Dundee Free Press*, however, came out strongly in support of the "Advanced School", praising Carmichael, Duncan and Grieve.[170] This prompted another critic to comment:

> "Around the pictures of Alec Grieve and Stewart Carmichael and others a war-dance takes place annually, and in the past newspaper critics have vied with each other in denunciation… [T]he advent of a new local newspaper which exalts them unashamed has quickened the appreciation of its rivals."[171]

98. Top left: George Dutch Davidson, Cover design for Graphic Arts Exhibition catalogue, 1899 *(Dundee City Council: Dundee's Art Galleries & Museums).*

99. Top right: Elizabeth Burt, *Title unknown*, embroidered and appliqué hanging based on a design by George Dutch Davidson, c.1900 *(Dundee City Council: Dundee's Art Galleries & Museums).*

100. Above: Rosa Baxter, embroidered portfolio cover based on a design by George Dutch Davidson, 1899, reproduced in the *Memorial Volume*, 1902 *(private collection).*

101. Opposite page: Nell Baxter, Sketch of John Duncan's mural design for Friarton Grove, from *The Piper o' Dundee*, 1900 *(Libraries, Leisure & Culture Dundee).*

A H Millar, however, did not mince words when reviewing the following year's exhibition for the *Advertiser*:

> "The second Gallery has a prevalent note of that 'intenseness' and 'precious symbolism' which has run its brief course elsewhere and expired of inanition, but which still lingers superfluously on the outskirts of art… it is a backward step of portentous dimensions to seek to revive mediaevalism at the close of so practical a century as the nineteenth."[172]

This review prompted a lengthy battle of words between critics and members of the public (see also chapter eight). Some of the correspondents followed those earlier critics of *The Evergreen* in branding some of the artists' work as an imitation of Beardsley, while others picked up on Millar's attack on "mediaevalism" to compare the Dundee artists to members of the Pre-Raphaelites.

There is no doubt that those artists were an important influence, as has already been noted in the case of John Duncan, though his colleagues all shared with him the higher ideals of art in favour of *fin-de-siècle* decadence. Just a few weeks after these comparisons were made, George Dutch Davidson wrote to Duncan: "I dread the thought of the unrelated artist. We want no more Beardsleys."[173] The Pre-Raphaelites, however, were more wholeheartedly embraced, as can be seen from another encounter with A H Millar related by Stewart Carmichael:

> "Mr A H Millar read a paper [to members of the Art Society] on Dante Gabriel Rossetti, Painter and Poet. To our ardent minds his praise was so stinted that it only evoked a torrent of criticism. Mr Millar replied humbly 'All night I have been trying to place another stone on the cairn of the painter-poet but you have criticised me as if I had laid the cairn in ruins.'"[174]

That the work of this group of Dundee painters was seen as part of the Celtic Revival is also clear. In his infamous 1900 review, Millar attacked "the lachrymose and lackadaisical pictures of the Symbolists" (singling out works by Carmichael and Grieve), praised some of Dutch

Davidson's work but condemned the rest as savouring "too much of the pseudo-Kelticism which was over-pronounced at the last Graphic Arts Exhibition."[175] The *Piper o' Dundee* defended Davidson's work, claiming of one unnamed example: "This little picture, so beautifully drawn and coloured, was in itself a sufficient justification for the existence of the harshly derided Dundee Celtic School."[176] The same critic later relayed a conversation he had had with a friend about the next GAA exhibition. "You'll get an eye-opener," he was told. "Some are good, others beyond speech." "Celtic school again?" asks the reviewer, to which the answer was rather "Westgreen school" (Westgreen being the location of Dundee's lunatic asylum).[177]

Closely connected to this development of a distinctive Celtic and symbolist school was John Duncan's encouragement of decorative art in Dundee. With odd exceptions such as William Norwell and James Bremner, the members of the GAA had not shown much interest in this field of art prior to Duncan's return to Dundee (although Stewart Carmichael had shown a decorative panel called *The Dancers* in 1896, and Nellie – now known as Nell – Baxter made her GAA debut the same year). In 1898, a proposal to have a separate section of industrial art in the annual exhibition was dropped, but a number of decorative pieces were shown. As well as work by Duncan and Dutch Davidson, Nell Baxter showed three works (two design pieces and a scene based on Hans Andersen's *The Little Mermaid*), Robert Donn (a student at the Technical Institute) showed a symbolist copper panel, *Death and the Futurity*, and Nell's sister Rosa Baxter also exhibited for the first time.[178]

In May 1898, Duncan laid out his vision for the future of decorative art in Dundee in a letter to Patrick Geddes:

"In Dundee here where I know everybody who do [sic] anything in an artistic way I could easily get together a number of assistants to carry through any work that presented itself… We might form ourselves into a Studio of Design and undertake work of various kinds. Embroidery interests me very much… and wood-carving. There is a kind of awakening in these things all the country over."[179]

Duncan's first major opportunity to showcase what such a studio could achieve came with the 1899 GAA exhibition, for which he and James Bremner were tasked with arranging an "ornamental section".[180] The exhibition proved to be the GAA's most ambitious thus far, extending into a second room and, more importantly, making a profit for the first time. In its annual report, the Association concluded that the "experimental section in applied Art" had helped to make this "the most interesting show yet held" by them.[181] John Duncan was rarely given public credit for this success – only the *Evening Telegraph*'s review noted the "attention and admiration" given to the "embroideries, needlework, and art decoration contributed by Mr John Duncan's pupils".[182] Only after Duncan's departure from Dundee did the GAA themselves acknowledge (in their annual report) that "Mr Duncan's cultured enthusiasm gathered round him a group of Art workers interested in Decoration".[183] The group included Nell and Rosa Baxter as well as Elizabeth Burt, M Hart Congleton, Margaret Cunningham, Edith Hamilton, Mrs J G Lees, Barbara Matthew, Annie Moon and Duncan's sister Jessie Westbrook.[184] Their work included a copper panel in repoussé, a plate warmer, a china vase and an embroidered tea cosy. James Bremner's influence can also clearly be seen in the number of wood carvings and furniture designs shown (the "JB" credited with designing several of these was presumably Bremner). Although most of the decorative art was by women, there were also designs by Robert C Eaton and Thomas Pryde, both recent students of Dundee School of Art.

George Dutch Davidson contributed numerous pieces including a striking design for the cover of the exhibition catalogue, combining a minimalist modern graphic style with Celtic imagery (figure 98). Many of his exhibits were embroidered panels and book covers worked from his designs by the women in his and Duncan's circle, including his cousin Elizabeth Burt and Rosa Baxter (figures 99 & 100). By this time a complex love triangle seems to have been developing between these three. David Foggie recorded in his diary: "As far as I have seen George loved Rose and Rose loved him in her own beautiful sweet manner (Mrs Baxter objected), but Lizzie loved him with all the passion of her great heart. She asked me once what the attitude of one should be who loved with her whole might but the love and kind of it unknown." Although

Burt evidently felt unable to tell Davidson of her love, Foggie felt it was she, not Baxter, "to whom George opened the heaven of high thoughts and ideals".[185]

John Duncan also designed craftwork for his students to execute (a china trinket box and embroidered bretelles) as well as collaborating with Davidson on a decorative painting illustrating a quotation from Fiona Macleod, "When the dew is falling I have heard a calling / Of aerial sweet voices o'er the low green hill". His most notable contribution to the exhibition was *The Peacock among the Cypresses*, one of six decorative panels that he was commissioned to create for the drawing room and hall of Chateau du Donjon in Savoy, which had been purchased in 1898 by a Cairo law professor, Pierre Arminjon.[186] The *Courier* claimed, "the design and execution [are] alike admirable. The scheme of colour is at once bold and harmonious."[187]

Closer to home, at the beginning of 1900 Duncan was commissioned to create a series of murals for Lord Dean of Guild Paul for the library of his home at Friarton Grove on Magdalen Yard Road, which he completed in a remarkably short time.[188] Duncan's central design embodied Paul's civic duties, depicting a female figure spinning yarn (possibly Mary, Dundee's patron saint) surrounded by symbols of the city's trade (jute, whaling, marmalade, etc), the emblem of the Nine Incorporated Trades and with a view of the city and the Tay behind. A particularly notable feature was Duncan's adaptation of the city's coat of arms, the traditional wyverns being replaced with Pictish-inspired beasts. Surrounding panels depicted the various places around the world connected by trade to Dundee – a Norwegian scene featuring pine forests; an Arctic scene with "an Esquimo in his kyak spearing seals"; the carting of jute on a river bank in India; and a Spanish scene with a palace courtyard surrounded by orange trees. Judging from the description published in the *Evening Telegraph*, Duncan evidently took great care to depict the flora and fauna of each location in some detail.[189] A line drawing of the central design by Nell Baxter was published in *The Piper o' Dundee* (figure 101), suggesting that she assisted him in its execution.[190]

Despite commissions like this and the growing success of his decorative group, Duncan was feeling increasingly uncertain of his future prospects in Dundee. Writing to Mrs Geddes in 1898, he confessed: "I often yearn to be in Edinburgh again amongst all the folks I learnt to love there but yet I feel more at home here [in Dundee]. My life is less distracted in the smaller place and then it has older associations. Sometimes I feel pulled one way, sometimes another."[191]

A year later, however, he wrote to Geddes saying that he was "praying to be delivered out of the body of this death, to be plucked from the miry clay of Dundee, and to have my feet again 'stablished on the Rock of Edinburgh."[192] Geddes had suggested that a position might be found for him at Rowand Anderson's School of Applied Art in Edinburgh, but nothing came of this. In December that year, however, Geddes travelled to the USA on behalf of the International Association for the Advancement of Science, Arts & Education, and during a visit to Chicago he met Mrs Emmons Blaine, a progressive educationalist like himself who was patron of the Chicago Institute, an experimental new teacher training college. Geddes managed to persuade Blaine and the Institute's president,

102. Top: John Duncan and James Ramsay, Quaich, c.1900 *(Bonhams Scotland)*.

103. Opposite page: George Dutch Davidson, *Ullalume*, ink on paper, 1900 *(Dundee City Council: Dundee's Art Galleries & Museums)*.

104. Above: Alec Grieve, *La Rosière (Souvenir of George Dutch Davidson)*, watercolour on paper, 1901 *(Dundee City Council: Dundee's Art Galleries & Museums)*.

Col Dr F W Parker, that Duncan should be appointed as the inaugural director of their arts department, telling them that he was "incomparably better and more original than... any other Professor of Fine Art I have heard" and noting how his own children had been inspired by Duncan's tuition.[193] To Duncan, Geddes outlined the duties of the post as being

"not only, as everywhere else, to arrange a model art department (the necessary space with collections of examples, photographs, casts, books of reference, etc., and the necessary assistants also, all being assured), but to keep all this agoing. Not only to interest and to develop young teachers in training, and the children alike, in drawing, handicraft, etc., and accustom them to chalk and pencil, colour and clay, and the rest, but to exercise an influence everywhere outside his department, e.g. upon those of Nature Study and Geography, of History and Literature."[194]

Duncan accepted the position with alacrity, excited by the prospect of such interdisciplinary teaching: "as you know [I] have in my own way been gradually developing some of the same ideas. I quite feel the necessity of again relating the fine Arts to Natural Science and Literature, to Life and Actuality, and see that this must be reached through the improvement of education."[195] The salary of $3000 a year plus $200 travelling expenses would doubtless have helped quell any doubts about leaving Dundee, where he regularly complained of "all these miserable little money embarrassments that take the energy out of me."[196]

Duncan's last few months in Dundee were busy ones. As well as preparing work for the GAA exhibition, it is believed that he collaborated with local silversmith James Ramsay to create a beautiful Celtic-style Quaich, the lugs of which depict two figures representing Night and Day (figure 102).[197] He also renewed his association with Helen Hay, encouraging her to exhibit four repoussé panels at the GAA exhibition, one of which he designed for her. He also created a panel, *The Handkerchief of St Veronica*, for embroidery by his sister, Jessie Westbrook. Besides these he also showed two paintings in the exhibition, *Rosamunde* and *Mona Rosa*.

The exhibition reviews largely ignored Duncan's work, but in his opening address, the painter and Royal Scottish Academician J Campbell Noble noted that "Dundee had been specially favoured in having a man like Mr Duncan, well known in Edinburgh. They had not thought too much of him in Dundee, and now he was going to leave them. It was always the same with a prophet in his own country."[198] The *Wizard of the North* followed suit, claiming that "in Mr Duncan Dundee loses a true artist, and one who was probably not appreciated at his full value."[199]

Noble also singled out George Dutch Davidson for praise, having been "greatly surprised to find exquisite work in the exhibition by a young lad of only twenty years of age. He had not seen finer work than this".[200] Davidson showed several of his finest pictures, including *The Hills of Dream*, and designed further pieces for Elizabeth Burt, Rosa Baxter and Miss Jane F Meek. Also showing in the decorative section were Margaret Cunningham, Annie Moon, Henry Taylor Wyse from Arbroath and Duncan's brother-in-law Richard D Winter, a commercial artist now based in London.

Four days after the exhibition opened, Duncan sold the contents of his studio at William Fyfe's Central Fine Art Gallery in the Overgate. The *Advertiser* advertised the sale as "a unique collection of decorative pictures, sketches and

drawings... All are characteristic of Mr Duncan's careful drawing, bold outline, accurate colour, and finished detail."[201] The *Courier* afterwards reported "a good attendance of buyers, and bidding was brisk throughout."[202] Perhaps suggestive of the audience's taste, it was Duncan's early painting *Phaedria* that fetched the highest price of £7.

Before leaving for America, Duncan joined Geddes in Paris, where the latter had arranged a Summer School to coincide with the *Exposition Universelle*. Attendance was disappointing, but it gave Duncan the chance to renew his acquaintance with the work of French symbolist painters. In August Duncan caught a steamship from Liverpool to begin his new life in Chicago. On his way he wrote to Geddes:

"I am your very faithful disciple. And I carry your notes with me as my Scriptures, and shall diligently strive to live up to them. I have your suggestions and regard them as definite instructions to be punctually carried out. This will come all the easier as they so completely coincide with my own aspirations – aspirations <u>which</u> you have evolved in me."[203]

A few days later the *People's Journal* reported Duncan's initial impressions of Chicago, his favourite attraction being the zoo.[204] It would be the last that Dundee would hear of him for some time.

The city's artists lost no time in trying to prevent Duncan's departure from atrophying the decorative art movement. On 30 April, a special meeting of the GAA was held

"to meet with a party of ladies and gentlemen in the district who were interested in Decorative Art. It was pointed out that this particular phase of Art had been fostered in Dundee for some years largely under the leadership of Mr John Duncan who had now left the city to take up an appointment at Chicago. Those workers who had taken up the Decorative side of Art, felt the need of being united together in some form of Society and the purpose of this conference was to ascertain if the desired end could not be attained under the wing of the Graphic Arts Association."[205]

Although there was clearly a move by some of those present to establish a separate organisation, it was ultimately agreed that a Decorative Art Section of the Association should be formed, and twenty new Members and Associates signed up immediately including Thomas

105. Mrs Emma Sinclair, c.1905. Photograph from a volume of newspaper cuttings owned by Stewart Carmichael *(Dundee City Archives)*.

Delgaty Dunn, Mrs Moon, Emma Sinclair, Margaret Cunningham and May Watson. Others followed later – Elizabeth Burt became an Associate Member in 1901, Rosa Baxter in 1902 and Nell Baxter in 1905. The close association with the Technical Institute was underlined by the fact that Delgaty Dunn and architectural design tutor Patrick Thoms were asked to arrange the decorative section of the next annual exhibition.

The new members clearly hoped to stage something that John Duncan would have been proud of, but their efforts were overshadowed by a shocking tragedy. After five months in Florence and shorter stays in Ravenna and Venice, George Dutch Davidson returned home in August 1900. He was immediately affected by the cold climate, and initially struggled to resume his art. With Duncan gone, Davidson took over his studio in Albert Square, and here he embarked on what would turn out to be his final works. The influence of Italian art and nature is apparent in the drawing *Ullalume* (figure 103), inspired by an Edgar Allan Poe poem, one of a number of works which, according to William Hardie, "place Davidson in the highest rank of Scottish draughtsmen."[206]

Davidson became increasingly concerned with the relation of art to life. His time studying the early Italians had convinced him that most modern art was "trickery only – a mere parading of dexterity".[207]

"Wherever you find affectation and the accepting of other men's conventions without an understanding of their truth, the art is degenerate… Much modern work – the Glasgow School of Designers is a notable instance – is full of this affectation. I do not question that it is artistic – nay, to me it is always very charming – but it is not great art…There must always be present the strenuous striving after rightness."[208]

Among his final works, the watercolour *The Apotheosis of the Child* and the planned oil painting *Love Retreating* (for which only a pencil study was completed) both show his attempts at "rightness".[209] David Foggie described the *Apotheosis* as "the consummation of George Davidson's art; he had never revealed himself so fully, nor given such beauty

in the tenderness of it all… I think, however, that it is but a beautiful indication of the better work he thought of doing on the morrow."

Such work was not to come. On the night of 8 January 1901 Davidson spent the evening at home with his parents in Seafield Road, and wrote a final letter to John Duncan:

"I have lost something of the purely decorative quality which my previous work possessed, but this lack is I think a necessary accompaniment of increased and intensified expression. My Art has become more human, and without throwing off that quality of strangeness peculiar to the Celtic temperament, from Italy I have succeeded in incorporating a sweetness which tends to make the result more rational."[210]

David Foggie recounted his friend's last moments: "At midnight, after all had retired, he was heard to call 'mother' twice. His parents hurried to his side, but he died at once, without pain. He was twenty-one years and five months old."[211] Writing privately in his diary just hours after Davidson's death, Foggie evoked the poetic sensitivities that the Celtic artists sought after: "George lay as one of his own pure creations, ivory yellow in a white robe with a bunch of lilies in his beautiful hand. I loved him well alive and now the ineffable peace he is in has gone also into my soul."[212]

Davidson's parents asked his artist friends to act as pall-bearers at the funeral – the task was undertaken by Foggie, Grieve, Carmichael, Delgaty Dunn, Frank Laing and Charles S Mills. Mills was an amateur painter, mostly of atmospheric landscapes (see figure 2). Although not a Celtic Revival artist himself, his personality ("refined to the full, hypersensitive, critical, tender, with an appreciation of knowledge of nature in all its moods" according to David Foggie) made him a close friend of the group.[213] The tragedy was thus deepened when Mills was taken ill at the funeral and himself died two days later, aged 41.

Davidson's death deeply affected the whole artistic community in Dundee. Before his own sudden death, Charles Mills had written a poem dedicated to him, which was published in the *Evening Telegraph* and was used by Alec Grieve in his tribute watercolour *La Rosière – Souvenir of George Dutch Davidson* (figure 104), which drew on Davidson's own decorative style and was shown at the GAA exhibition along with an extensive display of Davidson's work, the majority of which was later gifted by his mother and uncle to the city's permanent collection. Determined to commemorate his life and work more fully, the GAA embarked on the publication of a *Memorial Volume*. With the financial help of 100 subscribers, they created an exquisitely beautiful publication with finely woven jute binding, collotype illustrations of Davidson's work, extracts from his letters, a tribute by John Duncan and a

106. Opposite top: Helen Kippen, *Where Oxlips and the Nodding Violet Grows*, watercolour on paper, c.1918 *(Dundee City Council: Dundee's Art Galleries & Museums)*.

107. Opposite bottom: Helen Kippen and Rose Baxter, *The Fairies*, embroidered panel, c.1905 *(Dundee Art Society)*.

detailed memorial by David Foggie. Among those praising the book was the poet W B Yeats:

> "The book is beautiful with a kind of ritual beauty – as of things which have by very energy of feeling passed out of life, as though precious stones were made by the desire of flowers for a too great perfection. All such art delights one, as if it was part of some religious service speaking to the whole soul, the passions not less than the moral nature uniting it to an unchanging order."[214]

In his last letter, Davidson had complained to Duncan: "The Decorative Section of the Association lags behind somewhat – there is a strange apathy shown towards it by most of its youngest members. I think I can imagine you pointing out my duty as regards this... [but I] have no time to go out of my way to enthuse people about Art, and besides, whilst the state of my health imposes many limitations upon me, I lack that faculty which makes for interesting others and setting them awakening."[215]

There were other challenges to the cause of decorative art. The Technical Institute had always been an important centre for the movement, but following a nationwide reorganisation of technical and art education in 1901, a new Code of Regulation was introduced for evening classes, and James Bremner's woodworking class would be the first casualty. Bremner was informed that the new approved syllabus "will exclude all the ladies who 'make' things" and that "the class must be for working lads alone". Rather than be "curbed in [his] work by government restrictions", Bremner resigned, and was soon followed by the cabinet-making teacher David Ireland.[216] Thomas Pryde took over the teaching of woodworking, and lost no time in advertising a separate, privately funded class in "Wood Carving for Amateurs and Lady Students".

Despite such setbacks, the decorative group thrived, partly thanks to the press attention it received. The nature of the work and the number of lady artists involved in its creation led to a notable increase in art coverage in the women's columns of the local papers, particularly the *Telegraph*. Its female reporter Marguerite had a fondness for writing exhibition reviews in the form of conversations reported over afternoon tea, such as this one discussing one of the GAA exhibitions:

> HOSTESS: I hear that the Arts and Crafts Section is very good indeed. Milly has got some new ideas of needlework from the exhibits, she was telling me.
>
> FANNY: Yes, you would admire that part of it, Ethel. There's a lace collar designed and worked by Annie Moon, and a couple of blotters by the Stewart Carmichaels – and, oh! a wonderful piece of appliqué by Miss Burt...
>
> MARGARET: The wood-carving is very good, too, and there's jewellery and china painting and designing and leather work. Mrs Sinclair's carving is perfect, of course... Piano fronts seem to be favourite vehicles for decoration,

108. Stewart Carmichael, *Portrait of the Artist's Wife*, oil on canvas, c.1900. Photograph of a painting formerly owned by J T Ewen *(Special Collections, University of St Andrews Library)*.

too. I am thinking of getting my faded green silk one taken out and replaced by a bit of embroidery."[217]

The loss of John Duncan as a teacher was made up for by the development of other private design classes in the city. Most notable were the decorative art classes of Mrs Emma Sinclair, based at 15 Castle Street (figure 105).[218] Born in Caithness in 1864, Sinclair first made her name as an amateur wood carver in Perth, where her husband worked as a modern languages teacher.[219] She taught wood-carving classes in Perth and Newport and first attracted notice in Dundee in 1897 when she showed off the work of her pupils in Thomas Justice's shop window.[220] A class at the YMCA followed later that year, while throughout this time she was making regular visits to London, studying at South Kensington. It seems likely that financial necessity was behind all this activity – she was made a widow while still in her early 30s. In 1898 she relocated to Dundee and soon commenced classes in St Andrews and other neighbouring towns. Within a few years she was described as "a force to be reckoned with in artistic circles... She possesses a charming personality, and inspires her pupils with some of her own enthusiasm for art, with a capital A."[221] In 1907, she received a commission from the Town Council to create a large carved shield to represent the city in the hall of the Royal Caledonian Society of London.[222] By that time she was an active member of Dundee Art Society, serving as council member, librarian and a member of the hanging committee. Her daughter Lily was also an artist, but the two left Dundee for Edinburgh in 1911.[223]

Nell and Rosa Baxter continued to be active members of

the decorative group, and in 1902 joined with Elizabeth Burt and others in starting a school of embroidery in Tayport. After the death of George Dutch Davidson, Burt continued to create embroideries based on his designs as well as creating her own pieces, but although a "keen student and steadfast worker... [she] did not enjoy robust health" and died in January 1903 at the age of 28, two years after the cousin she loved so much.[224]

In 1900, Nell Baxter married Tayport physician John Kippen but continued to exhibit (as Mrs Helen Kippen) into the 1930s. Reviewers often singled out her work for praise – in 1905, for example, the *Advertiser* highlighted her "lovely needlework, including a highly effective casement curtain embroidered in New Art style with bright colours".[225] "New Art" referred to Art Nouveau, and Baxter seems quickly to have abandoned the bold, geometrical style of her *Evergreen* work in favour of a more conventionally fashionable approach. Two notable works by her survive today – a striking watercolour design for an embroidery, *Where Oxlips and the Nodding Violet Grows* (figure 106) illustrating *A Midsummer Night's Dream*; and an embroidered panel on linen, *The Fairies*, (figure 107), designed by her and worked by her sister.[226] Its text and images were drawn from a poem by William Allingham that was included in Patrick Geddes's *Lyra Celtica*. She died in 1952 aged 78.

Rosa Baxter (usually referred to as Rose after 1903) exhibited more actively, creating her own designs as well as continuing to execute work by George Dutch Davidson and others. In 1905 the *Evening Telegraph* featured her as one of Dundee's leading needlework artists: "Her work is exquisite of its kind, a veritable labour of love. Restraint characterises it alike in design and in colouring, and there is a certain harmony between the article decorated, whether cushion, table centre, sideboard cloth, or book cover, and the purpose for which it is intended."[227]

Baxter also continued to be an active member of Dundee Art Society into the 1930s, though evidently her style did not vary during that time (a review in 1927, for example, describes

109. The Dundee banner, reproduced in the *Dundee Courier*, 1909 *(used by kind permission of D C Thomson & Co Ltd)*.

110. John Duncan, *Sunset, Iona*, oil/tempera on canvas, 1908 *(Fife Cultural Trust (Kirkcaldy Galleries) on behalf of Fife Council)*.

her "tender Burne Jones-like tones... overpowered by the higher note of the very modern embroidery" shown by younger artists).[228] She never married, and died in 1947 aged 70.

Another notable embroiderer was Stewart Carmichael's wife Marion Willis (figure 108) – "known as the clever and capable exponent of her husband's artistic ideas in needlework, and she is with her needle as deft an artist as he is with his brush."[229] Willis had had a successful independent career before she met Carmichael, having taken an LLA degree before working as a governess and then English mistress at Worcester Ladies' College. In this path she was following her elder sister Susan, who had a very successful teaching career and in 1896 became one of the first two female Inspectors of Schools. Marion was also a talented organist, invited regularly to play in St Andrews as well as her home town of Forfar. She married Carmichael in 1893, and four years later her younger sister Emma married Alec Grieve. "[T]he four of them were great chums," recalled Emma's niece. "At that time artists' wives like [them] were really money-wise poor but they were rich in culture".[230] Carmichael was a noted advocate for women's rights, so presumably it was Marion's choice rather than his to give up her teaching career (and to some degree her music) but she turned instead to embroidery and exhibited regularly with the Art Society, also becoming an active council member. In 1904 she gave a lecture on needlework to members of the society, and her work was frequently singled out by reviewers.

Several other women were regular contributors to the decorative section of the Art Society's exhibitions, including Misses Florence Lee, May Watson and A Ure Wilson. The reputation of the group also encouraged decorative artists from further afield to exhibit, including Meta G Napier-Brown from Edinburgh and J T R Blair and Bessie McElwee from Glasgow.[231] In 1905 the Art Society held a special exhibition of decorative art in its clubrooms, opened by Mrs Longair, the Lord Provost's wife. The *Advertiser* praised it as a "remarkably interesting and beautiful exhibition" while the *Courier* noted: "It is impossible by mere description to do justice to the beauty of the designs and the artistic sympathy with which they have been worked out."[232] As well as embroidery there were also examples of metalworking, enamelling, leatherworking and marquetry.

The success of this show led to a larger Arts & Crafts

selling exhibition five years later in the Queen's Hotel. Stewart Carmichael later recalled: "A manifesto with a call to Dundee was printed and widely circulated... There were stalls for pictures, embroideries, jewellery, metalwork and decorated wearing apparel."[233] Carmichael's original proposal was to combine the sale with a pageant to be held in the Kinnaird Hall. A committee was formed to organise the event, chaired by David Foggie, and it was soon reported that "a number of suitable pictures from the History of Dundee were selected as likely to make excellent tableaux".[234] The idea was ultimately abandoned due to the costs involved, but the exhibition proved a great success, making an extraordinary profit of £109/14/11.[235]

Events like these, however, remained infrequent, and although prolific, the city's decorative artists were largely amateurs. Annette Carruthers has claimed that at this time "Dundee had neither the clientele nor the educational infrastructure to support a home-grown craft revival".[236] However, one indication of the growing reputation of decorative art was the commissioning by Lord Provost Longair in 1908 of a new civic banner for Dundee (figure 109). Featuring the familiar coat of arms on the front (with Celtic-style knotwork on the wyverns' tails) and a circular motif featuring Dundee's patron saint Mary on the reverse (based on an ecclesiastical seal of 1492), it was designed by Stewart Carmichael and embroidered by Mrs Carmichael, Rose Baxter and Elizabeth Laing (Frank's widow). The banner represented Dundee at the Scottish National Pageant in Edinburgh in June 1908 (for which John Duncan designed the Celtic group). The *Courier* reported that Geddes was "one of the prime movers in making the arrangements for the representation of Dundee" so he may have suggested the commissioning of the banner. It was carried by two young Dundonians wearing 12th century costume. The following month Geddes arranged for the banner to be shown in Dundee at a small-scale procession which was part of the 25th anniversary celebrations of UCD.[237] Geddes attempted to raise interest in a grand pageant for Dundee, but although a committee was formed to take this forward (including Geddes and Carmichael), nothing came of it.[238] The banner was then displayed in the Albert Institute and the Council Chambers until 1914, when it was loaned to an exhibition in Ghent. In the rush to return it on the outbreak of war the supporting poles were lost and the banner was put into storage and remained forgotten until its rediscovery in 1938.

With so little of the decorative work from this period surviving today, it is difficult to know how much the Celtic Revival continued to influence the artists and designers involved, beyond the occasional mention of a Celtic motif in a newspaper exhibition review. In December 1904, however, John Duncan began to renew his connections to Dundee, attending an event organised by the Art Society.[239]

Duncan had become increasingly frustrated with his work at the Chicago Institute, which in 1901 was taken over by the University of Chicago. He complained to Geddes that "the principles are good, the practice is abominable" and found he could do little to influence the latter.[240] At least in the faculty president, Col Parker, Duncan had found an inspirational leader that he could look to for guidance as he had previously

111. John Duncan, illustration from *The Woodman and the Elves*, c.1910 *(Libraries, Leisure & Culture Dundee)*.

done Geddes. In March 1902, however, Parker died and Duncan once more turned to Geddes for help. On the day of Parker's death, he wrote to his former mentor:

> "In his [Parker's] constant insistence upon social duty he has educated me to appreciate more and more fully the work you were engaged in in Edinburgh during the years when I was your very unworthy servant, when I tried to help in my feeble despairing way and no doubt often hindered and discouraged you. I see now what I could have done to further your plans but I was poor in hope."[241]

Despite the failure of the Old Edinburgh School of Art, Duncan still dreamed of forming a new art school in collaboration with Geddes: "Its work to be the decoration of schools and public places and the making of picture books such as your soul loves and furniture and pottery and embroideries".[242] Geddes, by that time, had moved onto other projects, and at the end of the academic year in 1903 Duncan returned to Scotland and took a studio in Torphichen Street, Edinburgh. Here he embarked on his career as a full-time painter, and it was during this period that he created some of his finest work.

Duncan's interest in Celtic mythology had continued

unabated during his time in America, and soon after his return to Scotland he was drawn to the Western Isles, "fired with the ambition to master Gaelic and to steep himself in the atmosphere of Celticism", in the words of singer Marjory Kennedy-Fraser.[243] He spent long periods on Eriskay, Barra and Iona, and it was on the latter island that he claimed to have his first encounter with the fairy world. According to Charles Richard Cammell, during a long, solitary walk Duncan had been approached by two tall, unearthly beings who floated silently towards him before fading away.

> "He recognized them instantly as people of the Sidh and from that moment knew that he was fey… Thenceforward he felt he was living in two distinct worlds, or spheres of being, and that he was slipping daily further from the old human sphere into the world of Faery. He saw others of the Sidh, always obliquely, and realized that he was at the cross-roads, and had little time to choose his path. With a supreme effort he tore himself away from the island."[244]

Thereafter Duncan claimed to have numerous supernatural encounters on the islands, including visions of angels and goblins and the sounds of fairy harps and bagpipes. But any

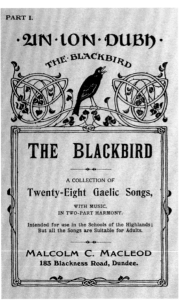

112. John Duncan, *The Riders of the Sidhe*, tempera on canvas, 1911 *(Dundee City Council: Dundee's Art Galleries & Museums)*.

113. Cover design for *The Blackbird*, published by Malcolm C MacLeod, 1905 *(private collection)*.

114. John Duncan, Reredos in St Mary's Church, Broughty Ferry, 1917 *(author's photograph)*.

attempts to capture these visions on paper were failures: "When I attempt to draw these people my work becomes very grotesque. The silence and purity and awe of their faces becomes a kind of selfish coldness and they look starved and mean."[245]

Whatever the truth of Duncan's experiences, they inspired in him a profound spiritualism which suffused all of his work from now on. In 1905 he wrote in his notebook, "I register a vow to devote myself to the realisation of a spiritual art."[246] The islands also renewed his interest in landscape painting, and indeed he played an important role in encouraging the Scottish Colourists to paint on Iona (figure 110). When he returned to Dundee to show at the Art Society's 1905 exhibition, it was two Hebridean scenes that he chose to include. Duncan renewed his membership of the Society and soon returned to give a lecture in the Victoria Galleries on "Celtic Art: Its Character and Meaning". In it, he described the "mystery, exuberance, and restraint" of Celtic art, and the "uncanny" quality of the interlacing knotwork on Celtic crosses. "It was in the proportion and shape of the cross and the interlacements that the genius of the Celtic art expressed itself, and rose beyond criticism, and was carried forward into competition with the best art of the world."[247] A programme of Highland music followed, organised by Mrs Sinclair.

Over the next few years Duncan showed work annually with the Art Society, and frequently attended the openings. Among the paintings shown were *How Arthur got Excalibur, his Sword, of Morgana Le Fay* (in 1906), *Lover and Lady* (1908) and *Yorinda and Yoringel in the Witches' Wood* (1911). In 1910 Duncan was made an Associate of the RSA and the Dundee Art Society decided to give a dinner in his honour at the Queen's Hotel. At the time, Duncan was showing *Angus*

Og (now in the National Galleries of Scotland) at the Dundee Fine Art Exhibition, prompting a spoof cartoon by Joseph Lee in the *City Echo* showing the winged figure being overtaken by a modern aeroplane.

A more unusual Dundee project also took place around this time, when Valentine & Sons published Duncan's only attempt at writing a children's book, *The Woodman and the Elves*, which he illustrated in full colour (figure 111).[248] An old man finds some large eggs which he takes home, but they hatch into mischievous elves that cause chaos. In a strange anti-climax, at the end, after being entranced by a strange light in the woods, the elves simply disappear and are never seen again.

In 1911, Duncan showed the work which is arguably his masterpiece, *The Riders of the Sidhe*, at the Art Society's most prestigious exhibition to mark its 21st anniversary (figure 112). His first major painting in tempera, it features the four "Lords of Life, bearing as symbols the Tree of Experience, the Love Cup, the Sword of Will, and the Stone of Quietness".[249] It was hailed by the *Courier* as "one of the outstanding pictures" of the exhibition, and was widely reproduced, including in the Dundee Highland Society's yearbook, the *Celtic Annual*.[250]

"Here is Mr Duncan's Fairyland, and he has made it our Fairyland, and we feel its undeniable charm and feel its beauty… he addresses himself to all who love beauty for

115. Stewart Carmichael, Ward Chapel Mission Hall mural design, line reproduction from the *Dundee Advertiser*, 1899 *(used by kind permission of D C Thomson & Co Ltd)*.

116. Stewart Carmichael, Rosebank Parish Church mural design, line reproduction from the *Dundee Advertiser*, 1904 *(used by kind permission of D C Thomson & Co Ltd)*.

beauty's sake and who see beyond the horizon of everyday life, the land of mystery and idealism and doom, which is wonderful as twilight and strange as a dream".[251]

The painting was bought by Patrick Geddes's former patron James Martin White and presented to the permanent collection, the first work by Duncan to be acquired for Dundee.

Duncan was also invited to give the opening address at the Art Society's exhibition, in which he recalled his early memories of Dundee and discussed the development of art exhibition and education in the city. In particular, he praised the new sculpture gallery in Barrack Street and the fact that as well as classical casts it also featured "reproductions of the Celtic Stones of Scotland. If any town has a duty to these ancient monuments it is Dundee, which, as you know, is set in the centre of the thickest cluster of stones of the best period of the art. It is an art which, though little known, is of profound interest and of high beauty. And it is our own."[252]

The city's on-going interest in all things Celtic was also soon to be seen in the design of St John's Cross Church in Blackness Avenue. The church opened in 1914 after a lengthy campaign, the congregation's previous home in the Gaelic Chapel on South Tay Street having been inadequate for many years. The new church (built by local architects H & F Thomson) featured Celtic knotwork decoration throughout its interior woodwork.

A growing interest in Celtic literature was also apparent at this time. In 1905 the treasurer of the Dundee Highland Society, Malcolm C MacLeod, began to publish a considerable number of books in both Gaelic and English, including *The Gaelic Concepts of Life and Death*, *Modern Gaelic Bards* (with illustrations by Joseph Lee, of whom more later), *Old Highland Legends*, *Popular Tales of the West Highlands* and a number of children's books such as *Gaelic Fairy Tales* and *The Tale of the Cauldron*, with full colour illustrations by Gordon Browne – a body of Celtic literature produced over two decades that easily rivalled that of Patrick Geddes & Colleagues in Edinburgh (figure 113).[253]

Other publishing ventures at this time showed a more direct debt to Duncan and Geddes. *The Meal-Poke* was a one-off illustrated book produced in 1903 to raise money for the University College Students' Union, and in both format and content was clearly modelled on *The Evergreen* (figure 244). Although Geddes is not credited, he may well have been involved as both Charles Mackie and James Cadenhead were among the contributors. Dundee artists involved included Stewart Carmichael, Alec Grieve, David Foggie and W B Lamond. Thomas Delgaty Dunn designed the book's covers. Among the authors contributing were J M Barrie, Andrew Lang, Annie S Swan and T M Davidson.[254] In a similar format, though featuring only images, was the Arbroath periodical *Imprints* (1901) to which Carmichael and Foggie also contributed along with Frank Laing and Angus artists such as Henry Taylor Wyse and James Watterston Herald.

The Dundee Highland Society also saw an increased interest in visual culture at this time, thanks to the election of Dr Angus MacGillivray as chief of the society in 1912. MacGillivray was an ophthalmic surgeon at Dundee Royal Infirmary and the Dundee Eye Institution and was a lecturer in ophthalmology at University College. He had a passion for archaeology and history and proudly claimed the title of 28th chief of the Clan MacGillivray, without apparently much in the way of documentary evidence to back this up![255] He was also chair of the Dundee Fine Art Association, which was responsible for the exhibitions and collections of the Victoria Art Galleries. Unlike his predecessors in that role, MacGillivray actively supported the Dundee Art Society, and Stewart Carmichael later credited him with encouraging local art patrons to make significant acquisitions of work by Dundee artists for the permanent collection, including *The Riders of the Sidhe* and Carmichael's *The Countess of Buchan* (figure 266). The *Celtic Annual* also regularly featured artworks from the collection, and in 1918 published an important article on Dundee artists.

John Duncan continued to exhibit his work in Dundee and maintained his links with the Art Society and with artists like James Torrington Bell (a fellow painter in tempera) right up to his death in 1945.[256] But his most enduring contribution to art in the city came in 1917 when he was commissioned to decorate the reredos of St Mary's Episcopal Church in Broughty Ferry (figure 114).[257] The work was part of an extensive series of alterations and improvements to the church that had been carried out since 1911 under the direction of Sir Robert Lorimer, one of Scotland's most eminent architects. Col W H Fergusson, a member of the vestry, presented the reredos as a memorial for his late wife, and Lorimer's design for it featured an ornate Gothic framework of carved oak, into which Duncan's painted gesso panels were set.[258]

Duncan conceived five panels featuring Christ and the four archangels. While his sketch design was being considered by the vestry he wrote nervously to Lorimer, "I shall be so disappointed if it doesn't come off. My heart is in that design."[259] Luckily, the proposal "met with universal acceptance" and arrangements were made for Duncan to visit the church to see "the kind & amount of light in which the pictures will be placed."[260]

The striking panels that Duncan created show Gabriel (the angel of Annunciation), Uriel (the angel of the Sun), Raphael (the angel of Music and Healing) and Michael (the angel of Justice). In an echo of the symbolic themes of *The Evergreen*, Duncan conceived the panels

"as four moods, that of East, South, West and North; Spring, Summer, Autumn, Winter; Youth, Manhood, Maturity and Age; Morning, Noon, Evening and Night… The Central panel represents Christ enthroned as King of Kings and Lord of Lords. His left hand holds the Book of Life. His right hand is raised in blessing. He is seated upon the White Throne spanned by the rainbow. The seven planets are about Him, the earth is His footstool."[261]

The reredos was dedicated on Christmas Eve 1917.[262] Duncan later reworked the design for the reredos in the chapel at Sneaton Castle, Whitby, completed in 1925.

While Duncan's connections with Dundee continued despite his move to Edinburgh, Geddes's active involvement with the cultural life of the city was much more sporadic. In 1907 he published a series of articles in the *Dundee Advertiser* under the heading "Recent Art Movements of Dundee", for which he received assistance from both Stewart Carmichael and Frank Laing.[263] In them he made an outspoken appeal for better appreciation of the city's artists:

"Without coals we know our engines will not run; but we forget sometimes, do we not, that, without oats, even Pegasus cannot be expected to fly? Considering the irregularity and scantiness of his feeding, is it not surprising that he now and then leaps upward as far as he does? Does the Scottish history, of which we are so proud… show very much more than this perpetual wasting of genius? But genius in our townsmen! Why, certainly! And in an appreciable percentage, too, could we but better extract it."[264]

In the same article Geddes also asked that Dundee's artists be commissioned to paint murals to decorate public buildings, a theme he had discussed at length eleven years earlier when opening the GAA exhibition in 1896. There, he suggested that fine work could be done on the new Post Office or public baths. He noted how much the Council Chambers had been improved by Morris and Burne-Jones's glass, but implored the city fathers to draw on local talent instead:

"it appeared to him [Geddes] that the most important, practical and economic secret of art development was the continuity of employment and purpose which would begin in the decoration of private houses and still more in the decoration of their public buildings… [T]hese decorative and ornamental designs would by and by become applicable to the different manufactures of the town, and Dundee would then make its manufactures more widely respected and enjoyed."[265]

Stewart Carmichael enjoyed the greatest success in creating public art for his native city. Like Geddes he believed that art should be seen and enjoyed everywhere, famously comparing it to "little green leaves that grow between the stones of the city."[266] In 1898 he was commissioned to paint a large panel for the Ward Chapel Mission Hall in Brown Street on the subject of Christ receiving little children (figure 115). On seeing the painting in progress, the *Evening Telegraph* hailed it as "the finest work which Mr Carmichael has accomplished. It marks a new era in the history of local art. Henceforth it is

117. Stewart Carmichael, *The Leaders of Scottish Liberty*, mural painting, 1901, reproduced in *The Scottish Patriot*, 1904 *(Dundee City Archives)*.

hoped that Dundee will bestow greater attention to decorative work of this kind."[267] Carmichael may have been inspired by seeing James Christie's painting *Christ's Welcome to the Children* exhibited in Thomas Murray's gallery in April 1898.[268] The finished work, measuring ten feet by six, received overwhelmingly positive reviews. The *Advertiser* praised its symbolic qualities and subtle colours, concluding: "The artist is to be highly commended for having so successfully carried out his idea without overstraining the theme or lowering the religious sentiment of the subject."[269] The *Courier* hailed the modernism of the painting as "strictly unconventional" and noting the "abundance of light in the centre of the picture. In every line there is absolute harmony".[270] The *Telegraph* again referred to Carmichael's "genius" and noted: "The conception of the picture is marked by the poetry which pervades all Mr Carmichael's works. The treatment is neither too conventional nor too realistic, but a happy blending of both."[271]

Despite this success, similar decorations for church buildings were few and far between. It seemed that many in Dundee were uncomfortable with the whole concept. In 1896, Geddes's "bold suggestion of pictures in churches provoked a stir of amused surprise" according to the *Evening Telegraph*.[272] Carmichael received only one further religious commission – for a large mural (23 x 14 feet) on the south wall of Rosebank Parish Church on Constitution Street, painted in 1904 as part of an overall redecoration of the church (figure 116).[273] Depicting two angels flanking a central radiating figure, the mural was (unlike the work in Brown Street) painted *in situ*, using a blue and gold colour scheme with no varnish. The *Advertiser* hailed it as "the first important attempt in this locality to elevate the style of ecclesiastical decoration by introducing figure subjects appropriate for the place".[274] Although the *Courier* claimed that the painting "will last as long as the church itself", there is no trace of it in the building today, which has been repainted in plain white.[275]

The only other similar church decorations known about from this period are the murals by C G L Phillips for the Baptist Church on Ward Road, depicting scenes from the Holy Land with Art Nouveau borders. Phillips was a member of the church and was appointed Convenor of the Decoration Committee responsible for a complete refurbishment of the interior in 1903. William Norwell undertook the principal decoration, with Phillips designing "many beautiful colour schemes" within the church and the murals ("quite unique in their way")

in the adjacent hall.[276]

Carmichael's most ambitious piece of public art in Dundee was political rather than religious in intent. In 1901 the Dundee Liberal Association unveiled in its new rooms at 51 Reform Street a massive mural (30 x 10 feet) entitled *The Leaders of Scottish Liberty* (figure 117). The work had been acquired from Carmichael thanks to a subscription campaign led by John Maclauchlan and supported by (among others) John Robertson of Elmslea and William Low. Although no price was stated in reports of the time, the artist was evidently underpaid: "Mr Carmichael was in a sense handing over the work to the Liberal Association, because they could never repay the artist for the immense amount of labour and brains he had put into the picture."[277] The painting was "intended to show the progress of Scottish liberty by typical figures selected from the history of the nation from early times to the present day... It shows the epoch-makers of Scottish nationality who led the way in war, in the Church, in literature, and in politics."[278] Its fourteen subjects covered nineteen centuries, and comprised (from left to right) Galgacus, St Columba, Michael Scot, Alexander III, John the Graham, William Wallace (the central figure), Robert the Bruce, Blind Harry, John Knox, Andrew Fletcher of Saltoun, Robert Burns, William Gladstone and Thomas Carlyle. A female figure symbolising liberty was shown in the foreground laying a wreath at the feet of Wallace. Carmichael set these figures against a representatively Scottish landscape, featuring mountains, Scots firs, a ruined abbey and a Celtic cross. The painting, executed on canvas and attached to the wall in the billiard room, was unveiled to considerable acclaim on 21 December, with A H Millar giving a lecture on the figures depicted. As well as extensive local press coverage, the mural was publicised in the *London Star* and the *Daily Chronicle*, and was the subject of an illustrated feature in the *Scottish Patriot*, which noted:

> "A taste for the pictorial decoration of interiors appears to be springing up among the people of Dundee, who possibly feel that something must be done by way of compensation for the external meanness which still characterises the great majority of the buildings of the town."[279]

Carmichael exhibited his original study for the mural at the GAA exhibition the following year, and it was bought by J T

118. Alec Grieve, *Miss Agnes Husband*, oil on canvas, 1909
(Dundee City Council: Dundee's Art Galleries & Museums).

Ewen, a Schools Inspector and art patron based in Forfar (also associated with Patrick Geddes). Two years later Ewen bought another mural study by Carmichael, this time showing *The Scottish Poets*.[280]

One of the differences often cited between the Celtic Revivals in Scotland and Ireland is that the latter was far more politicised. But while Geddes and Duncan saw their work in Edinburgh more as an internationalist movement than a nationalist one, the Dundee school was far more political in its activities. As Carmichael later recalled, "Many of us were ardent socialists and were students of that ideal taught by William Morris and Walter Crane that in the coming new state every man and woman whatever their work must be an artist. And we did not hesitate to preach our ideas in and out of session."[281] In 1895, for example, Carmichael wrote to the *Advertiser* in reply to a scathing article on nationalism, saying: "Abolish this worship of land, gold and property by making them common property, as the streets of our towns, our parks, our museums are common property. Then the desire of such things will evaporate, and merge into the recognition of the idea that all things belong to one and all."[282] Carmichael's ideal of socialism was "the development of man to his highest in his mental, moral, and physical nature, this only being possible by striving to give all men equal opportunities of development." Art played an important role because "beautiful environment of life, home, and law will gradually efface from our earth mental and physical ugliness."[283] Carmichael enlarged on this in another newspaper piece the same year, focusing on the role of the decorative artist:

"Under Socialism the popular ideals of the workers would be the doing of their best in all handicrafts; thus delight and joy in their work would dominate, and thus the artist craftsman would develop, and his works however humble would be marked with that stamp of sincerity and delight which would operate upon all, permeating the community with the love of well-made articles, which in time might nourish and advance each worker in the community to a sense of beauty which the artist of to-day possesses. And the artist of to-day. What is he? A slave to fulfil the caprice and whim of his plutocratic patron, sacrificing his artistic conscience and aims for his life, a steady incentive for the abasement of the best in him."[284]

This is unlikely to have endeared Carmichael to Dundee's art patrons, and he offended them even further at the opening of the GAA exhibition in 1900, declaring during the vote of thanks that "The Soul of Dundee was buried under Jute"![285] Paintings such as his *Labour Triumphant* (exhibited in 1897), "must have given real cause for alarm."[286] In 1907 he wrote to Patrick Geddes of the "peculiar and remarkable need of a body of artists to Dundee" due to "its quick growth – feverish anxiety to be rich – the machine-worship – the trodden out souls of the workers... Art and its influence might breathe the life breath into the people."[287]

Alec Grieve was another firm believer in socialism. During his time in London he became a close friend of Keir Hardie, and was the cartoonist for many years on Hardie's periodical the *Labour Leader*. He was a member of the Independent Labour Party (ILP) and the Dundee Central Workers Committee and, like Carmichael, often spoke about the role of art in the labour movement:

"An artist at present must paint to sell, otherwise he will go to the wall. This is death to true art, and the creator of a commercial art that is worthless. The Labour movement, is a movement to bring order out of this chaos; to produce things, not money. Its consummation will be the destruction of commercialism, that of art along with the rest... It is my firm conviction that with the realisation of Socialism, there will dawn a new era of all the arts, that will far surpass that great artistic period of the Greeks".[288]

In 1909 Grieve expanded further on this in a lecture to the Dundee Art Society on "The Fine Arts under Socialism". Grieve's figurative work had always shown a keen sympathy for the working class. In 1894, for example, he created a set of twelve etchings under the title *The Blind at Work*, showing scenes of life in the Dundee Blind Institution, where the inmates worked to make mattresses, brushes, baskets and the like. The etchings were published by Robert Scott to help promote the work of the Institution, and were praised by the

Piper o' Dundee as "conceived in a truly suggestive and artistic style."[289]

Grieve also painted a number of portraits of prominent labour supporters. In 1909 he received considerable acclaim for his painting of Agnes Husband (figure 118), a member of the Dundee School Board and honorary president of the Dundee branch of the ILP. The portrait was presented to the permanent collection the following year after a subscription movement that included the ILP, the Dundee Social Union and the Women's Enfranchisement Movement (Husband was also a noted suffragist). It was thus the first presentation portrait of a woman to enter the collection. Ten years later, Grieve's posthumous portrait of his friend Robert Stirton, another ILP stalwart and former president of Dundee Trades & Labour Council, was also presented to the city's collection, gifted by the Council.

Grieve's many rural landscape paintings did not generally reveal his political sympathies, a notable exception being the

119. Opposite page: Alec Grieve, *The Ploughman and the Crows*, oil on canvas, 1903 *(Perth Museum & Art Gallery)*.

120. Above: Joseph Lee, 'Dawn in a Dundee Lodging-House' from *The City Echo*, 1908 *(University of Dundee Archive Services)*.

1903 painting *The Ploughman and the Crows* (figure 119). It was exhibited at the GAA exhibition that year and later at the Paris Salon, where it was hung on the line and attracted considerable attention for its political symbolism – the crows as capitalists living off the fruits of the working man's toil. A line drawing of the painting was published in Joseph Lee's socialist magazine, *The Tocsin*, as one of a series of illustrations of artworks with a relevant message for the labour movement. Lee had a different interpretation: "As we look, the two horse, the dark and the light, become night and day. Very shortly, and they shall lead the wearied ploughman to the end of the world, for him, and he shall lie quietly in just such a track as he has here laid open."[290]

Although not generally associated with the Celtic Revival, Lee was a member of Dundee Highland Society and illustrated at least one of Malcolm MacLeod's *Modern Gaelic Bards* series in 1913. His career will be discussed in chapter five, but his socialist interests are worth pointing out here. *The Tocsin* was billed as "An Illustrated Labour and Socialist Journal", and although it only lasted seven issues in 1909, it was read by influential figures in the movement including (possibly through Grieve's connection) Keir Hardie.[291] Lee wrote much of the content (though Agnes Husband was another notable contributor) and drew all of the illustrations. Lee's first magazine, the *City Echo* (begun in 1907), had been more humorous in content but had also included more serious pieces with political intent, including 'Darkest Dundee', a series of illustrated articles on life in the most deprived parts of the city (figure 120). These jostled rather oddly with cartoons poking fun at working class visitors to the Victoria Galleries (see figure 5).

Along with Grieve and David Foggie (see chapter four), Lee was actively involved with the ILP, and in January 1908 the party's publication *Forward* reported that the three artists were creating drawings and cartoons for the Dundee ILP's first

premises at 107 Victoria Road:

> "We are now a living active force in this city… We have women and men who are prepared to make sacrifices. All are workers. Each gives according to their own talents… Messrs Grieve, Lee and Foggie provide pictures and sketches which to adorn the walls of our temporary abode".[292]

Unfortunately, their efforts seem not to have been appreciated by the members, and in 1909 Lee found them "punctured and bespattered and spoiled".[293]

Stewart Carmichael later felt that the political nature of the city's artists was one reason why the public were so reluctant to support them. There was a long tradition in Dundee of artists making their political opinions known. Robert Mudie, for example, came to Dundee in 1808 as drawing master at the Academy. His interest in politics led him to join the Town Council, but when he began writing satirical accounts accusing his fellow councillors of corruption, they took a dim view of his sense of humour and he moved to London in 1821.[294] That same year, Henry Harwood created his famous caricature of Dundee worthies, *The Executive*, which was widely reproduced as an engraving.[295] Unlike Mudie, Harwood seems to have been forgiven, since he later received various commissions by town councillors for more flattering portraits.

More actively involved in political activity was the first secretary of the GAA, David Ramsay Sellars (figure 263). Born in 1854, Sellars' childhood was interrupted at the age of eleven when his father died and he had to work for his living. For some time he worked in the offices of the *Advertiser* from 4am to 9am every morning before attending school. He learned shoemaking as a trade, moving to Glasgow at sixteen. "He early took an interest in the conditions of labour," reported the *Piper o' Dundee*, "and attracted attention by the able manner in which he conducted a newspaper correspondence on behalf of his fellow-workmen during a trade dispute."[296] Over the next few years, Sellars worked for the Glasgow Trades Union then was appointed secretary for the Dundee Trades Union, Dispute Investigator and ultimately (when he was still only 23) Organiser and Strike Manager for Scotland. His trade union career halted in the 1880s while he studied at the School of Art, gaining his Art Teacher's Certificate in 1884. He joined the Dundee Art Club, exhibiting with them as well as the Dundee Fine Art Exhibitions and the RSA. At the same time he began publishing poems in the local press, one of which was later included in the anthology *The Bards of Angus and the Mearns*, its editor describing him as "a man of exceptional power."[297] In the 1890s he returned to politics, having been chosen by the Bootmakers' Society as their Parliamentary candidate for Northampton, an area with a reputation for political radicalism.[298] Ultimately, Sellars chose art over politics and returned to Dundee to teach at the High School. He died in 1922.[299]

It is perhaps unsurprising that Dundee's artists should follow such interests given the reputation of the place as a 'Radical Town'. In practice, however the city's politics were largely shaped by the *Dundee Advertiser*, whose editor for

many years was a Liberal MP, John Leng. The *Advertiser* was certainly not supportive of political extremism and often attacked the Labour Party, seeing it as a threat to the Liberals. However many of the artists on its staff were far more left-wing, and political cartoons were a common feature in both the *Advertiser* and its weekend companion, the *People's Journal*. Joseph Lee contributed frequently, and ultimately rose up the ranks to become editor of the *People's Journal*. As such he commissioned numerous political cartoons including one by Tom Ross showing Dundee suffragettes on the warpath (figure 121). It was based on an incident on 28 June 1912 when a hammer was thrown by a suffragette through the window of the main post office. Dundee was one of the principal centres of the Scottish suffrage movement, and one of the women depicted may have been Ethel Moorhead, a Dundee artist who was also one of the most active members of the movement (figure 122).

Moorhead was born in Kent in 1869. Her father was an army surgeon and as a result she had a peripatetic childhood in India, Mauritius and South Africa before the family eventually settled in Dundee in 1900. By that time Moorhead had already studied art in Paris, chaperoned by an older friend. Years later she wrote a fictionalised autobiography in which she described this "adventure":

> "There was never any talk in the home about her being a painter, they had never known any such thing but they would let her indulge in that low streak. Even her father's enthusiasm stopped short at that and her mother was disdainful. Cissy [her sister Alice] said she should go, and saved money and sent it to her regularly. And there she found the Atelier Carmen [where] she worked furiously with an eager group of American students."[300]

Although no details of her study are known (the Atelier Carmen is fictitious), the *Celtic Annual* described her as "a pupil of Whistler for painting, and of Mucha for drawing".[301] The *Evening Telegraph* also described her as having studied under Whistler.[302] She joined the GAA in 1900 as a Member (ie a professional artist) rather than an Associate, and the following year took a studio with Miss Oliphant in the Arcade Buildings, King Street. She became a significant contributor to the GAA exhibitions, and from her first appearance her work was singled out by the critics for praise:

> "Ethel Moorhead, who exhibits here for the first time, is a distinct acquisition to the Graphic Arts Association. Her pictures are unquestionably the gems of the collection from an artistic point of view. Three of them are studies of heads, worked out in a manner which suggests Parisian training – careful drawing, subdued colour, and that indescribable glamour which artists call 'tone'."[303]

In 1902 she exhibited at the RSA for the first time with *The Conspirator*, "a very striking head of a youth with long auburn hair and a sinister expression in his eye".[304] She was

now gaining a strong reputation for the "intelligent and well-studied work shown by [her] at various Exhibitions throughout the country."[305] Reviewers noted that her work was more progressive than that of other women artists – the *Piper o' Dundee*, for example, described her as "an artistic 'new woman.' She has shaken off the Christmas card traditions that bind so many of her sisters, and faces reality with open vision."[306]

The death of Moorhead's mother in 1902 left her less time for painting as she had to care for her father (whose portrait she painted that year) and further tragedy struck in 1910 when her beloved sister Alice (who had studied medicine and became one of Dundee's first female GPs) died at an early age. It was after this that she began to get involved in the women's suffrage movement, joining the Women's Social & Political Union. Her first recorded action was in December 1910 when she threw an egg at Winston Churchill during a political meeting. The following month she became the first woman in Dundee to invoke the WSPU's 'No Vote, No Tax' motto. On refusing to

121. Opposite top: Tom Ross, *On the Warpath*, ink on paper, 1912
(Libraries, Leisure & Culture Dundee, licensor www.scran.ac.uk).

122. Opposite left: Tom Ross, 'Dundee Artist Suffragette', a caricature of
Ethel Moorhead from *The Wizard of the North*, 1912
(Libraries, Leisure & Culture Dundee).

123. Above: Ethel Moorhead, 'Ernest Walsh' from *This Quarter*, 1925
(private collection).

pay her taxes a valuable candelabrum was seized from her house and sold at auction, but her fellow suffragettes bought it back and returned it to her. Moorhead's father died in 1912, and she is believed to have designed the strikingly modern gravestone erected over the family plot in the Western Cemetery.[307]

From this point she became increasingly militant in her activities, causing havoc in London, Edinburgh and Aberdeen among other places.[308] She served the first of several prison sentences in Perth in September 1912, and two years later became the first suffragette to be force-fed in a Scottish prison, this time in Edinburgh. It has been claimed that she was Fanny Parker's accomplice in the attempted arson attack on Robert Burns' cottage in July 1914 – if so it was probably her last militant activity before the suffragettes suspended their actions on the outbreak of war.[309] Moorhead worked with Parker doing relief work for the National Service Organisation during the war, then sold her house in Dundee (which she had rarely occupied during the past few years) and moved to Dublin and other places before eventually settling in Paris in the early 1920s. Thanks apparently to a legacy left her by Fanny Parker, she founded and co-edited a literary and art journal, *This Quarter*, along with a young Irish-American poet, Ernest Walsh (figure 123). The journal's contents reveal that Moorhead was in contact with leading avant-garde artists and writers of the time, including Francis Picabia, Wyndham Lewis, Constantin Brancusi, Ezra Pound, Ernest Hemingway, Gertrude Stein and James Joyce. Moorhead eventually returned to Ireland where she died in 1955.

Many of Dundee's artists supported the suffragist cause. It is notable, for example, that the local branch of the Women's Freedom League held their meetings in the Dundee Art Society's rooms for several years. In 1906, Frank Laing chaired a packed meeting in Tayport which Alec Grieve also attended at which a motion for enfranchisement of women was carried unanimously.[310] Things became more problematic, however, when the suffragettes started attacking paintings. Carmichael added a cutting to his scrapbook about the slashing of the *Rokeby Venus* in the National Gallery, though without adding any comment to it. Joseph Lee was more vocal when a portrait of the Prime Minster was vandalised:

"we must have no more pasting of legends on the faces of portraits, even if they be of the stony-hearted and hard-avisaged Asquith. The windows of Downing Street as much as you please, but the glass fronts of pictures must be held sacred, and taboo. And what if there had been no glass front? And what of the unfortunate artist in any case? All artists are in favour of Votes for Women – saving only such as have had their pictures desecrated."[311]

Carmichael showed his support in other ways. He followed his *Leaders of Scottish Liberty* mural design with one depicting *The Scottish Heroines*. It was exhibited by the GAA in 1902 and the Tayport Artists' Circle in 1905, but was never turned into a full-size mural. The *Advertiser* described the piece:

"he has grouped in an artistically decorative manner a succession of historical personages, beginning with St Margaret, Queen of Malcolm Canmore, and including many women who have made a name in Scottish history… [A]lthough exception might be taken to some of the characters selected by Mr Carmichael, the idea is excellent."[312]

One of the selections the reviewer might have taken exception to was Carmichael's decision to place 17th-century militant activist Jenny Geddes in the central position rather than the expected Mary Queen of Scots.[313]

Over the years Carmichael was associated with a number of remarkable women. In 1905 he showed a portrait of mystic poet Rachael Annand Taylor ("the remarkable poetess, the unknown", as he described her) at the Tayport Artists' Circle exhibition, and she attended the opening with him.[314] She was living in Dundee at the time, and gave a lecture to the Art Society on the Italian Renaissance.[315]

Carmichael later became a close friend of the future nationalist politician Wendy Wood, who moved to Dundee in 1923 and worked as an illustrator.[316] He painted her portrait that year, and may well have stimulated her interest in Scottish nationalism.[317] Carmichael became increasingly involved in the growing Scottish nationalist movement – it seems likely that he joined the Scottish Home Rule Association, and was later associated with the National Party of Scotland and subsequently the SNP.[318] It was at this time that his work

was being championed by another outspoken nationalist, the poet C M Grieve (better known by his pen-name Hugh MacDiarmid), who lectured to Dundee Art Society on 'The Scottish Renaissance Movement' in 1929. Grieve was famously dismissive of Dundee, describing it in 1925 as "the dreariest waste of materialism that contemporary Scotland possesses."[319] While the Victoria Art Galleries were full of "bloated portraits of all manner of local nonentities", he claimed that "Carmichael's studio in the Nethergate is like an oasis in the desert."[320] He praised Carmichael's mural designs but noted:

> "his most distinctive vein is represented by his symbolical compositions. Here the poet side of his nature emerges... [A]s manifestations of the Scottish psyche – as glimpses into the soul of Celtic imagery – they stand in a category of their own. They are very different from the ornamental designs of John Duncan...

Carmichael is less concerned with outward trappings. His visions are more profound, and personal to himself while distinctively Scottish in quality... [They] confront us with this aspect or that of a powerful imagination that has difficulty in compressing cosmic conceptions or remote spiritual problems into terrestrial human terms at all. These are wild, weird designs, full of unique psychological interest. If I was asked 'What is a Scotsman?' I could scarcely do better than show my interrogator one of these compositions".[321]

By this time, the other Dundee artists who had embraced symbolism and the Celtic Revival, such as Alec Grieve, had returned to a more conventional style. Carmichael, on the other hand, continued to paint Celtic and Highland subjects as part of a wider fascination for Scottish history and culture (figure 124). During the 1910s (possibly thanks to the influence of Angus MacGillivray) he had become an active member of the

124. Opposite page: Stewart Carmichael, *Anima Celtica*, oil on canvas, 1932 *(Dundee City Council: Dundee's Art Galleries & Museums)*.

125. Above: Stewart Carmichael at his Exhibition of Celtic Pictures, 1936. Photograph from a volume of newspaper cuttings owned by Carmichael *(Dundee City Archives)*.

Dundee Highland Society, and would later become one of its chieftans. He was also elected a member of the exclusive Piper's Bairns, who honoured him with a complimentary dinner in 1928.

Of his later Celtic paintings, the most ambitious was surely his mural design *The Gaelic Bards*. The five-foot-long study was first exhibited in 1935 in one of his annual studio exhibitions, and was described by the *Evening Telegraph* as "a decorative treatment of Ossian, Mary of the Songs, Iain Lom, Alexander MacMaighstir Alasdair, Duncan Ban Macintyre, and the rest."[322] In all there were seventeen poets featured, with Iona cathedral in the background. The *Telegraph* concluded: "One day the finished work should decorate the new Celtic College, or some other public building", probably a reference to an attempt by the Iona Society to create a college in Scotland for teaching and preserving Gaelic.[323] The full-scale mural seems never to have been commissioned, but the study attracted considerable interest at the Dundee Art Society exhibition in 1936, and that same year Carmichael loaned the painting to the Dundee Highland Society as an illustrative backdrop to a lecture he gave on the Gaelic Bards. It is worth noting that although Carmichael read out English translations of the poems during this lecture, someone else rendered them in Gaelic, raising the question of whether or not Carmichael was a Gaelic speaker. Having come from Highland Perthshire, his parents probably had been, and Carmichael's scrapbooks contain many newspaper cuttings about the preservation of Gaelic, clearly demonstrating its importance to him. He certainly knew a number of Gaelic songs – at a concert given by the Dundee Gaelic Musical Association of Hebridean songs in February 1920, Carmichael acted as translator, explaining "the meaning and origins of the songs, after the manner of Mrs Kennedy-Fraser, in a fashion which added greatly to the appreciation of the audience."[324] Between 1918 and 1930 he also contributed illustrations to the Gaelic-language periodical *An Rosarnach*, printed originally in Perth then later in Dundee.

In 1937 the Highland Society was actively involved in bringing the Gaelic Mod back to Dundee. Carmichael seized on the opportunity to stage an exhibition of Celtic artworks in the Caird Hall, where the event was held. The *Courier* reported:

"The Mod… has the good fortune in its present session to have at its call a painter, Mr Stewart Carmichael… who, with rare enthusiasm, has created year after year large-scale decorative studies of the bards and saints and heroes of the Gaelic age."[325] The accompanying photograph (figure 125) showed Carmichael holding one of the eighteen paintings included in the exhibition – *Three Celtic Women*, depicting Mary of the Gael, Deirdre and Mary MacLeod, an oil version of which was later included in the 1939 RSA exhibition. On the left is the far end of the *Gaelic Bards* study. Other paintings shown included *The Meeting of St Kentigern and St Fergus* (another watercolour later worked up into an oil painting, now in the city's collection) and *The Gleam* (now in the University of St Andrews under the title *Allegory of Scotland*).

Carmichael would return to several of these subjects during the remainder of his life, while still remaining prolific in still life and landscape painting. The death of his wife Marion in 1941 was a major blow to him and his workload reduced significantly, though he continued to support the Dundee Art Society and to serve as a governor at Dundee College of Art. He died in 1950 at the age of 83, the last of an extraordinary generation of Dundee painters. A memorial exhibition was held the following year, the tribute in the catalogue noting:

"There is a deep strain of poetic romance in many of his productions and Celtic history and tradition are repeatedly portrayed. There seems to be often a yearning over the buried beauty of the past… yet he looked forward too, with an optimism that seldom dimmed. He was ever quick to welcome good work from young painters and poets, and there was no melancholy or bitterness of spirit in the man who possessed within himself courage, gaiety, and the quiet mind… [His] death removed from us not only a picturesque and familiar figure but one of the best-loved and most distinguished of our citizens."[326]

During his long career he had continued to pursue a visionary, Celtic-infused style of art that had begun thanks to the influence of Patrick Geddes six decades earlier. Writing in the *Advertiser* in 1907, Geddes had attempted (as Carmichael had on so many occasions) to encourage a greater sense of art appreciation among his readers, encouraging them not to be put off by the modern, dream-like style of painting:

"Have we no sympathy with dreams? In this hard world of every-day toil, of dull matter of fact, what can the… artistic imagination do but dream? … The artist but dreams in better company than ours, yet is peculiarly able and willing to lift us into his. Here, then, is one main element for the case of art, never more needed in history than here and now in the gloom of our modern manufacturing towns."[327]

CHAPTER FOUR
Artists at Work

126. John Stewart, *Alexander Bell*, oil on canvas, c.1850s *(University of Dundee Museum Services, Tayside Medical History Museum)*.

The Celtic Revival and symbolist movement represented Dundee's most distinctive contributions to the art world at this time, but there were many other professional artists in the city working in more conventional genres. Their work may not have been ground-breaking, but its quality and success undoubtedly makes it worthy of attention. This chapter will look at some of the many Dundee artists not yet discussed, with a particular focus on portrait and landscape painters.

Before the 19th century, success for any prospective painters in the town usually lay elsewhere. This was due as much to the lack of educational prospects as to the absence of suitable clientele. Without an art school, the only way artistic ability was to be nurtured was for the painters in question to leave Dundee – and indeed Scotland. Katherine Read, for example, studied in Paris in the 1740s before becoming a successful pastel portraitist in Rome and London. Soon after, George Willison began his artistic career in Italy, then moved to India where he amassed a considerable fortune as a portrait painter. Other notable talents emerged from Dundee in the early 19th century – John Zephaniah Bell began in Edinburgh as an assistant to Sir David Wilkie, then worked in London, Paris and Rome painting portraits and frescoes. The Simson brothers – George, William and David – found fame in Edinburgh and London as landscape and portrait painters.[1]

By the mid-19th century, it was beginning to be possible to stay in Dundee and make a living by painting portraits. Writing

in 1906, T S Robertson recalled: "There were three artists in Dundee 50 years ago who were all portrait painters – Harwood, Stewart, and Macgillivray [sic]... Dundee in those days was not able to support three portrait painters, and although Harwood, as far as I know, never painted out of Dundee, the others occasionally had to find employment in neighbouring towns."[2] Of these three painters, George McGillivray is better known for his topographical paintings, which we shall return to later.[3] Henry Harwood remains the best known today thanks to his much-reproduced satirical cartoon *The Executive* (see chapter three). Born in Ireland in 1803, Harwood was the son of Lieutenant Coleshurst, who had retired from the Royal Navy and married an actress, changing his name to Harwood when he too took to the stage. He died when young Henry was still in infancy and his widow came to Dundee seeking work in the theatre. Henry earned a reputation as a painter and numerous portrait commissions followed including Provosts William Lindsay and Alexander Lawson. His clients also included the local aristocracy – Lord Kinnaird commissioned him to paint *"Whistle o'er the lave o't"*, a humorous scene of a hen-pecked husband which was later acquired by Dr John Stewart and was singled out by the *Courier* as a particular highlight of his extensive collection.[4] Although he struggled financially during his lifetime, Harwood's paintings became fashionably collectible in the decades following his death in 1868, and over twenty were included in the Old Dundee exhibition, many of which were later gifted to the permanent collection.

Also well-known locally was John Stewart, born in Angus in 1810. He worked (and presumably studied) for a while in Paris, where he painted a large-scale *Adam and Eve* (1847-8), intended for entry in the competition to create artworks for the new Houses of Parliament in London. Unfortunately Stewart got caught up in the Paris revolution of 1848 and failed to complete the painting on time, but it was exhibited internationally to considerable acclaim. He returned home and established himself as a portraitist in Dundee, his subjects including Rev George Gilfillan and several medical figures such as surgeons James Arrott and Alexander Bell (figure 126), and Capt Patrick Scott, chairman of the Board of Directors of Dundee Royal Lunatic Asylum.[5] Presumably in an attempt to broaden his client base, he branched out into photographic portraits in the 1850s, but the lack of any newspaper obituaries at the time of his death in 1887 suggests that he had been largely forgotten. His son (also John) became an art teacher in Dundee.

The commissions to paint Christopher Kerr and James Yeaman in 1871-2 (see chapter two) seem to have encouraged Hugh Collins to relocate to Dundee permanently, taking a studio initially at 7 Ward Road and then settling in 10 Shore Terrace, with a house in Broughty Ferry.[6] Within a few years, he would establish himself as Dundee's leading portrait painter, being eulogised by the *Piper o' Dundee*, for example, as 'Our Portraiteur' – "his careful and studious work has kept growing in excellence... His portraits... display a delicacy of touch and mastery of technique only seen in the work of the true artist."[7]

Born in Tillicoultry in c.1834, Collins was brought up in Alloa and served as an apprentice to a house painter before studying art in Edinburgh, working both there and in Stirling before his move to Dundee.[8] He began showing at the RSA in

example the *Courier* praised a painting of a child surrounded by his pet dogs as "a remarkable display of artistic skill – the outcome of long experience and native ability in the painter")[10] and was also called upon on several occasions to undertake posthumous portraits (for example George Kinloch and John Morgan, both now in the city's collection), though the results of these were usually less impressive. Far more successful were his striking portraits of Inuit men who came to Dundee on whaling ships (figure 127).[11]

Although portraits were Collins' principal source of income, he was also fond of landscapes – his most haunting painting is his *Wreckage from the Tay Bridge* (figure 128), in which a peaceful river scene is torn apart by sections of broken girders in a surprisingly modernist composition. There were also more conventional scenes of rural life and humble domestic interiors, which Collins produced in great quantities in between commissions. "He worked with great rapidity," the *Piper o' Dundee* claimed, "and was a wonderfully prolific." Collins' personality, however, was not always a likeable one:

> "With regard to Mr Collins' personal characteristics, it never could be said by his warmest admirers that he erred on the side of reticence in speech… When Mr Collins thought he was slighted by someone, he never minced his words, but hit straight out at the offending party, not always in the most diplomatic fashion. Indeed his invective was generally more pointed and pungent than prudent and polite."[12]

127. Hugh Collins, *Portrait of the Eskimo Shoodlue*, oil on canvas, 1894 *(private collection; photo © Christie's Images/ Bridgman Images)*.

128. Hugh Collins, *Wreckage from the Tay Bridge*, oil on canvas, 1880 *(Dundee City Council: Dundee's Art Galleries & Museums)*.

1860 and the RA in 1868. As well as showing works in the Dundee Fine Art Exhibitions, he was also a regular lender of paintings to the permanent gallery. Many of his portrait commissions came from successful working-class businessmen who were aspiring to middle-class respectability – the whaling captain William Adams, the framer and gallery owner Thomas Murray (who often showed Collins' work) and the manager of Her Majesty's Theatre William McFarland. Collins also had a number of commissions from the local Masonic Lodges, including paintings of Past Master Sir John Ogilvy and Brother Thomas Buik RWM, and restoration work on portraits of Past Masters which had been damaged by fire.[9]

Collins' work generally was well-painted if uninspiring. He was acclaimed for portraits of children and animals (for

He also seems to have had something of a drink problem for a while, which did not help his reputation.[13] Whether due to this, a falling out, or simply because commissions were drying up, Collins returned to Edinburgh in 1882 or 83, staying with his daughter for a few years. There he claimed: "I have a fine studio, working hard, lots of pictures here but cannot get money."[14] By the end of the decade he was back in Dundee where, occupying a studio at 65 Nethergate (later used by Stewart Carmichael), he continued to work with great energy right up until his death. The *Courier*'s art correspondent reported on a visit to his studio just five months before his death, when he had just completed a series of views of North Berwick and a number of large-scale paintings of religious allegory.[15] Not long after, Collins suffered a stroke from which he only partially recovered. He died of heart failure at his home in Church Street, Broughty Ferry on 21 June 1896. His daughter Janet (who often styled herself Jennett) also had success as an artist, based in Edinburgh and London.

At the time of Collins's death, a younger artist, Charles Louis Mitchell, was rapidly establishing a reputation as a portraitist, which would be consolidated in 1899 with the Campbell Smith commission referred to in chapter two. Despite having to stand comparison with so many other fine portraits in the permanent collection, Mitchell's painting of the local judge was well received, and was certainly evidence of a more original talent than Collins'. Edward Pinnington described it as "the painter's high-water mark so far, reserved in colour, superb in characterisation, a lawyer's face, shrewd, genial, and humorous."[16]

The son of a farmer, Mitchell was born in Laurencekirk in 1860, and studied in Montrose, Aberdeen and Germany.[17] He quickly abandoned a career as an Aberdeen bank clerk in favour of art, becoming a member of the Aberdeen Artists Society in 1887. He first exhibited at the Dundee Fine Art Exhibitions in 1889, while living in Montrose (where he had been taught art by James Irvine, a pupil of Raeburn). The following year he moved to Dundee, taking a studio first at 26 Castle Street and then 28 Ward Road. His home was across the water at Downiemount, Tayport. He was soon attracting clients of significant social standing – at the Old Dundee exhibition he showed portraits of iron merchant and former Dean of Guild Thomas Nicoll, and of the art collector G B Simpson. Three other collectors, C C Maxwell, A B Spence and John Robertson of Elmslea, also had their portraits painted by him.[18] He would be given another commission for a presentation portrait in 1909, that of Chief Constable David Dewar.

Mitchell supplemented his income by teaching. In 1892 he advertised the opening of an atelier which he had purpose-built on the corner of Ward Road and North Lindsay Street (figure 129), taking the upper floor of a new coach-building establishment: "The flat will be divided into a large gallery, 35 feet by 22 feet, and with two studios, each about 20 feet square. Special arrangements have been made for these apartments so as to give the best possible light for the art pupils."[19] The following year the *Courier* reported: "Mr C L Mitchell has started in Dundee with a very charming studio, of which a great many art students have been quick to avail themselves. All this winter they have been working under Mr Mitchell's tuition".[20] It's not clear how long Mitchell continued to teach from his own studio, but in 1902 he was appointed to teach Fine Art at University College, Dundee (see chapter six).

Although his reputation was founded on portrait painting, Mitchell's real love seems to have been Highland scenes, particularly depictions of crofter's cottages, both inside and

PLAN OF STUDIOS.

129. Plan of C L Mitchell's studios in Ward Road, 1892 (*Libraries, Leisure & Culture Dundee*).

130. C L Mitchell, *Struan Bridge*, oil on canvas, reproduced in *The Meal-Poke*, 1903 *(University of Dundee Archive Services)*.

131. David Comba Adamson, *Five o' Clock Tea*, oil on canvas, c.1880s *(Dundee City Council: Dundee's Art Galleries & Museums)*.

out. As the Dundee Art Society's obituary explained, "he loved to paint the rugged, well-coloured Scottish types – both men and women – delighting also in the quaint farm kitchen interiors of a by-gone century, and feeling the lonely, calm spirit that broods over the Highland hills and glens of his native countryside."[21] Mitchell showed such paintings in large numbers at the Art Society's exhibitions with prices ranging from £3 to £50, but he also found ready buyers much further afield. The rest of Mitchell's family (his parents and ten siblings) had emigrated to a farm in Dalton, Minnesota in 1880, and Mitchell had come to recognise that there was a significant market for quaint or couthy Highland scenes in America.[22] Andrew Carnegie and the Mellon family were among his clients there, and he made increasingly frequent visits across the Atlantic, ultimately settling in Pittsburgh where he died in 1918. The Dundee Art Society (of which he had been both President and a long-standing Treasurer) held a memorial exhibition the following year.[23] "He was a handsome man," according to their obituarist, "well educated, retiring, seeking no honours, but eager always to excel in his chosen art of portraiture."[24]

An artist who might have had a successful career as a portraitist was William Yule, the son of Dundee's Harbour Master and a cousin of George Dutch Davidson. Born in 1868, he studied art at the High School and then in Edinburgh, London, Paris and Madrid. Before his premature

death in 1900 aged just 31, he produced, according to the *Celtic Annual*, "many fine portraits".[25] These included one of ex-Lord Provost Mathewson, shown at the Fine Art Exhibition in 1895. Two years later his portrait of Jack Darling was shown by the Society of Portrait Painters in London, where the *Times* hailed it as one of the highlights of the exhibition.[26]

Only one other Dundee painter from this time became particularly acclaimed for his portraits. David Comba Adamson was born in 1859 in a miner's cottage in Kilbarchan, Renfrewshire, though contemporary accounts of his life described him variously as coming from Ayrshire, Glasgow and Edinburgh.[27] His obituary in the *Dundee Advertiser* claimed that his father was a medical practitioner, but the truth was rather less socially respectable – David Adamson senior tried his hand at various jobs including ironstone miner and music hall proprietor, but seems to have had more success running an advertising business, which allowed the rapidly expanding family (the Adamsons had nine children altogether) to move to a larger house in Cambuslang. At around that time David junior left school and was put to work in an architect's office, but evening classes at Glasgow School of Art led to further art training in Belfast and Edinburgh. In 1882 he left Britain for the Continent, enrolling at Antwerp Academy at the same time as E A Hornel and two Edinburgh artists who would go on to have significant connections to Dundee, W G Burn-Murdoch and J Michael Brown. Two years later he moved to Paris to attend the Ecole des Beaux Arts and the Ateliers of William-Adolphe Bouguereau, Benjamin Constant and others. He soon began to exhibit his work at the Paris Salon and made friends with many of the popular French painters of the day. Adamson therefore decided to remain in Paris, opening his own atelier (where his students, according to Stewart Carmichael, included two Romanian princesses).[28]

At the same time, one of David's five brothers, Andrew Adamson, was trying to establish himself as a professional photographer in Glasgow, and the renaming of his firm as Adamson Bros around 1884 indicates that other members of the family were also involved – in 1891 they promoted themselves as "Photographic Artists and Portrait Painters", suggesting that David was making regular trips back home to work with the firm.

Adamson's first connection with Dundee had been in 1880 when he showed a scene from *King Lear* at the Fine Art Exhibition, but it would be another ten years before he sent further work. It may have been on a visit to the city in connection with the 1890 Fine Art Exhibition that he met and wooed Jane Cappon, sister of the Dundee architect T Martin Cappon. As the *Wizard of the North* reported the following year, "Tho' not a Dundonian, Mr Adamson has shewn his good taste by carrying off one of the ladies of the city, to share his honour in Paris".[29]

One of the two paintings Adamson showed in 1890, *Art* (showing a lady painting at an easel), was reproduced in lithograph in the *Piper o' Dundee*, but he really came to public attention in Dundee the following year when his painting *The Unexpected Guest* (which had hung on the line in the Royal Academy in 1889) was singled out for praise in the *Wizard of the North*, the editor James Russell saying: "Might we suggest to some of our merchant princes, who are in the habit of making

132. David Comba Adamson, *David Rutherford Dow*, oil on canvas, 1898 *(courtesy of Crail Museum Trust)*.

presentations to our local Picture Gallery, that the above would form a large and very handsome Christmas gift, and could be admirably accommodated in the Victoria Gallery?"[30] Although no one took up the offer (the £250 price tag probably being the main deterrent – only artists with notable letters after their name were charging that much for their work), word of Adamson's abilities quickly spread. His new family connections brought him back to Dundee on a regular basis, and Russell rarely missed an opportunity of promoting his discovery whenever he was in town. In 1894 the *Wizard of the North* reported:

> "Perhaps the strongest point of Mr Adamson's work is in portraiture, and his portraits have been greatly admired at the annual exhibition on the Continent and in London. He has, during the past three months, been engaged in painting portraits of some well-known ladies and gentlemen in this neighbourhood. These portraits are at present on view at 2 India Buildings, where the artist has collected some of his summer's work".[31]

Adamson began to hold regular exhibitions of his work in Dundee, and it was his portraits that captivated the critics. Russell particularly liked a painting of T M Cappon in his Volunteer Officer's uniform: "The *pose* is full of strength and dignity, and the colour is rich and harmonious. The likeness is unmistakable, and the modelling of the features gives a force and reality that make the head stand out from the canvas."[32]

The art critics of the *Courier* and the *Advertiser* soon became equally effusive in their praise. Reviewing an exhibition of Adamson's at the Royal Hotel in 1897, the *Advertiser* was particularly impressed by a portrait of grocer William Low:

> "This is not only one of those works that attracts by fidelity of resemblance, it is one in which character, as well as likeness has been described by the artist… for the longer we look, the better we know the man. In ease of attitude, vivacity of countenance and exquisite taste in the disposition of vestments, the figure is quite a triumph of technical skill."[33]

The same reviewer (possibly A H Millar) went on to praise a flower study by Adamson in such over-the-top terms that the *Piper o' Dundee* lampooned it in their next edition, though they were quick to agree that Adamson "well deserves such tribute from the local Ruskin."[34]

Adamson was still based in Paris but was spending more and more time back in Britain. In 1896 he had spent some months in Manchester painting portraits of prominent citizens, but Dundee seemed to hold a stronger attraction and in 1898 he made the decision to settle there permanently. He began exhibiting with the GAA that year and rewarded James Russell for his support by painting his portrait, shown at the GAA in 1899 (figure 175). That was also the year of Adamson's first local public commission – not from Dundee but from Forfar, where he executed a presentation portrait of ex-Provost Doig (now in Angus Council's collections).

Adamson's already-substantial reputation was rewarded with a steady stream of commissions, including Dr Alexander Campbell and his wife (1898), businessman and art collector William Rettie and his wife (1899), Bailie (later Lord Provost) Barrie and his wife (1901) and an on-going series of portraits of the family of ex-Lord Dean of Guild Paul (starting in 1899), seven of which were exhibited together at Scott's gallery in 1907. He became particularly noted for children's portraits (figure 132) – a 1900 oil of the daughter of "a well-known Newport gentleman" drew particular praise from both the *Courier* and the *Wizard*, the latter noting: "The dress of white satin is exceptionally well done. The shading is so effective that you can almost feel the richness of the material. There is no stiffness in the pose of the subject, who seems to have thrown herself in a careless, easy posture on the chair".[35]

Paintings of cute Victorian children appealed far less to the following generation, and it may have been due to changing fashions that Adamson's work was seen and reviewed less often as the new century progressed. According to Stewart Carmichael, "he became somewhat of a recluse, mixing but little with other people." This was a notable change for the man described as "courteous and distinguished... cultured and erudite in the history and theory of his art, and gifted in expressing himself on art – or, indeed, any question – in a scholarly and vivid way. His knowledge of literature was extensive. His love of music was very great; he possessed a beautiful tenor voice, and sang with charm and genuine artistry."[36] Adamson's last years were blighted with illness (he seems to have suffered from Parkinson's disease, which would certainly have affected his ability to paint) and the last four were spent permanently confined in Royal Victoria Hospital where he died in 1926.

Dundee boasted only a small number of professional sculptors at this time, mostly undertaking private commissions for portrait busts or decorative work for architects. Undoubtedly the most commercially successful were the Gonnella family from Italy. Joseph Gonnella had come to Dundee in the late 1850s and was joined by Allessio Gonnella a few years later.[37] At a time when Dundee's wealthy merchants were building grand new villas and needing to decorate them, the Gonnellas built up a successful business working as modellers, figuremakers and importers of Italian sculpture. After small shops in Reform Street, Coupar's Alley and Union Street, they opened a Fine Art Saloon on Sea Wynd, off Nethergate. The *Courier* reported:

> "The lovers of the fine arts will find a rich field
> to gratify their curiosity in the large, varied
> and valuable collection which crowds the
> saloon of the Messrs Gonnella… and which
> has been enriched by additions of exquisite
> pieces of statuary and other sculpture, which
> Mr Allessio Gonnella has selected at great
> expense from the studios in Florence, Carrara,
> Pisa, Leghorn, and Volterra."[38]

As well as copying Italian works, the Gonnellas began to create their own sculptures to appeal to local tastes – statuettes of Burns' Highland Mary, for example, and a bust of the campaigning orator and man of letters, Rev George Gilfillan. The *Courier* concluded: "A more interesting collection of sculptured works of art is not in Dundee, and were it situated in the Nethergate, instead of the narrow wynd where it is, thousands would stop to inspect and admire it." Two years later, Joseph succeeded in moving the business to 81 Nethergate, where it remained for many years (figure 133). The company's fame was spreading – in 1882 they were commissioned to create a marble statue of Robert Burns for Dumfries, to a design by Amelia Hill.[39]

By that time Allessio had left Dundee and Joseph was assisted by his son Louis and nephew Giuseppe, handing over the business to them on his retiral in 1889.[40] Giuseppe soon took the lead and "his ability as a modeller and sculptor brought him a large clientele in the city."[41] The Gonnellas provided decorative statues for McFarland's Music Hall, classical casts to the art school at Dundee Technical Institute and scientific models for D'Arcy Thompson at UCD. They showed off their wares at the Dundee Industrial Exhibitions of 1887-8 and 1893-4 and won the prize for marble statuary at the Chicago Exhibition of 1893. Giuseppe taught modelling at both the Technical Institute and the High School, and of all the family he seems to have been the most artistically gifted. He was an active member of the Dundee Art Club and exhibited at the Fine Art Exhibitions. Among his private commissions were busts of the dentist and art collector Dr John Stewart and steamboat captain David Edwards. In 1896 he and Louis dissolved their partnership and Giuseppe continued the business on his own. In 1909 he was appointed Italian consular agent in Dundee (a position also held by at least two other members of the

133. Gonnella's Fine Art Saloon, Nethergate. Photograph from the Wilson Collection, 1893 *(Libraries, Leisure & Culture Dundee)*.

134. Below: Line drawing of Alexander Neilson's bust of Martin Anderson, from a volume of newspaper cuttings owned by Stewart Carmichael *(Dundee City Archives)*.

1008—"CYNICUS."—*Alex. Neilson.*

family over the years), and he returned to his homeland after retiring in 1922. His brothers Francesco and Luigi carried on the business, but it had closed down by 1936.

Alexander Neilson was born in 1854 in Edinburgh, where his father was also a sculptor and worked on notable projects such as the Scott Monument. Alex trained under Edinburgh sculptor John Rhind and came to Dundee in the 1880s. According to the Dundee Art Society he "warmly identified himself with the art life of the town", joining the Art Club and becoming one of the founder members of the GAA.[42] His work as a portraitist included busts of fellow Art Club member Martin Anderson (figure 134); Thomas Carnelley, Professor of Chemistry at UCD; and another depiction of Rev George Gilfillan, which Neilson donated to the permanent collection in 1893. At the same time he was undertaking decorative work for churches, notably the font at Brechin Episcopal Chuch, and was engaged in restoration work on earlier sculptural work, including the famous market cross at Culross. He won prizes at the Dundee Industrial Exhibition in 1888 and the Home Industries Exhibition in 1891. Prior to his early death in 1906, he worked from a studio at 12 Ward Road, and before that at two different studios on Nethergate. The year after he died, his widow held a large sale of all his remaining works, which included plaster busts of the Duke of Argyll and the late John Bright MP, various decorative panels and other ornamental works.[43]

135. Above: George MacDougald, carved figure decorating Five Kings House, London *(author's photograph)*.

136. Below: Margaret Suttie, *Stewart Carmichael*, plaster bust, 1895 *(Dundee Art Society)*.

137. Top right: James Fenton, *View of Dundee from Balgay Hill*, engraving from a painting by D A Andrews, 1836 *(Libraries, Leisure & Culture Dundee, licensor www.scran.ac.uk)*.

George Macdougald was described in the *Celtic Annual* as "possibly the most talented sculptor connected with Dundee."[44] The son of a notable city analyst, he began exhibiting with the GAA in 1902. Within a few years he was in London and in 1910 had three works shown at the Royal Academy, including a bust of chemist Sir James Dewar (now in the National Portrait Gallery). A member of the Royal Society of British Sculptors, he undertook various public commissions in London, including a striking pair of carved stone figures adorning the entrance to Thames House (now Five Kings House, figure 135). His work for Dundee included a bust of surgeon David M Greig, donated to the permanent collection; and bronze busts of Andrew Carnegie and William Ogilvy Dalgleish, commissioned for the new library in Barrack Street. He died in 1945.

Two other sculptors stayed only briefly in Dundee. Margaret Suttie was both a painter and sculptor, and could more appropriately be termed one of the 'Glasgow Girls', for (as the *Celtic Annual* explained), "she was fellow student and friend of E A Walton, Alex. Roche, Arch. Kay, and others of that school, when the 'Glasgow Boys' were making their name."[45] She came to Dundee in 1893 and quickly became actively involved in the GAA, opening up her studio at 15 Castle Street for the use of members one night a week. She exhibited a bust of Alec Grieve at the 1895 Fine Art Exhibition, and also one of Stewart Carmichael at the GAA exhibition the same year (figure 136). Writing in the *Courier*, Marie Imandt described the latter as "an able piece of sculpture, powerful and bold in its modelling – for it only affects to be a rapid sketch – of quite remarkable fidelity; and whilst it is a true mental and physical portrait of the sitter, it reflects with integral truth the charac-teristic style of the sculptress, and it is, above all, fresh and original, refined and artistic."[46] It certainly became a prized possession of Carmichael's and featured in his 1947 *Self Portrait in the Artist's Studio*. After his death it was presented to Dundee Art Society and is now permanently displayed in Roseangle Gallery. No further sculptural work by Suttie is known in Dundee, and she had returned to Glasgow by 1897.[47]

Charles Adamson learned his trade as a sculptor in Ireland – according to the *Courier*, "At an age when youth commonly finds it difficult to support itself with cigarettes and collars, Mr Adamson was earning a man's wages, and chipping and chiselling away, dreaming the dreams of a sculptor."[48] Returning to his native Dundee, he joined the GAA in 1901 and

138. Arthur Lee, *Dundee Docks*, oil on board *(Dundee City Council: Dundee's Art Galleries & Museums)*.

over the next four years produced several sculptures including busts of Sir John Leng MP, the Very Rev Canon Holder, painter W B Lamond (now in the city's collection) another of Stewart Carmichael (whose studio in Nethergate was next door to his) and one of his father, musician Alexander Adamson. The *Evening Telegraph* described him as a "youthful enthusiast. No dreamer he. Intensely sensitive to all the subtle Appeals of Idealism, he is still splendidly wide awake to the practical."[49] In 1905 (or shortly thereafter) Adamson emigrated to Canada, where among other important commissions he worked on a war memorial in Toronto and the House of Commons Memorial Chamber in Ottawa.

If portraits were the principal source of commissions for Dundee's artists, landscape paintings were the most likely to appeal to collectors. But as an industrial city with a skyline dominated by smoke-belching chimneys, Dundee was not an obvious source of subject matter for artists in the late 19th century. Opinions certainly differed on its aesthetic merits. The nickname given to Jacobite hero James Graham of Claverhouse – 'Bonnie Dundee' – was often applied to the town itself. Writing in 1891 to outline some suggestions for local garden designs, Patrick Geddes claimed: "I am not a native of Dundee... but I am constrained on all occasions to uphold its title to 'Bonnie'."[50] Two years later, however, the artist W G Burn-Murdoch described Dundee as "a very ugly blot on the beautiful face of Nature".[51] In 1899 the *Piper o' Dundee* noted that the "clouds of heavy soot-laden smoke [which] continually belch from our hundreds of tall mill and factory chimneys hang like a funeral pall over the city."[52]

Writing in *The City Echo* in 1907, Joseph Lee satirised Dundee's claims to be an art centre in a mock interview with "Madder Brown, the celebrated local artist" that reveals much about how the city was perceived aesthetically:

" 'Then, Mr Brown, you consider Dundee a sufficiently picturesque place for an art centre?'

'Most assuredly I do. No city more so. See Naples and die; see Dundee and live. One has its Vesuvius, the other its Law. Both are volcanic, though the Law is undoubtedly safer. Venice *had* its Campanile; Dundee still has its Cox's stalk [sic]. The city has streets and lanes as dirty and narrow surely as anything to be found on the Continent. Some authorities hold that Blinshall Street [then densely populated with mills] shares with Princes Street, Edinburgh, the honour of being one of the finest thoroughfares in Europe. By moonlight the mill stalks look not unlike an array of Cleopatra's Needles.' –

'And by daylight they resemble a lot of huge penny smoking cheroots,' ventured our representative, who is devoid of artistic imagination."[53]

John Duncan, on the other hand, revelled in the romance of Dundee's docks, which linked the city to exotic places around the world. Speaking in 1911 he recalled the times he spent there in his youth:

139. C S Lawson, *Foundry Lane*, pencil on paper, c.1880s *(Libraries, Leisure & Culture Dundee)*.

140. David Small, *Old Custom House*, watercolour on paper, c.1880s *(University of Dundee Museum Services)*.

"Strange ships from many strange places; huge swollen Dutch hulls that looked too lazy for anything but a canal, and lean sea-going ships; and full of foreign folk; swarthy creatures like pirates from the Spanish Main; Chinamen and Hindoos, and an occasional Lapp; lanky, blue-eyed Scandinavians talking together an unintelligible tongue. And the queer rigging, and the carving, the figureheads, and windows in the stern, the gilding, and the paint, and the whitewash, and the tar; and the moving water that caught all this picturesqueness, and shook it into twisting Chinese dragons of liquid dancing fire. What a wonder it all was, what a delightful place for a Sunday afternoon."[54]

One thing that everyone could agree on was Dundee's spectacular setting on the Tay, and it was on this that most early depictions of the town focused. Following the tradition of earlier artists such as John Slezer, many of Scotland's best-known landscape artists of the 19th century visited Dundee and chose to paint it from a distance, emphasising the river and hills beyond. Notable examples include E T Crawford's *Dundee from the East* (c.1820), Alexander Nasmyth's *Dundee from Princes Street* (c.1823-4), John Cairns' *Dundee – On the River Tay* (1861) and David Farquharson's *Dundee from Harecraigs* (1879), all now in the city's collection. As the town became increasingly industrialised, the distance from which it was painted tended to increase, as the *City Echo* recognised in judging its aesthetic qualities from the other side of the Tay: "Dundee, shrouded in the mystery of its own smoke, lies across

the river, its harshnesses and incongruities subdued into soft impressionistic tones. A place paintable at such enchantment lending distance".[55]

As Dundee became known as a centre for art collecting, visiting artists recognised that there would be a ready market for such views – particularly among those who made their home in neighbouring Broughty Ferry. Hence J C Bell bought Sam Bough's *Broughty Castle in Olden Times*, G B Simpson acquired *Broughty Ferry Castle* by John Cairns and W O Dalgleish owned *Broughty Ferry* by Arthur Perigal.

Local artists also realised the commercial potential of such scenes. As with portraitists, Dundee had boasted only a small number of topographical painters in the first half of the 19th century. David Angelo Andrews was the one whose surviving landscapes are most like those of Nasmyth and Crawford – the best-known being two distant views of the town (from Balgay Hill and from the river), both of which were reproduced as engravings in 1836 and sold widely (figure 137).[56] By contrast, George McGillivray's views were more documentary in intent, as well as more naively painted. They included records of notable events such as *The Opening of the Dundee and Arbroath Railway* (1838, now in the city's collection) and *Burning of the Town's Churches* (1841).

As the market for engravings increased, many artists came to specialise in this form of topographical scene. Gershom Gourlay Cumming was one of the most successful of the mid-19th century, running an extensive engraving and publishing business in Reform Street from the 1830s. His most celebrated achievement was the book *Forfarshire Illustrated: Being Views of Gentlemen's Seats, Antiquities, and Scenes in Forfarshire, with Descriptive and Historical Notices* (1843), which he illustrated and published. In later years he turned his attention to oil and watercolour painting, exhibiting at the Fine Art Exhibitions. When in 1898 he died at his home in Broughty Ferry aged 88, he was described as one of the oldest residents of the burgh.[57]

Frustratingly little is known of Arthur Lee, an accomplished painter who specialised in views of Dundee from the river, often focusing on sailing ships in the foreground, sometimes bathed in evening sunlight (see figure 138). Several fine examples are held in the city's collection, all undated, but the fifteen paintings by him included in the Old Dundee exhibition span dates from 1832 to 1866, and he is listed as a painter in the Dundee Directories from 1845 to 1876. It seems probable that Lee's concentration on ships and harbour scenes was not merely for aesthetic reasons – before the mills became Dundee's predominant industry, shipbuilding and seagoing trade were the main sources of wealth, and the titles of some of Lee's paintings (such as *Launch from Brown & Simpson's Yard* or *Earl Gray Dock, with Ship 'Jamesetjee Family,' built by Messrs Stephen*) clearly indicate where his commissions were coming from. This sometimes got him into difficulty – in 1868 he went to court to pursue a debt of £2 for the value of a painting of the Arbroath schooner *Favourite*, which he claimed was owed by its master David Findlay. The latter claimed never to have asked for the painting and in the absence of witnesses the case was thrown out of court, causing much amusement to everyone present except the unfortunate artist.[58]

141. William Gibb, *Fish Street Looking East*, lithograph based on a drawing by David Small, c.1890s, published in A C Lamb's *Dundee: Its Quaint and Historic Buildings (private collection)*.

Lee earned some more unusual commissions during his career. In 1863 he created two painted flags for the shore porters to carry during the opening of Baxter Park, depicting the harbour and dock with various insignia including the Dundee coat of arms and the figure of Neptune.[59] In 1876 the Dundee Public Baths unveiled a new Turkish Bath with murals painted by Lee depicting Neptune again, Venus, Minerva, Diana and Leda. The *Courier* praised Lee's work as "being specially fine and worthy of commendation."[60]

As well as maritime and bathing scenes, Lee had a more unusual interest in making copies of old painted signboards that he spotted around Dundee – eighteen of these were lent by him to the Old Dundee exhibition, including *The Plough Tavern, St Clement's Lane* (1836), *Thomas Fenton, Taxidermist, Nethergate* (1839) and *Arthur Lee, Ship Tavern, East Shore* (1829), presumably referring to a relation of his.

Many of the topographical views produced by Lee, Cumming, Andrews and McGillivray (as well as others of the period whose work there has not been space to mention, such as James Paterson of Broughty Ferry) ended up in the collection of A C Lamb, the main organiser of the Old Dundee exhibition, described in chapter one. Lamb's lasting achievement was his weighty tome, *Dundee: Its Quaint and Historic Buildings*, published in 1895 after many years of preparation and research. In 1881 Lamb had begun looking for suitable images for a book that he initially conceived of as comprising "a series of pictures of the older buildings in Dundee, especially of those that had been removed."[61] From the start, the work was led by its illustrations, and Lamb found it "a very difficult task"

to obtain suitable pictures. The 1871 Improvement Act gave a group of trustees the power to make radical alterations to the physical character of Dundee, from the High Street down to the harbour. By the time Lamb came up with the idea for his book, large parts of the medieval maritime quarter had already been destroyed to make way for wider Victorian streets and buildings. "I saw that someone must take up the subject and prosecute it with spirit," claimed Lamb, "if anything was to be done at all to preserve the appearance of old Dundee."[62]

Lamb used three principal artists to create the illustrations for his book. The first and most prolific of these was Charles S Lawson. Born in Forfar in c.1838, Lawson came to Dundee as a boy and was initially apprenticed to a draper before turning to printing, setting up business in Murraygate with his brother.[63] Among their many publications were *A Guide-Book to Dundee (Ancient and Modern)* (1870) and *Lawson's Illustrated Dundee Almanac* (1874), both of which were illustrated with engravings of traditional Dundee views. For the most part these pictures are naïve and often bizarrely out of perspective, but Lamb would have been drawn to a series of far more realistic depictions of Dundee closes that also appear in the Lawson Brothers' guide, which are unlike any views of the town that had hitherto been produced.

It seems likely that, on the strength of such documentary-like observational drawing, Lamb commissioned Lawson to start recording the buildings that were to be affected by the improvement scheme. This proved to be a race against time in more ways than one – not only had many of the buildings already been emptied ready for demolition, but Lawson himself was under considerable strain – his business had collapsed and he was suffering from failing health, physically and mentally. He died as an inmate of the Royal Dundee Lunatic Asylum in 1884, but had still managed to create many hundreds of drawings of both exteriors and interiors, ranging from rough sketches to finished artworks (figure 139). Charles McKean claimed that the "collection of drawings far outreaches any other visual record of any other Scottish town or city".[64] Yet the drawings remained largely unknown thereafter, and Lamb did not include any of them in the Old Dundee exhibition. It seems he viewed Lawson's work purely as reference material for other (better) artists to draw upon.

David Small picked up the baton dropped by Lawson. Born in Kinross in 1845, Small began his working life as cashier to a firm in Glasgow, but soon decided that his career lay with art.[65] An early member of the Glasgow Art Club (alongside such luminaries as George Henry and John Lavery), Small worked as a commercial illustrator but also painted topographical watercolours. Lamb may have seen his work in the Dundee Fine Art Exhibitions (where he exhibited from 1877) or may have been introduced to him by Small's brother-in-law, fellow Dundee antiquarian A H Millar. Small and Millar worked together on the popular books *Quaint Bits of Old Glasgow* (1887) and *By-Gone Glasgow* (1896).[66] Lamb subsequently commissioned Small to work up Lawson's sketches into more professional drawings and to continue his efforts to record the rapidly disappearing historic buildings of Dundee (figure 140). In 1890 Small moved to Dundee permanently to replace Martin Anderson (see chapter five) as chief illustrator for the *Dundee Advertiser*, a position he would hold for over 30 years.

142. Richard D Winter, *St Mary's Tower and Old Cross*, etching on paper, 1891 *(private collection)*.

143. Duncan Cameron, *Harvest Time*, oil on canvas, c.1880s *(Lyon & Turnbull)*.

He joined the GAA and regularly exhibited his watercolour views of Dundee and the East Neuk of Fife, many of which were also turned into postcards. Sadly Small suffered from blindness in his later years and died aged 82 in 1927. Lamb certainly promoted his work far more than Lawson's, including over 40 drawings and watercolours by him in Old Dundee.

Lamb decided to use a high-quality lithographic process for his book. Asked why he did not go for photographic illustrations, he replied: "people are growing tired of these mechanical processes. They want pictures that will have some tokens of human art about them, not mere facsimiles reproduced chemically... [You] could not have had the artistic touch in a photogravure which is evident in these pictures."[67] The final artist working on the book, therefore (and the one who got most of the credit), was professional lithographer William Gibb, who had produced the plates for James Drummond's book *Old Edinburgh* (1879).[68] It was Gibb who turned Lawson and Small's drawings (as well as images from various other sources) into finished lithographs (figure 141). Lamb described the process:

> "The drawings were made by Mr William Gibb upon the stone, so that the plates are really direct from the artist's hands. The objection I have always had to the usual lithograph is that it is thin in appearance unless there are several colours introduced that necessitate numerous printings. But as my pictures were only to be in black and white, I had to make the repeated printings in tones of grey, and by this method I got the requisite depth in the shadows such as is usually found in fine etchings. Some of the plates had as many as twelve printings, and yet they seem to be only in two colours...

144. A S Edward, *Fishing Boats at the Mouth of the Tay*, oil on canvas, 1879 *(Dundee City Council: Dundee's Art Galleries & Museums)*.

Mr William Gibb, the artist, saw every plate when it was in progress, and examined the proofs after every printing, so that it may be said that the pictures were produced by him just as a water-colour drawing would be by a painter in water-colour… Several artists who have seen the pictures have been astonished to find that lithography was capable of producing plates so artistically fine as those in the Dundee book."[69]

When the book finally appeared in print in 1895, it was met with rave reviews, not least for the quality of its illustrations. "It is evident that masterly and loving care has been lavished on the production of the plates," claimed the *Evening Telegraph*.[70] The *Advertiser* hailed it as "a signal triumph for the British art of book illustration."[71] The *Glasgow Herald* noted that the images, "both in point of artistic merit and of delicacy of finish, [are] as beautiful and as perfect as anything we have ever seen."[72] Comparing the book to James Drummond's the *Scotsman* admitted that "Dundee has come abreast, and even gone ahead, of the Scottish capital."[73]

The publication of Lamb's book, and the success of the Old Dundee exhibition which preceded it, encouraged many local artists to try their hand at topographical views of their native city, including those who had already left it. One of those already making a name for himself in this field was Richard D

Winter. Born in Dundee in 1862, Winter was apprenticed to the engravers Douglas & Smith from an early age, while taking evening classes at Dundee School of Art.[74] In 1885 he married John Duncan's sister Marjorie, and it was apparently Duncan who encouraged him to take up etching as an art. He joined the Dundee Art Club and began showing work there and at the Fine Art Exhibitions. By 1888 he was already getting work from London publishers and seems to have been based there for much of the same time as Duncan. In 1889 Robert F Mackay (who also released Duncan's work) published his etching of Mains Castle, and its success may have led to him being chosen to etch C G L Phillips' popular painting *Dundee from Balgay*, published in February 1891. That July Winter held a joint exhibition with John Duncan (whose studio in Sea Wynd he was now sharing) where he showed off a new folio of etchings he had created under the title *Old Dundee* (figure 142). The *Advertiser* praised "the happy union of technical skill with refined sentiment" and also described two "vigorous and brilliant" etchings he had done based on Constable paintings.[75] In October that year Mackay published Winter's etching of Reekie Linn, and in December he was the main featured artist in an exhibition of etchings held by framer Grindlay Liddle. After all this success he returned to London, where he eventually opened an engraving business with his son. Although he continued to exhibit with the GAA, he remained in England, based in Essex then Hertfordshire, where he died in 1947. Several of his fine etchings of Dundee are currently on permanent display on the walls of the Local History Centre at Dundee Central Library.

145.Allan Ramsay, *The Wild Music of the Glen*, oil on canvas, 1898-9
(courtesy of the University of St Andrews).

146. John S Fraser, *Arbroath Fishing Cobble 43AH off the Coast*, watercolour on paper, 1891
(private collection).

147. E S Hodgson, *Christ's Hospital from the Treasurer's Gardens*, oil on canvas, c.1900 *(by kind permission of Christ's Hospital Foundation)*.

Following in Winter's footsteps as a popular recorder of local scenes was Tom Ross, one of the most versatile of Dundee artists. Born in 1878, Ross's principal career as a press artist will be described in chapter five. He seems to have been something of a perpetual student – he enrolled in the art school at Dundee Technical Institute, winning the Prize for Painting in 1898. 25 years later he was still studying there, and still winning prizes![76] "There his perfectionism in the posing of the model could be a trial to the instructor in charge, whose function he sometimes usurped," a friend of his later recalled. "His usurpations also included making forceful amendments to the work of his fellow students, not always appreciated."[77]

Ross was a regular exhibitor with the GAA and occasionally had work shown at the RSA. He was also a frequent visitor to the Continent and was once featured in French art magazine *La Revue Moderne* (1924). Such international connections were a surprise to his friends in Birkhill, where he lived with his sister for most of his life in a house called 'Bide-a-Wee', being better known as the editor of a popular local newsletter, *Birkie Blethers*. He was recalled later in his life as

> "a somewhat homespun character… he always wore a black rough woollen overcoat. His trousers were on the short side revealing tackety boots and he wore a cloth cap. He wore steel-rimmed spectacles. He had a guid Scots tongue pronouncing his words in a forthright manner. His sentences were impeccably constructed giving his speech something of grandeur."[78]

Ross had some success as a portraitist in paint, print and pastel, but was better known for creating both lithographs and etchings of picturesque parts of Dundee, particularly a series showing the area around the old Town House that was purchased by the Free Library committee for the permanent collection in 1921. Ross was not the only artist documenting this part of town during the 1910s – David Foggie and C G L Phillips were among several making prints to sell of the Town House, Strathmartine's Lodging and the Vault.

The timing of these was deliberate – in 1914 James Caird offered £100,000 to build a new city hall, giving weight to earlier proposals for the demolition of the Town House (built to a design by William Adam in 1732) and its neighbours. The Dundee Art Society was one of several bodies who objected to the plans. Forty years earlier, it seemed that only Lamb lamented the destruction caused by the 1871 Improvement Act – now the Town Council were planning a whole new series of city improvements and Dundee's artists were keen to draw the public's attention to the aesthetic qualities of what was under threat. This fact was not lost on the *Courier*'s art critic in reviewing the 1911 Dundee Art Society exhibition:

> "the plea for the picturesque put forward at the Art Society's meetings when Lord Provost Urquhart's town improvement scheme was mooted naturally makes one look about to see what beauty lurks in those portions of our city which are threatened… Who, for instance, would have imagined that such dignity and power resided in the view of 'Dundee from the Stannergate' as Mr J Calder Smith has found there, or that the smoke of the torpedo boats could make our familiar 'Dock Street' so striking as it appears in Mr J Milne Purvis' brilliant picture? The 'Old Steeple,' (uncrowned) never looked finer than it does in Mr John D Revel's splendid etching, and Mr John Maclauchlan Milne has built up in his 'Dundee Harbour' a singularly pleasing composition, while in his 'Wet Night' he has grasped the possibilities of the Greenmarket."[79]

While these artists and others continued to explore the artistic possibilities of the city itself, the surrounding countryside proved a far greater attraction to many Dundee artists, and their clientele. Reporting on the GAA exhibition in 1896, the *Piper o' Dundee* noted: "The mountain and coast scenery of some of these capable artists will be refreshing at a time when city-dwellers are beginning to weary for a whiff of ozone."[80]

John Duncan recalled some of the many places that he and his fellow artists visited in the late 19th century:

> "We young landscape painters found many happy hunting grounds: the Den o' Mains; the Emmock Wood; the Denhead o' Gray. West Ferry had a row of fisher houses then, and great boats beached. Then there was Scotscraig, and Tayport, and Tents Muir – enchanted land: And Earls Ha' was a ruin, its garden roses smothered in wild garlic; and wild roses grew at Ninewells, and rasps and brambles; and the Den of Fowlis was full of primroses in their due season."[81]

An important inspiration to the landscape painters of John Duncan's generation was the considerable success of Duncan Cameron. Born in Perthshire in 1837, Cameron became one of the first intake of students at Dundee School of Art before going on to further study in London and Edinburgh. Although based in the latter for the rest of his career, the local press were always quick to label him "a Dundee artist", the *Courier* for example proclaiming that Cameron "has reflected credit on our city by achieving a prominent position and an unblemished reputation in the wider art world of the Metropolis... For some considerable time he has been recognised as one of the ablest of the great Scotch school of landscapists, specially distinguished among that brilliant band by his beauty of colour and his ability to infuse his own characteristic spirit into a picture".[82]

Cameron's particular speciality was haystacks depicted in an autumn light – a fine example can be seen in figure 143. Referring to a similar work, the *Courier*'s art critic waxed lyrical: "the artist has caught the very spirit of autumnal nature, conveying to the spectator by lovely harmonious tints a profound feeling that it is harvest time indeed; that the year's work is done; and that we have come to dwell in that land where it is always afternoon."[83]

Cameron kept his ties with Dundee, exhibiting in the Fine Art Exhibitions, lending works to the city's permanent gallery and in 1895 holding a major one-man show (billed as one of the first such exhibitions in Dundee) in the Imperial Auction Rooms, Murraygate, comprising 84 paintings. He died in Edinburgh in 1916.

There were many other successful landscape painters who spent only part of their careers in Dundee, and it is worth briefly describing a few of the most notable here. Alfred S Edward was born in Dundee in 1852, the son of an architect. He studied at Dundee School of Art then in Edinburgh and London, where

148. William Barclay, *The Mouth of the Tay, Moonrise*, oil on canvas, 1875 *(Dundee City Council: Dundee's Art Galleries & Museums)*.

149. James G H Spindler, *A Forest Pond*, watercolour on paper, 1906 *(private collection)*.

150. Jane E Spindler, *Springtime*, oil on canvas, 1880s *(Dundee City Council: Dundee's Art Galleries & Museums)*.

he settled in the late 1870s. He returned to Dundee regularly, painting around the Tay and the Angus and Fife coastline (figure 144), and exhibiting at the Fine Art Exhibitions and with the Dundee Art Club and GAA. He was elected an RBA (Member of the Royal Society of British Artists) in 1894 and in 1912 gifted his painting *Dordrecht* (1906) to the permanent collection. He died in 1915.

Allan Ramsay (no relation to the 18th-century painter) was born in Forfar in 1852 and came to Dundee as a chemist's apprentice, but was unable, in his words, to "keep his hands frae the brushes".[84] As noted in chapter three, he was taken on as an apprentice by interior decorator Alexander Drummond, while studying at the Dundee School of Art. He was an early committee member of the Dundee Art Club, exhibiting with them and at the Fine Art Exhibitions. Although he undertook occasional portrait commissions his reputation was based on dramatic oil paintings of the Angus landscape, particularly Edzell, where he moved in 1887. When asked by a friend why he didn't vary his subject matter, he replied "Enough for me on the banks of the Esk". According to his effusive obituary in the *Arbroath Guide*, "there could be no satiety in the invariably beautiful and subtly varied moods in which he portrays the sweeps and bends or lucid pools of the rough brown river he loved so well."[85] He continued to exhibit his work in Dundee until his death in 1912.

Born in 1856, John S Fraser initially decided to follow a seafaring life. He made several sea voyages as a youth before settling down to work for the shipbuilders Gourlay Brothers with the aim of becoming a marine engineer. This necessitated taking evening classes at Dundee School of Art which made him realise that art was his true vocation, and he earned his Art Master's certificate in 1880. According to the *Dundee Advertiser*, his "experience on board ship had led him to study unconsciously the splendid effects of colour which are to be seen in their fullness at sea, and thus he [became] one of the foremost of Scottish marine painters in water-colours."[86] The *Celtic Annual* claimed that "the first note of the modern spirit in Art in Dundee was struck when John S Fraser gave us his free and ably handled water colours... [f]resh and sparkling in colour".[87]

After finishing his studies, Fraser took up a studio in Edinburgh and quickly gained a strong reputation for his watercolours, exhibiting at the RSA and RA. He returned to Dundee regularly, painting Angus and Fife coastal scenes and exhibiting at the Fine Art Exhibitions and the Art Club. A serious heart condition unfortunately curtailed his activities and he took a house on the coast near Carnoustie, where he died in 1893 aged just 38.[88]

Edward S Hodgson was born in Arbroath in 1866. Like Fraser, he came to Dundee intending to follow a life at sea but a leg injury scuppered this and he turned instead to art, studying at the School of Art before becoming a teacher in various private schools.[89] During his time in Dundee he exhibited with the Art Club and GAA, having first won critical attention with a selection of paintings shown at Thomas Murray's gallery in 1888.[90] In 1891 he produced his first important etchings – a set of six under the title *Round the Old Steeple* which included views of the Royal Exchange, the Custom House and the Hilltown and was accompanied by a descriptive letterpress by C C Maxwell

and John Maclauchlan.[91] Further Dundee scenes followed including *Mains Castle* (1892) and *The Mars Training Ship* (1893). Hodgson was evidently influenced by Whistler in taking a minimalist approach to his etchings – the *Courier* praised his 1892 print *The Ebbing Tide* as "the best that Mr Hodgson has yet produced, and shows that he has learned the lesson – so difficult for young etchers to understand – that there is as much art in keeping details out of a picture as in putting them in."[92]

In 1893 Hodgson had his greatest success with a large-scale etching, *Dundee from the River*, published by Grindlay Liddle, a copy of which was "accepted and specially acknowledged" by Queen Victoria. The *Piper o' Dundee* described it as Hodgson's "*chef d'oeuvre*. The picture is masterly in scheme, wrought at with artistic deftness, and throughout displays keen observation and truthful transcription."[93]

In 1895 Hodgson left Dundee for England and settled in Bushey, where he studied under the celebrated Hubert von Herkomer. As well as continuing to draw and paint landscape scenes, he became a popular book and magazine illustrator, known particularly for naval and aeronautical scenes. He died in 1937.

All of these artists chose to move away from Dundee to further their careers, and those painters that did stay usually earned most of their income from teaching or commercial work. The first landscape painter to make a living in Dundee solely from his art was William Barclay. How successfully he achieved this is unclear – T S Robertson claimed two years before Barclay's death that "he has lived outside the atmosphere of art, and on that account has barely made a living" but it is known that he sold pictures in London for as much as 50 guineas.[94]

Barclay was born in the Nethergate in 1831 and began his career as a merchant, initially apprenticed to Lipman & Co before starting his own business in the Cowgate. Speaking fluent German as well as French and Italian, he could have achieved success in international trade, but art was a greater attraction to him, and he studied in Edinburgh before heading to London then the Netherlands, where he evidently fell in love with the distinctive style of Dutch landscape painting. Robertson claimed that Barclay was so impatient to move on to landscapes that he never learned to draw the human figure, and certainly the scenes he depicted were largely depopulated. He was also said to have been fairly anti-social and distrustful of other people. "He seemed to be always suspicious that some one was to take advantage of him", Robertson noted, and he does not appear to have joined either the Art Club or GAA.[95] He was, however, friends with some notable painters outwith Dundee, including James Cassie who introduced him to watercolour painting. He also knew many of the Scott Lauder school of Scottish painters, and through them acquired a considerable knowledge of art that many local patrons drew upon in building their collections.

The critics were often unkind about Barclay's work. In 1871, the *Courier* reviewed his contributions to the RSA exhibition by saying: "Mr Barclay seems to have been labouring

151. James Douglas, *Dundee (from the harbour)*, watercolour on paper, 1888 *(University of Dundee Museum Services)*.

152. James Douglas, *Sheep in an Orchard*, watercolour on paper, 1891 *(private collection)*.

It was perhaps experiences like this that led Barclay to paint increasingly from memory in his studio rather than on location. The *Advertiser* concluded that his "merits as a painter rested on the refinement of his style, his sense of fine, true colour, and his extreme delicacy. His range was not a very wide one, but no vulgar, loud or garish picture ever left his easel."[100] One of his finest works, *Mouth of the Tay, Moonrise* was hung on the line at the Royal Academy in 1875, and was purchased for a private collection (figure 148). When it came up for sale again, a group of Dundee men clubbed together in 1903 to secure it for the city's permanent collection. The Free Library committee welcomed it as "local in the sense that it depicts a scene not far from our civic gates, where Tay's crystal waters merge with the grey German Ocean, but possessing in full measure those rare qualities which make art universal".[101] Barclay died in 1906, and was described by the Dundee Art Society's obituary as "an excellent judge of pictures, a good linguist, and an intellectual and scholarly man."[102] According to the *Advertiser*, "his finite mind was ever in absolute communion with the infinite loveliness of nature."[103]

Many Dundee painters followed in Barclay's footsteps and established strong reputations (albeit usually of more local reach) as landscape painters. One of the first was James G H Spindler, born in Edinburgh in 1843. He came from a talented family – his father was a respected German-born musician, his brother John also followed that profession and his younger sister Jane would also become a successful painter. By the age of eighteen James was already calling himself a professional artist, and he began to exhibit work at the RSA two years later.[104] Most of his income probably came from teaching – he established himself in partnership with Robert Cowie as "teachers of drawing and painting" in Reform Street,[105] but soon began teaching solo and continued to do so in both Dundee and St Andrews for many years – at the time of his death the *Courier* referred to "the many hundred pupils who have passed through Mr Spindler's hands".[106] He and Jane (thirteen years his junior) soon became regular exhibitors at the Fine Art Exhibitions, then at the Dundee Art Club. In the late 1880s Jane left Dundee to establish a studio in Blairgowrie, and although James painted there often, he remained based in Dundee. One of the founding members of the GAA, he became its second President and one of its most copious exhibitors. He also gave a number of lectures to the society and other bodies over the years, including "Art Culture in Ancient and Modern Times" (1884), "What is an Impressionist Picture?" (1896), "The Value of Pigments in Art" (1907) and "Humour in Art and Art Work" (1910).

Although he painted locally (and in Spain, Switzerland and the Netherlands), James's greatest passion was for Highland scenery, particularly around Loch Tummel, and in his early years he was influenced by the Pre-Raphaelites. His work was always of a high quality, but critics rarely troubled to give it more than brief attention. In 1894, however, he held a solo exhibition at McEwan's Art Saloon in Nethergate which won praise from the *Evening Telegraph*: "The freshness and

painfully upon one idea. This may indicate patience and perseverance, but those qualities, either combined or separate, are not necessarily productive of high art."[96] Fourteen years later, they attacked his painting *Sea and Sky* by describing it as "a unique example of a 'patent reversible' picture. Surely the artist could have introduced some features that would have taken away the blankness of the picture without detracting from the general effect."[97] "The public as a rule did not appreciate his efforts," Robertson claimed, but he obviously considered him significant – in his series of newspaper articles on famous Scottish painters, Barclay was the only Dundee artist included.[98] His anecdotes help to bring life to this otherwise reclusive artist, such as this one about a sketching expedition that Barclay took with James Cassie:

> "[They] were on one occasion painting on the Forth, near Crail, within sight and hearing of each other[.] Barclay occasionally left his picture to see how he [Cassie] was getting on, and to rest and smoke with him for a little. During one of these visits children were seen lifting sand from the beach and throwing it about near the distant picture. Barclay got up and ran off like a shot, while Cassie bawled for all his might to the children to run for their lives, and they did so. When Barclay reached the place, he found not only his picture, but all the moist colours in his box covered in sand. Cassie was of opinion that had he caught a child it would certainly have been thrown into the sea."[99]

153. Frank Laing, *Les Invalides*, etching on paper, c.1898
(private collection).

elasticity of spring, the rich autumnal colours of autumn, the light and shade of moonlight and the greyness of gloaming are all beautifully reproduced."[107] The following year the *Piper o' Dundee* referred to him as "one of Dundee's rising stars" when his painting of Ben Vrackie was shown in a good position at the Royal Academy.[108] This success prompted the *Courier* to send Marie Imandt to interview him in his studio, where "he talked with enthusiasm of the German artists".

> "Whilst listening attentively and appreciative-
> ly to the din of the war of the rival 'schools'
> [of art]… Mr Spindler has not become a
> blind partisan of any of these – old or new.
> He has ever studied in the oldest but what
> is the perennially newest of all schools, that
> of Nature herself. She alone he calls mistress
> and strives to reproduce her changing but
> always beautiful moods, not with the dull
> slavishness of a mere copyist, but with the
> loving intelligence which trained skill, keen
> perception, and striking individuality combine
> to produce".[109]

That same year Jane had her first major exhibition – over a hundred pieces were shown at the Dundee Auction Rooms in Ward Road to be sold at auction. The *Piper o' Dundee* claimed this as "the first time in the history of Dundee art that a lady artist has exhibited a collection of pictures entirely her own".[110] While Imandt had found in James's work an "eye for splendour of colour", surviving examples show Jane to be much more of a colourist – *Springtime*, for example (figure 150,

painted sometime in the 1880s and in the city's permanent collection by 1889) has a vivid brightness comparable to the work of James Guthrie and the Glasgow Boys. It also has an impressionistic painting technique which James's work rarely showed, despite the enthusiasm with which he lectured on the subject in 1896:

> "Men were first natural, but had always had
> a tendency to become conventional, and
> impressionism was simply a going back to
> truth, and time and again great artists had
> made efforts to shake off these unrealities and
> show the loving soul of the world glowing
> through its outward obscuring material
> aspect." [111]

James seems to have become fascinated by attempting to capture this glow on canvas, and in visiting his studio, Marie Imandt had noticed numerous pictures "which are unfinished for want of sunshine."[112] Nevertheless, James's work continued to find favour both nationally and internationally – in 1899 it was claimed that "he has had the unique distinction among Scottish artists of having his pictures accepted three seasons consecutively by the Paris [Salon] hangers."[113] That year he held a large exhibition of work to be sold at auction at the Central Fine Art Gallery, Overgate, and had a painting of St Andrews presented to the permanent collection.[114] The *Piper o' Dundee* claimed: "None of our local artists more deserve such encouragement and recognition".[115] He died in 1917 and a memorial exhibition of over 50 paintings was held soon after. Jane had held another Dundee exhibition in 1900 at Scott's Stationery Warehouse on Perth Road, but after her brother's death she largely confined her activities to Blairgowrie and Edinburgh. She died in 1939.

While the Spindlers' success was principally local, that of watercolour artist James Douglas was truly international. According to the *Celtic Annual*, he "carried the Art of water colour to a very high level."[116] Born in Dundee in 1858, by the age of thirteen he had left school to earn money as a messenger boy before becoming a solicitor's clerk. He already held artistic ambitions which fortunately were encouraged by his employer, and at the age of sixteen he exhibited his first painting at the Albert Institute, where apparently it was "sold on the opening day."[117] In 1877 he left Dundee to follow a legal career but after the successful sale of one of his paintings, "he suddenly threw law to the winds and plunged into the career of a water-colour professional artist." Stewart Carmichael recalled: "With characteristic pluck he rented the studio just vacated by Sir Noel Paton, one of the largest in the capital, and at once took his place in the art life of Edinburgh."[118] In 1881 he showed at the RSA for the first time, and around this time painted in the Borders with future Academicians Tom Scott and J Campbell Noble.

Visiting Paris for a holiday, he ended up staying a year to study at the Académie Julian.[119] According to Carmichael, "Douglas presented his admission drawing in water colours instead of the usual life study in chalk, a very unusual proceeding, as that medium was then looked upon in France as one hardly befitting the attention of a serious artist."[120] By 1885 he was back in Edinburgh and making a name for himself. The *Piper o'*

Dundee featured him in 1888, noting that his "travels and hard work have so perfected his style as to place him in the front rank of the water colourists of Scotland."[121] They also complained that so little of his work was shown in Dundee. Douglas made up for this with his most ambitious painting, *Dundee from the Harbour*, which was unveiled at Robert Scott's gallery in 1888 (figure 151). Now in the University of Dundee's collections, the watercolour was greatly praised. The *Piper* wrote:

"The artist has chosen the sunset for his time, and in the lovely flood of light that falls over the scene the harsh lines of the town are lost, while all the more public buildings stand out in fine relief. Detail is not awanting, and Mr Douglas's exquisite drawing of the more prosaic objects of our harbour is not less admirable than his beautiful colouring of the sunset haze. The water of the harbour shining in the foreground seems to glow and move."[122]

Stewart Carmichael added: "The drawing is precise and spirited, the arrangement true and pictorial and the colour pure and cool, and very Scottish in quality."[123] Here was a view of the city to rival the paintings of D A Andrews, and like them the work was soon reproduced in print. "Not for forty years has such an important engraving of 'Bonnie Dundee' been produced", the *Piper* claimed.[124] In fact Robert Scott decided not to follow the traditional method of engraving but went all the way to Berlin to have the work reproduced in photogravure and sold as 100 artist's proofs. Both the original painting and the print were shown to great acclaim in the Fine Art Exhibition that opened the Victoria Galleries in 1889. The painting was then shown at the RSA where it was priced at £160, exceptionally high for a watercolour. It was bought by jute merchant David Dawson, whose daughter Anna was receiving tuition from Douglas. Although continuing to base himself in Edinburgh, by this time Douglas had acquired a second studio in Longforgan. He and Anna were married in 1890 and bought a caravan which they toured around the Carse of Gowrie. Stewart Carmichael recalled:

"That whole district was explored and studied, and the camp fixed in sunny orchards. There the artist, inspired by the free life of the camp, the joyousness of spring, and his happy family, painted his beautiful apple blossom pictures that are so characteristic – pictures that are distinguished by a delicacy of colour, a sensitiveness in drawing, and a deftness in handling".[125]

In 1891 the family caravan moved south to the Lake District. After a few years living in Keswick, they took the bold decision to relocate to Bavaria, where they settled in Rothenburg for two years. This gave Douglas important connections and during the following years his work was exhibited in Munich, Dresden, Leipzig and Vienna.

Douglas returned to Dundee in 1897 and exhibited several works at the GAA. The following year he opened a new Edinburgh studio but continued to paint around Angus and Perthshire. In 1900 he was off again, this time to London.

That year he showed work at the Paris International Exhibition and was also elected to the Royal Scottish Society for Painters in Watercolour (RSW). After three years living in London and Surrey he returned north and settled in Spring Cottage, Tayport. He had been commissioned by Martin Anderson to create postcards for the Cynicus Publishing Company (see chapter five), and over the next few years at least 40 of his paintings were printed as postcards. Jim Barnes has noted that by this time he was using a camera to record scenes that he would later translate into paintings for Anderson.[126]

By this time Anna Douglas had also achieved some success as an artist in her own right, specialising in portrait miniatures. In 1905 they became part of the Tayport Artists' Circle, an exhibiting body described in chapter eight. Reviewers were now hailing James as "one of the foremost water-colourists in Scotland", his work "glowing with colour and pulsating with light."[127]

Douglas contributed substantially to all the Circle's exhibitions, but particularly its final one in 1907, which featured 40 of his watercolours. The same year he held a large sale of paintings at the Dundee Auction Rooms. He seems to have been in urgent financial difficulties – around this time he was struck off the RSW's membership roll for not paying his subscription. The cause of these problems was probably his growing mental health problems – in 1908 he was admitted to Murthly Hospital, and later transferred to the asylum at Liff. According to Barnes, "His decline and end were to be protracted, sad and painful for himself, his wife and family."[128] In 1910 the Dundee Art Society's annual report gave Edinburgh as Douglas's address, but he was still at Liff, where he died the following year aged 53. Stewart Carmichael summed up his talent in an appreciation written for the *Advertiser*: "Few have had his unerring craftsmanship in the medium [of watercolour], his decisive yet playful and varied touch, his clean and sweet colour, and his unfailing perfect use of his material."[129]

Douglas's success in watercolour was paralleled by that of Frank Laing in etching, and his career also was cut short prematurely. Laing was born in 1862 in Ferry-Port-on-Craig (later renamed Tayport) and would go on to play a prominent part in the life of his local community, serving on the Town Council, leading a campaign to save the village common, chairing meetings of the Tayport Literary Society and serving as President of the Choral Union.[130] His working life had begun as an apprentice to the Town & Country Bank in Dundee, and was later posted to various branches in the north east of Scotland. It was during this period that he realised that art was his real interest and he spent all his spare time drawing.[131] The Dundee artist and architect Charles Ower introduced Laing to etching, and in 1888 he left the bank to study at the RSA Schools in Edinburgh and then in London. In 1892 he moved to Paris, where fellow Dundee artist William Yule was also based at the time. Laing's principal teacher there was Jean-Paul Laurens of the Académie Julian but his primary influence was Whistler.[132] On arriving in Paris, Laing had sent a portfolio of his etchings to Whistler via art dealers Goupil & Co in the hope, presumably, that the great artist would take him under his

wing.[133] It is not clear whether Whistler ever met with Laing, but his style of etching was certainly an inspiration, and it was thanks to "warm commendations from such high authorities as Sir Seymour Haden and Whistler" that Laing was elected an Associate of the Royal Society of Painter-Etchers.[134] His work was compared favourably to that of Haden in the French journal *L'Art*, which described him as "a very strong etcher" using the negative process devised by Haden, in which the plate was engraved in the acid bath.[135]

While spending much of his time in Paris, over the next few years Laing also visited Spain, Belgium and Italy. In 1893 he showed some of his Continental etchings at Robert Scott's gallery, earning a glowing review from the *Courier*: "The quality of the work is fresh and vigorous, wonderfully graphic effects being obtained by the merest touch of the needle."[136] By this time, Laing had become the first Dundee artist to join the new Society of Scottish Artists (SSA).[137] In December 1895 he was invited by the organisers of the Dundee Fine Art Exhibition to give a lecture on "Original Etching", illustrated using works by Rembrandt, Whistler and others lent by Orchar, T S Robertson and fellow collectors. Laing showed several works at the Fine Art Exhibition including his best-known watercolour painting, *The Yellow Girl* (1894, figure 273), which had been shown at the Paris Salon. The *Black Cat* magazine claimed, "I imagine a Parisian looking at this picture would say '*C'est du chic!*' [sic]".[138] After Laing's death it was purchased by James Martin White for donation to the permanent collection.

In 1896 Laing produced a set of etchings comprising six views of Dundee and Tayport contained in a leather portfolio. Thanks to the support of John Maclauchlan at the Albert Institute, a circular was issued to promote the works, claiming: "Dundee is often accused of not being sufficiently appreciative of local talent, and it will be readily admitted that when a native of the City does really display genuine ability ... it ought to be a duty, as it must be a pleasure, to support it."[139]

The full series was shown along with a set of twelve created in Paris and various others in an exhibition at Robert Scott's gallery in 1897 – the first time that a one-man show of etchings had been staged in the city. The *Evening Telegraph* praised the Parisian scenes above all: "Mr Laing has evidently worked here *con amore*, and his transcripts of views on the Seine and bits in and around Paris are delightfully rendered – clear, forceful and artistic."[140]

While his Dundee reputation was growing, Laing continued to spread his wings elsewhere. In 1898 he was awarded a solo show at the Bibliothèque Nationale in Paris; the library had already acquired a set of Laing's Parisian etchings for its print collection. In 1899 he held an exhibition of prints in Aberdeen and was featured in the French journal *Gazette des Beaux Arts*, whose editor Roger Marx praised his "innate feeling for the picturesque and [his] power of observation, highly sensitive to the variations of light and the surroundings".[141] Marx became a regular champion of Laing's work, later marvelling at his ability "to condense and capture the impression of the appearance and feeling of things on copper as if by magic and fast as lightning."[142]

In 1900 several of Laing's etchings of Edinburgh were published in the *Magazine of Art*, while at the Paris Exhibition he won a jury commendation.[143] The same year, he was featured in the Vienna art journal *Die Graphischen Künst*, which included an original etching by him of Spiershill in Tayport (figure 154).[144] In 1901 he showed a series of etchings at the Glasgow International Exhibition at Kelvingrove (Stewart Carmichael being the only other Dundee contributor to this prestigious event), while 60 of his etchings were shown in an exhibition at the Albert Roullier Galleries in Chicago.

For all this success, Laing was never fully appreciated in Dundee. Although most reviews of his work were positive, some were decidedly less so. "Of Frank Laing's 'Portrait arranged in Black and Canary,' the best that can be said is – nothing!" claimed the *Piper o' Dundee*, reviewing the GAA exhibition in 1901. "Mr Laing must cherish supreme contempt for his audience when he ventures to place such a picture before it".[145] As will be described in chapter eight, Laing had an often fractious relationship to his fellow artists in the GAA. David Foggie described him as "sometimes method without genius, sometimes genius without method".[146] His personality seems to have been childlike, and he loved playing with children and having them around him in his studio. A fellow artist described his workplace:

"The studio itself, bare-raftered and rough, was just his gigantic boy's pocket. It was littered with work of all kinds; copper plates and prints, brushes and colours on the floor, sketches on the chairs, canvas on canvas up to the gigantic unfinished oils giving us the measure of his ambition and energy. Whilst in every corner were seen toys, a wasp's 'bike,' Japanese masks, the gleam of a Chinese embroidery, skins of birds he had cured himself, pine branches, feathers, scraps and curiosities gathered on his way."[147]

154. Frank Laing, *Spiershill*, etching on paper, c.1900 *(private collection)*.

Thanks to the support of John Maclauchlan, in 1902 Laing was honoured with the first one-man show to be held in the Victoria Art Galleries, a popular exhibition which attracted several thousands of visitors.[148] It revealed the full range of his work – his much-acclaimed etchings (praised by the *Advertiser* as works of "indisputable genius") were joined by watercolours of French scenes, a series of seascapes painted on Tiree and a large-scale oil painting, *God's Brown Earth*, a symbolic representation of labour featuring potato diggers, with a carved frieze above it showing a procession of workers on their way to the field.[149]

Laing held another exhibition at Robert Scott's in 1904, and an exhibition of drawings in his Tayport studio the same year. In 1905 he became one of the principal founders of the Tayport Artists' Circle, which became the main outlet for his work over the next two years. Laing was now a familiar name in Dundee and a very vocal proselytiser for the role of art in society. In 1907 he wrote an article on the subject for the *Advertiser*, claiming that:

> "some imagine fine art to be a luxury, a
> thing that is not utilitarian and practical.
> This is a mistake. Fine art is utilitarian in
> the highest sense. A touch of art redeems the
> meanest thing. The art in a thing lengthens its
> chance of life and extends its influence; and
> the principles of fine art are beneficial and
> helpful to all the activities of such a city as
> Dundee".[150]

Just a few months after, however, Laing died at the age of just 45, having never fully recovered from a severe bout of typhoid three years earlier. The Tayport Artists Circle held a memorial exhibition for him including 79 paintings and 160 etchings, and later gifted a collection of the latter to the city's permanent collection. His international reputation continued after his death – nineteen of his etchings were included in an exhibition of modern graphic art in Toronto in 1912, and he was praised in the German monograph *Die Moderne Graphik* (1920).[151] In Dundee, Laing's death prompted several tributes in both prose and poetry, including one written by "one of the 'Circle'":

> "Brilliant, elusive, pawky, with his numberless
> Scottish character stories, it is simply
> impossible to realise that he is gone. Laing, the
> graceful, the debonair, the airy and subtle, yet
> withal the intense and strenuous – strenuous
> in a lifelong fight with the world in which he is
> stricken but dies unconquered. He was indeed
> a fighter. He fought for the recognition of the
> beauty of the world, for art, for liberty, and
> justice."[152]

Dundee's most successful landscape painter in oils at this time was undoubtedly William Bradley Lamond. Born in Newtyle in 1857, he came to Dundee as a child and attended Balfour Street School. His father was an engine driver (and indeed had driven the first engine on the Dundee-Newtyle Railway) and the young William initially followed the same

career, obtaining a railway job in Doncaster.[153] Industrial action led him to return to Dundee, and it was at this point that he decided to make art his profession. He had long held a passion for drawing: "When little more than a toddler at Newtyle he had decorated the fly-leaves of his grandmother's Bibles with childish productions".[154] Later, attending church as a young boy "he spent the drearier hours of the service in making surreptitious outline sketches of his reverend pastor, George Gilfillan".[155] These would stand him in good stead years later when he painted a masterful posthumous portrait of Gilfillan, hailed as far more true-to-life than the more formal portraits painted of him in his lifetime.

Apart from a brief period of study in Paris, Lamond's remarkable skills were entirely self-taught – the *Courier* claimed that "his ability to transfer beauty from the palette to the canvas was 'a gift from the gods.'"[156] He first publicly exhibited his work at Dunfermline's Fine Art Exhibition in 1883, followed by Dundee's in 1884. In 1890 he became one of the founding members of the GAA and had work shown in the window of Robert Scott's gallery, which earned him good publicity. His first notable commission came the following year – a presentation portrait of Sgt Major Kilgour of the Dundee Highlanders.[157] Soon after, he painted a memorably lugubrious portrait of the Poet McGonagall, which was acquired by A C Lamb. Other portrait commissions followed, most notably a wonderfully characteristic painting of Councillor William Blair (1895), but landscapes remained his speciality. Around 1894, he hit on one of his most profitable subjects – shore scenes featuring seaweed gatherers at work with horse and cart (see figure 155). One of these, *A Breezy Day* (1896), was praised by the *Courier* for its "bold and vigorous drawing", though they acknowledged that it added to his reputation "as a painter of strange subjects".[158]

It was also around this time that he discovered his favourite sketching ground in the fishing village of Auchmithie, and he would spend almost every August there for the rest of his life. Here he painted the coast, the sea and the fisherfolk's cottages, including a series of atmospheric interiors. In 1895 he had his most successful year yet, showing at the Glasgow Institute and the RSA and ending with an exhibition of paintings and sketches in his studio at 61 Reform Street. The *Courier* published a feature on him that year, noting the influence of William McTaggart and J L Wingate on his work, but saying "it is impossible not to feel the strong individuality of the painter's style and tastes."[159] "There is a firmness in his touch, truth in his colour, and rare health and life in his composition" the *Evening Telegraph* opined later that year, claiming that Lamond "revels alike in the foamy, sandy strand of the sea shore, the darkling hurrying clouds and mists of the mountain tops, and the sweet peacefulness of woodland begirt quiet waters."[160]

With unusually broad, vigorous brushstrokes, Lamond succeeded in capturing impressionistic effects with rare skill:

> "Mr Lamond has the happy knack of catching
> the evanescent sun effects which haunt our
> memories, but which it is next to impossible
> to define. A momentary gleam on the crest
> of a wave, a flitting flash across the shingle,
> a shimmer upon a grassy ridge, there they
> are transfixed upon the canvas, making the
> picture a thing of beauty and a joy for ever."[161]

155. W B Lamond, *Gathering Seaweed, Auchmithie*, oil on canvas *(Angus Council Museums)*.

Although he himself eschewed modern art, his compositions were often regarded as distinctive due to his preference for capturing particular effects rather than selecting subject matter because of its social or symbolic meaning, in contrast to the Celtic Revivalists. The *Piper o' Dundee* noted that his 1901 painting *Noonday* "may be uninteresting to one seeking for 'subject'; but the effect of flooding sunlight on water is attained perhaps as nearly as is possible by means of paint."[162]

Lamond's work evidently appealed to collectors and his prices steadily increased. In 1898 60 of his paintings were auctioned by William Fyfe at the City Assembly Rooms, fetching prices of up to 19 guineas. In 1900 he showed at the Royal Academy for the first time, and soon began to cultivate a London audience. In May 1901 he spent time painting scenery in Kent, and a year later he opened his first one-man show in London, at Clifford's Gallery in Haymarket. Before leaving Dundee, his fellow artists gave a dinner in his honour. In giving a toast to his future success, sculptor James Bremner claimed that Lamond's "great tutor was Nature. She unfolded to him the treasures she had in store, and he had the eye to see, the mind to comprehend, and the hand to execute."[163]

Although many Dundee illustrators and cartoonists enjoyed considerable success in London (see chapter five), the city's painters had rarely made such an impact in the capital. Lamond's exhibition (entitled 'The Glens and Shores of Scotland') was therefore followed with considerable interest by the local press, who reported gleefully on its success

in critical and commercial terms. "Quite a commando of men and women of note have visited the Clifford Gallery," claimed the *Evening Telegraph*, the most celebrated of whom was millionaire Scottish businessman Andrew Carnegie.[164] The Dundee critics were full of praise for the show:

"One is at once impressed by the striking advance Mr Lamond has made in his art. His colour is purer, richer, and more positive; he gets his sunny effects without a sacrifice of tone, and his work is pervaded throughout by that breezy, open-air freshness and vigour that are indispensable to a sympathetic treatment of northern landscape."[165]

Those London critics that reviewed the show were also positive. The *Morning Post* (whose art correspondent James Greig began his career as a Dundee illustrator) hailed Lamond as "the most distinguished member" of Dundee's "coterie of artists... His mastery of technique is indisputable. Sure and firm in drawing, his colour is delightful in its fresh beauty and truth".[166]

One of the most admired paintings in the exhibition was *A Reedy River*, a scene on the Tay near Perth. "Mr Lamond, I think, has never done anything finer," claimed the *Telegraph*,[167] while the *Courier* noted that the painting "is held by competent critics to be the best that has come from Mr

Lamond's easel."[168] It was reproduced in the magazine *Black & White* and was shown in further exhibitions in London, Edinburgh and Leeds before being reproduced as an autotype print by Valentine's in Dundee and displayed at Thomas Murray's gallery in 1904.

The dinner held in Lamond's honour and the presentations made to him prior to his departure for London clearly implied that his fellow artists were not actually expecting him to come back. When the exhibition finished, however, he returned to his tenement in Hawkhill and continued to paint from his studio in Reform Street. He returned to London in 1903 to undertake a number of commissions and later that year was elected a member of the Royal Society of British Artists. Had he remained in London at this point and cultivated the right patrons his commercial success would undoubtedly have been secured, but once again he returned home, moving to Tayport to share Alec Grieve's studio at West Lights and joining the Tayport Artists' Circle. He continued to show work at the exhibitions of the RBA, RSA, Glasgow Institute and GAA, but in 1906 his health broke down and he withdrew from all of these, his only recorded work that year being one painting, *A March Morning*, shown at Murray's gallery. Instead Lamond took up golf (winning the Scotscraig Golf Club medal in 1907) and gradually regained his strength.

By summer 1908 Lamond was back in Dundee and back in action, holding an exhibition of his latest work in his new studio at 3 Constitution Road; the following year he moved to 27 Bank Street where he would remain for the rest of his life.

Several paintings by him were donated to the city's permanent collection over the next few years – his portraits of Rev Gilfillan (in 1909), Cllr Blair (1910) and Dr George Lawrence (1913), and coastal scenes *Seagulls* (1910) and *A Breezy Day* (1911). In 1915 he gained a celebrity patron in the person of music hall legend Harry Lauder, who commissioned two paintings from him and visited him periodically in either Dundee or Auchmithie. That same year, Lamond placed an advert in the local papers seeking "commissions to Paint Memorial Portraits of Officers who have fallen in the Great War".[169] During the next two years, his youngest son was wounded and his eldest died. He continued to paint as much as ever, spending his summers in Auchmithie then showing the results in exhibitions in his studio each autumn. He rarely showed his work elsewhere in his later years, and was described by the *Courier* in 1922 as "the most unassuming man in his profession".[170] He was said to be unsparing in his criticism of modern art – his purpose, claimed the *Dundee Advertiser*, was "to purge Art of effeminate affectation."[171]

Lamond died of pneumonia in 1924 at his home in William Street. He died intestate, and following a exhibition in his studio to try to sell off his remaining paintings, a memorial exhibition was held at the Victoria Galleries in 1925, featuring 68 works loaned by various collectors, along with numerous paintings donated by his fellow artists in order to raise money to provide for his widow and to erect a stone over his grave in the Eastern cemetery. The exhibition was opened by Sir Harry Lauder, who summed up Lamond's homely qualities: "He did not search the world for themes for his art. He painted what

156. Opposite page: W B Lamond, *Farm Cart at Sunset*, oil on canvas (*collection of Dumfries & Galloway Council*).

157. C G L Phillips, *Invergowrie Bay*, oil on canvas, 1920 (*Dundee Heritage Trust*).

he could see from his own doorstep, and he showed to his fellow-men the wonder and the glory which might be found in the humblest scenes and familiar faces around them."[172]

The artist who enjoyed the longest period of success in landscape painting, though his reputation was largely a local one, was Charles G L Phillips. The son of a sea captain, Phillips was born in Montevideo in 1863, but the family soon returned to their native Aberdeenshire. After a few years in Aberdeen, Phillips came to Dundee and began to study at Dundee School of Art, winning a National Bronze Medal among many other prizes (see figures 201-2). He began showing work at the Fine Art Exhibitions from 1880, and joined the Dundee Art Club in 1885. The following year he advertised his first classes in drawing and painting from his studio at 28 Union Street (later moving to no 14), despite the fact that he did not earn his Art Master's Certificate until 1892, following further evening class study at the Lochee Science & Art School and Morgan Academy. His classes proved popular and in 1891 a group of his students showed decorative work at the Home Industries Exhibition. He would continue to teach painting classes every year until 1916.

Phillips' detailed but atmospheric landscapes soon earned him critical attention – in 1889 the *Courier* described him as "one of our most talented young artists" when his painting *Sunshine and Shadow among the Grampians* was shown in Thomas Murray's gallery. In 1891 he showed at the RSA for the first time, and that same year his impressive painting *Dundee from Balgay Hill* (from an almost identical viewpoint to one of D A Andrews' paintings 55 years earlier) was turned into an etching by Richard D Winter.[173] The painting was bought by Simon G Fraser and later gifted to the permanent collection. Also in 1891, the *Weekly News* gave its readers a free colour print in chromo-lithography of his painting *After the Battle*, an unusually imaginative subject for Phillips, showing a Gordon Highlander finding the body of his fallen comrade.

Extremely prolific, Phillips became one of the most voluminous contributors to the GAA exhibitions, while also showing his work in Edinburgh and Glasgow. Reviews of his paintings (both oils and watercolours) tended to focus on their technical accomplishments with appreciation if not overwhelming enthusiasm. In 1899, 60 of his paintings were shown at the Central Fine Art Gallery to be sold at auction by William Fyfe. "The collection reveals the artist at his best," claimed the *Evening Telegraph*, "and critics who have not always seen eye to eye with Mr Phillips must now join in congratulating him on his achievements in colour toning and technique."[174] The sale attracted a large audience with notably keen bidding over some of the smaller works, suggesting it was not just the wealthy collectors who were buying his art.

While many of his pictures were rural and coastal scenes, Phillips also recognised the commercial interest in views of old Dundee, and in 1903 issued a folio titled *Brown Studies* comprising six hand-coloured reproductions of watercolours of historic buildings such as the Trades Hall, Union Hall and Lady Warkstairs' House (all demolished during the 'improvements' of the 1870s-80s). A decade later he joined other artists in recording through a series of prints and watercolours the High Street and surrounding areas when the Town House was threatened with demolition (figure 158). His historical knowledge was extensive and he gave various public talks such as 'A Day in Old Dundee' (1911) and 'The Old Steeple and

158. C G L Phillips, *High Street, Dundee*, etching on paper, 1914
(*University of Dundee Museum Services*).

Round About' (1913). Before the Town House eventually came down in 1932, Phillips (who had publicly campaigned to save it) helped to create an elaborate scale model of the whole area, which has been a popular exhibit in the city museum ever since.

In 1905 – a time when many Dundee artists were attracted across the Tay to join the Tayport Artists' Circle – Phillips moved in the opposite direction, commissioning the artist and architect Charles Ower (one of the founders of the GAA) to design a villa for him at 310 Strathmartine Road, then at the northernmost edge of the city. With half-timbered gables and red-tiled roof it was notably English in style, a quaint contrast to the distinctively Scottish landscapes he depicted in his paintings. One of these, *A Highland Storm* (figure 267), was purchased from the Dundee Art Society's 21st-anniversary exhibition in 1911 and presented by an anonymous donor to the city, the first painting by Philips to enter the permanent collection.

Two years before that, Phillips had been elected onto the Free Library's Museums & Art Committee, which ran the Albert Institute and Victoria Galleries. This was a major breakthrough for the representation of professional artists in the city and it was a measure of Phillips' standing in the community, and also perhaps his more conservative nature – more politically radical and outspoken artists such as Stewart Carmichael and Alec Grieve would never have been chosen. Carmichael later claimed that Phillips "saved many an awkward situation with his tact and wisdom."[175]

In 1913 Phillips was commissioned to paint a presentation portrait of Rev Monsignor Holder (figure 292) – a rare instance of a local artist being given such a commission. Painting the subject in his ecclesiastical robes, Phillips achieved a striking colour scheme and composition, and the work was highly praised. That same year, he was awarded a solo exhibition in Lamb's Hotel by the Dundee Art Society, which included in the 40 or so works shown his new portrait of ex-Baillie and Councillor Simon G Fraser, an important patron of his work.

Phillips was now concentrating his interests within Dundee – he had largely given up exhibiting at the RSA after 1910, and would only sporadically show his work there after that. He threw himself into local affairs – in 1917 he became a member of the Dundee War Savings Committee, and was later made a Justice of the Peace and a Deacon of the Baptist Church in Ward Road (where he had painted murals in 1903). In 1917 he was elected Convenor of the Free Library's Museum Committee, a position he held until 1928. He became actively involved in the museum displays, painting scenic backgrounds for the natural history cases and painstakingly restoring the collection of ship models at Dudhope Museum. Although he continued to paint in his later years, at the time of his death in 1944 it was for his public service rather than his art that he was chiefly remembered. Only more recently has Phillips' work come to public attention again – in 2002 Dundee Heritage Trust received a substantial collection of paintings and etchings by bequest from his son, which have been exhibited several times since then.

Some other artists deserve briefer mention here. Although based in Edinburgh for most of his life, Joseph Milne spent the greater part of his career painting in and around Dundee. Born in Aberdeen in 1859,[176] Milne studied at the RSA Schools in Edinburgh and achieved early success, exhibiting at the RSA while still a teenager. He first showed in Dundee in the 1879 Fine Art Exhibition and, realising the appetite of the city's art collectors, quickly came to concentrate on local landscape scenes painted in a clean but energetic style. In 1884, for example, he showed several Tayport scenes which impressed the critics, and was hailed by the *Courier* as "a rising student of great promise".[177] Soon after, he took a studio in East Wemyss, though the Tay continued to be his main inspiration. He began to take an active part in the social events accompanying the Fine Art Exhibitions – in 1891 he painted the scenery for a series of *tableaux vivants* in which paintings from the exhibition were brought to life; he did the same the following year, and also acted one of the main parts (alongside E S Hodgson) in a short play performed in the gallery. Milne had evidently established a strong friendship with curator John Maclauchlan – when his son was born in 1885 he named him John Maclauchlan Milne.

In 1889, Milne's *Crossing the Moor* was hung on the line at the Royal Academy, and it became one of the centrepieces of the following year's Fine Art Exhibition. The *Advertiser* hailed it as "an almost phenomenal advance on some of his earlier work... the manner in which the spirit of the scene has been caught by the painter is worthy of high praise."[178] The *Courier* admitted that "here is a young artist who has made a big attempt and succeeded wonderfully", but they had significant reservations: "we should like, also, to point out to Mr Milne a necessity to keep seeking after quality in his work. He must fight against a strain of commonplaceness which now and then creeps into it."[179] The painting was purchased by J G Orchar and Robert Scott commissioned James Kinnear to turn it into an etching.

In 1894, 80 paintings by Milne were shown at the Dundee

159. Joseph Milne, *Steam Tug, Dundee Harbour*, oil on canvas, 1893 *(Calton Gallery)*.

Auction Rooms to be sold by John C Crabbe. The advertisement in the *Courier* claimed: "This is the first occasion that one of the 'One-Artist' sales, so popular in London and Edinburgh, has been held in Dundee", and as we have seen, its popularity paved the way for many more.[180] In reviewing the collection, the *Evening Telegraph* summed up Milne's talents:

"In the landscapes Mr Milne seems to work at his best in quiet evening effects. He is successful in the brighter and sunnier pictures, but excels in the depiction of the done day, and some of the village and field pictures are delightful examples of this phase of the artist's work. In the seascapes and shorescapes he revels in brightness, and not a few of the exhibits are sure to be coveted by connoisseurs."[181]

The sale was a triumph, fetching in total around £600, the highest price being 45 guineas for *A Glimpse of the Tay*. It seemed that Milne was all set for a brilliant career, and as well as his Dundee successes he was also showing work in Edinburgh, Glasgow, London and on the Continent. For whatever reason, however, Milne failed to capitalise on this early success. In 1909, reviewing Dundee's art collections, the critic Edward Pinnington referred to Milne as "a name never read without regret that the promise of his early day has not been fulfilled in his prime".[182] The *Scotsman* later claimed that he "was at one time considered to be on the road to Academic honours, and on

more than one occasion was in the running for Associateship rank of the Royal Scottish Academy."[183] Such hopes never came to fruition. Despite his Dundee connections, he never joined or exhibited with the GAA, and although in Edinburgh he was one of the founder members of the SSA, he seems not to have cultivated any influential friendships in the capital. In 1903 he was declared bankrupt, and soon after moved to London to try to rebuild his career there. The attempt failed and he returned to Edinburgh and then to Dundee, where took a studio in Commercial Street and in 1909 held another sale (again through Crabbe), this time including work by his son, who had followed him into the same profession. In January 1911 he died of a heart attack. His obituarist praised him as "a colourist of considerable strength", noting that "his landscapes were pervaded by a poetic sentiment".[184]

Milne's son developed his father's skills as a colourist. John Maclauchlan Milne was born in Buckhaven in 1885, and seems to have been taught art entirely by his father and his uncle (William Watt Milne, also a painter). At the age of 18 he boarded a ship for Canada where he is said to have had an adventurous few years as cowboy and artist![185] Milne was back in Dundee by 1911, when he joined the Art Society and began exhibiting. The following year he was included in the British Association exhibition (see chapter nine) and over the next few years showed his landscape paintings regularly in Dundee and at the RSA. By 1918 (when he was away fighting in the Great War), he was praised by the *Celtic Annual* for "rapidly gaining a reputation in landscape, and for his studies of the sea. [He]

has already produced beautiful work, and what is better, gives promise of greater things."[186]

At the end of the 1910s, Milne was still painting in a similar style to his father, clearly demonstrated by his *Fife Landscape* of 1920 (purchased for the city's permanent collection in 1924). That year, however, he returned to France and took a studio in Paris, where he was immediately inspired by the cultural reawakening of the city after the war (see figure 161). In March 1921 he showed some of the results at an exhibition at Murray's gallery. The *Evening Telegraph* welcomed this opportunity to "plunge into Paris, steep one's self in a sun bath and revel in the glowing colour of the boulevards or the gardens", noting that Milne's work had "gained in breadth... [and] attained to a firmness of touch, and a clarity of colour that does not always accompany the modern impressionistic picture."[187]

Although his style was still developing, Milne quickly adopted a much bolder colour palette, and many of his paintings from this time show clear affinities with the work of Peploe, Fergusson, Cadell and Hunter – the artists who would later be termed the Scottish Colourists. When his new work was shown alongside theirs at the 1924 Dundee Fine Art Exhibition, critic Robins Millar compared the work of modern French painters to "our own innovators, Peploe, Leslie Hunter, Cadell, and, very stirringly, those strong Dundee men, David Foggie and McLauchlan Milne [sic]."[188] Milne would soon get to know the Scottish Colourists, painting with them in the south of France and Iona and exhibiting with them as well, and there is certainly a case for considering him as the fifth Colourist, though he has never received the same critical attention.

Thanks to the support of Dundee patrons Alexander Keiller, William Boyd, Matthew Justice and John Tattersall, Milne was able to spend much of the 1920s and early 30s in France, though he continued to base himself in Dundee (in David Foggie's former studio in Nethergate) and play an active role in the Art Society. In 1922 he held an exhibition in his studio, and delighted in telling the *Courier*'s reporter who asked what rules he painted by, "There are no rules of art!" The writer attempted to sum up Milne's increasing turn towards abstraction: "it is an effort to represent what is in the artist's mind by an arrangement of shapes and colour, more or less arbitrary." On commenting that Scotland lacks the same vibrant colours shown in his paintings, the reporter was told by the artist: "Scotland is glowing with colour, ...it is we who have failed to see it, and our painters have too often hidden it under a haze."[189] Three years later, Milne again showed his latest work in his studio. This time the critics were more certain of its qualities. The *Courier* noted that Milne "has brought back from the azure shore [of the South of France] pictures that palpitate with hot sunlight and dazzle with their audacious colour... [T]hey radiate a joyousness which will affect the most casual beholder."[190]

Milne's later career falls outwith the scope of this book, but it is worth noting that in 1933 he was part of a group exhibition with Stewart Carmichael and Alec Grieve in the Victoria Galleries (the three had previously shown together in the Dundee Art Society rooms in 1920) and in 1937 was made a Royal Scottish Academician. He settled in Arran in the 1940s and continued to paint there until his death in 1957.

A strong Colourist influence is also apparent in the later landscape paintings of Alec Grieve. As we have seen in the previous chapter, Grieve made his first notable contribution to art as a symbolist painter, but he had always shown a fondness for landscapes, and was particularly inspired by the 'Nocturnes' of Whistler. Their influence is apparent in many of his early exhibits at the Graphic Art Association – *Nightfall* (1894), *Nocturne in Grey – the Tay Ferries* (1895), *Nocturne – A Moonlight Sonata* (1896) and *Nocturne – Moonlight on the Tay* (1897). John Duncan later argued that such associations were natural given the unique quality of light on the Tay, as seen from the Newport ferry, or 'Fifie':

> "The wonderful beauty of opalescent water at morning and at night. How we all loved it… the dusky town, the golden sunset haze, the creeping mists upon the water. We knew Whistler's range of effects before we heard his name. His nocturnes had nothing strange for us but an old familiar face, and we could say as we saw each new shadowy dream, 'We have seen things as lovely as that from the Fifie.'"[191]

At first the critics were unsure what to make of Grieve's moody landscapes, though they knew which artist's work they resembled. *Nocturne – a Moonlight Sonata* "shows the rear-lights of a train gleaming through the mirk darkness of the night, and is reminiscent of some of the weird pictures which Whistler first made popular", said the *Advertiser* in 1896.[192] The following year, *Nocturne – Moonlight on the Tay* was described as "a sketch in the Whistler vein... very cleverly managed."[193]

Grieve's colour scheme gradually brightened, as can clearly be seen by comparing his two views of *Pont du Cheval, Bruges* in the permanent collection. The 1911 painting is muted in colour, concentrating on composition and subtle water effects. The 1922 version is considerably brighter, and is far more concerned with colour and light effects. *The Moor, Tayport* (1924, purchased for the Orchar Gallery's collection in 1949; figure 162) takes this further, the expanse of sand dunes in the foreground creating an almost abstract composition behind which the setting sun creates striking colour harmonies. *Newburgh-on-Tay* (1926, also in the Orchar Collection) is a purely Colourist work with bold outlines and blocks of pure colour, closely resembling one of Peploe's landsapes.

Grieve continued to paint on the Continent (particularly Bruges, Ghent, Paris and Rouen), but he found his greatest inspiration in the views from his studio in Tayport, as Stewart Carmichael recalled:

> "the river and the city beyond, with its thousand reflections, the great ships coming and going, proved the inspiration of much of his best work. But beauty he saw and painted in every aspect of nature; amongst the hills, on the moors, scenes of harvest life, ice on the river, flowers and apple blossom… the artist's personal vision is rendered with the skilful hand and seeing eye of the craftsman and poet."[194]

160. Joseph Milne, *Boating at Sunset*, oil on canvas, 1897 *(private collection)*.

161. John Maclauchlan Milne, *Tuileries Gardens, Paris*, oil on canvas, 1920 *(Lyon & Turnbull, © the Estate of John Maclauchlan Milne, represented by Portland Gallery, London)*.

162. Alec Grieve, *The Moor, Tayport*, oil on canvas, 1924 *(Dundee City Council: Dundee's Art Galleries & Museums)*.

Grieve died in February 1933 just a few days after the opening of his group exhibition at the Victoria Galleries (described as "a veritable revelation of his genius") with Carmichael and Maclauchlan Milne.[195] Both men helped to carry his coffin at the funeral, along with John Duncan and another young landscape painter, J Calder Smith. A memorial exhibition of Grieve's work was held two years later, at which it was noted that his work had "steadily advanced from a sort of poetical obscurity to notable brilliancy of colour."[196]

Of all Dundee artists working in the conventional genres of landscape, portraiture and still life, the most talented was arguably David Foggie, to whom the rest of this chapter is devoted (figure 163). Foggie is in many ways the quintessential artist of this period, having worked in all of the aforementioned genres as well as flirting briefly with decorative art. He was also actively involved in the GAA and Tayport Artists' Circle, and since his career is exceptionally well documented thanks to various papers held by his family, he provides an excellent case study of the life of a professional artist in and around Edwardian Dundee.

Foggie was born on 31 December 1878, the last of fourteen children (only half of whom survived to adulthood) born to James and Margaret Foggie of 141 Ann Street, Dundee.[197] James Foggie was an architect who also served on the Town Council for many years. It must quickly have become apparent that art was Foggie's main talent, for he started in the first grade of the Dundee School of Art's day class at the age of eight, and won the first of numerous prizes the following year. In 1893 he showed off his acting skills for the first time, appearing as the Jesting Fairy in a performance of *The Grammar Fairies* (see chapter three). David's father had wanted his son to take up pharmacy as a profession, but his exceptional artistic ability allowed Foggie to work towards becoming an art teacher. As it turned out, James Foggie never lived to see his son fulfil this goal - he died in 1895. A year later, David Foggie was made a Pupil Assistant at the art school (see chapter six).

It was during this period that Foggie first came into contact with the members of the GAA. "They were a talkative and argumentative lot," Foggie later recalled, "and their conversations and example were the most formative influence I ever met... With the stimulus of this atmosphere I determined to be an artist."[198] Following in the footsteps of Duncan and Carmichael, in 1898 Foggie set off to Belgium with £30 left to him by his father, and enrolled at the Antwerp Academy. It was here that he honed his drawing skills, which would become the basis for his art.[199]

163. Stewart Carmichael, *The Anatomist (Portrait of David Foggie)*, oil on canvas, 1897 *(private collection)*.

After two sessions, Foggie returned to the family home (now at Pearlbank, 53 Albert Street, Tayport) and began his attempts to make a living as an artist. Attempting to subsidise his income by doing part-time manual labour for some of the local farms, Foggie had ample opportunity to observe and sketch his fellow workers. On his 22nd birthday he wrote in his diary: "Today has been particularly happy. Due, as far as one can assign, to my finding the drawing of these outworkers in line with my life. There is one of these women magnificent in character – like a growth, direct from the soil."[200] A few days later, he noted: "Been working well... at the turnip gatherers and am proceeding very cautiously and carefully with my studies."[201]

Shortly after writing this, Foggie was to be devastated by the death of his close friend George Dutch Davidson. They had been art students together at the High School, and Davidson had followed Foggie to Antwerp in 1899. His death left Foggie (a lifelong atheist) questioning his lack of faith. That night he wrote in his diary: "Strange to me tonight to think that I, who have [been] doubting all transcendentalism the last months, should in the presence of the victory of materialism as it appears, be strong enough to quite overcome my past thoughts and feel the rest in which George sleepeth."[202] The funeral brought more typically acerbic comments: "I realized anew the poverty of the orthodox religion which calls itself Christian. The minister understands nothing of the beliefs of our dear friend and read what would have sounded in his ears... as trash".[203]

The following year brought a far happier occasion, when Foggie married Margaret Anne Jack of Spring Cottage, Tayport. A gifted musician, she had studied at the Berlin Conservatory and earned an LLA degree. Less than four months after his marriage Foggie's mother died and he decided to return to further study in Antwerp, this time taking Margaret with him. From there they moved on to Florence (Foggie later claimed to "love Florence more than any place I was ever in"), then visited Paris and London on their way home.[204] On their return in 1904, they settled in Fife – originally Logie, then Lucklaw Hill overlooking Leuchars and Balmullo. Missing the regular contact of his Dundee friends, a few years later he began renting a studio at 28 Ward Road, to which he bicycled every day via the Tay Ferry.

To earn his keep he returned to teaching (this time mainly private pupils), gave public lectures and wrote critical articles. He was also exhibiting his work regularly, having shown at the GAA exhibitions every year from 1897. Gradually his work started to gain critical attention – in 1900 the *Evening Telegraph* praised his "exquisite chalkwork", while the *Piper o'Dundee* shared the opinion that his work "was amongst the finest and most interesting in the Exhibition".[205] The following year he contributed two drawings to the Arbroath art periodical *Imprints*, which the *Arbroath Herald & Advertiser* claimed were "distinguished by singular clearness and precision, with a softness and a truthfulness not often found in chalk work."[206]

At the time when decorative art was at its height in Dundee, many of the pieces Foggie submitted for exhibition in these early years were embroidered book covers and lace patterns, designed by him and executed by Margaret. In 1906 Foggie gave a lecture to the Dundee Art Society on 'The Appreciation of Beauty', in which he showed his socialist convictions by complaining of the "grasping capitalism of manufacturers... [which] crushed out all art instincts among workers".[207] His skills as a public speaker became well-known – his friend George Wilkie Gahan described him as being "gifted with a clear, subtle mind, and also with a splendid power of expression, vocally and elecutionally."[208]

In 1905, Foggie became the youngest member of the Tayport Artists' Circle, and contributed significantly to their exhibitions (twelve pieces in the first exhibition, 28 in the next). The prices he was charging for his work also increased. In the third exhibition (1906) his maximum price was £8/8 for *Turnip Thinning*. A year later he was asking £25 for *Memories*. At the Dundee Art Society exhibition of 1911 he asked £50 for *Girl in White*. Not all of his work sold, of course, but Foggie was now making a reasonably good living. His surviving accounts show that his average expenditure throughout the 1910s was £72, compared to an annual income of nearly £234.[209]

The exceptional quality of his head studies led to a number of notable portrait commissions, including oil paintings of his brother James K Foggie (1905), Lord Dean of Guild Dickie (1906), department store owners Thomas Justice (1905) and D M Brown (1909) and ex-Bailie (later Lord Provost) Don (1908). In 1912 he held the first of what would become annual solo exhibitions in his studio, revealing the full range of his work, including some fine watercolour landscape paintings.[210] The following year he moved to a new studio at 132a Nethergate, where he would remain for the rest of his time in Dundee.

By this time he was also having work accepted by the RSA – in 1911 a *Head Study* and a beautiful *Mother and Child* showing his wife and baby son (figure 164). The latter was exhibited at Thomas Murray's gallery for a few days prior to its Edinburgh showing and was praised by Joseph Lee in the *City Echo*: "Both as regards conception and colouring it will rank with anything he has yet done. The unconventional treatment of the child, in particular with its almost elfin characteristics, is quite notable... Mr Foggie is going forward."[211] From 1914, Foggie would exhibit at the RSA every year for the rest of his life. In 1910 he was elected a member of the SSA, and his watercolours were also proving popular at the annual exhibitions of the RSW, to which he was elected in 1918. In 1930 he became Vice President of the Society.

During the Great War, Foggie twice attempted to enlist – despite his earlier association with the Independent Labour Party, many of whose members opposed the war – but was rejected on medical grounds, having suffered badly from asthma from some years.[212] He found new but somewhat depressing employment in commissions of posthumous portraits of beloved sons and husbands killed in the war. One of these, *The Late G W Paisley, 2nd Lieutenant*, he exhibited at the Dundee Art Society in 1919.[213] Perhaps his most memorable wartime image, however, was the bold graphic cover he designed for the programme of a concert held in aid of Belgian refugees in 1915, the original of which was auctioned at the event.

By this time, Foggie was the father of four children, and he and Margaret were assisted in their upbringing by the late George Dutch Davidson's mother, who had come to live nearby. Advised by Patrick Geddes, Foggie was against sending the children to school, and it was partly the desire for better private tuition that led the family to move to Edinburgh in September 1919.

As it turned out, Foggie was back in Dundee just two years later, staging a solo exhibition of his work at Murray's gallery in the Nethergate (owned at the time by his brother James).

The show comprised sixteen oils, eight watercolours and seven pastels, and included some superb works such as *Forfouchten* (now in the city's collection), *Pickling Eggs* (family collection) and *The Dressing Table* (figure 166). The latter two revealed a vivid use of colour that had not been notable in his work before. The *Courier* noted that "his work has acquired greater decision and freedom, and a higher key makes for greater brilliance."[214] The introduction to the catalogue was written by John Duncan, who had become a close neighbour of Foggie's in Edinburgh. His description of Foggie's work stresses first the contrast then the similarity to his own fantastical creations:

> "Mr Foggie does not dress his figures in bygone modes, nor rely on mythologies or poetic associations, but is satisfied to render his folk as they are, and as he sees them, believing that they are wonderful enough and beautiful enough for the purposes of the highest Art. But this does not entail a merely objective or epidermic realism; he aims, as all modern artists aim, at simplification and elimination of all that is indifferent or insignificant to liberate the aesthetic and human elements."[215]

"It seems to me that art is one of the greatest means for the elevation of mankind," Foggie wrote in a letter to one of his former Antwerp friends.[216] In a later essay he explained his own approach in some detail: "Whatever the theme or the treatment the result in a good picture must be the complete absorption of the subject by the expression. The picture must be personal and alive by its own reality and aesthetically independent of any outside reference. It must... be the embodiment of an idea."[217]

Foggie believed that there was no automatic correlation between the beauty of art and of nature. He explained: "the beauty of art I take to be chiefly expression. It is not enough to copy beauty, we must achieve it. The artist must create his synthesis by dominating natural beauty to his own idea. Personally this seems to me easier to do when the elements with which he deals are not beautiful in themselves."[218] This would certainly explain Foggie's distinctive style of portraiture, and why he was mostly denied commercial success in this field. While other artists could create elegance on demand, Foggie could not deny his own vision. Even from his earliest portrait commissions he quickly gained a reputation for unflattering truthfulness, and his sympathetic portrayals of working class subjects may have put off prospective clients from higher up the social scale. His occasional later commissions included two more Dundee

subjects – the pair of portraits of Sir James Caird and his sister Emma Marryat created in 1928 for the foyer of the Caird Hall (where they still hang today), with copies being ordered for Dundee Royal Infirmary (now in the Tayside Medical History Museum collection).[219]

Generally, though, Foggie was obliged to pay models to sit for him, and he was particularly attracted to those whom one of his obituarists described as "lower-class, middle-aged, robust types of Scottish people, which he invests with a sense of weight and a quiet dignity at times recalling the simplicity of Greek art".[220] He held a particular fascination for men and women who worked with their hands – something he clearly empathised with, as his early diary entries showed. In 1901 he wrote: "The greatest gift to me now would be a wage of 20/- for 20 hours per week working at one of the manual occupations I would choose. It seems impossible to make enough, in the little time I would allow myself per day, by the labour of one's hands."[221] A great many of his subjects were craftsmen – *The Smithy* (1918), *The Mushfaker* (or umbrella-mender, c 1926), *The Shipwright* (1931) and *The Old Engineer* (undated, all in family collections). Foggie's socialist principles also informed much of his work in this area. During the strikes of 1926, for instance, he helped to support a mining family by paying all of them to sit for him individually.[222]

Children were another favourite subject, especially his own (being cheaper). Since Foggie could take several weeks to complete even his smallest paintings, many of them ended up as composite portraits – one child would get fed up modelling and be replaced by another, with no obvious detriment to the finished picture! Mother and child compositions were also common, one of the finest being of a friend of the family, Mrs MacDonald, with her baby son in 1925 (now in Paisley Museum & Art Galleries).

Foggie's wife was certainly his favourite model, a role she tolerated but did not exactly relish. His early drawings of her are among his most tenderly beautiful works, and she was the model for the fine *Portrait of a Lady* which was bought for Dundee's permanent collection in 1924. A reporter once asked Margaret if she had been the model for one of her husband's early nudes. "How dare you suggest such a thing?" she retorted, knowing full well that she had posed for the picture in question![223]

Thanks possibly to the influence of John Duncan, Foggie was appointed to the teaching staff of Edinburgh College of Art soon after his move to the capital. During term-time he worked almost entirely in his studio, but when the holidays came, he took to the countryside of East Lothian and Fife to indulge his love of watercolours. He also devoted an increasing amount of his time to the RSA, who had made him an Associate in 1925 and a full Academician in 1930. In 1931 Foggie became the Academy's Treasurer, and in 1932 took over as Secretary, a position he retained until his death.

Foggie died aged 69 on 2 June 1948 after a severe attack of asthma. *The Scotsman*'s obituary summed up his career simply but effectively, describing him as "a figure painter who found beauty in ordinary life and expressed it with honesty."[224] Foggie's own opinion, made the year before he died, was this: "I have had a very good life and I would gladly live it again – missing out some of the bumpy bits."[225]

164. Left: David Foggie, *Mother and Child*, oil on canvas, 1911 *(private collection)*.

165. Above: David Foggie, *Untitled figure sketch*, charcoal on paper, 1916 *(private collection)*.

166. Next page: David Foggie, *The Dressing Table*, oil on canvas, 1921 *(Paisley Art Institute Collection, held by Paisley Museum, Renfrewshire Council)*.

CHAPTER FIVE

Art & Journalism

DIAGRAM OF THE TAY BRIDGE
AS ON THE 28TH DECEMBER 1879.

DIAGRAM OF THE TAY BRIDGE
AS IT NOW IS, 1st JANUARY 1880.

The above diagram gives an idea of the present appearance of the Tay Bridge, but it may be explained that in order to bring both diagrams within the width of our page they are shortened by five spans—from Nos. 15 to 21—on the south side. In other respects the relative lengths of the standing and fallen parts are accurate.

167. Unknown artist, 'Diagram of the Tay Bridge', from the *Dundee Advertiser*, 1880 *(used by kind permission of D C Thomson & Co Ltd)*.

The phenomenal success of D C Thomson's comic publications (most famously *The Dandy* (1937-2012) and *The Beano* (1938-present)) has given Dundee international significance as one of the most important centres for comic-book production.[1] But the story of the city's success in bringing art and journalism together dates back considerably further and involves little-known work by some of the Dundee's most significant artists.[2]

Two large companies dominated the newspaper business in late-19th century Dundee. W & D C Thomson were responsible for the *Courier & Argus*, the *Evening Post* and the *Weekly News*, but the greatest empire was that of John Leng & Co, publishers of the *Dundee Advertiser*, the *Evening Telegraph*, the *People's Journal* and the *People's Friend*.[3] Leng had been editor of the *Advertiser* since 1851, using it as a platform for his liberal political campaigns, which culminated in a period of seventeen years as MP for the city, from 1889 until shortly before his death in 1906.

In the 1870s, daily newspapers were generally unillustrated. The occasional map or plan could be inserted into the letter press as an engraved block, but the effort required to do so was generally prohibitive.[4] The event that would change this was one of the most infamous disasters of the age. On 28 December 1879 the central section of the Tay Bridge (which had been completed just two years earlier) collapsed during a heavy storm while a train was passing through it, causing the death of everyone on board.[5] As part of its coverage of the tragedy, the succeeding editions of the *Evening Telegraph* and the *Advertiser* featured an engraved diagram showing the bridge before and after the event (figure 167).[6]

Inevitably, the issues sold well, and a special notice appeared in the *Advertiser* the day after announcing that readers could order copies of Tuesday's edition "with Diagram of Bridge" that could be posted to friends at a distance.[7] The same illustration was repeated on 1 January 1880, this time with a new diagram entitled 'Composition of Train and Position where it now lies'. Realising he was onto a good thing, Leng repeated both of these on 6 January and followed them with a new one ('Present Appearance of the Bridge') on 9 January and yet another ('Diagram showing the Tay Bridge and Fallen Girders as seen at Low Water of Spring Tide on Tuesday 13 January'), which appeared a week later.

The success of these led Leng to consider investing in the necessary equipment to allow such illustrations to become a regular feature, something no other daily paper had ever attempted. While on a visit to London later that year he discovered machines that could engrave pictures onto a plate of prepared plaster of Paris, using a combination of pantograph and vertical drill. Leng quickly ordered one of the machines to be brought to Dundee and erected in the company's headquarters in Bank Street.[8] He then employed a young illustrator called Martin Anderson to become the first regular staff artist for a daily newspaper in Britain.

Born in Leuchars in 1854, Anderson went to school in St Andrews and in 1868 left home to attend what was later known as Glasgow School of Art. Ten years later he was providing small but regular illustrations for a Glasgow paper called *News of the Week*, and had his first painting (*The Music Lesson*) hung in the RSA. In 1878 he made an unsuccessful attempt to break into the London art world, and the following year returned penniless to the family home in Tayport.

Leng was clearly aware of Anderson's work, and not just from *News of the Week*. Just a few months before his appointment, a review in the *People's Journal* had singled him out in an exhibition of local landscape paintings at Thomas Murray's gallery, noting his skill "in a nice little coastal scene."[9] Anderson's topographical skills were soon required for his work in Leng's papers. The first illustration that we can assume to be his is a sketch of Dumbarton Castle in the *People's Journal* of 5 June 1880. In the *Advertiser*, diagrams of a proposed re-

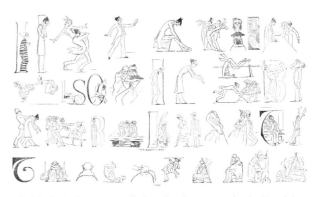

168. Martin Anderson, compilation of early cartoons for the *People's Journal* and other Leng titles, 1880s *(Libraries, Leisure & Culture Dundee, used by kind permission of D C Thomson & Co Ltd)*.

PUSSY'S FIRST MOUSING.

THE DISCOVERY.

THE ATTACK.

CAPTURED.

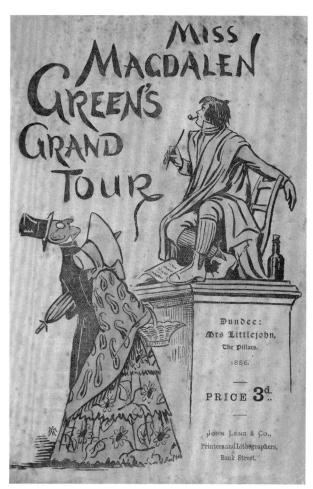

169. Martin Anderson, 'Pussy's First Mousing', from the *People's Journal*, 1885 *(used by kind permission of D C Thomson & Co Ltd)*.

170. Martin Anderson, *Miss Magdalen Green's Grand Tour*, cover illustration, 1886 *(private collection)*.

construction of the Tay Bridge appeared on 16 and 17 June, and illustrations of the new Commercial Bank in Dundee were printed on 22 June. These set the pattern for the kind of work Anderson was expected to produce for Leng, but he soon began to create more distinctive pieces. On 9 October he provided the *People's Journal* with its first humorous cartoons, two small bathing scenes to illustrate a column called 'Job's Reflections', which also appeared in the *Evening Telegraph*. He was soon producing regular thumbnail sketches for this series as well as serial features such as 'Blunders of a Bashful Man' and 'Alvira Slimmens' Search for a Husband'. Anderson's biographers, Elspeth Reid and Flora Davidson, described these early works: "The young artist enjoyed embarrassing situations: a lady lost her wig in company; a dignified gent took a tumble; a drunk clung to a lamp post. The figures were caught in mid-action, in ridiculous attitudes, their surprise and fury captured in a few lines" (see figure 168).[10]

In 1884 Leng replaced his pantographic system with a new zincographic process. Illustrations could now be produced on special paper to be transferred to a zinc plate. A bath of nitric acid would then eat away the white parts of the image, leaving the black ink lines untouched. Attached to a wooden block the plate was thus ready to be inserted directly into the letter press. The process was not only quicker and cheaper but could also reproduce shading effects hitherto impossible.

By this time Anderson was head of his own department and had at least two assistant artists working for him, one of whom was the teenage John Duncan. A significant innovation from this period that we can ascribe to Anderson was the introduction of comic strips. On 31 October 1885 the *People's Journal* included a three-picture sequence entitled 'Pussy's First Mousing' (figure 169).[11] Others followed at irregular intervals, usually subtitled "a story without words", presumably to help explain this brand-new art form to the readers. Although not the earliest examples known to exist (in Britain, Ally Sloper made his debut in 1867), these certainly predate the American pioneers of the form, and seem to have been among the first cartoon strips to appear in newspapers rather than illustrated magazines, thus introducing the form to a far wider audience.[12]

Work like this was proving popular, and Leng issued a series of booklets of the papers' illustrated features, including *Humorous Readings Maistly Scotch* and *Readings Pithy and Pawky*, in which Anderson was for the first time credited for his work. The young artist was also developing his style in other publications away from the Leng stable. Between 1879 and 1883 he contributed numerous cartoons to the lively Dundee periodical *The Wizard of the North*, and was at the same time sending work to Glasgow for a similar magazine called *Quiz*, begun in 1881. The success of these pieces and the Leng booklets encouraged him to attempt a publication of

his own. The result was *Miss Magdalen Green's Grand Tour* (figure 170), published by Mrs Littlejohn in 1886, in which the title character "meanders gently round all the principal sights [of Dundee], giving curious historical, anecdotical, and enigmatical information."[13] The book was a hit, earning at least two reprints and a sequel, *Miss Magdalen Green's Christmas*.

For Anderson, this was only the beginning. As founder and leading light of the Dundee Art Club, he was now one of the best-known artists in town. The journalist and poet Norval Scrymgeour later recalled:

"In Dundee streets no figure was more conspicuous. Though he was not big in stature, the brisk beady-eyed artist compelled notice. He was a live wire, flying along with his Highland cloak blowing about him. He radiated fun. In a somewhat squeaky voice he distributed the best of humour. He could tell stories in an exquisitely droll way. In the best sense of the term he was a 'comic'."[14]

In 1887 Anderson adopted a new pseudonym for his contributions to *Quiz* – 'Cynicus'. His work was now reaching new levels, and in 1890 he resigned from Leng's "in order to prosecute his profession in London."[15] Before leaving, his friends honoured him with a complimentary conversazione featuring singing, dancing and speeches. Anderson was presented with two illustrated books on design, a palette and a box of paints.[16]

Abandoning a steady annual income of £250, Anderson headed south for the second time and recruited his former employer's London office to print his first major publication, *The Satires of Cynicus*. It was issued in a deluxe edition with each picture hand-coloured by his sisters back in Tayport. By the summer of 1891 the book and its author were hailed as "the success of the season in London."[17] Visitors flocked to his studio, from old friends such as John Duncan to new admirers such as William Morris and Ramsay MacDonald. Later that year came a sequel, *The Humours of Cynicus*. By this time Anderson's sister Annie was training local youngsters in Tayport to assist with the colouring process.

Cynicus was now much in demand for London periodicals, and over the next few years he contributed to the *Pall Mall Budget*, the *Labour Leader*, *Ariel* and *The Idler*. In 1892 he published a further collection of cartoons, *Symbols and Metaphors*, and a story book, *The Fatal Smile*. His fifth and final hand-coloured publication, *Cartoons Social and Political*, came out in 1893. As the title suggests, its tone was far sharper than its predecessors – too much so, in fact, for his fashionable London readers. Sales were poor and Anderson was forced to return to Tayport and sell a number of original paintings through the Graphic Arts Association in order to boost his funds.

Cynicus now looked to a new art form to suit his unique talents, and found it in the comic postcard. He created his first designs in 1898, and by 1902 had raised enough capital to set up his own printing company in Tayport. As well as using his own designs he also employed other artists (including at least two from Dundee, James Douglas and C G L Phillips).

"Soon our staff numbered over a hundred," he later claimed, "and we had won the highest award for colour printing in the country."[18] Among his most popular designs were those that poked fun at the holiday experience, most famously the ludicrously overcrowded 'Last Car from...' which could be overprinted with the name of any holiday resort in the country.

The postcard craze lasted only a few more years, and the Cynicus Publishing Company began to make a loss in 1909. Two years later it was put into liquidation. The rest of Anderson's career comprised a series of attempts to get back on his feet, most of them failures. At the time of his death in 1932, however, he was enjoying a brief reawakening of public interest in his work, partly spearheaded by the publication of his memoirs in the *Glasgow Evening News* in 1930. In them he provided a summary of his artistic philosophy: "Brevity is the soul of wit. It was my earliest endeavour by elimination to oust the unnecessary line, to take away that which obscured and to discover that minimum that suggested in itself all that I intended to convey."[19]

Cynicus was the first Dundee newspaper artist to achieve real success in London, but many others would follow – by 1897 the *Evening Telegraph* claimed that "Juteopolis has more 'leaders in black and white' in London than any other city in the kingdom."[20] John Duncan, however, was not destined to be one of them. He left the *Advertiser* in early 1887 (nearly three years before Anderson) and spent some time in London doing what he later described as nothing more than "hack work".[21] This included contributions to the *Magazine of Art* and *English Illustrated Magazine*, but much of the work by him that we know from this period was actually printed in Dundee. On 9 April 1887 the *Piper o' Dundee* reported on a supper held by the Dundee Literary Society, noting that "The menu card was an artistic gem, designed by Mr John T Duncan, of London, a member of the society."[22] On 18 June, the *Piper* noted the publishing by Robert F Mackay of "a fine etching of Her Majesty Queen Victoria, with an environment of designs, illustrating the British colonies and possessions. Mr Mackay selected Mr John T Duncan, artist, London (late of Dundee), to carry out the idea, and with rare artistic taste and right loving labour has Mr Duncan accomplished the work."

But Duncan was clearly not satisfied with his duties as an illustrator, and soon left the capital to study in Antwerp and Düsseldorf. As we have seen, on his return to Dundee he spent some time working as a portrait painter before Patrick Geddes set him on an altogether different course.

By the turn of the century the Leng company's artistic output had "assumed gigantic dimensions."[23] To celebrate the *Advertiser*'s centenary in 1901 they published a souvenir booklet which described the zincographic department thus:

"Three artists are constantly employed in this department exclusively, and they turn out a weekly average of about 60 drawings of all kinds – portraits, architectural subjects, memorable events, and maps… The work

of the artists is almost equal to that of the London weekly illustrated papers, and if the pictures in the newspaper are not always as fine in appearance as the carefully printed plates in the Graphic or Illustrated London News, this must be attributed to the exceptionally high speed at which the printing presses are driven, whereby some of the finer effects are lost."

By this time the *Courier* had also embraced the use of illustrations, though its technology was somewhat behind the *Advertiser*'s and most of the early images to appear in its pages look like lino-cuts. The most talented artist at Thomson's in the 1890s was undoubtedly Max Cowper. Born Thomas Maxwell Cowper in Lochee in 1870,[24] we have an amusing glimpse into his childhood from the 'Art Reminiscences' of George Wilkie Gahan:

> "Like most boys … I was addicted to drawing on the pavement slabs. I suppose I had shown a certain amount of aptitude, for I had aroused the jealousy of one of my companions, who, on seeing himself defeated, said he would 'bring a boy round to-morrow who could beat me easily.'
>
> On being told to do so, he turned out to be as good as his word. The boy came, a space was allocated to each, and we were allowed to draw whatever we fancied.
>
> The lad proved to be more than a worthy opponent, and after grave deliberation, it was decided that I had lost as far as drawing was concerned…
>
> This same little fair haired, blue-eyed boy lived to become a very Napoleon in the 'Black and White' world. His name was Max Cowper…"[25]

Cowper spent the first three years of his working life as an apprentice in the jute business – the *Courier* later reported that in order to pursue his art career he "gave up his place at the desk of a firm in the staple trade, even in the face of a most tempting offer to stay at it".[26] He began studying art in the evenings at Harris Academy, and first exhibited under the name Maxwell Cooper at the Dundee Art Club in 1888. By the following year he had adopted his snappier pseudonym and was contributing cartoons to the *Piper o' Dundee*. He joined W & D C Thomson in 1889, and was first given credit for his work in a book called *Picnic Resorts around Dundee* (1890), based on features in the *Courier* and *Weekly News*.[27] Although the sketches themselves are undistinguished, Cowper's work immediately stands out due to his use of Art Nouveau-inspired lettering and sinewy border lines.

Cowper was soon an active member of the Dundee art scene, exhibiting at the Fine Art Exhibitions and joining the GAA soon after its foundation; he drew the back cover image for their conversazione programme in 1892 and the front cover for their first exhibition catalogue in 1893.[28] By that

171. Top: Martin Anderson (as Cynicus), '*A Law Suit*' from *The Satires of Cynicus*, 1892 *(private collection)*.

172. Middle: Unknown artist (probably Martin Anderson), 'Artists' Room', illustration from *How a Newspaper is Printed*, John Leng & Co, 1890 *(used by kind permission of D C Thomson & Co Ltd)*.

173. Above left: Max Cowper, 'Amaryllis', from *To-Day*, 1895 *(private collection)*.

174. Above right: Max Cowper, 'London Street Scene', from *Moderne Kunst*, c.1900s *(private collection)*.

175. Opposite page: David Comba Adamson, *James Russell*, oil on canvas, 1898 *(Dundee City Council: Dundee's Art Galleries & Museums)*.

"I often wish I had four hands instead of two," Cowper told an interviewer in 1899, having become so much in demand that he was unable to keep up with the work.[35] Soon after this he gave up his piecemeal commissions and joined the staff of the *Illustrated London News*. For them he created his most memorable pieces, elegant yet amusing portrayals of the latest trends, from roller skating to lady motorists. Yet he could also handle more serious topics – in 1905 the *Daily Mail* asked him to cover the advance of the Japanese army into Russia; the work he produced for them was far more objective than the strongly anti-Japanese cartoons from America that the *Dundee Courier* was reprinting at the time.[36]

Cowper's career was sadly cut short, as Gahan recalled:

> "He worked unsparingly to achieve a comfortable competency, so that he might be able to attain to what was all along his *real* ambition, that of a master in 'oils,' and at the age of forty … he had set himself to win the laurels in the greater field of art when, unfortunately, appendicitis claimed him as a victim… His fellow-workers all admitted that none knew as fully as he the possibilities and the limitations of the art of reproduction."[37]

After his death in 1911, the editor of the *Illustrated London News* donated an original drawing created by Cowper for the magazine to Dundee's permanent collection.

Almost all of the artists mentioned in this chapter earned their living in Dundee working for either Leng or Thomson, but their most distinctive work appeared in illustrated magazines, most notably *The Wizard of the North* and *The Piper o' Dundee*. The earliest publication of this kind was *Our Special Artist at the Dundee Fine Art Exhibition*, a curious mix of rather childish cartoons with lithographic reproductions of paintings from the exhibition. The "Special Artist" in question was James Russell (figure 175), a chemist by trade who was fondly known as 'Druggy' Russell, and who was President of the Dundee Amateur Art Association. Three editions were published by William Kidd during the course of the 1877 exhibition, followed by a compilation reprint. Later editions (which appeared sporadically up to 1883) were published by James P Mathew and were of altogether better quality (the 1879 one was considered of sufficient importance to be included in the time capsule placed under the statue of Robert Burns). This was largely due to the involvement of other (and better) artists, with Russell acting as editor. The series also branched out onto other topics – for example *Our Special Artist at the Dog Show* (1879).

In 1878 Kidd published the first edition of *The Piper o' Dundee*, and since its style and several of the artists working on it are the same as *Our Special Artist* it seems likely that Russell was its editor. Several cartoons were included, all of them fairly crude and mostly identified only by cryptic monograms such as XYZ. The result seems not to have met with much enthusiasm,

time he was already sending his work to London – his cartoons appeared in the magazine *Fun* in 1892, he was given a full page in *The Strand* the same year, and in 1893 contributed a comic strip to the early children's paper *Chums*.[29] In late 1893 he left Dundee and moved to Edinburgh, where he had recently had his first painting accepted by the RSA. At the Academy's Life Schools, according to the London *Evening News*, he "won more prizes than he could with convenience get into his portmanteau".[30] Just over a year later he settled in London, and over the next few years had his work published in a host of publications including *Punch*, *Cassell's Magazine*, *Lady's Realm*, *Harmsworth London Magazine*, *The Rambler*, *The Longbow*, *Pick-Me-Up*, *Illustrated Bits*, *The Quiver*, *Pall Mall Magazine* and *Penny Pictorial Magazine*.[31] He also spent some time as art editor of *Black & White*, and he described his work for that paper to the *Art Record* in 1901:

> "it is my duty to portray the leading event of the week. Society functions are my especial *forte*. The work has often to be done in great haste. It not uncommonly happens that I attend a banquet or drawing-room on Friday, and the drawing has to appear on the following Monday. After working all night, the morning brings the milkman, and a telegram urging me to hurry up a little more."[32]

Cowper did not forget his native city, however, continuing to show works at the GAA exhibitions and staging a solo exhibition of his illustrations at Robert Scott's gallery in 1900, where he claimed to have "sold nearly all my originals."[33] One of the pictures he exhibited with the GAA was an oil painting of Auchmithie fishermen – Cowper often spent time there painting with W B Lamond, and the latter sometimes included Cowper's work in his own exhibitions.[34]

176. David Burns Gray, Advertisement for Paterson Sons & Co, from *The Piper o' Dundee*, 1890 *(Libraries, Leisure & Culture Dundee)*.

as the *Piper* did not reappear until 1886. Far more successful was Russell's next venture, *The Wizard of the North*, which first appeared in 1879 and ran monthly until Russell's death in 1912. It was printed in Kirkcaldy until 1880 when James P Mathew of Dundee took over.[38]

A mixture of humorous stories, cartoons, local news and gossip, the *Wizard* soon took off. One reason may have been that from its second issue the magazine's pages were significantly enlivened by the work of Martin Anderson. In 1891, when Anderson was the toast of London, Russell was proud to relate that "for fully three years he was a regular and valued contributor to its [the *Wizard's*] pages, supplying upwards of 100 sketches and over a dozen cartoons."[39]

In 1881, a very young John Duncan joined the *Wizard's* ranks, his first identifiable contribution being a centre-spread in September showing two fashionable ladies enjoying the Fine Art Exhibition (figure 25). At least nineteen further drawings (usually monogrammed JTD) can be found up to July 1883, when presumably Duncan's *Advertiser* duties took over.[40] Many years later, when Duncan was made an Associate of the RSA, Russell informed his readers that "28 years ago, when a youth of 14, Mr Duncan had his first experiences in newspaper work by being employed on the *Wizard* staff." Duncan evidently enjoyed the experience, writing to Russell, "It was with you I made a serious start on the long journey, and your kindness I will not easily forget. I remember those days with much gratitude."[41]

For many readers the highlight of the *Wizard* was its Portrait Gallery, a regular series of full-page sketches of local worthies accompanied by a potted biography. Usually

unsigned, we know that many of the earlier examples were created by Robert C Farquharson (see chapter eight), while some of the later portraits were the work of George Salmond Peddie; both died young, Peddie aged only 27. His obituarist (presumably Russell, who seemed never to give his artists any credit until they were famous or dead) wrote: "Gifted with a keenly observant eye, his power of transferring his impressions to paper was strong and acute, and his sense of the harmony of colour won him an amount of success which few artists achieve."[42]

Born in 1883 (the same year Farquharson died), Peddie won a competition in the *People's Journal* which (in the midst of the Russo-Japanese war in 1904) asked readers to send in cartoons of "The Funny Little Jap".[43] Two years later he joined the Dundee Art Society and exhibited with them in 1909. He was described as "one of its young and promising members" when he died after a long illness in 1911.[44]

In 1886 the *Wizard* had its first serious competition when George Scrymgeour resurrected *The Piper o' Dundee* as a weekly paper (also published by James P Mathew). In 1884-5 Scrymgeour had edited a fortnightly literary and artistic review called *The Dilettante*, but this was unillustrated. At first it seemed that the new *Piper* would be the same, but in March 1887 a two page supplement was introduced featuring sketches by "DBG". This was David Burns Gray, who became one of the most frequent contributors to the magazine over the next few years. Gray had begun his working life in commercial practice, but "the bent of his mind was towards art and the artistic".[45] He first showed his work at the Fine Art Exhibition in 1885, and became an early member of the GAA. Perhaps his most recognisable work today is the portrait of William McGonagall that illustrates the first volume of *Poetic Gems* (originally printed by Winter, Duncan & Co in 1890). In 1894 he created a modern version of Henry Harwood's famous satire on Dundee's social and political elite, *The Executive*. The following year he moved to London where he enjoyed some success in book and magazine illustration, including occasional contributions to *Punch*. Suffering poor health for some time, he died in 1907.

The *Piper* soon began to copy the *Wizard's* portrait gallery feature, to which Gray contributed along with David Clark, John Francis Pollock and James Michael Brown. The latter was based mainly in Edinburgh and is best known as a landscape and genre painter, but he spent some time in Dundee, undertaking local illustration commissions (see figure 33), exhibiting at the Fine Art Exhibitions and playing golf for the Carnoustie Visitors.

Pollock was also better known as a landscape painter, and many of his topographical views also featured in the magazine. Born in Dundee c.1856, he first studied art in Dumbarton, returning about 1887 and exhibiting at the Fine Art Exhibitions in 1889 and 1891. In 1890 he became one of the original members of the GAA but his career as a painter never really took off. In 1906 the *Evening Telegraph* praised his Highland scenes, but the following year he was branching out in an entirely different direction, selling tinted light bulbs and flashing advertising signs.[46]

David Clark seems to have been the longest-serving lithographic artist in Dundee. He came from Kirkcaldy (via

Aberdeen) in about 1885 and worked for both the *Piper* (see figures 19 & 32) and the *Wizard* as well as taking up employment as a "lithographic writer" with the Leng company.[47] After five years at Leng's he was taken on as a designer by Burns & Harris, remaining there until his retirement in 1930. One of his most widely known designs was the tartan label used by Keiller's on their world-famous jars of marmalade. He died in 1937.[48]

John Duncan made one lasting contribution to *The Piper o' Dundee* before his move to London. His elaborate front cover design (figure 177) first appeared in May 1887 and remained in use until 1901 – it features a roguish piper in the centre surrounded by knights in armour on winged horses, one carrying a quill pen and one an artist's palette. Clara Young has noted the similarity to an advertising card created by Duncan which also features a figure on a winged horse holding a palette, this time bearing the words "John T Duncan, Artist, 26 Overgate, Dundee" accompanied elsewhere with the description "Illustrating, Designing, Etching".[49] Prospective clients visiting this address to see the artist might have been somewhat put off by the fact that it was actually his father's butcher's shop!

Also joining the *Piper*'s ranks in 1887 was Alick P F Ritchie, another who would go on to far greater success in London.[50] Born in Dundee in 1868, he began his drawing career in Brown & Simpson's shipyard (Simpson being his uncle), and was showing landscapes in oil at the Fine Art Exhibitions from the age of fifteen. He created small (and fairly undistinguished) cartoons for the *Piper* until 1890, then moved to London and succeeded in earning enough money to study in Antwerp.[51] Returning in 1892 he began sending increasingly stylised cartoons to a variety of magazines including *Eureka, The Ludgate Monthly, Penny Illustrated Paper, Pall Mall Budget, St Paul's* (to which Max Cowper was also contributing at the time) and *Sketchy Bits*. Like Cowper, Ritchie continued to exhibit with the GAA, sometimes showing original examples of his magazine work, like his *Studies in Straight Lines & Curves*, created for *Pick-Me-Up* (figure 178).[52]

He was also much in demand for theatrical and advertising posters – the *Celtic Annual* claimed that "some of the best known London posters are from his designs."[53] His series of chromolithographs entitled 'Men of the Day' was issued as a supplement to *Vanity Fair* from 1911-13 – a set is now held by the National Portrait Gallery. In 1912 he "compiled, invented, designed, rhymed, and pictured" a book entitled *Y? A Study in Zoo-all-awry*. The *Scotsman* explained: "Young people and their elders will be amused to make the acquaintance of such droll hybrids as the 'Octopussycat,' the 'Magpike,' the 'Crabbit,' and the 'Elephantelope'."[54]

During the Great War, Ritchie was also involved in creating an early animated film, *A Pencil and Alick P F Ritchie*, in which he creates lightning sketches which then come to life. It was shown in 1915 at the King's Theatre in Dundee under the title *Cartoons by Alick P F Ritchie* and was reissued in 1916 as *Alick Ritchie's Frightful Sketches (No 1)*, suggesting that more may have followed.[55] Ritchie died in 1938.[56]

Max Cowper and James Eadie Reid (who worked briefly for Anderson at the *Advertiser*) also contributed to the *Piper* in its first few years, as did an Arbroath-born artist called James Greig

177 John Duncan, *The Piper o' Dundee*, cover illustration, 1885 *(Libraries, Leisure & Culture Dundee)*.

178. Alick P F Ritchie, 'Study in Straight Lines & Curves', from *Pick-Me-Up*, c.1898. The original caption read, "Well, Uncle, I can hardly believe *you* are in *straightened* circumstances!" *(private collection)*.

No. 9.]   FEBRUARY 1898.   [ONE PENNY.

ART EDITOR.—Beautiful! beautiful! my friend, but where is the joke?

ARTIST.—The joke? Well, that comes in if you accept the sketch. Then the joke is on you.

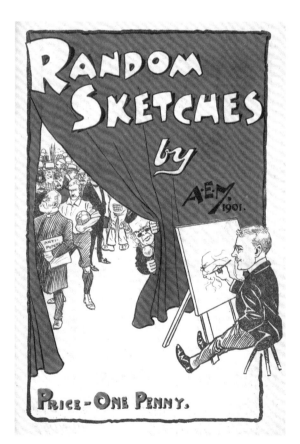

179. A E Morton, cartoon from *The Wasp*, 1898 *(University of Dundee Archive Services)*.

180. A E Morton, *Random Sketches by AEM*, cover illustration, 1901 *(Libraries, Leisure & Culture Dundee)*.

who worked on the magazine from 1889-92 before joining the veritable exodus to London and working on numerous magazines in the 1890s and 1900s. He would become better known, however, as art critic on the *Morning Post*, and for his influential books on Gainsborough and Raeburn.[57]

Scrymgeour was determined to establish a reputation for the *Piper*, and sent copies far and wide hoping for favourable reviews. Most if not all of these were soon quoted within the magazine's own pages – in 1891 the *Detroit Free Press* hailed it as "That bright northern light of journalism," while the *London Star* described it as "Dundee's *Punch*".[58] When the celebrated *Punch* cartoonist Harry Furniss visited Dundee later that year, a copy of the *Piper* was presented to him, and his hastily sketched reply was reproduced the following week.[59] In 1892, at an exhibition of work by British caricaturists in London, the *Piper* was "honoured with a special place".[60]

Another celebrated *Punch* cartoonist, George du Maurier, also visited Dundee in 1891 to give an Armitstead Lecture on "Social Pictorial Satire". Three years later, his wildly successful novel *Trilby* featured a painter from Dundee, Sandy McAllister, known as the Laird. Given that other characters in the novel were based on specific people (Whistler, for example), it's likely that du Maurier had one or more Dundee artists in mind here.

The Wizard of the North, meanwhile, was struggling to fill the gap left by Martin Anderson. Some good work was done by an artist signing himself 'Mac' (possibly DC Thomson staff artist Duncan McCallum), but the most frequent contributor at this time was 'AEM' (real name Alfred Elijah Morton, born in Dundee in 1878), who would go on to greater success nearly two decades later.

'Mac' and Morton were also the two principal illustrators of a short-lived rival periodical, *The Wasp*, subtitled 'The Dundee Flagellator' (figure 179). A monthly "chronicle of the latest gossip" which started in 1897, its editor J Edward Taylor stated in the first issue that "sketches and cartoons by the best local artists will adorn its pages".[61] In fact, none of their early results was particularly noteworthy, but that didn't prevent the editor proclaiming in issue seven that "cartoons have been *the* feature of the publication... welcomed by his [the editor's] fellow citizens as a revelation of the capabilities of the art of caricature."[62]

For its first three years, 'Mac' and Morton were the sole illustrators of the magazine, and by the end of that period the quality of their work had improved dramatically. In 1900 they produced two magazines of their own under the title *Squibs*. Consisting entirely of their caricatures of Dundee's politicians and other worthies, the two specials were published by James P Mathew. The following year, Mathew also published a solo effort by Morton, *Random Sketches by AEM* (figure 180).

The Wasp, meanwhile, had to find new contributors, including Tom Livingstone (see below) and George Wilkie Gahan. The latter was a decorator and sign writer who also turned his hand to painting, sculpture, music and poetry. Born in Newcastle in 1871, he moved to Dundee to set up business with his brother James (later an antique dealer) and although some of his work is of considerable merit, he never managed to escape from his commercial practice: "I would say that the

Dundee public don't buy my work simply because they have arrived at the amazing conclusion that a man who letters signs cannot be an artist."[63] He died in 1956.[64]

An unusual feature introduced to *The Wasp* in 1901 was a series of lithographic portraits of female beauties from the jute mills. Each factory was encouraged to nominate its most attractive workers, and the readers were asked to vote on their favourite! The magazine was now under its third publisher (there were four in all: Mrs Littlejohn, J B White, James Fraser and George Montgomery), but managed to survive (albeit with increasing irregularity) until August 1905, with one final issue in January 1910.

It was a *Wasp* (and *Wizard*) artist, Tom Livingstone, who by the turn of the century had emerged as the Leng company's principal artist. Born in 1864 and self-taught as an artist, he seems to have largely abandoned a career in painting to enter the more lucrative world of illustration. A member of the Dundee Art Club, he also exhibited with the GAA and the Fine Art Exhibitions during the 1890s. In his spare time he was a keen cyclist, and designed the trophy for the Forfarshire Cycling Club.[65] Although he joined the Leng staff in 1882, it would be another decade before his work became a regular feature, which it then remained for another 20 years.[66] It may have been Livingstone who introduced the first political cartoons to the Leng papers – though not yet a regular feature, these did appear sporadically, usually whenever there was a municipal election.

The finest cartoonist on the Leng staff during this period was arguably William McMann. Born in Rye, he had come to work at Leng's in the lithographic department about 1897, graduating to the "newspaper artists' room" about 1903-4.[67] His distinctive cartoons were usually accompanied by his own doggerel verse, most notably in two popular and long-lasting features – 'Kirsty at the Cooncil' in the *Evening Telegraph* (figure 181) and 'Granny's Gossip' in the *People's Journal*. He was still at work in Bank Street on the day he died in 1922, struck down by a heart attack on his way home at the age of only 56. An "intimate colleague" described him as follows:

> "A hard and conscientious worker, an inspiriting companion, and a warm and generous friend, one's pen hesitates when it would fain summarise William McMann's rare talents. His touch with pen and brush was as natural as it was perfect. Brain and hand never loitered to consider; everything came easily and immediately, and nothing was left out. In drawing or in verse his feeling was intuitive; it represented the thing as it was. A few strokes – and a portrait leapt to life… Always the effect was true, with the infinite beauty of the familiar."[68]

For sheer versatility, Tom Ross's work certainly stands out at this time. Best known for his lithographs of local scenes and a number of portrait commissions, his newspaper work included the *Courier* and *Wizard of the North*, though it was the *Advertiser* that employed him long-term – when he joined the GAA in 1896 he gave the *Advertiser* office as his address.[69] By this time photographs were taking the place of the more mundane illustrations, and Ross concentrated on topical cartoons and illustrations for serial adventures like 'The Convent Girl' or 'The Brand of Cain' – all of which he achieved in a much livelier and more detailed style than his predecessors.

181. William McMann, 'Kirsty at the Cooncil', from the *Evening Telegraph*, 1914 *(used by kind permission of D C Thomson & Co Ltd)*.

182. Tom Ross, 'The Black Watch arriving in Dundee', illustration of the Carters' and Dockers' Strike from the *Dundee Yearbook*, 1911 *(University of Dundee Archive Services)*.

183. The Artists' Room at D C Thomson's new Meadowside headquarters, from *The Pageant of the Press*, c.1905. Second from the left is Joseph Lee *(used by kind permission of D C Thomson & Co Ltd)*.

Thomson's, meanwhile, were undergoing a significant expansion. Having taken over *My Weekly* in 1888, they introduced new illustrated papers the *Weekly Welcome* (from 1896) and the *Red Letter* (from 1904). In 1905 they were reformed as D C Thomson & Co Ltd. One result of this was an increase in political cartoons, supplied mainly by Frank Coutts (figure 184) and Leonard Lowson. The two artists studied together at Dundee School of Art in the late 1890s, Coutts then spending five years training as an architect with Leslie, Ower & Allan before joining the Artistic Department of the *Courier* in 1907. Lowson, meanwhile, was contributing to the *Piper o'Dundee* before being reunited with Coutts at the *Courier*. He later emigrated to Canada, becoming cartoonist on the *Manitoba Free Press*, but died in 1916 at the age of just 30.

Another important development was the company's desire to attract female readers. Both the daily and weekly papers now featured regular fashion and society sections as well as romantic serial stories, and Thomson began to employ a number of 'lady artists', as they were known at the time. By the 1910s the *Courier* had at least three on its staff – Ruby Scott, Agnes Nicoll and Meta Mitchell (figure 185). As well as working together the three also attended evening classes at the new School of Art in the Technical College, suggesting that D C Thomson may have encouraged (or even insisted upon) this training for all its artists. One of Scott's sketchbooks still exists which shows life studies of a male model alongside fashion sketches (figure 186).[70] As well as illustrating the women's columns, the three ladies (all still teenagers when they joined the staff) were also responsible for designing the many adverts on which the papers depended. A publicity photograph was taken of Scott showing her deep in thought, with a book entitled *The Psychology of Advertising* carefully positioned on her desk! The social restrictions of the day were still in force, however – when Scott married Frank Coutts in 1925, she had to give up her work to keep house for him.

Leng also began employing female artists, and may have beaten Thomson to it – the popular 'Aunt Kate' column in the *People's Journal* led to numerous spin-off booklets in the 1900s, all distinctively illustrated. Marion Gardiner's name appears on at least one of these,[71] while Jean C Rollo may also have worked on them; in 1910 Mrs Churchill sat for a portrait by Rollo which appeared in the *Journal* (credited to "a *People's Journal* lady artist") on 10 December. Rollo had also studied at the School of Art, winning a King's Prize for Design in 1903. A member of the Dundee Art Society for several years, she was also well-known as a musician. She retired from Leng's after 21 years and died six years later in 1935.[72]

The Leng papers, meanwhile, were increasingly coming to use work by artists outwith Dundee. On 12 February 1910 the front cover of the *People's Journal* proclaimed "Cartoons by David Wilson" above the title, the first time any illustrator had had his work specifically promoted. Wilson was a regular *Punch* artist who that year would become chief cartoonist to the *Graphic*.[73] His stylised creations immediately stand out from the less adventurous work of his Dundee-based contemporaries, as do the occasional cartoons contributed by Tom Browne, a Nottingham-born artist widely credited with having pioneered the distinctive style of British comics.[74]

184. Top: Frank Coutts, *Winston Arrives in Safety*, ink on paper, 1908 (*University of Dundee Museum Services*).

185. Middle: 'Lady artists' at the *Courier* – Ruby Scott, Agnes Nicoll and Meta Mitchell, 1910s (*private collection*).

186. Bottom: Ruby Scott, *Untitled fashion sketch*, watercolour on paper, c.1910s (*private collection*).

187. Opposite page: Tom Ross, 'Dundee's Press Artists Outing', from *The Wizard of the North*, 1912 (*Libraries, Leisure & Culture Dundee*).

With such an increase of illustration in the newspapers, the *Wizard* and the *Piper* were evidently losing their popularity. The *Piper* ceased playing altogether in 1901, only to be resurrected in 1905 and finish again less than a year later. H G Low (see figure 6) was the principal artist during this last run, with Leonard Lowson contributing some good work. The *Wizard* survived until 1912, by which time Tom Ross was seemingly the sole contributor, though Jean C Rollo was also working on it in its penultimate year. The magazine came to an end with the death of its editor, James Russell, by now popularly known as 'The Wizard'. His obituary described him as "a loveable Bohemian, whose warm heart answered to many an appeal."[75]

By this time the city's newspaper artists were a recognised group, coming together for social gatherings such as the one shown by a Tom Ross cartoon of 'Dundee's Press Artists Outing' to Kinneswood in the summer of 1912 (figure 187). Six of the artists are shown in close-up, but are identified only by punning remarks in their speech bubbles. James Carrie and Nellie Coupar studied at the School of Art alongside Jean C Rollo, while the "sma' jaunt" may refer to the topographical artist David Small, who worked for the *Advertiser* for some 30 years.[76]

Included in this cartoon is the artist who had already come to dominate Dundee's newspapers and magazines in these pre-war years. Joseph Lee was born in Dundee in 1876 and began work at the age of fourteen in a solicitor's office.[77] It failed to inspire him, however, and in 1890 he enrolled in evening art classes at the YMCA. Much of the next few years he spent travelling, particularly in Canada, and his journeys inspired him to sketch and write poetry. As the century came to its close he attended Heatherley's School of Art in London,[78] and began to submit his drawings to magazines.[79] It was in London that he gained his first experience as a journalist, but was anxious to return to Dundee and edit his own publications.[80]

In 1907 Lee launched *The City Echo*, a monthly magazine similar in style to the *Wizard* and *Piper*, though smaller in size (figure 188). Lee wrote most (if not all) of the articles and certainly supplied all of the cartoons, originally signing them 'Crowquill'. His interest in art led to a number of fascinating articles, including an amusing parody headed 'Interview with Local Artist', in which the *Echo*'s representative asks the celebrated local artist 'Madder Brown' about Dundee's development as an art centre:

"'A glorious proposal,' cried Madder Brown enthusiastically, 'a glorious proposal. Too long has Dundee been a place of mere mills and marts, jutes and jams, we shall now try a little–'

'Tart,' suggested our representative, absently.

'Yes, art,' went on Madder Brown. 'Dundee will take a foremost place not only as the home of industry but as the nursery of rats – arts I mean.'"[81]

Although Lee's tone in the *Echo* was humorous, he was always keen to get his political message across, and in 1909 he launched a socialist paper, *The Tocsin*, described in chapter three. Photographs were more common than cartoons in this, but Lee did include number of satirical depictions of Dundee's new MP, Winston Churchill. *The Tocsin* ended after seven issues, and the last *City Echo* appeared in 1912, replaced almost immediately by Lee's re-launch of *The Piper o' Dundee* ("with which is incorporated *The City Echo*"). It was really the *Echo* in all but name, and Lee was still illustrating the whole thing himself. This new monthly version of the *Piper* lasted only a year.

In 1909 Lee joined the staff of Leng's as artist and art and music critic, but soon rose to become editor of the *People's Journal*. Also on the staff at that time was the writer R J B Sellar, who recalled him years later in an article for the *Scots Magazine*:

"He was a striking-looking man. He was not tall, but he was broad and powerful-looking. He had a noble head, a resolute mouth, and unforgettably interesting eyes, glowing, slumbering eyes. He was immensely masculine and vital. In mood, he could be as capricious as Arran weather. He was gay but prickly, genial yet passionate. But his anger went as quickly as it came, expelled by a gust of explosive laughter. He argued fiercely for the things he believed in, but there was no more generous opponent. A fascinating, friendly fellow, abrim with character and humour. He had an immense gusto for life, and it was because of his foibles that one loved his sterling virtues."[82]

188. Top left: Joseph Lee, *The City Echo*, cover for the first issue, 1907 (*University of Dundee Archive Services*).

189. Above: Joseph Lee, *Untitled sketch*, watercolour on paper, c.1916 (*University of Dundee Museum Services*).

190. Top right: Joseph Lee, *Beeskow*, pencil on paper, 1918 (*University of Dundee Museum Services*).

Lee was also becoming established as a poet – his first book, *Tales o' our Town*, was published by George Montgomery in 1910 and contained many of his distinctive line drawings. He was also in demand to illustrate other works, such as *Dundee from the Tramcars* (1908), *The Regality of Kirriemuir* (1909) and *Lochee as It Was and as It Is* (1911).

When the Great War erupted, the male staff of Leng's and Thomson's rushed to enlist, and Lee (though 38 and suffering from bronchial asthma) soon followed suit. Along with many others from Dundee he enlisted in the 4th Battalion of the Black Watch. At Neuve Chapelle, Loos and the Somme he experienced first-hand the horrors of warfare, and found expression for his experiences in poetry and art, both of which he sent back to Dundee for publication in the *People's Journal*. His first book of war poems, *Ballads of Battle*, was published in 1916 while he was still at the front, and received favourable reviews both in Britain and in the United States.[83] Undoubtedly a major part of the book's powerful sense of authenticity came from Lee's own illustrations, twelve of which he also sent to the Dundee Art Society for their 1916 exhibition. They included *Dawn in the Trenches* (which Lee left unfinished on the first morning of the Battle of Neuve Chapelle) and were praised by the *Courier* for their "intense pathos... drawn with a firm hand and much keen characterisation."[84] In December that year the *Scotsman* named Lee along with Rupert Brooke and A P Herbert as the most popular poets of the war.[85]

Lee was able to send further drawings for the 1917 Art Society exhibition, including a "sympathetic drawing of

'German Prisoners'", [86] and his second volume of poetry, *Work-a-day Warriors*, was published later that year. In November, however, Lee and many of his comrades were taken prisoner during the Battle of Cambrai. Their destination was Karlsruhe camp in Germany, where Lee joined officers from seventeen different nationalities. Despite numerous attempts, no one ever managed to escape from Karlsruhe. En route, Lee had persuaded one of his captors to buy him a sketchbook and pencil, and after careful scrutiny he was allowed to keep these and use them freely within the camp. His portraits of his fellow prisoners soon attracted attention. As Lee later recalled:

"One day I found the Commandant looking over my shoulder. He was keenly interested, suggested that he might give me a sitting, and reverted several times to the question of price. Finally I hinted that while I could not dream of accepting monetary recompense, he could, if he cared to be so complaisant, connive at my escape by way of part payment!"[87]

To keep themselves entertained, the prisoners had created their own theatre where they performed plays and staged musical concerts, something Lee already had experience of from his time in France with the Black Watch. He soon found himself pressed into service as "scene-painter, scene-shifter, poster-artist, actor, prompter, 'noises-off,' and playwright."[88]

In July 1918 Lee was moved to another camp at Beeskow (figure 190). Here security was much more lax – a parole system was introduced which allowed Lee to wander unaccompanied into town and sketch his surroundings.

When the Armistice came Lee returned briefly to Dundee then settled in London and became sub-editor for the *News Chronicle*. From 1919-23 he attended classes at the Slade School of Fine Art, where his fellow students included Stanley Spencer. He remained at the *Chronicle* until 1944 then retired to Dundee, where he died in 1949.

During the Great War the Dundee papers had followed Lee's progress with both pride and apprehension. On 27 November 1915 the *People's Journal* devoted a full-page spread to "'Dundee's Own' Artist at the Front", reporting on his whereabouts and reproducing fifteen of his sketches along with two poems. But Lee was just one of many newspaper artists fighting overseas, and the female illustrators who remained anxiously awaited news of all of them.[89] Ruby Scott kept an album in which she pasted cuttings relating to her friends and colleagues from D C Thomson's art department at the front. They tell the stories of Sergeant-Piper Dan McLeod of the Black Watch, a process blockmaker who was awarded the Military Medal; of Private Walter Auld of the Argyll & Sutherland Highlanders, a linotype operator awarded the DCM but then reported missing in action; of Private Alex C Brown of the Black Watch, a *Courier* artist killed in action at Aubers Ridge; and of Private George Rushworth of the Fife & Forfar Yeomanry, a *Weekly News* artist who died at Gallipoli.[90]

Scott's main concern, however, was her husband-to-be Sergeant Frank Coutts, serving with the 5th Black Watch. One of his letters to her survives, in which he describes his billet, somewhere in France: "This one is built over with sandbags and contains two beds, a table and some shell boxes used as shelves. It might stop a direct hit from a very tiny shell, but I hope it isn't tested during my tenancy... If you want to know about dug-outs and such, ask Joe Grey, or go to his exhibition."[91]

"Joe" was Joseph Gray, a press artist who, like Lee, sent his war sketches home to be exhibited.[92] Born in South Shields in 1890, Gray came to Dundee around 1912 to work as an illustrator for the *Courier*. On the outbreak of war he enlisted in the 4th Black Watch and, like Lee, was with them at the Battles of Neuve Chapelle and Loos. His biographers have written about his wartime career:

"Once he reached the trenches Gray's talents as a draughtsman were quickly recognised. Captain Boase appointed him his observer, a role which involved countless expeditions into the firing zone to make sketches of enemy positions. He was also called upon to duplicate trench maps, as he did before the Battle of Festubert, marking out the positions of the men of his battalion."[93]

In December 1915 he was invalided home suffering from deafness due to shell shock, but managed to find a new role as war artist and correspondent to *The Graphic*.[94] He began work on a series of pictures documenting the life of the 4th Black Watch, which were exhibited at Robert Scott's gallery in February 1917. The *Courier* hailed them as "a vivid panorama of life on the Flanders front, its squalor, its perils, its moments grim and gay, and its extraordinarily varied and picturesque accessories."[95] Gray later presented several of his pictures (and their copyright) to the Scottish branch of the Red Cross, to be auctioned to raise funds. Starting in December 1917, Gray also wrote a series of articles on the history of the 4th Black Watch which were published in the *Advertiser*.

At the end of the war, a selection of Gray's drawings were shown in a special Victory Exhibition at the Kinnaird Hall. The director of the Imperial War Museum, Sir Martin Conway, opened the exhibition and declared Gray's work to be "a record which was of priceless value". Unlike so many war pictures in the past, he claimed, these were "the work of a man who had fought."[96]

In the years that followed, Gray turned many of his drawings into large-scale oil paintings, including *Ration Party of the 4th Black Watch* (in the Imperial War Museum) and *The 4th Black Watch in the Attack* (figure 191). His most ambitious work was *After Neuve Chapelle*, a depiction of the battalion on the day of their first engagement with the enemy on 10 March 1915. The *Evening Telegraph* claimed: "It is a work vivid with the glow of personal experience and surcharged with the tragedy of a great and disastrous day."[97] The painting was begun in Gray's Barnhill studio in 1921 (see figure 192) and presented to Dundee's permanent collection the following year by the few surviving officers of the battalion.

While Lee largely gave up his artistic career after the war, Gray continued to work with great success as both painter (receiving several other commissions for memorial paintings of wartime regiments) and particularly as a printmaker, becoming highly acclaimed for his drypoint etchings. He moved to

London in 1931 and during the Second World War became an acknowledged expert on camouflage (having begun research into the topic in the mid-1930s).

In 1941 Gray wrote to Mary Meade (who would become his second wife):

> "In the last war, most of my best friends were killed along side of me. As they went, one by one, all in their early twenties – all men of subtlety and imagination – intellectuals or 'intelligents' with the supreme and trained bodies of the first armies – really the best in the country – I remember the conviction that I formed that it was ridiculous and absurd to assume that because their bodies were shattered and finished that they were finished too. Of course they went on – Just as we will go on…"[98]

He died in 1963.[99]

With so much of the younger talent away at the front, only the older male artists remained on the Leng papers in the late 1910s. William McMann continued to be a strong presence,and was now joined by the Glasgow cartoonist Dyke White, who supplied regular football and political caricatures.

The highlight during this period was the *People's Journal's* first regular cartoon strip, 'Haw Wull', created by former *Wasp* and *Wizard* artist Alf Morton (figure 193). Wull was a hapless loafer who first appeared in April 1912 and by February 1913 had been promoted to page one. The format was simple – Wull was constantly out of work and each week saw him try his hand at some kind of gainful employment, with disastrous results. The

war knocked Wull off the front cover but his exploits continued unabated, often featuring his attempts to enter military service – with equally unfortunate consequences! Never remotely deterred by his consistent failures, Wull continued to appear until July 1918. The following March, Morton attempted a new series, 'Private Smiler', about a soldier returning from the war and trying to re-adjust to civilian life. Possibly the humour was too politically sensitive, since the strip only lasted five weeks and was then replaced by the return of Haw Wull, whose adventures continued just as before until finally coming to an end in October 1919.

191. Top: Joseph Gray, *The 4th Black Watch in the Attack, 1915*, oil on canvas, 1922 *(The Black Watch Museum)*.

192. Above:Joseph Gray at work on his painting *After Neuve Chapelle*, 1921 *(used by kind permission of D C Thomson & Co Ltd)*.

193. Opposite page: A E Morton, 'Haw Wull', from the *People's Journal*, 1914 *(used by kind permission of D C Thomson & Co Ltd)*.

The *Advertiser*, meanwhile, had been sourcing most of its wartime illustrations from other publications – mostly *Punch*, though they sometimes reprinted German cartoons as well. By 1916 there were more illustrations in the paper than ever before, but none of them by a local artist! The *Courier*, on the other hand, downsized dramatically during the war – each issue was only four pages long and was notably bereft of illustrations. By contrast, pictures were a key feature of the *Post Sunday Special* (later renamed the *Sunday Post*), introduced by Thomson in 1914 as a direct result of readers' insatiable desire for war news – it included a regular feature called 'How the Cartoonists View the War' which reprinted cartoons from around the world.[100]

As the Dundee papers entered the post-war world, local cartoons began to creep back in, but photographs were now entirely dominant. A younger audience was now being targeted, and Leng scored a surprise hit with the long-running serial adventures of Billy and Bunny, introduced to the *Advertiser* in 1919 by staff artist James Crighton.[101] Both Leng and Thomson lost many of their staff (including several artists) at the time of the General Strike. Soon after, the two great newspaper empires merged to form Thomson-Leng Publications (though in practice Thomson had held a controlling interest in Leng's for over twenty years), and the joint *Courier & Advertiser* became Dundee's new daily paper.[102]

Before concluding this chapter it is worth mentioning five Dundee illustrators who had only brief connections with the city before their careers really took off, but whose success in their field demands their inclusion here. The first is Malcolm Patterson, who was born in Twickenham in 1873 to Dundee parents. Educated in Bristol, he originally trained as an engineer but abandoned this for art, studying in Paris and London and then contributing illustrations to publications such as *Punch*, *Fun* and the *Penny Pictorial Magazine*. In 1897 he showed original artwork from *The Idler* and *Pick-Me-Up* at the GAA exhibition, giving his address in the catalogue as "Inverlaw, Dundee". After the Great War he settled in St Andrews, becoming an art teacher at St Leonard's School. He developed an exceptional talent for etching, and his detailed views of St Andrews and the surrounding countryside are still much reproduced.[103] He died in 1941.

The second is Hutton Mitchell, famous as the first artist to draw legendary schoolboy Billy Bunter. Born William Hutton Mitchell in Kennoway, Fife in 1872, Mitchell began his art career on the *Piper o' Dundee* and as a member of the GAA before studying at Heatherley's in London and the Académie Julian in Paris.[104] He spent some time painting in the Netherlands, and became known for his Dutch-style watercolours. He was contributing to London magazines by 1892 and over the years had work in *The Tatler*, *The Bystander*, *The Longbow*, *The Graphic* and many others. Thanks partly to the influence of Sir Arthur Conan Doyle, he became an acclaimed novelist in 1923 with *The Deviations of Diana*. The *Courier* predicted "one of the greatest literary successes of recent years" but only one further novel followed.[105] Mitchell joined the weekly boys' paper *The Magnet* from its first issue in 1908, and among other things illustrated Frank Richards' stories of Greyfriars School, which quickly became the most popular feature. Billy Bunter was just a minor character at first but soon took centre-stage, though Mitchell's illustrations of him are somewhat different from the classic look the character later adopted. The original Bunter was apparently based on Mitchell's sons, who later recalled "stuffing pillows into their trousers to achieve a satisfactory rotundity."[106] After 39 issues, Mitchell was replaced and other artists would develop Bunter into the instantly recognisable figure he would soon become. Later in life, Mitchell moved to Canada (where one of his sons, Bruce, became a successful artist) but died in England in 1935.

The other three artists were brothers, following the same profession and all enjoying significant success.[107] The three Adamson boys (Sydney, Howard and Stanley) grew up in Mount Pleasant House, Hawkhill Place, and attended the West End Academy in Tay Street.[108] Their artistic talents were presumably inherited from their father James – a coal and brick merchant by occupation, he was a sculptor in his spare time, showing his work in the Fine Art Exhibitions. According to the *Courier*, he was also "a buyer and critic of pictures, whose friendship and criticism were esteemed by John Pettie and other artists of eminence."[109] Born in 1872, Sydney was his eldest son, and seems to have been the only one to work professionally in Dundee, exhibiting at the Fine Art Exhibitions from the tender age of eleven while studying at the School of Art. After a time in Edinburgh learning lithography, he took a studio at 61 Reform Street (later occupied by E S Hodgson and W B Lamond) and began seeking portrait commissions

LESLIE'S WEEKLY
ILLUSTRATED

NEW YORK, SEPTEMBER 23, 1899.   PRICE, 10 CENTS.

THE FIRST INTIMATION OF THE ENEMY.

AN INCIDENT OF THE CAPTURE OF CALUMPIT—WHILE MAJOR BELL, WITH TWO TROOPS OF CAVALRY, WAS ADVANCING TOWARD QUINGUA, THE FILIPINOS SUDDENLY OPENED FIRE, KILLING AND WOUNDING A NUMBER OF OUR BRAVE CAVALRYMEN.
DRAWN BY SYDNEY ADAMSON FROM PHOTOGRAPHS AND DESCRIPTIONS FORWARDED BY THE SPECIAL CORRESPONDENTS OF "LESLIE'S WEEKLY" IN MANILA.

while contributing cartoons to the *Piper o' Dundee*.[110] He soon left for London and achieved rapid success as illustrator for the likes of the *Pall Mall Magazine* and *Harper's Magazine*, and in 1894 was appointed art editor of Jerome K Jerome's magazine *To-Day*. His association with Jerome continued on *The Idler*.[111] The same year he also began contributing to the celebrated *Yellow Book*.

In 1895 Adamson became co-director of the Artistic Supply Company, a short-lived agency that helped promote the interests (and guard the copyright) of several commercial illustrators, including his brother Stanley, Max Cowper and other notable artists such as the Beggarstaff Brothers. It may not have been a coincidence that most of the artists on their books were Scottish.

Adamson spent some time studying in Paris before sailing for New York in 1898, where an unexpected new career opened up for him as a war correspondent. He was sent to the Philippines by the magazine *Leslie's Weekly* (figure 194), but earned his reputation as "one of America's most venturesome and clever war artists" during the Boxer rising in China.[112] Travelling with the American 9th Infantry, Adamson was able to create some of the first published images of the conflict, at considerable risk to his own safety. One of the soldiers involved in the campaign to take Tientsin recalled: "He was under fire all day long... he was all over the field and absolutely fearless, and the wonder is he wasn't killed."[113] While there Adamson endured malaria, dysentery and temporary blindness, and according to the *Evening Telegraph* "had the distinction of being mentioned in despatches for bravery in the field."[114]

Adamson himself wrote about his experiences with the 9th at Tientsin, suggesting he thrived in this terrible environment:

"There was nothing lacking, in this arena of fire and death, of those elements of spectacular and dramatic interest which the world associates with war – the dead horses and human corpses; the ruined smoking buildings; the roar of guns and the rattle of infantry; the long train of wounded and the hideously mutilated dead; the shells bursting in mid-air or exploding on the earth...; the quiet heroism of the officers, and the dash of the men... With all its horrors it was grand. On such a day the commonplace and the ordinary are driven from one's mind. The game is a mighty one and the stakes are life and death. Until one has seen men in battle it is impossible to truly understand the human race".[115]

Adamson became as well known for his journalism as for his art, and he continued to act as travel writer for *Leslie's* and *Harper's Magazine*. In 1914 he was one of the first artists at the front, but little is recorded of his wartime activities.[116] A member of the Society of Illustrators, he exhibited with them as well as the RA in London and the New Salon in Paris. He died in London in 1958.[117]

Born in 1873, Howard Somerville Adamson studied engineering at Dundee Technical Institute and later in Glasgow (his sister Mabel claimed he was "something of a genius" at mechanics[118]) but gave up the profession to follow his brothers into the art world. With Mabel he sailed for New York in 1897 and began his career as an illustrator on magazines such as *Life* and *Pearson's*. In 1900 a collection of his original drawings was shown at Robert Scott's gallery in Dundee, by which time he was already "becoming known as an original and vivacious illustrator."[119] The year before that he had settled in London and under the name Howard Somerville contributed to *Punch*, *The Red Magazine* and *Illustrated London News*. He became best known as a portraitist, exhibiting his work at the RA, the RSA, the National Portrait Society and the Royal Society of Portrait Painters among others (figure 195). In 1939 he won the Gold Medal at the Paris Salon for *Norah*, one of two portraits he undertook of the stage actress and film star Norah Baring.[120] He retired to Bristol and died there in 1952. Despite all his successes as an artist, his proudest achievement – according to his sister – was winning a medal for Machine Construction in the National Competition at the age of nineteen.[121] After his death she arranged for the distribution of many of his surviving paintings to public art collections across Britain.

The third brother, Ernest Stanley Adamson, was born in 1877, but left Dundee at the age of thirteen to find work both in London and America.[122] Taking the delightfully magniloquent 'Penrhyn Stanlaws' as his professional name (after variations

194. Top: Sydney Adamson, 'The First Intimation of the Enemy', cover illustration for *Leslie's Weekly*, 1899 *(private collection)*.

195. Opposite page top: Howard Somerville, *In the Studio (Self Portrait)*, oil on canvas, c.1916 *(The Atkinson, Southport)*.

196. Opposite page bottom: Penrhyn Stanlaws, cover illustration for *Hearst's*, 1919 *(private collection)*.

including 'Penryn Stanley' and 'Stanilaus'), he earned enough money as an illustrator of the latest female fashions to attend Princeton University and then the Académie Julian in Paris. One of the more unlikely acquaintances he made while there was the infamous Satanist Aleister Crowley, who recalled him in his memoirs:

"One day one of the Americans introduced the 'great American artist, Penrhyn Stanlaws'. His name was Stanley Adamson and his birthplace Dundee. He had begun his life in the traditional manner of the great by holding horses' heads and earning dimes. Somehow or other, while quite a youth, he had sprung into popular favour and was already earning £2,000 a year or more by dashing off a succession of spidery scrawls representing fluffy American flappers in various attitudes. He had come to Paris to study art seriously.

I was delighted with him… His innocent earnestness, without any root to it, his infatuation for 'uplift', his total ignorance of the morality of the artist, his crude prejudices based upon Sunday School, his attitude to everything assumed in blissful unconsciousness of a background: this was all perfectly charming. He had all the fascination of a new penny toy."[123]

In 1907 Stanlaws returned to New York and became more fashionable than ever as cover artist for the *Saturday Evening Post*, *Hearst's*, *Metropolitan* and others (figure 196). As one of the most sought-after artists in America, his models became instant celebrities. One was Anna Q Nilsson, whose success as

the 'Stanlaws Girl' led directly to Hollywood stardom. In 1920 Stanlaws himself entered the film business as a director, and two years later was directing Nilsson alongside Bebe Daniels and Adolphe Menjou in the film *Pink Gods*.[124] He was also a playwright, having plays staged in London in 1912 and at Yale in 1915. One of his scripts was accepted by Sir Henry Irving, but it is not known whether this was ever performed. In 1915 he became founder of the *Hotel des Artistes* in New York, a large-scale artists' collective building featuring about 100 apartments and studio spaces, constructed at a cost of $1.25 million. These various enterprises distracted him only briefly from his painting, and in the 1930s he held a number of solo exhibitions, including one in London. He moved permanently to Los Angeles in the late 1940s and painted portraits until he was tragically burned to death when his studio caught fire in 1957.[125]

Stanlaws' career is perhaps the most extraordinary of all Dundee's newspaper and magazine artists, yet what is arguably even more astonishing is the fact that the city should have produced so many highly successful illustrators and cartoonists in this relatively short time. But despite the energetic efforts of editors like James Russell and George Scrymgeour, the city's own magazine industry was in no position to rival that of London, and it was there that so many of Dundee's 'black and white' artists had to go to realise their ambitions. All that was to change when D C Thomson decided to launch their first children's story paper, *Adventure*, in 1921. It proved an instant success and was soon followed by *The Rover* (1922), *The Wizard* (1923), *The Skipper* (1930) and *The Hotspur* (1933). With these 'Big Five' Dundee proved that it could take on London, and when *The Dandy* and *The Beano* were added to its arsenal, the city finally emerged triumphant.

CHAPTER SIX

Art & Education

Dundee has long been recognised as a centre for art education. Duncan of Jordanstone College of Art & Design is now one of the leading art schools in the UK, with an impressive roll call of teachers and graduates. Yet the development of the College was a slow and complicated business – particularly as regards James Duncan of Jordanstone's bequest – and in its early days it was just one of several institutions competing to offer training for the city's aspiring artists.

The British art education system began in 1852 when the Board of Trade set up a department of Practical Art (later to become the Science & Art department (S&A)) led by the influential Henry Cole. Cole established a rigid system of art training centred around what would eventually become known as the National Art Training Schools, which would set exams and award certificates for students at provincial art schools around the country. The government awarded grants for local authorities to run these schools, in return for which they had to suffer strict control by Cole's department.[1]

Only a few towns created new art schools from scratch – most extended or adapted existing resources, and Dundee was no exception. The High School of Dundee (referred to as the Public Seminaries prior to its official naming in 1859) was the leading source of education at the time and in 1853 its directors set up a special committee to report "on the subject of a School of Art or Design".[2] Although fears were expressed that "the people of Dundee did not sufficiently appreciate the advantages of such an institution", it was agreed to pursue the idea with the Board of Trade.[3] Within a few months, the necessary agreements were thought to be in place, and on 23 December a notice appeared in the *Advertiser* announcing that

> "the Dundee School of Art and Science, for instruction in the principles of Drawing, Colouring, &c, conducted by a certified master of the Department of Science and Art, will be Opened in the Seminaries about the end of January next. The master will teach all kinds of Painting in Oil and Water Colours, Figure and Landscape, Perspective, Mechanical, Architectural, and Geometrical Drawing."[4]

The master employed was a Mr Croome, formerly head of a School of Design at Waterford. The existing drawing master at the Seminaries, D R Andrews, was offered a pension to retire.[5] Unfortunately, it soon emerged that the directors of the Seminaries had misunderstood the terms under which the S&A were willing to sponsor Croome's appointment. While the directors were expecting "an immediate grant of at least £70", all the government proposed to give was £10.[6] Croome, having just moved to Dundee with his family, was forced to resign his post and leave again immediately, with £20 awarded to him for his trouble. Andrews was told he would no longer get his pension "but must just resume his easel and his brushes."[7]

197. John Kennedy *(Libraries, Leisure & Culture Dundee)*.

Although the Town Council and the Seminaries tried to place the blame for this fiasco entirely onto the government (who were said to be generally "shabby... in Scotch affairs"), the *Courier* concluded that the directors should "in future go about their business in a more business-like way, and make no engagements without having first provided the means of fulfilling them."[8]

It would be another two years before a second, and this time successful, attempt was made to establish an art school. In April 1856 John Kennedy (figure 197) came from Dublin to begin teaching evening classes under the title Dundee School of Art. During the day he would also teach art to pupils at the Seminaries and other local schools, as well as holding private classes for "ladies and gentlemen".[9] The government this time agreed to pay Kennedy a salary of £20 based on his existing qualifications, to be increased by £10 a year for each additional certificate gained. They would also make up any shortfall should his total annual income (including fees) be less than £70.[10] In reporting on the matter to the directors of the Seminaries, the convenor of the organising committee noted "the satisfaction with which this appointment would be hailed by the artisan class in town", having found himself inundated with names of potential students.[11]

The new School of Art proved a success, raising the teaching of art "from the fancy picture cult it had been to a serious science".[12] By 1860 Kennedy was teaching 132 day students and 239 evening students (as well as 1,376 school children at the High School and elsewhere).[13] He was evidently an inspirational teacher, and many of his students went on to considerable success. As early as 1859, for example, one of them, Andrew Stevenson, was appointed head of a new School of Art in Halifax.[14] Speaking not long after Kennedy's death in 1904, another former student, Councillor James Gordon, claimed "I owe [him] a debt of gratitude that I gladly acknowledge here. Kindly, refined, acute, and able, zealous as a teacher, he gained the esteem of all his pupils, and I am sure his memory is dear to many as it is to me."[15]

Only a few school registers seem to have survived from Kennedy's time, but they show that the evening students were generally in their late teens or early twenties, and the most common professions listed were joiners and mechanics.[16] This was in line with the government's original intentions in financing such schools – to teach art to the so-called 'artisan' classes as a means of improving the quality of British workmanship

198. David Hutton and Robert Cowie, illustration from *The First Grade Freehand Drawing Book*, a set of drawing manuals created by John Kennedy in 1863, illustrated by his pupil assistants *(Libraries, Leisure & Culture Dundee)*.

and manufacturing. As we shall see, however, such laudable intentions would soon be compromised by the system of funding Henry Cole had initiated.

In 1875 Kennedy retired and was succeeded by one of his former pupils, William Mortimer Grubb. Born in 1849, he had been educated at the Seminaries then started his teaching career in London before returning to his *alma mater*.[17] As an artist his main talent was landscapes (John Duncan recalled his "expert touch in watercolour"[18]) and he exhibited several of these at the Dundee Fine Art Exhibitions, the RA and the RSA during the 1890s.

Under Grubb the School of Art flourished – by 1880 there were 743 students enrolled.[19] It was under Grubb that most of the artists discussed so far in this book received their first art training – in the 1870s Allan Ramsay and Frank Laing, in the 1880s John Duncan, Stewart Carmichael, Alec Grieve, Charles G L Phillips, David Ramsay Sellars, Sydney Adamson and Richard D Winter, and in the 1890s Alick Ritchie, David Foggie, George Dutch Davidson, Frank Coutts and Leonard Lowson. Some of the city's leading architects also studied under Grubb, including T M Cappon and James Langlands. There were also many young artists who came from outside the city to study at the school – some would go on to achieve fame in other parts of the country, such as Henry Wright Kerr and James Watterston Herald.[20]

Speaking to the Dundee Art Society some two decades after his student days, John Duncan gave a vivid description of the School, describing it as a "great centre of artistic life in Dundee":

"The room – it was only one room – was divided by a great black mysterious curtain [see figure 199]. In front of the curtain was the outer court, … given up to mechanical drawing, and to elementary drawing. We did elaborate stippled drawings in black chalk pencil… The half of the room behind the curtain was reserved for the elect, the initiated, the art students proper. I still remember the solemn feeling with which I peeped into the occult place, which I was afterwards for a few years to know so well.

"The School of Art in Dundee was not a first-class Art School… It was only one room with a few casts and a few pictures. But to us who knew nothing better, it was a whole world. And it is astonishing that so much that was fine was packed into so small a place, and that we, with so little training, managed somehow to get so much out of it."[21]

Duncan was less certain about the way art had to be taught at the School, endlessly copying from the casts or lithographs: "one is not quite so sure whether it was very good art study to make the patient imitations of them we did. Some students would spend the whole quarter of a year on one drawing."[22]

Grubb may well have agreed with Duncan about this, but there was little he could do – as a government-sponsored art school, Dundee had to follow the National Course of

199. Antique Room, Dundee School of Art, c.1890s. William Grubb is standing centre, facing away from the camera *(Dundee City Archives)*.

200. William M Grubb, *Our Back Garden*, watercolour on paper, c.1897 *(Dundee City Council: Dundee's Art Galleries & Museums)*.

Instruction laid down by the S&A. As Stuart Macdonald has written, "no examination could be passed, no prizes won, no grants made, nor certificates obtained, except in specified stages of this course."[23]

This National Course was generally known as the South Kensington system, which was where the National Art Training Schools were based from 1863. Originally drawn up by Henry Cole and his art superintendent Richard Redgrave, it was divided into 23 stages within four sequential courses. First and most important was the Drawing Course – ten different stages of drawing and shading from models, casts and (eventually) the human figure. Following that was the Painting Course (seven stages), the Modelling Course (four stages) and finally the Design Course (two stages).[24] All but these last two stages were strictly imitative, and the department specified the various casts and prints that they expected the Schools of Art to use, all of which were copies of ones held in the South Kensington Museum (now the V&A), of which Cole was also the first

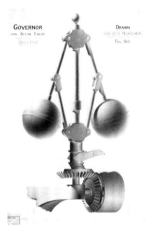

201. Top: Charles G L Phillips, *Untitled drawing of a classical cast (head of the horse of Selene)*, created as a 3rd grade student at Dundee School of Art, c.1882 *(Dundee City Council: Dundee's Art Galleries & Museums)*.

202. Above left: Charles G L Phillips, *Governor for Steam Engine*, technical drawing created as a student at Dundee School of Art, for which he won a National Bronze Medal, 1882 *(Dundee City Council: Dundee's Art Galleries & Museums)*.

203. Above right: Robert D Cairns, cover illustration for *The Book of the Bazaar*, 1896 *(Libraries, Leisure & Culture Dundee)*.

director. The theory was that repeated imitation would lead to better co-ordination of hand and eye, which was thought to be the basis of ability in art – it was a commonly held view among Victorian educators that drawing could be learned in the same way as writing, such that any intelligent person (child or adult) could learn how to do it by repeated copying.

Allied to this system were the three grades of examinations laid down by the department. The 1st Grade was the Elementary School level, which it was hoped most school children would pass. Following a review of art education in 1889, Dundee was pleased to boast that 1st Grade drawing "is taught in every public school without exception" and that the number being taught at this stage "has increased 10 times in 10 years".[25] The 2nd Grade was the Art Students Certificate Level, and it was these certificates that most students at the Dundee School of Art were aiming towards. Only a few would ever reach the 3rd Grade (figure 201), the Art Masters Certificate Level, which would qualify them to teach in a government-sponsored art school.[26]

Allied to the exam system was the National Competition. When a South Kensington inspector came to visit a local art school to supervise the 2nd and 3rd Grade examinations, a display of students' work would be prepared, from which he would select the best examples for entry into the competition. Gold, silver and bronze medals were awarded for the best drawings (figure 202). The top prize was a National Scholarship, which would pay for a year's study at the National Schools – this could only be won by students who had already gained medals in the final two stages of the National Course. As such it might have seemed like an impossible dream for most Dundee School of Art students, were it not for the fact that Grubb himself had achieved it. In 1878 David Anderson became the first of his students to win a Scholarship, and in the Fine Art Exhibitions of 1880 and 1881 he sent work up from London to be exhibited.

By this time a Scotch (later Scottish) Education Department (SED) had been formed to co-ordinate its own national system of education, but the South Kensington system remained in force. Although the strict teaching curriculum gradually began to be relaxed, the examination system remained unchanged until 1896, and the National Competition continued until 1915. Funding was allocated by government solely on the basis of exam results – a fixed grant would be paid for every piece of work that was accepted for a certificate or medal. This was why, as Duncan observed, Grubb encouraged his students to spend months working on specific drawings – he knew exactly what the examiners would be looking for. This often meant that the students most likely to succeed were those with enough time to devote to creating exam-worthy drawings, which generally excluded most of those from the working classes that the government schools had been set up to serve. Schools started to direct their energies towards day classes for students who didn't have to work for a living, and for which they could also charge higher fees. The High School was at an obvious disadvantage here, since it had school pupils to teach during the day, but this did not stop Grubb (like Kennedy before him) allowing a limited number of adults to attend his day classes alongside the children.[27]

Given its limited resources, there is no doubt that the School achieved outstanding success. At the winter prize-giving in 1880 it was claimed that only two other schools in Britain had achieved such good results.[28] Grubb evidently tried his best to vary the teaching where possible, inviting fellow artists to the School to speak to his students, and building up his own collection of prints and watercolours to show them.[29] He allowed his students to take inspiration from their local surroundings as well as the prescribed teaching aids from South Kensington – in 1880 student John McInroy won a bronze medal for his perspective drawing of the high girders of the Tay Bridge.[30]

A clear index of the success of the School is the number of its students who went on to win important teaching positions either locally or further afield. John Duncan recalled that "Seven of my fellow-pupils have now Art Schools of their own".[31] One of the most interesting of these was Henry Taylor Wyse. Born in Glasgow in 1870, Wyse moved to Dundee as boy and studied under Grubb before starting a successful teaching career, initially as assistant to D S Murray (see below)

at Morgan Academy, then more senior posts in Coatbridge, Arbroath and Edinburgh.[32] He also wrote a number of books to aid art teaching, starting with a set of designs for 2nd-grade freehand drawing, published in Dundee in 1891.[33] Later publications included more theoretical works such as *Modern Methods of Art Instruction*.[34]

Another example was John Gray, who was born in Dundee in 1877 and studied under Grubb before continuing his training at Glasgow School of Art. He then moved to the Borders where he taught art in Hawick for over 25 years. In 1927 he returned to Dundee as art master at Grove Academy. After his retiral he served as a governor of Dundee College of Art as well as becoming president of both the Dundee Art Society and the RSW. Following his death in 1957, McIntosh Patrick wrote that "he has been a tireless worker on behalf of art education in Dundee."[35]

Each year, Grubb was able to employ two or more assistants, most of whom were students who were working towards their Art Masters certificate. One of the first was his younger brother Alexander, but many more notable people were to come.[36] David Scott Murray, for example, was a silver medal-winning student who assisted Grubb in 1888-9 and went on to teach at Perth Academy before returning to Dundee as the first art master for Morgan Academy.[37] H T Wyse described him as being "full of idea and experiment".[38] Robert D Cairns (see figure 203) came up from Edinburgh to succeed Murray as Grubb's assistant, remaining until 1896 when he moved to take up a teaching post in Brechin. Both Murray and Cairns exhibited regularly at the Fine Art Exhibitions, and the latter also with the GAA. Working alongside both of them at the High School was Thomas Delgaty Dunn, who assisted Grubb from 1887 until 1892; we shall return to him shortly.

Probably the most famous of Grubb's pupil assistants was an 18-year-old David Foggie, whose work during 1896-8 earned him £15 a year, but involved only the "most elementary teaching, mostly occupied with sharpening pencils".[39] Foggie described the South Kensington system as "absurd" and over the next two decades he did only occasional teaching.[40] It was not until Foggie moved to Edinburgh that he would properly return to art education. In 1920, he was offered a part-time post as teacher of Life Drawing at Edinburgh College of Art, possibly at the recommendation of John Duncan, who was then on the Board of Management. During the next nineteen years, Foggie would teach some of the College's most celebrated students, including William Gillies, John Maxwell, William MacTaggart, Wilhelmina Barns-Graham and William Gear. Jack Firth claimed that Foggie "honed his students' drawing skills to the limits of their achievement".[41]

Foggie's criticisms of the South Kensington system were made many years after it had disappeared, but there were plenty who spoke against it at the time. In 1899, for example, Max Cowper gave an interview in *Brown's Book-Stall* in which he claimed that the pleasure he had from drawing the antique casts was "the only good I ever derived from the Dundee Art Schools." He acknowledged that the teachers "were clever fellows, and thoroughly able to impart their knowledge of South Kensington Art, but, as you can easily understand, this was quite a different form of it from the free and easy paths of the painter."[42]

The authorities themselves were also starting to question the system. In November 1895, Her Majesty's Inspector of Science & Art for the North of Scotland, W R Blair, exhibited examples of artworks by school pupils from around the country at an event held at the Dundee YMCA. The works were displayed with the marks from South Kensington on them, so that the teachers present could see what was considered good or bad. The event was hosted by the Chairman of the Dundee School Board, ex-Bailie Macdonald, who was reported by the press as saying that

"he was very much puzzled when the results came [from South Kensington] to find that some of the boys and girls whom he thought best had failed, whereas some of those of whom he had little hope gained prizes. (Laughter.) He had no doubt it was his want of knowledge, because the South Kensington people never committed a blunder – at least they never confessed to making a blunder. (Renewed laughter.)"[43]

Not only does the audience's laughter suggest that such errors were not uncommon, but Blair then proceeded to agree with Macdonald, and even gave some examples of his own! He also commended the Dundee School Board for having made drawing compulsory for boys in all their schools – something that was not yet happening at a national level.

Five years after this, the Victoria Galleries were chosen as the venue for an exhibition of highlights from the National Competition – some 250 gold and silver medal-winning works by students from throughout Britain and Ireland. The *People's Journal* promoted it as "perhaps the most interesting and instructive exhibition ever seen in Dundee", but went on to note: "As much controversy has existed regarding the art teaching given under the inspection and direction of the Science and Art department, this exhibition will offer a fine opportunity of judging of its highest development", clearly suggesting that criticism of the system was widespread.[44]

204. YMCA building, Constitution Road, Dundee, c.1895. Art classes were held in the top left room. Photograph from the Wilson Collection *(Libraries, Leisure & Culture Dundee)*.

That same year William Grubb celebrated 25 years at the High School, and was presented with an illuminated address by his students. At a function held in his honour in March 1901 it was stated that "no fewer than 42 of his students had taken art masters' certificates, and 30 of them were art masters at the head of large institutions throughout Scotland and England and abroad."[45] He had continued to expand his own knowledge and abilities (becoming an Associate of the Royal College of Art in 1899) but major changes were soon to take place in the teaching of art in Dundee, and the School of Art would be one of the principal casualties.

In 1872, the Dundee branch of the Young Men's Christian Association (YMCA) moved into the former Watt Institution building on Constitution Road (figure 204), and began to run a series of evening classes in various aspects of technical education.[46] Their classes proved a success, and they soon branched out into other practical subjects such as elocution, book-keeping and shorthand. In 1875, they decided to introduce art classes, and appointed George Malcolm to teach them. Malcolm had been John Kennedy's principal assistant at the School of Art, where he had earned his Art Master's certificate.[47] He began offering lessons three nights a week; within two years he would be teaching five nights and have 150 students on the register.

From the start the classes were South Kensington-directed, and Malcolm concentrated on the art courses required by technical students: Practical, Plane & Solid Geometry, Machine Construction & Drawing, and Building Construction (collectively known as the Graphic Sciences). A separate Drawing class was soon introduced, based around the early stages of the National Course. A special Pupil Teachers' Class was also arranged three nights a week, for the study of 2nd Grade art. Although only men could join the YMCA, it is notable that women were also allowed to attend these classes.

Malcolm's students quickly found success in the South Kensington exams. In 1880 it was reported that 75% of 2nd Grade students had passed in one or more subjects, compared to a national average of just 25%.[48] In 1884, YMCA students won eight prizes in the National Competition, but the popularity of Malcolm's classes came at a price: "The room occupied by them [the students] is so crowded that they have too little space to work with ease and comfort."[49]

Unlike at the School of Art, almost none of the YMCA's art students went on to become professional artists (Joseph Lee being a notable exception). Most were studying art as part of their technical education – they included Robert Gibson (later to teach Engineering Drawing at the Technical College) and Angus Fulton (later Principal of UCD). Of Malcolm's own artistic interests we know little, though he regularly exhibited landscapes in oil at the Fine Art Exhibitions.

Malcolm left the YMCA in 1886-7, after a record year which had seen nearly 3,000 drawings submitted to South Kensington, winning eleven prizes in the National Competition. His successor, James S Gibson (another of

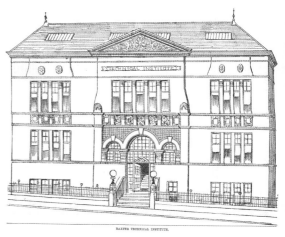

205. William Gillies and William Ryle Smith, *A Corner of Kirrie*, watercolour on paper, 1912. This joint effort suggests that Smith was closely mentoring his nephew during their sketching expeditions (*Royal Scottish Academy collections*).

206. Technical Institute, Small's Wynd, 1888 (*University of Dundee Archive Services*).

Grubb's students from the High School), was altogether less successful. He stayed just one session, during which student numbers plummeted and many of those who came dropped out before exam time (which had obvious financial implications when the following year's grants were being awarded). A replacement was quickly found in William Ryle Smith, who would remain in post until the YMCA classes were dissolved.

Born in Kirriemuir in 1862, Ryle Smith came to Dundee as a teenager to study under William Grubb while working as an apprentice to a carriage builder. After further study at South Kensington and in Leipzig, he commenced his teaching career in Elgin in 1884. Three years later he returned to Dundee as drawing master for the Broughty Ferry School Board, as well as taking on part-time work teaching at two private schools in the

city. He also started an evening class in Broughty Ferry, and his success with this doubtless helped to secure him the YMCA position.[50]

Smith soon regained the ground lost under Gibson and within two years numbers were higher than ever, though exam results were still down (something the YMCA blamed on the S&A for making the papers harder). In 1890 the institution proudly noted the eagerness of their students for the subject: "Persons visiting the Art Classes could not fail to be struck with the superior discipline maintained without apparent effort on the part of the Teachers. All seemed interested in the progress of each, and each in the progress of all."[51]

Smith joined the GAA in 1891, regularly exhibiting landscapes in their annual exhibitions. He had a keen interest in art culture generally, subscribing to art magazines, visiting exhibitions and building up his own collection of art. All this was to prove a decisive influence on his young nephew, none other than the celebrated landscape painter William Gillies (see figure 205). As a boy, Gillies made regular visits to Smith's home in Broughty Ferry, where he pored over back issues of *The Studio* and was particularly taken by two watercolours in his uncle's collection by James Watterston Herald. In the summer months Smith would visit the Gillies family in Haddington, and Gillies later recalled: "[He] went out each day to sketch the older parts of the town in a series of delicate watercolours. How delighted I was when I was allowed to go with him and try my hand. That really was the beginning of my long enthralment with watercolour painting."[52]

On the other side of town from picturesque Broughty Ferry, Lochee was also able to boast a Science & Art School. It was founded in 1874 by John Y Gray, whose early career had been spent at Camperdown jute works and Ward Foundry. He also studied under Grubb, earning his Art Master's certificate in 1881 (exhibiting two watercolours at the Fine Art Exhibition that same year), and in 1883 became one of the first students of the new UCD.

Gray ran the Lochee classes until 1885 then left to become drawing master and workshop instructor at Sharp's Institution in Perth. A year later he returned to Dundee to teach mechanics and run the technical workshop at the High School. In the evenings he joined the YMCA staff, mostly teaching mechanics but also assisting with the graphic science classes.[53]

For a few years his brother David Gray took charge of the Lochee school, but in 1892 he was succeeded by another of Grubb's students, Ninian R Jamieson. He too had started in the jute works (and indeed continued to be employed at Clepington Works while teaching in the evenings) and also studied at UCD.[54] A notable innovation introduced by Jamieson (and subsequently adopted by similar art schools elsewhere) was a series of regulations designed to combat the "wholesale class failures, which are the rule and not the exception in many subjects".[55] For example, any students who failed to complete a course would be charged at a higher rate. He also included detailed information in the syllabus about the different subjects and how they could be studied together, the net result being that by 1898 "little has been known at Lochee of pupils dropping away."[56]

The Lochee Science & Art School was essentially a one-man operation, as was the Central School of Art at 128½ Nethergate.[57] It was run by Peter D Lauder, who was born in Dundee in 1859 and earned his Art Master's certificate under Grubb in 1880. From that year he exhibited landscapes regularly at the Fine Art Exhibitions. His classes were held three nights a week and on Saturdays, and were officially sanctioned by the S&A. One notable student was Stewart Carmichael, who apparently earned a place there after winning a school prize for a wallflower study.[58] Around 1885, Lauder left Dundee and moved to Dollar, where he became art master at the local High School.[59]

Numerous other private tutors were offering their services in Dundee at this time. Freed from the restrictions of South Kensington, many provided the chance to practise a far wider range of skills. During the 1880s Rea Stevenson (who had been one of the first students of Dundee School of Art) ran drawing and painting classes at the Templar Hall in Broughty Ferry which included "painting on plaques, silk, china, enamel &c".[60] He exhibited landscapes and fishing scenes at the Fine Art Exhibitions until his death in 1891 at the age of 48.[61] Many women artists found an outlet for their talents through such classes – Miss Whyte and Miss Goodfellow taught "Drawing, Water-Colour Painting, and Painting on China and Terra-Cotta" in their studio at 9 Ward Road in the 1880s while Miss Lowson taught drawing, painting, and clay modelling at the Imperial Temperance Hotel in Commercial Street.[62]

Some of the city's best known painters supplemented their income by teaching, including J G H Spindler, C L Mitchell and C G L Phillips. Mitchell and Phillips offered private classes in their studios, while Spindler also taught at various independent schools such as the Dundee Institution and the Broughty Ferry Collegiate School. Peter D Lauder did the same, acting as drawing master in the Constitution House Institution and the East of Scotland Institution for the Board & Education of Young Ladies.[63]

The Dundee School Board (established in 1873) also held evening classes at this time, with the idea of encouraging "some deserving boys to remain at school a year or two longer than they otherwise would".[64] Plans were first made for this in 1874, and George Baird began teaching science and art classes at Victoria Road School in 1877. The art classes were soon taken over by Robert T M Allan, who earned his Art Master's certificate from Grubb in 1879. Allan held art classes in Balfour Street School on Wednesday nights and Victoria Road on Friday nights. John Duncan was among those who attended these classes as a teenager.[65] In 1885, the S&A gave a further grant to set up an art school at the new Harris Academy, which Allan took over full-time.[66] A similar school followed at Morgan Academy when the School Board took control of it in 1889.

All of these various evening classes would be either ended altogether or substantially re-organised as a result of the overwhelming success of the Dundee Technical Institute, from which would eventually grow both Duncan of Jordanstone College of Art & Design and Abertay University. Its origins date back to 1872, when Sir David Baxter died leaving £20,000 to

found a Mechanics Institution in Dundee. His trustees decided this was not enough, and it was not until UCD was founded in 1881 that any progress was made. Initially the College tried to persuade the trustees that it should be allowed to use the money for its own scientific teaching – John Y Gray was one of the first to speak out publicly against this. By 1887, a different agreement had been reached whereby an independent Technical Institute would be founded next door to UCD on Small's Wynd, and College staff would help to devise its curriculum and serve on the Institute Committee and Board of Studies, as well as sharing a number of key posts.[67]

Designed in "the Renaissance style" by J Murray Robertson, the Institute (figure 206) was formally opened on 15 October 1888 by a Yorkshire manufacturer, Swire Smith.[68] Classes had already begun by that time, and they included the teaching of art and the graphic sciences by none other than George Malcolm.[69] There were also seven science subjects taught. By the following session the syllabus had expanded to include Carpentry & Joinery (also taught by Malcolm), Wood Working (taught by John G Clarke and including carving and decorative work) and a course of popular lectures on the Decorative Arts by Prof G Baldwin Brown of the University of Edinburgh.[70]

The Institute's account book shows that Malcolm was by far the highest paid member of staff – in 1889-90 he received £217/15/1, three times that of any other teacher. This sum included a quarter share of the grant paid by the S&A, and from it he had to pay £15 to employ two assistants.[71] The accounts also give us details of the other expenditure necessary to equip a would-be art school: in 1889-90 this included £7/12/5 to Chapman & Hall of London for illustrations and other teaching materials; £1/18/5 to James Farmer for easels; and £1/18/6 to D Brucciani & Co of London for models.[72] Over the next few years there were further orders to Brucciani and Chapman & Hall (both South Kensington-approved suppliers) but also to local sources – J Gonnella & Co supplied further models and casts (including the ubiquitous statue of Discobolus), Robert Scott provided picture frames, Peter Feathers supplied a lantern for slides and the building's architect J Murray Robertson (who in 1890 also began teaching a course on the Principles of Design and Colouring) sold the Institute his own copy of Owen Jones's *The Grammar of Ornament*.

In the syllabus for 1892-93, a crucial turning point in the history of art teaching at the Institute was recorded: "Mr T Delgaty Dunn has been appointed Teacher of Fine Art, Modelling and Design; and a Special Syllabus of Elementary

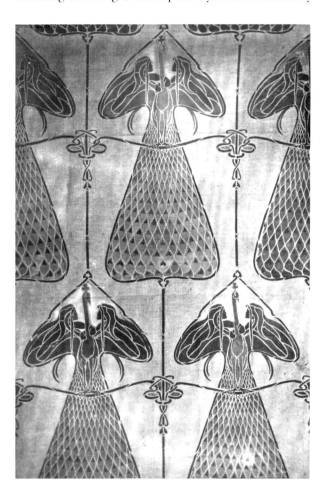

207. Top left: Thomas Delgaty Dunn, c.1908 (*Duncan of Jordanstone College of Art & Design*).

208. Left: Technical Institute Syllabus, 1893, designed by Thomas Delgaty Dunn (*University of Dundee Archive Services*).

209. Above: Alex M Richardson, *Design for Stencilled Jute Hanging*, c.1899, which won the artist a National Book Prize (*Duncan of Jordanstone College of Art & Design*).

and Advanced Art Subjects, both in Day and Evening Classes, will be issued separately."[73] In fact, when the separate art syllabus appeared, it was just for evening classes (day classes would not be advertised until the following year), but it still represented a major expansion of art teaching.[74] Since Malcolm remained to teach the graphic science classes, Dunn was able to offer a wider range of subjects: "Technical Drawing, Shading, Painting, Design, Principles of Ornament and Decoration, Architecture (History and Ornament), and Modelling. A Class for Assistant Teachers will also be arranged. This Class will include the Principles of Class Teaching."

Thomas Delgaty Dunn (figure 207) was born in Edinburgh in 1864 and studied at the RSA Schools while working for George Waterston & Sons as a designer, draughtsman and engraver. He came to Dundee in 1886 to work as an assistant to Grubb at the School of Art, where he also continued to study – in 1889 alone he won five prizes, three first-class certificates and had some of his applied designs purchased by the S&A. He was soon promoted to second master, taking charge of the girls' school, where "he was allowed to introduce his own methods, and was very successful in developing a taste for art, especially printing and design."[75]

Dunn came to the Technical Institute on a salary of £200, but as Malcolm was still receiving the government grant share, he was notably better off with £234/0/5 (their salaries would not equalise until 1897). By comparison, the Director of Studies Frank W Young was only paid £50. The new teachers of cabinet-making and woodworking, David Ireland and James Bremner, were paid £10 each, while Malcolm's assistant David Stewart earned £15.

The new art classes had been arranged with specific local requirements in mind. In the day classes, this included "Technical Design for Embroidery, Painting, Lithography, Engraving, Pottery &c" as well as "Drawing in 'Black and White' for process reproduction", something in which South Kensington showed little interest. An evening course in Art Metalwork was also offered. But what the city of jute needed above all was a school of textile design and discussions began in February 1895 to consider how this could best be achieved.[76] The Chamber of Commerce agreed to fund a School of Design to a total of £200 a year for five years, and in October Thomas Woodhouse was appointed to the new school to teach textile design and manufacture.[77]

Woodhouse was brought up from Yorkshire and quickly established strong links with the local jute manufacturers.[78] He seems to have been an unconventional teacher, sometimes at odds with his masters at the Institute, and on at least one occasion he threatened to leave and take up a more lucrative post in India.[79] During his career he wrote over twenty textbooks, often in collaboration with former students – these included *Jute and Linen Weaving* (1906), *Textile Design: Pure and Applied* (1912), *The Finishing of Jute and Linen Fabrics* (1916) and *The Handicraft Art of Weaving* (1921).[80]

From 1896, Woodhouse offered day classes, including an advanced course in which students were expected to create original designs and apply them. It was slow to take off – nine students in the first year, only one in the second – but eventually proved its worth, and Woodhouse would continue to teach at the Institute for 33 years.[81]

Dunn's art classes, meanwhile, were becoming ever more popular. 125 fees were paid in 1895-6, rising to 265 by 1901-2.[82] He was now assisted by two of his best students, Alex Richardson (figure 209) and James Wyse (figure 84).[83] Additional courses were now being offered, including lectures on Historic Ornament by Dunn, Architectural Design by Patrick Thoms and John Duncan's course in Figure Drawing & Composition, described in chapter three.[84]

In 1895, Drawing from the Living Model was advertised in the syllabus for the first time. It is possible that the subject had been taught prior to

210. Joseph Lee, 'Art School for Dundee', from *The City Echo*, 1907 (*University of Dundee Archive Services*).

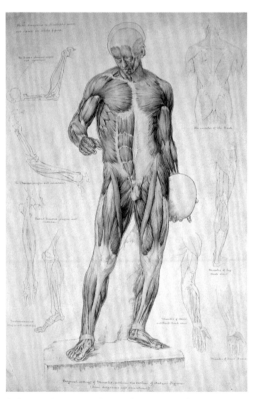

211. Unknown artist, *Original Setting of Muscles within the Outline of the Antique Figure*, drawing made at Dundee Technical Institute, c.1895 (*University of Dundee Museum Services, Duncan of Jordanstone College Collection*).

212. Tom Petrie, *Vathek* and George Wilson, *Craftsman*, prize-winning furniture designs reproduced in *The Studio*, 1902 *(Duncan of Jordanstone College of Art & Design).*

213. Harry Smith, *Design for Stencilled Wall Filling*, reproduced in *The Studio*, 1901 *(Duncan of Jordanstone College of Art & Design).*

214. Examples of jewellery by unidentified students at the Technical Institute, c.1900s *(Duncan of Jordanstone College of Art & Design).*

this but not listed, for Victorian morality had great difficulty coming to terms with the naked life model, and the S&A never openly encouraged it. It was left up to individual schools to decide, and for a long time it was common for such classes to be privately arranged without any evidence appearing in the published syllabus.[85] Dunn was certainly careful in advertising it, noting: "Students desirous of taking this Class must submit evidence of their previous study, and admittance will only be given to those whose work satisfies the Art Master of their ability to profit by it."[86]

From the annual prize lists we can find out who the early art students at the Tech' (as it was soon known) were. They included George Ogilvie (who was also employed as an assistant to George Malcolm), the newspaper artist Tom Ross, textile designer Andrew B Findlay, furniture designer Tom Petrie (figure 212) and carpet designer Harry Smith (figure 213). The Dundee Master Painters Association began awarding prizes for students' work – in 1894 this included James Robertson for Ornamental Lettering and Heraldry, David McLaren for Decorated Door Panels and Frieze, and Joseph Smith for Imitation Marbles and Glass Gilding.[87]

In 1901, the SED commenced a major reorganisation of technical and art education. The Technical Institute was designated a Central Institution with a remit to provide education for both the city and its surrounding area. Frank Young left and was replaced as Director of Studies by John S Lumsden. A new code of regulations was imposed which every class had to meet. As previously noted, this led both James Bremner and David Ireland to resign. Thomas Pryde (a former student of Grubb's at the School of Art) took Bremner's place running the woodworking class.

The most dramatic effect of the reorganisation was the termination of all other evening science and art classes in the city. The School of Art at the High School was closed down and the YMCA classes absorbed within the Technical Institute. For William Grubb, this marked the end of an association with the school going back 34 years. In 1902 he took a new post as art master at Madras College in St Andrews, but died the following year.

Central co-ordination of the various evening classes had been on the cards for some time – in 1895 the Technical Institute had made an unsuccessful bid to take over the YMCA and Lochee classes, offering both William Ryle Smith and Ninian Jamieson the opportunity to continue their teaching at the Tech'.[88] By 1900 a Joint Committee on Overlapping was in operation comprising staff of the Institute, the YMCA and the High School, one of their aims being "to promote the large scheme of a School of Industrial Art", suggesting altogether more ambitious ideals than the SED had in mind.[89]

In the event, Ryle Smith was employed by the Technical Institute, along with John Y Gray, Robert Gibson (another of Smith's graphic science assistants) and other YMCA teachers. Since there was no space in Small's Wynd to cope with the extra influx of students, the former YMCA staff continued to teach in the YMCA rooms, meaning that for the most part it was business as usual for all concerned.[90] Delgaty Dunn's day classes continued to expand, and now included "technical design applied to embroidery, wood carving, gesso, pottery, repoussé, weaving, and block printing."[91] As well as supplying the Institute with models, Giuseppe Gonnella was now giving occasional demonstrations in casting as well.

Since 1899, Dunn had also had a talented new assistant, John D Revel. Born in Dundee in 1884, Revel had studied under Dunn, winning various prizes including a free scholarship in 1901 and bronze medals in the National Competition in 1903 and 1904 (see figure 215). After this he left Dundee to work at Shipley School of Art in Yorkshire, moving in 1905 to become second master at Preston School of Art.[92] He evidently missed Dundee – when Lumsden wrote to him enclosing his final prize money, he noted:

> "Mr Dunn was telling me tonight that he had received a letter from you, which was not very cheerful. Keep up your heart, the best part of the session is over and next year the work will go more smoothly. I am afraid you will never be right until you get a place in Scotland again amongst your old friends."[93]

In fact it would be another twenty years before Revel came back to Scotland. He moved to London to study at the Royal College of Art, gaining diplomas in both architecture and painting. In 1911 he was appointed headmaster of Chelsea School of Art. During the Great War he served as a war artist in India, Mesopotamia and Russia. In 1925 he finally returned to Scotland as Director of Glasgow School of Art until 1932. He died in 1967.[94]

Revel was one of the last of the old style of pupil assistants, which the SED had decided to dispense with as part of their reorganisation. The Institute, however, did not give them up without a fight. In 1902 they wrote to the department extolling the virtues of the system, and noting that of the five pupil assistants that had so far completed their training under Delgaty Dunn, two were now art masters elsewhere, one was a first assistant, one had won a National Scholarship to the Royal College of Art and the last (Revel) had been promoted to first assistant in the Institute. Three months later they tried again, writing: "It is so difficult to get efficient assistants for Evening Art Classes that we think it desirable to continue the practice of training our own assistants."[95] The SED thought otherwise, but still allowed the Institute to take on two final pupil assistants, John M Moyes and Philip R Paul. Moyes would prove particularly successful, and promoted to first assistant would remain on the staff until 1912.[96]

The Institute also employed two assistants from the High School, John A Myles and Robert Donn. Although both had also studied at the Tech', they had far greater experience – Myles had been on the High School staff for ten years, having risen from student to assistant art master under Grubb, becoming second art master when Grubb left. As a consequence he demanded a higher salary than the other assistants, at one point threatening to leave unless he received £50.[97] The best the Institute could offer was £40, so after less than a year he was off to the more lucrative position of art master at Montrose Academy.[98] His replacement, Robert Donn (who also took over his post at the High School) had similarly been a pupil assistant under Grubb but had left to study at the Royal College of Art before teaching at Glasgow School of Art and at schools in Fife. A regular exhibitor with the GAA, he had also had work accepted by the RSA and had written a textbook entitled

215. John D Revel, *Modelled Design for a Carved Bench End*, c.1900 (*Duncan of Jordanstone College of Art & Design*).

216. Technical Institute certificate, designed by Thomas Delgaty Dunn, 1900s (*Duncan of Jordanstone College of Art & Design*).

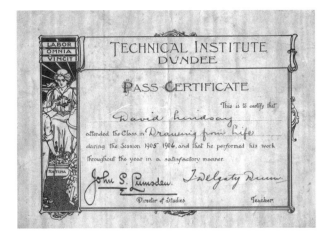

Object Drawing.[99] He too remained only a year at the Institute, though he would continue to teach in Dundee schools for several years.[100] After the Great War, Donn emigrated to New Zealand where he played a pioneering role in the development of art teacher training.[101]

By now there were over 1,000 students enrolled at the Institute and overcrowding had become a serious problem. In 1905-6 the former evening classes run by the Dundee School Board were reinstated as preparatory classes, allowing the Institute to raise its entrance standard. Art students would no longer be able to enrol straight from school, but would first have to attend a Preliminary Art Course at either Harris or Morgan Academy. Similar courses in the graphic sciences were offered at Victoria Road, Hill Street, Blackness and Liff Road Public Schools.[102] This cut the numbers by about 100, but the relief was short-lived as the founding of Dundee Training College in 1906 led to a considerable expansion in art training for teachers. Having no initial home of its own, the College rented those parts of the Technical Institute that were unoccupied during the day.[103] Delgaty Dunn was appointed as a part-time lecturer, and as Drawing was a required part of the General Knowledge course for all teachers, he was much in demand. Right from the start, the College also offered

STAFF—DUNDEE SCHOOL OF ART.

217. Top left: Dundee Technical College & School of Art, Bell Street, 1912 *(University of Dundee Archive Services)*.

218. Above: Drawing & Painting Rooms, School of Art, Bell Street, c.1910 *(University of Dundee Archive Services)*.

219. Top right: Joseph Lee, 'Staff – Dundee School of Art', featuring Perry Hill, John Milne Purvis and John M Moyes, from *The City Echo*, 1911 *(University of Dundee Archive Services)*.

specialist training for art teachers – originally a 'special subject' lasting 120 hours, by 1914 this had evolved into a three year certificate course lasting 2,330 hours, of which 1,050 hours had to be spent at an Art School.[104]

It was clear that the Institute could no longer cope with the demand for art teaching given the cramped accommodation at Small's Wynd – one studio for general work estimated at 35 by 40 feet and a much smaller room for life drawing and modelling.[105] To make matters worse, the rooms were poorly lit and ventilated, as Delgaty Dunn recalled many years later:

"In these days, the incandescent mantle had not been invented, consequently our rooms were illuminated by gas flares. The fumes of the gas made the overcrowded rooms intolerably stuffy, but we had no remedy, for the moment we opened the ventilators the glaring and the flickering of the naked lights made work impossible."[106]

In February 1906, Stewart Carmichael gave a lecture to the Eastern Branch of the Scottish Art Teachers' Association on 'The Possibilities of Art for the Future Citizen', in which he berated UCD for its failure to offer instruction in the fine arts, which had been one of its founder's intentions (see chapter seven). This prompted a series of letters in the press from Dundee's artists advocating better art instruction, as well as a special feature, 'The Neglect of Art', written for the *Courier* by Carmichael, Frank Laing and David Foggie. The focus was entirely on UCD, and little attention was paid to art education at the Technical Institute. Later that year, however, the chairman

of the Institute Committee, William Henderson, launched a major fund-raising campaign to provide the Tech' with a new home. One possible catalyst for this was a visit to the city by the eminent architect Sir Rowand Anderson, acting as a representative of the SED, who were keen to see further developments in art education. A scheme was proposed whereby UCD would arrange classes that would be taught in the Tech', though in the end this was never carried out.

In 1907 a site on Bell Street was purchased for a new building and plans drawn up by Robert Gibson, with architect James Langlands winning the competition to design its frontage.[107] The announcement of these new expanded facilities led to a high-profile campaign for the establishment of a fully fledged art school in Dundee. Leading this cause, as before, were some of the city's most notable artists. Writing in the *Advertiser*, Stewart Carmichael claimed:

> "The new Technical School is being built, and there will come a body of students, so many with talent and a few with genius. For these few an art school is the necessary and crowning education: an art school where drawing, modelling, painting, architecture, and art history will be taught, and opportunities given for a perfect equipment in these branches, for the culture of these subjects for themselves alone, just as a University should exist for the higher culture, for the perfection of the spiritual life. Your student at the Technical College might be gifted in modelling, painting, stained glass, wood carving or figure design – where is he to gain that complete knowledge of the figure unless in a well-equipped life school? On the town itself the art school would have an enlargening, deepening influence. The horizon of crafts and arts would widen and have much more significance. Many wonderful crafts that are known in France to-day are unheard of in Dundee. Our town has produced brilliant engineers, why not great craftsmen and artists?"[108]

The Town Council were evidently impressed by the possibilities, particularly on finding that they would have the support of the SED, who offered to match whatever sum of money could be raised locally to commence such a school. According to the *Advertiser*, the Department "feel strongly that in this matter Dundee, having allowed itself to fall behind the three other principal towns of Scotland, ought to make good its leeway and take its place in line with them".[109] On 22 January 1907 a deputation led by the Lord Provost visited Glasgow School of Art and were encouraged by its close collaboration with the city's Technical College.[110]

On 30 January a public meeting was held in the Town Hall to discuss the possibilities. Among those present were representatives of the Technical Institute (Delgaty Dunn among them), the High School, the School Board and UCD, as well as architects including T M Cappon, Charles Ower and Patrick Thoms, and artists Stewart Carmichael, Frank Laing, James Douglas, David Foggie, Alec Grieve, C L Mitchell and J G H Spindler.[111] The idea that a school of higher art could

220. John Milne Purvis, *Santa Sophia, Constantinople*, oil on canvas, 1912 (*University of Dundee Museum Services, Duncan of Jordanstone College Collection*).

be established on the same site as the new Technical Institute met with almost unanimous approval, the only voice of caution being that of J E A Steggall, Professor of Mathematics at UCD, who questioned whether it would not be more economical simply to send their students to existing schools elsewhere. He added rather facetiously that if they were planning a school of art, why not also a school of poetry, "as it would be nice to catch their poets young"![112]

Despite a motion to pursue the matter being carried unanimously, nothing more seemed to happen. Although William Henderson had stated at the meeting that the improved facilities in Bell Street "would not be sufficient for a highly graded School of Art",[113] this crucial fact seemed to get forgotten amid the excitement as construction work began. Expansion of the art classes continued – in 1907 the course structure was re-organised, removing some of the basic subjects which were now being taught in the preparatory classes.[114] New subjects were introduced at the YMCA – Ryle Smith began teaching Clay Modelling, and Arthur A Dunbar was appointed to teach Lithography.

The most ambitious announcements came in 1908. Firstly, the Institute would from the following year be known as Dundee Technical College *and School of Art*, and secondly, it intended to offer a full four-year Art Diploma course, with students in their final year specialising in Architecture, Sculpture, Painting or Design.[115] The question was, could they deliver the goods? The SED clearly didn't think so, and on 17 September 1908 Lumsden had to write a humbling reply explaining that only two or three years of the course would be taught in Dundee and claiming, "It has never been thought to

221. George Reid, *James Duncan of Jordanstone*, oil on canvas, c.1890 (*University of Dundee Museum Services, Duncan of Jordanstone College Collection*).

make an attempt to reach the standard of the Art Schools in Edinburgh and Glasgow", which was clearly untrue.[116]

The old Institute was emptied in 1908, but by 1909 the new building was not yet ready so the art classes had to be taught entirely within the YMCA before finally moving into Bell Street in 1910. The new College (figure 217) was formally opened on 9 January 1911 by Sir William Ogilvy Dalgleish (nephew-in-law of Sir David Baxter), who had donated almost a third of the £35,000 raised by Henderson's campaign. The SED matched this with an equal sum to cover the remaining costs of the new building, which now provided the art school with accommodation six times the size of its predecessor (figure 218). Joseph Lee's *City Echo* described the new premises in detail:

> "The new School of Art consists of a suite of ten specially designed and equipped rooms situated on the top floor of the front block of the Technical College… Mounting the east stair the main landing is reached with the headmaster's room adjoining; two full-sized antique statues at once suggest the purpose of this part of the building. All the rooms are large and airy, extremely light and cheerful in tone…

> "The entire equipment of the school has been arranged by Mr Dunn, the headmaster; and fitments, furniture, and lighting arrangements represent the result of his wide experience and study of class needs. Some of these are decidedly ingenious, as for example the electric lighting of the life room. In it a cluster of shaded lights is suspended from a radial arm, which can be moved from the centre round a circular rail, 14 feet in diameter: the lights can also be run to any position on the radial arm itself, raised or lowered by a coun-ter-weight, or tilted to any convenient angle, lighting at the same time the model and the student's work… Painting rooms and central hall are lit during the day by great roof-lights and high windows on the north side, all having adjustable blinds…

> "Architecture and Design rooms are both equipped with individual desks, the former has a collection of casts for reference, to be added to from time to time; the latter room is hung with framed illustrations of designs done in the school and with coloured examples of museum specimens. A feature of the design room is the large wall space provided for students working out cartoons or other subjects which require greater area than drawing boards give."[117]

After giving many more details, the article concluded: "For the first time in its history Dundee has now adequate accommodation for advanced students". To meet the anticipated demand for more specialist training, the School of Art employed new members of staff – Moyes was promoted to General Art Assistant, and was joined in 1910 by John Milne

Purvis to teach Painting & Drawing from Life and Perry Hill for Modelling & Handicrafts (figure 219). In 1912, Ernest Gill replaced Moyes and Edith Cheyne was employed to teach Embroidery.[118] Ryle Smith was now teaching Perspective in the School of Art as well as his continued work with Malcolm, Gibson and others teaching the graphic sciences in the Technical College.

Masterminding all of this was Delgaty Dunn as headmaster, who finally had an art school of which he could be truly proud. By this time, Dunn had become a significant figure in the artistic life of Dundee. He exhibited at the Fine Art Exhibitions in the 1890s and with the GAA from 1901, helping to organise the decorative art section of their exhibitions for several years. In 1911 he was chosen to design the ceremonial mace for UCD. He also took a keen interest in the development of his profession, serving as President of both the North East of Scotland Art Teachers' Association and the Scottish Art Teachers' Association.

Of all the new teachers, the most notable was undoubtedly John Milne Purvis. Born in Perth in 1885, he had first studied art at Perth Academy (becoming pupil teacher then assistant to D S Murray) before continuing his training at Glasgow School of Art.[119] In 1908 he earned both a Diploma in Painting and a scholarship which took him to Italy, Germany, Belgium and Holland. He would remain at the School of Art for the next 40 years, making an unsuccessful attempt to succeed Dunn as headmaster on the latter's retiral in 1927.[120] During the summer breaks he continued to travel widely (see figure 220) and exhibited his landscapes along with genre subjects at the RA, RSA, RSW and SSA. In Dundee, he quickly got involved in the artistic life of the city, designing ten Stations of the Cross and other decorative work for St John's Episcopal Church shortly after his arrival in 1910.[121] He later served as president of the Art Society and combined a love of art and theatre by designing stage sets for the Dundee Dramatic Society and murals for the Nicoll Street home of Dundee Rep Theatre.[122]

Despite its impressive new facilities, the School of Art was still only able to offer the first two years of the Diploma course – students would have to go to Edinburgh or Glasgow to complete their training. But in February 1909, while the new building was still under construction, a generous bequest was publicly announced which seemed to offer the answer to everyone's prayers, but which would turn out to be the cause of a long and bitter dispute.

Born in 1825, James Duncan (figure 221) studied at the High School of Dundee before earning his fortune trading in South America and in New York.[123] Having already acquired the estates of Drumfork and the Forest of Alyth, Duncan purchased the Jordanstone estate in 1892, living there until his death in 1909.[124] Although he took some part in the life of the community there, he was little known in Dundee beyond the livestock traders of the Cowgate, and had certainly not shown any public interest in art. It came as a complete surprise, therefore, when in his will Duncan bequeathed part of the residue of his estate (five of 29 shares, amounting to some

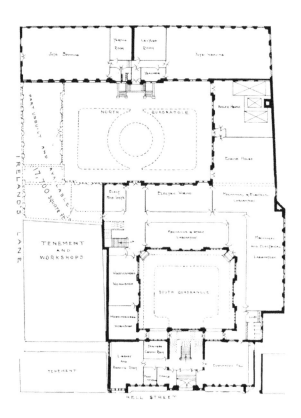

222. Plan of the new Technical College & School of Art, showing the space potentially available for the Duncan of Jordanstone Art School, 1909 *(University of Dundee Archive Services)*.

223. Margaret Lamond, *Untitled design exercise*, made at the School of Art, c.1910 *(University of Dundee Museum Services, Duncan of Jordanstone College Collection)*.

£60,000) to "be applied by my trustees in founding in Dundee a School of Industrial Art, to be named and known in all time to come as the 'Duncan of Jordanstone Art School.'"[125] Half the money was to be spent on the building, the other half on equipping and maintaining it. Duncan was quite precise as to the subjects to be taught there:

"The chief object of the school shall be the

teaching of textile manufacture and design, but instruction should also be given in the ornamentation and decoration of buildings, and the designing of furniture, art metal work, lithographic drawing, wood carving, art pottery, and the like… There should also be erected in connection with and as part of the Arts School a Women's Institute, in which instruction could be given in such subjects as household thrift and management, cookery, laundry work, dresscutting, and needlework".

In relation to this latter stipulation, it should be noted that Duncan died a bachelor! He concluded this section of his will by noting that

"while the school to be built and endowed as aforesaid is to remain in all time to come a separate and distinct institution, it shall, so far as is practicable and so as to prevent overlapping and waste, be managed in conjunction with the University College and the Technical Institute, and I recommend my trustees, if at all possible, to erect the school in the neighbourhood of the College and Institute."

The problems for Duncan's trustees and those of the Technical College were quickly apparent. Duncan had made his will in 1899, clearly aware of the College in its original form on Small's Wynd, but wanting his school to be a separate institution. By 1909, however, most of the subjects he expected it to teach (the Women's Institute aside) were already being catered for by the College. The appeal for co-operation with the College was enough to allow its trustees to make a swift bid for the money. A plan was drawn up to use available land on Ireland's Lane, immediately adjacent to the new building, as the site for the Duncan of Jordanstone School (figure 222).[126]

It soon became clear, however, that the Duncan trustees were not going to be rushed into a decision. Four years passed with no action taken. In 1913 the trustees were reported to be "considering the situation very carefully".[127] In 1914 the decision was reached to buy the Ireland's Lane site and begin work on the new school, but still nothing happened.[128] In 1921 the rise in construction costs was given as the reason for further delay, and in 1925 the Rent Restriction Act was said to be the cause.[129] During all this time the Technical College made repeated appeals to the Duncan trustees to begin work, but all to no avail.[130] At the time of his retirement in 1927, Delgaty Dunn was still hoping for increased accommodation for the School "as a result of the Duncan of Jordanstone Bequest".[131] It would be Dunn's successor, Francis Cooper, who finally won the bequest in the 1930s; his successor, Hugh Adam Crawford, who would see the opening of the new Art College on Perth Road in 1955; and his successor Chessor Matthew who would finally see the Art College become completely independent of the Technical College in 1975.[132]

Despite the frustrations surrounding the Duncan bequest, as the School of Art entered the 1910s it was making good progress. Numbers were up in both day and evening classes, and every year over 200 students from the Training College were also attending art classes. Among the lists of prize-winners

around this time are many familiar names, mostly press artists such as Tom Ross, G S Peddie, Frank Coutts, Ruby Scott and Jean C Rollo. The demand for well-trained illustrators for Thomson and Leng publications provided the School with an important market – Lumsden clearly recognised this when he referred to the evening classes in life drawing as "instruction and practice for newspaper artists".[133]

A brief glimpse into the life of a typical student is provided by a diary kept during 1910-1 by a young employee of Martin Anderson's at Tayport, David Graham.[134] He had been an evening student since at least 1906, spending his days producing illustrations for Anderson as well as other commissions (such as programmes for UCD and a poster for a suffragette bazaar). His diary entries are always brief, but record significant events in his life suc as getting his first pair of long trousers, having all his teeth out, seeing Little Tich at the King's Theatre, and dating two different girls at the same time. During this time he was also busy working on an oil study of a girl's head for submission to the Fine Art Exhibition. Starting work on 9 August he records a total of 12 hours 45 minutes spent on it. He had the work framed at Liddle's on 23 August ("Very satisfactory indeed."), submitted it on 12 September and had it rejected on 3 October.

Better news had come on 27 April when he noted: "Am told news that I am 1st in Life Class", for which he later chose Solomon J Solomon's book *The Practice of Oil Painting* as his prize. On 5 September he signed up for the new session at the Technical College, and a week later recorded: "No class tonight or this week. Saw work of new teacher [Purvis]. Splendid. He 25 years of age." On 19 September: "Up to 'Tech' and got card of admission. Spoke to Mr Purvis, very good impression of him. He very homily." His life drawing classes started on 21 September ("1st night of 1st Pose") and continued twice a week. Although most of his social life was

224. Group photograph from the School of Art's annual fancy dress ball, 1913. Among those present are: Top row: Tom Petrie (second from left), Ernest Gill (fifth left), Frank Coutts (seventh left), Jean C Rollo (third right), Philip R Paul (second right). Second row: James Cadzow (first left), Ruby Scott (fifth left), Winifred Hean (sixth left). Third row: John Milne Purvis (first left), Joseph Lee (second left), Louise Milne (seventh left). Fourth row: James Leslie (eighth left). Fifth row: Annie Nicoll (first left), Edith Cheyne (fifth right). Front row: Nellie Coupar (fifth left) *(private collection)*.

225. Joseph Lee (second right) in his production of *Fra Lippo Lippi* at Dundee School of Art, 1914 *(University of Dundee Archive Services)*.

spent on the other side of the Tay, he was evidently friends with George Peddie and Tom Ross and was involved in the School of Art Club (see chapter eight).

Social activity was a defining feature of the new School of Art. The improved accommodation allowed the Art Club to stage various events, most memorably the annual fancy dress ball (figures 224 & 274). Every Christmas the students designed and made their own costumes for these events, which were always favourably reviewed in the press:

"The beautiful hall, with its softly shaded lights, made a fine setting for the scene, the simplicity of the oak-panelled walls contrasting with the bright and bizarre colours of the different costumes. The students had put a great deal of originality into their costumes, and if they can transmit in equal degree the same faculty to more serious forms of art, they will have gone a considerable way towards achieving success."[135]

There were also one-off events, the most prestigious being the performance of a play written by Joseph Lee, *Fra Lippo Lippi* (figure 225). A fairly florid account of the life of the 15th-century painter, Lee dedicated the work to Delgaty Dunn "as a small recognition of his 25 years of valuable service to the art students of the city".[136] It was staged at the School of Art during Easter 1914; John Milne Purvis designed the scenery, Ernest Gill the costumes and Perry Hill the props. Lee starred in the play alongside students including Annie Nicoll (who married Purvis the following year), Nellie Coupar, Frank Coutts and James Leslie. The critics were generous in their praise, one noting that "for beauty of scheme and artistic realisation the production of Mr Lee's play by the Dundee School of Art has not been excelled in amateur circles for many years."[137]

Within a year, Lee would be in France with the Black Watch, and many of the students and staff of the Technical College also enlisted, including John Milne Purvis.[138] Student numbers dropped from 1,476 in 1913-4 to 757 in 1915-6, and some subjects (such as lithography and woodcarving) had to be abandoned. There were positive developments as well, however – following an official inspection of the School of Art in 1915 by no less than Walter Crane ("the most influential art teacher in Britain"[139]), the SED agreed that the School could now teach the full four-year Diploma course in Design. The first two successful graduates from the course were Winifred E Hean (born in Glasgow in 1895) and Louise R Milne (born in Dundee in 1893), both in 1916.[140] Embroidered panels by each student were reproduced in *The Studio* the following year (figure 226), the reviewer praising the "excellent colour-scheme" in Milne's work, but noting that as a result of the war, "the scarcity of dyes has limited very considerably the range of colours in which silk thread has been produced... [necessitating] a marked modification in the execution of her design."[141] *The Studio* also noted that Hean and Milne had produced skilful tapestry panels, weaving now being "an important feature in the curriculum... which the day students learn as a craft".[142]

By now the South Kensington system had been entirely eradicated, and the School of Art instead submitted work to a Committee of Assessors employed by the SED.[143] Enrolment was higher than ever after the war, and in 1919 new staff were employed – William Armstrong Davidson to head the Design department and James Steedman Hamilton to replace Perry Hill in Modelling & Handicrafts. Davidson already had a strong reputation having run his own design and metalworking studio in Glasgow, where he worked with Charles Rennie Mackintosh among others.[144] He and Hamilton collaborated on a stunning Art Nouveau war memorial for Dundee Training College, unveiled in 1924 (figure 227).[145]

A new pay structure implemented by the government in

226. Louise Milne, *Embroidered Panel for Screen*, reproduced in *The Studio*, 1917 (*Duncan of Jordanstone College of Art & Design*).

227. William Armstrong Davidson and James Steedman Hamilton, Dundee Training College war memorial, 1924 (*University of Dundee Museum Services*).

1919 led to better salaries for most of the staff (Delgaty Dunn was now on £450, Thomas Woodhouse on £400 and Purvis on £250) but also saw the forcible retirement of all staff over 70.[146] This included George Malcolm, who now left the College after some 45 years as an art teacher. During the 1920s the School of Art continued to concentrate on the Design Diploma, and it would not be until 1929 that an equivalent course in Drawing & Painting was approved by the SED. Despite increasing overcrowding (built for 150 students, the art rooms were now squeezing in 300 each evening[147]), the popularity of the School remained undiminished:

> "There was much enthusiasm amongst the students in the School of Art, and there was an atmosphere there different from that in the other departments of the College. Many of the art students attend for the love of making artistic things, and what they do has no relation to their daily employment. There is the absence of the desire to pass examinations, and a freedom and happiness in their demeanour which shows that they do not find this study a task."[148]

Before ending this chapter, we should briefly note the new generation of teachers in Dundee's secondary schools. At the High School, James Mackie Smith had taken over from William Grubb, having been second master there since taking over from Delgaty Dunn in 1892.[149] Born in Montrose, he had studied in Edinburgh and Antwerp and became a regular exhibitor of landscape paintings at the Dundee Art Society, of which he also served as president. Like Dunn, he also became president of the Scottish Art Teachers' Association.[150] The High School magazine referred to him as "our genial art master" and noted the success of his summer sketching expeditions (figure 228), taking his pupils to Invergowrie and across the river to Wormit Bay.[151] He died in 1945 aged 84.

In 1911 Mackie Smith was joined by James Cadzow as assistant master. Born in Carluke in 1881, Cadzow studied at Edinburgh College of Art (having earlier trained to be an architect) and began his teaching career in Dunfermline before coming to Dundee. He became an active member (and later president) of Dundee Art Society and a regular exhibitor at the RSA. A talented painter best known for his west coast landscapes, he eventually succeeded Mackie Smith as art master, remaining in post for the rest of his life – he died whilst playing a round of golf in 1941.[152]

At the Morgan Academy, James Watson took over from D S Murray in 1907, having come to the school as a pupil teacher when it first opened in 1889. He painted Scottish and Continental landscapes in a style similar to that of Arthur Melville, which were exhibited both locally and at the RSA and RA. His obituary claimed that he made the art department at the Morgan "something of an art school in itself", presumably referring to his work running the preparatory classes for the School of Art.[153] He too served as president of the Dundee Art Society.

Ryle Smith was now art master at Grove Academy (figure 229) while also undertaking his work at the Technical College

(he later recalled, "the pupils were ever eager and enthusiastic to learn... outstanding in brightness and cheeriness of outlook"[154]), and at Harris Academy, Robert J Plenderleith succeeded R T M Allan in 1907 (see figure 230). Originally from Biggar, Plenderleith had studied at Heriot-Watt College and would remain at the Harris for the next 28 years.[155]

All of these various teachers joined the growing number of artists at the Technical College in making a significant contribution to Dundee's art culture. But Dundee's other educational instutition, UCD, also played a part in the artistic life of the city, as we shall see in the next chapter.

228. High School girls sketching from nature, c.1896 (*Dundee City Archives*).

229. Grove Academy Art Room, 1914 (*Libraries, Leisure & Culture Dundee*).

230. Robert J Plenderleith, 'Good and Bad Old Days', illustration from the *Harris Magazine*, 1913 (*Libraries, Leisure & Culture Dundee*).

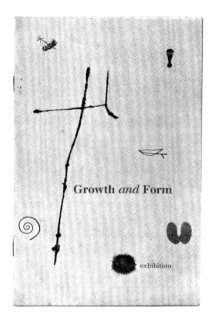

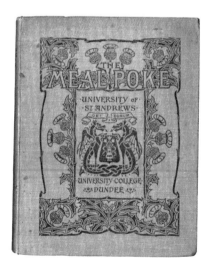

242. Catalogue for Richard Hamilton's *Growth and Form* exhibition at the ICA, 1951 *(University of Dundee Museum Services, D'Arcy Thompson Zoology Museum)*.

243. Andy Lomas, *Aggregation 24*, digital print, 2005. Lomas works as a CG effects designer as well as an artist, creating images of growth patterns generated by computer algorithms *(University of Dundee Museum Services, D'Arcy Thompson Zoology Museum)*.

244. Thomas Delgaty Dunn, cover design for *The Meal-Poke*, published in 1903 in aid of the Students' Union Bazaar, its format modelled on Patrick Geddes's periodical *The Evergreen (University of Dundee Archive Services)*.

USA, Jackson Pollock and other abstract expressionists were also reading the book, and one can imagine Thompson's discussions of splash patterns having a particular resonance for Pollock, whose apparently chaotic forms hide a carefully ordered underlying structure.

Thompson published a second edition of *On Growth and Form* in 1942 which was enthusiastically reviewed by Herbert Read. The new edition was taken up by a group of students at the Slade School of Fine Art in London in the 1940s, including Nigel Henderson, Richard Hamilton, Eduardo Paolozzi and Dundonian William Turnbull.[46] In 1951, Hamilton staged an influential exhibition called *Growth and Form* at Herbert Read's new Institute of Contemporary Arts (ICA) to accompany the Festival of Britain (figure 242). The show (a pioneering example of installation art), included models, photographs and drawings based on the illustrations in Thompson's book.

In 1953 Hamilton took up a teaching position at the Department of Fine Art in King's College, Newcastle, where he was joined a year later by the constructivist artist Victor Pasmore.[47] The new Basic Design Course they introduced made the department "one of the most advanced and progressive in the country"; it included many exercises based on Thompson's work.[48] Meanwhile early pioneers of computer art such as Roy Ascott and Desmond Paul Henry saw *On Growth and Form* as a key prefigurement of their work, and one can trace a direct line of descent from Thompson through Mandelbrot's work on fractals to the computer-generated imagery of Pixar and others today (see figure 243).

Through teaching such as Hamilton's, exhibitions at the ICA and the influence of various other artists, Thompson's seminal work of science – written at UCD in the 1910s – became fully integrated into British contemporary art years after his death in 1948. Many more artists have since been drawn to his work, including Andy Goldsworthy, Tony Cragg, Robert Smithson, Peter Randall-Page, Susan Derges, Will Maclean, Daniel Brown and Gemma Anderson. How aware Thompson was of the artistic impact of his work is unclear. Herbert Read wrote to him in 1942 saying "I wonder if I ever thanked you for the enlightenment I got from your book 'On Growth and Form': it helped me where perhaps you never intended it to help – in the understanding of art."[49] In another letter, Read told Thompson, "you have built the bridge between science and art."[50]

As for Thompson's opinions of the modern abstract painters and sculptors of the 1930s and 40s who were so inspired by his work, it's unlikely that he would have been a great enthusiast, though it does at least seem like he tried. In 1946 he wrote to Read praising his book *A Coat of Many Colours* and saying: "I envy you your knowledge of, and your sympathy for, a number of modern men whom I have had all too little patience to study and understand... Ben Nicholson [is] within my ken. But I have got along without Picasso, easily enough".[51]

The other great interdisciplinary thinker at UCD was Thompson's close friend and colleague Patrick Geddes, whose role in the Celtic Revival we have already discussed. Geddes came to UCD as Professor of Botany in 1888 and quickly gained a reputation as a stimulating if often frustrating teacher, as one former UCD student recalled:

"Geddes was something of a shock to the student who came expecting to get notes which he could learn by heart and recite at his forthcoming examination. A curious habit of dropping his voice made it necessary

for the student to listen closely. When the student caught what he was saying it was often something very different to what the student thought Botany should be. It might quite as likely have been Ancient History or Fine Art or Political Economy, as a note about the structure or habits of one of the prescribed plants."[52]

As well as his students, Geddes swiftly turned his attention to aesthetic matters – firstly the College grounds, which he "transformed into banks of greenery, and beds of flowers."[53] As the campus grew in size, Geddes continued to develop these gardens, and also began to suggest schemes in other parts of the city (see figure 245).[54] These included Law Park Way, which would have seen the bleaching green near the Royal Infirmary transformed into an open-air club for working women, featuring gardens as well as a rest room decorated with murals on the theme of washing.

Geddes extended such interests into the Art & Recreation committee of the Dundee Social Union, which had been founded just six weeks after his arrival in Dundee. It was clearly modelled on Geddes's own Edinburgh Social Union, which had championed the value of art and decoration in the lives of working men and women. Actively involved in the Dundee version were several of Geddes's fellow UCD professors, including Thomas Carnelley, J A Ewing, J E A Steggall and D'Arcy Thompson. At an address to mark the 50th Annual General Meeting of the Union, Thompson recalled: "Geddes was thinking of the dullness of men's lives and their need for something more than bread alone; and in 1889... a committee was formed with Pat Geddes for chairman, to deal (as the phrase went) with Art and Recreation."[55]

Thompson was, in fact, misremembering – Geddes served on the committee throughout its existence (it lasted until 1896) but was never its chairman, and the surviving reports do not indicate any active involvement on his part. Perhaps as a result of this the committee quickly turned its interests away from art towards providing social events for working women and children. Geddes served on various other Union committees, but his main contribution seems to have been in the inspiration he gave others – most notably Mary Lily Walker, a former UCD student who turned the Union into a more active, campaigning organisation and ultimately reformed it as the Grey Lodge Settlement Association. Although D'Arcy Thompson remained her strongest influence, she would later refer to her "deep sense of gratitude" for Geddes and "all he has taught me of the wonder and beauty of this world's life".[56]

Geddes frequently used art as a means of awakening this sense of wonder and beauty. In the pamphlets he wrote under the title *Every Man his own Art Critic*, he brought his own interpretation to bear on various artworks, often using these to demonstrate his belief in the synthesis of art, science and life as a whole. For example, his reaction to seeing a painting of a sleeping beauty in midsummer is that of a "speculative naturalist" who sees it as a "supreme visible rendering of ... that waxing potential energy of life in repose... And thus the fairy tale *is* science".[57] Geddes was well aware that art and science had become increasingly separated, "as Science

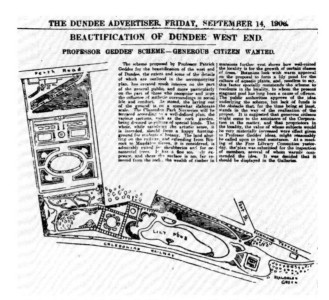

245. Patrick Geddes's West End Park proposal for Magdalen Green was exhibited in the Victoria Galleries and at the Whitechapel Gallery in London. It was also featured in the *Dundee Advertiser*, 1906 *(used by kind permission of D C Thomson & Co Ltd)*.

goes on isolating and analysing strange new fields of minute detail, Art refracting subtler aspects of nature through more individual moods of mind. Who now speaks of Leonardo's, Dürer's dream of reuniting Art and Science, save as a mere echo of the days of alchemy?" Geddes, of course, was one of the few who shared this dream, aiming for "a rebuilding of analyses into Synthesis, an integration of many solitary experiences into a larger Experience, an exchange of the narrow window of the individual outlook for the open tower which overlooks college and city."[58]

This was a reference to the Outlook Tower in Edinburgh, which Geddes purchased in 1892, intending to develop it as a new form of public museum. Museums were an important aspect of Geddes's belief in cultural education and a way of bringing together art and science. During his time in Dundee he worked on the manuscript for a book (never published) entitled *Museums: Actual and Possible*, and when the Museums Association held their annual conference in Dundee in 1907 he gave a ground-breaking paper outlining theories of contemporary museum displays that are still topical today.[59] He regarded the Albert Institute as an "admirable gallery... full of interest and value... so richly illustrative of this City's history", but noted also that "at present [it] attracts few save our antiquarians, a sadly dwindling class".[60] Geddes corresponded with the curator A H Millar, and at one point drew up plans for an extension to the building, though like so many of Geddes's schemes this was never carried out.[61]

Geddes also took a close interest in the development of art education in Dundee. As well as following the work of James Malloch, he was a keen supporter of Thomas Delgaty Dunn's work at the Technical Institute. In 1902 he wrote to his assistant in the Botany department, Marcel Hardy, encouraging him to meet Dunn "and see something of his work. Without being specially a botanist, he has interest in plant life, and appreciates its value in education. Ask him also about Mr Henry Wyse [see chapter six], and make his acquaintance; you will find him an excellent educationalist, and quite ready and willing to co-operate with us in our methods of teaching."[62]

Despite his very close connection to John Duncan, Geddes never established the same kind of relationship with Dundee's other artists. As noted before, he became an Associate Member of the GAA in 1891 and gave the opening speech at their annual exhibition in 1896. He undoubtedly knew many of the city's artists personally, most notably Stewart Carmichael, with whom friendly correspondence survives in Geddes's archive.[63] Geddes later included works by Carmichael in his pioneering Cities and Town Planning exhibition – indeed two of his pictures (*The Passing Crowd, Overgate* and a study for the mural *Labour*) were part of the version of the exhibition that was lost when the ship transporting it to Madras was sunk in the Indian Ocean in 1914.

Joseph Lee also became a friend of Geddes's during the brief period between his return from the war and Geddes's departure for Bombay (to take up the Chair of Sociology & Civics) in 1919. Sharing his socialist ideals, Lee wrote to Geddes: "Your chiefest difficulty, I imagine, is with the blindness of Authorities to the glitter of anything which is not gold. You have correctly diagnosed our social disease. There is hope for the irrigation of our ancient Earth if the streams of life can be diverted to flow through pleasant & unpolluted channels."[64]

Alec Grieve's work also attracted Geddes, and he bought Grieve's painting *Nocturne* from the 1896 GAA exhibition. David Foggie made a portrait of him as an etching, and was sufficiently inspired by Geddes's views on education to have his children taught at home rather than at school. George Dutch Davidson's work evidently made an impact on Geddes, and after his death Geddes referred to "these strange colour-traceries in which one young wistful dreamer has summed up his too short life".[65]

At his address to the GAA in 1896, Geddes made a plea to local collectors to support the artists involved.[66] He continued this theme in a series of articles published in the *Dundee Advertiser* in 1907 under the heading 'Recent Art Movements of Dundee', which he wrote at the request of the Tayport Artists' Circle.[67] In the first, 'Where are the Patrons of Art?' he noted the decline in art collecting within the city (and throughout Britain), lamenting that those aspiring to a higher social status "can now do this so much more successfully by collecting motor cars."[68]

In the third and final article, 'Art in Civic Progress and in Education', Geddes stressed the importance of art education, not just for artists but for workers and scientists also:

"…where can we look for real light, for practical leading, than to the arts? But to these not merely… in their humbler and more mechanical forms, but their supreme ones, the arts of co-ordination and of expression, the arts of skill, the art of seeing. And who … has ever expressed an ideal in most manifest and enduring yet subtlest form, in fullest mastery of matter, like the sculptor? Who has ever seen things real, and shown them as they truly are, like the painter, and who else can so worthily display them as they may be? … [As] Science herself rises from her analyses of nature considered as dead, to comprehend everything from actual evolution in nature and man and, in his cities, all discerned as living, she will be first to claim for art a renewed and higher place."[69]

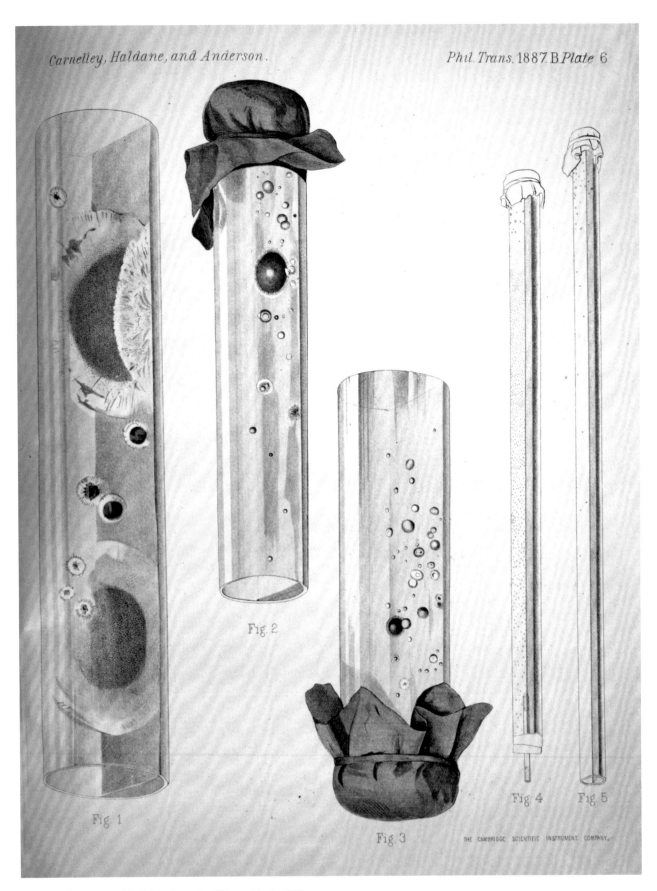

Fig. 1

Fig. 2

Fig. 3

Fig. 4   Fig. 5

THE CAMBRIDGE SCIENTIFIC INSTRUMENT COMPANY.

246. Opposite page: Patrick Geddes (seated, middle row) in the UCD gardens with a group of students. Etta Johnston is sitting to the right of him *(University of Dundee Archive Services)*.

247. Above: Diagram based on paintings by Etta Johnston from 'The Carbonic Acid, Organic Matter, and Micro-Organisms in Air, More Especially of Dwellings and Schools' by Thomas Carnelley, J S Haldane & A M Anderson, published in *Philosophical Transactions of the Royal Society B*, 1887 *(Libraries, Leisure & Culture Dundee)*.

248. W G Burn-Murdoch, 'Summer' from *The Evergreen: The Book of Summer*, 1896 *(University of Dundee Archive Services)*.

249. W G Burn-Murdoch, *Dundee Antarctic Whaling Expedition*, oil on canvas, 1893 *(Dundee City Council: Dundee's Art Galleries & Museums)*.

Geddes had himself brought science and art together in Dundee in 1891, when he approached the GAA through his assistant Etta Johnston (figure 246) with a scheme "for adding to the usefulness of the University College, wherein the assistance of the members of the Assoc. would be of great value".[70] The plan was to create a series of oil and watercolour paintings of plant life, showing "not only the plant, but also its surroundings, and... the climatic conditions under which it grows."[71] Geddes was dissatisfied with the standard botanical lithographs available commercially (which failed to reflect his interest in studying plants – and later cities – within their wider context), and had been inspired instead by the work of Marianne North at Kew Gardens. After hearing Geddes speak at length on the project, the Association embraced the project enthusiastically, 23 members agreeing to participate providing their costs could be met. The 1891 GAA Annual Report noted that "a number of most excellent works have been completed."[72] The following year Geddes persuaded the Albert Institute's curator John Maclauchlan to lead a subscription campaign, with J G Orchar also assisting. Maclauchlan noted that as well as members of the Association, "I have obtained promises from distinguished Artists in other places, who are interested in Dundee." His letter of appeal (probably written at least partly by Geddes) also described the works being undertaken:

"The studies are of considerable size – 24 x 16 and 16 x 12 inches, so that there may be room to properly depict the surroundings of each plant. Thus a distinguished artist has grouped in a picture the varied and beautiful bent-grasses which grow on Carnoustie Links, carefully painted in detail, and showing also the grass-covered undulating sand-dunes, and the blue sea beyond. Thus also the tall handsome reeds which fringe our estuary; the heather of the moors, and the aquatic vegetation of the moss; the endless variety of wild-flowers, which adorn wayside and waste land; and plant life generally, will be shown, and not foolishly detached from their surrounding, but in the habits as they live."[73]

How far the scheme advanced is unclear – after the fundraising appeal was sent out in June 1893, nothing further is heard of it until the following May, when Geddes invited the Association to hold their next meeting at UCD "in order that the scheme spoken of some two years ago might be again taken up".[74] That meeting never took place, and the scheme is not referred to again. Those works that were completed do not seem to have survived today.[75] Etta Johnston had organised a painting studio to direct the scheme, and Geddes soon had her running a similar studio in Edinburgh as part of his Summer Meetings. An intriguing account of the possible output of these studios can be found in a fictionalised account of one of the Summer Meetings by Riccardo Stephens, who describes the house of Professor Grosvenor (clearly intended to be Geddes):

"There were pictures by well-known artists on the walls, but they were of subjects which one could not believe the artists to have chosen, and indeed, I knew that form and colour were of secondary importance to Grosvenor, who got the pictures painted to order, trying to make art the servant of science and expecting his artists to express very queer things in paint."[76]

Possibly the Dundee artists had similar problems uniting art and science under Geddes's direction and the completed works were never used, but more likely the money to cover costs was never raised – though it seems like just the kind of project that would have appealed to James Martin White. Etta Johnston, however, was to have a fascinating career in both art and science.[77] Born in 1862, she studied under William Grubb at the School of Art, winning a National Book Prize in 1884.[78] In 1889 she won first prize in Paterson's Artistic Anatomy class.[79] She had been part of the first intake of students at UCD in 1883, studying a wide range of subjects but showing a particular interest in chemistry. Head of this department was Thomas Carnelley, who encouraged his students to publish their own research and to become actively involved in social welfare. Johnston published four papers during her student years, including 'The effect of floor deafening [a form of insulation] on the sanitary condition of dwelling houses', a study undertaken in a range of buildings around Dundee.[80] Johnston became an active member of the Dundee Social Union and was also appointed assistant to Geddes in the Botany department (becoming, along with Patti Jack, one of

the first two women to be employed by the College).

During all this activity, Johnston continued to work as an artist, exhibiting landscapes and flower studies at the Dundee Art Club and the Fine Art Exhibitions, contributing drawings to the student magazine *The College* and combining art and science by illustrating some of the Chemistry department's research papers (figure 247). After the 1890s, however, she seems to have abandoned both art and science, spending the rest of her life in Newport working for various charitable causes. As well as serving on the Forgan School Board, she was also secretary of the Newport, Wormit & Forgan Nursing Association and treasurer of the Newport branch of the British Women's Temperance Association.[81] She died in 1952.

Two other protégés of Geddes were responsible for a unique collaboration of art and science that stretched from Dundee almost literally to the ends of the earth. In 1892, Geddes learned of a planned expedition from the silvery Tay to the icy waters of the Antarctic. At that time, Dundee was one of the principal centres of the whaling industry, and when the Arctic whale population started falling, one of the leading whaling companies decided to investigate reports by early Antarctic explorers that whales had been sighted there in large numbers. Four ships were to set sail in September that year, the *Diana*, the *Active*, the *Balaena* and the *Polar Star*.

Geddes saw artistic parallels with Dundee's whaling and shipbuilding industries. In one of his *Advertiser* articles, he wrote:

> "Is it a mere coincidence that original and effective skill in shipbuilding and in art should appear together in the same city? … From ancient Athens to old Bruges or Antwerp – nay, from these to modern Hamburg and some of her rivals we may learn that the love and mastery of the sea, the love and mastery of the arts, have often appeared and culminated together. What thinking person who seeks to understand Dundee can fail to see in the supreme seamanship of the whale-fisher, with his long adventurous voyages and his pre-eminently keen look-out, qualities which have once and again expressed themselves in kindred ways, superficially different, though they seem. …indeed, is not the local record in photography, one so high alike in quality and output, also akin to these, for what is your photographer if not the keenest of look-out men?"[82]

Thanks to Geddes's influence, the expedition was to prove an important landmark in both scientific and artistic exploration. The chief scientific advisor to the expedition was a former student of Geddes's at Edinburgh, Hugh Robert Mill, and it seems to have been Geddes who introduced Mill to another of his students, William Speirs Bruce. Bruce helped Mill in compiling data for a report for the Scottish Fishery Board, and so when Mill succeeded in securing some scientific places on the expedition, he quickly thought of Bruce, who was appointed as naturalist on board the Balaena.[83]

At the time, Bruce was living in Riddle's Court, one of Geddes's halls of residence in Edinburgh. Geddes had commissioned another former student, the artist William Gordon Burn-Murdoch, to paint a frieze for the hall, and Bruce and Burn-Murdoch soon became close friends, and "devoted disciples" of Geddes.[84] As Burn-Murdoch was later to write, "Bruce and I… are deeply indebted to his genius… for raising our spirits a little out of the rut into what we may be allowed to call the dreamland of science."[85]

Burn-Murdoch readily accepted Bruce's invitation to accompany him on the Dundee expedition. Initially he had trouble getting a berth, but as he later recalled, "I wrote immediately to some friends who took a keen interest in the scientific prospects of the venture, and who were also good enough to believe that my drawings in the southern latitudes would be of value in science, and prayed them to exert their influence in my behalf".[86] It seems almost certain that Geddes was one of these. Just three days before the start of the expedition, Burn-Murdoch learned that he'd been given a place on the *Balaena*.

Burn-Murdoch did not think much of Dundee, though he singled out the Albert Institute as the "one beautiful spot in… a large and wealthy town."[87] On his return the gallery was to stage an exhibition of the artworks he produced during the voyage. Burn-Murdoch effectively became the Antarctic's first artist-in-residence, creating vivid recreations of his experiences there (figures 248 & 249).[88]

Captain Fairweather, master of the *Balaena*, apparently had little interest in scientific or artistic work, and expected Bruce and Burn-Murdoch to do their fair share of the manual work, leaving them limited time for anything else. Burn-Murdoch wrote in his diary: "Bruce and I have… seen only a fraction of what we wished to see, and have nothing to speak of in the way of collections either scientific or artistic".[89]

Nevertheless, what data and specimens Bruce was able to bring back had a significant effect in promoting interest in the Antarctic within the scientific community and Burn-Murdoch's drawings and paintings (he brought back over 200 of them) found an eager public who hitherto knew little of this remote part of the world. As well showing them in exhibitions and illustrating his own book about the voyage, Burn-Murdoch's images appeared in numerous other publications, including Geddes's *Evergreen*.

The Dundee expedition has been seen as a crucial catalyst for the whole 'heroic age' of polar exploration, and certainly the performance of the whaling ships in the Antarctic ice was a crucial factor in the decision to build Scott's ship, the *Discovery*, in Dundee. As far as the whalers were concerned, however, the mission was a failure – what whales they'd found there were of a different species to those in the north, too powerful to be captured. It's therefore largely due to Bruce and Burn-Murdoch that the expedition had such a powerful legacy, and Geddes was the key catalyst to that success. On their return, Geddes and his wife met Bruce and Burn-Murdoch at the docks and invited them home for a meal. He remained very proud of the part he had played in bringing the two men together, and would later tell Bruce, "you [have] been the actual initiator of this now world-wide movement of Antarctic Exploration".[90] It was a movement in which art and science played an equal, if unexpected, part.

Artists Together

The significant growth of art as a profession in Dundee at the end of the 19th century owed much to the artists' own attempts at improving their opportunities and increasing both public and official recognition of their role in the cultural life of the city. This could only be achieved by greater professionalisation of their work and by making their collective voices heard in unison.

An early example of artists supporting each other came in 1868 following the death of Henry Harwood, who had struggled with alcoholism in his later years. As was later reported in the *City Echo*, "several of those who appreciated his genius erected a memorial over his grave in the Eastern Cemetery... a portion beside his grave having been set aside as a burying ground for artists who may die in Dundee, having neither friends nor relatives to afford them a last resting-place."[1] This magnanimous scheme was led by Robert Cowie, owner of the Theatre Royal in Castle Street. Cowie had previously taught art and worked as a painter and decorator, known for his "exquisite natural taste".[2] He had sat for a portrait by Harwood (figure 250) and owned several other examples of the artist's work.[3] A group calling themselves "Robert Cowie Inst. Artists" purchased three lairs in the Eastern Cemetery, Harwood being interred in the first. As it transpired, only one other person was ever buried in one of these lairs – a decorative painter called John P Jerome who died aged 24 in 1873, leaving a widow and child.[4]

Given the clear need for support of professional artists like Harwood and Jerome, it seems ironic that it was a group of amateurs who first banded together to promote their joint interests. The town seems to have had a thriving community of amateur artists of all classes. In 1880, some 1400 pencil drawings were exhibited in Lindsay Street Hall, the work of a Dundee stonemason who practised art in his spare time.[5] Most such artists never gave up the day job, but some working men tried to take their talent further. A series of newspaper articles in 1888 on 'How the Poor Live' included a feature on a pavement artist working in Albert Square. Having been made unemployed from the shipyards, he had worked as an artist for twelve years and claimed to make more money at it than he had in his former profession. He found that the working classes generally paid him more ("the 'nobs,' you know, have collections of their own"), but the journalist's description of him hardly suggests that he was making a decent living: "He seemed to be a poor creature shaking and nervous through exposure and dissipation. His clothes were ragged and dirty and he was literally covered in mud".[6]

This was clearly not the intended audience of the Dundee Amateur Art Association, founded in 1876.[7] Little is recorded of its activities, but James Russell was its president, and its mostly middle-class members, numbering about a dozen, met initially in Mathers' Hotel and then at 61 Reform Street (later used as a studio by several professional artists). According to a 1900 description by the GAA, "Meetings of members took the practical form of Art Study and discussion."[8]

The Association seems to have dwindled away after just a few years, but many of its members were involved in the founding in 1880 of the Dundee Art Club.[9] This brought amateurs and professionals together for the first time "in the regular study and practice of Art... by Weekly Meetings for Study, Monthly Exhibitions for Criticism, and Annual Public Exhibitions."[10] Meetings were held initially in the same room as those of the earlier Association at 61 Reform Street and also at Lamb's Hotel, before settling permanently at 31 Reform Street (where Jane Spindler had her studio). Prospective members had to be proposed and seconded by existing members, and had to submit at least two original sketches to demonstrate their ability. There was a strict format to the Club's activities – the weekly meetings took the form of a Life Class, and once a month members were required to bring at least one sketch on a particular theme or genre to be exhibited:

"At these meetings, after the preliminary business, there shall be criticism of the Sketches brought by the Members, in illustration of the prescribed subject or otherwise. Contributors may reply at the close. The subject of illustration for next Meeting shall then be chosen; and thereafter, papers may be read or discussions engaged in, on Art subjects, as time may permit."[11]

250. Henry Harwood, *Robert Cowie*, oil on canvas (*Dundee City Council: Dundee's Art Galleries & Museums*).

251. Unknown artist, 'Amateur Street Artists' from *The Piper o' Dundee*, 1889 (*Libraries, Leisure & Culture Dundee*).

Stewart Carmichael later recalled that the criticism was not always well received:

"One evening the subject for illustration had been 'Helen MacGregor' – the warrior wife of Rob Roy. A water colour (with red hair, blood stained claymore and flaming tartan defiantly afoot on her native rock) was placed on the easel. It was the work of a choleric amateur whose brow grew darker and darker as each defamatory critique was launched at it, until in exasperation he seized the offending 'Helen', snatched his coat and hat and vanished."[12]

The "founder and moving spirit" of the Club was Martin Anderson, at this time still working for the *Dundee Advertiser*.[13] He served at various times as Secretary, Treasurer and President of the Club. The architect and art collector T S Robertson seems to have been the first President, succeeded by another notable collector, J G Orchar, who was later made Honorary President. Many other amateur artists also played active roles: Thomas Kyle, who served as both Secretary and Vice President, worked at the Harbour Chambers Office; another Vice President, John Jones, was a carpet merchant. Perhaps most successful as an amateur was Adam B Fairweather, a professional barber who achieved a considerable reputation as a painter, showing regularly at the RSA.[14]

Other members were, like Anderson, just beginning to establish their careers as professional artists. The Club's first Treasurer, Robert C Farquharson, was making his living as a jeweller but was a regular contributor to the *Wizard of the North* and was "well known in local art circles as a very successful artist and portrait painter", displaying his work regularly at the Fine Art Exhibitions. A relative of the sculptor Sir John Steell, his early death from typhoid fever in 1883 robbed the Club of "one of the most assiduous of its members."[15] Other artists serving on the committee over the years included Allan Ramsay, Stewart Carmichael, John Duncan, Etta Johnston, Jane Spindler, Alex Neilson and Giuseppe Gonnella.

The Club held its first public exhibition in June 1883 at Fraser's Art Saloon. Seventeen of its nineteen members contributed, alongside a memorial display of works by Farquharson, who had died just a few weeks before. Altogether 112 works were included, and the *Courier* referred to "the general excellence of the great proportion of the collection" and praised (among others) landscapes by Ramsay and Spindler, cartoons by Anderson and topographical pictures by architects T S Robertson, Charles Ower and T M Cappon.[16]

The success of this exhibition led to the next being held at the Albert Institute in December 1884. 24 artists contributed 95 works and Anderson designed an elaborately illustrated catalogue to accompany the show (figure 252). John Duncan and Stewart Carmichael were among the new exhibitors, and the success of the exhibition led to another just five months later, this time with 173 works including newcomers C G L Phillips and D Ramsay Sellars, the latter earning particular praise in the *Courier*'s review.[17] An exhibition of black-and-white work was held in the Club's Reform Street rooms in

252. Martin Anderson, cover illustrations for Dundee Art Club exhibition catalogue, 1884 *(Libraries, Leisure & Culture Dundee, licensor www.scran.ac.uk)*.

December 1885, and by the time of the next Albert Institute exhibition in May 1886, the *Courier* was noting how gratifying it was "to find so many in our midst devoting themselves to art study, and with so much success."[18] Further familiar names made their Club debut in this show, including E S Hodgson and R D Winter.

By 1886 the Club claimed to include among its members "nearly all the Professional Artists in Dundee and places round about".[19] It boasted 32 members but the commitment to producing work for criticism at each meeting seemed to discourage other prospective members. New rules were drawn up to distinguish between Ordinary Members (paying an annual subscription of 5 shillings) and Honorary Members (paying 10s) "who may desire to be connected with the Club for the purpose of encouraging Art" but who were not obliged to submit work at the meetings.[20] This increased the membership to 43 – 22 ordinary and 21 honorary members. The latter category included interested parties like J M Keiller, I J Weinberg and D C Thomson but also several professional artists such as A S Edward and Allan Ramsay, suggesting a reluctance on their part to engage fully with the Club's activities.

The 1886 exhibition was the last to be held in the Albert Institute, the Club retreating to its Reform Street rooms for the 1887 show. The *Courier* noticed that this was a smaller affair than usual, but still "speaks well of our local artistic ability."[21] Both the *Courier* and the *Piper o' Dundee* singled out John Duncan as the most notable exhibitor. More established painters such as Allan Ramsay were not represented, and it

is notable that the *Piper* referred to the Club as a "coterie of young artists".[22]

The Club may have been losing its claim to represent Dundee's professional artists as a whole, but its social activities continued unabated. In May 1888 they held a Club Picnic which was amusingly reported in verse by the *Piper o' Dundee:*

The artists had a picnic party,
And friends they invited them all;
There was G—lla the hearty,
And N—son the sculptor so tall.

And comic young artists they came by the dozen,
With paper and pencil tied up in a roll;
While Martin the painter listlessly listened
To the cheering praise of a congenial soul.[23]

The 1888 exhibition seems to have been the Club's last. The *Courier* pointed out "several specimens of crude art, suggestive of juvenility".[24] Once again John Duncan was singled out for the highest praise, while newcomers Max Cowper and Alec Grieve were favourably noticed by the *Piper*.

When Martin Anderson headed to London to find fame as Cynicus the Club was evidently unable to survive without him. The playwright R Fenton Mackay took over as President and Anderson continued to be listed as a committee member but was no longer actively involved.[25] Before its demise, the Club was successful in fostering a briefly popular off-shoot in the form of the Quill & Quaver Club, a literary and musical society which met in the Art Club's rooms on Saturday evenings, and featured many of the same members. Anderson served as Vice President before heading to London, but unlike the Art Club the Quill & Quaver survived his departure, at least for a few years. Artists continued to be prominently involved in it – sculptor George MacDougald and painter Charles S Mills both served as President, with Alex Neilson as Secretary.[26]

Another organisation of related interest was the Dundee Institute of Architecture, Science & Art. The study of art was a vital part of the curriculum for any would-be architect, and many architects were active members of the Art Club. On 9 June 1884 architect James MacLaren chaired a meeting of his profession at Lamb's Hotel, at which it was agreed to found an Institute "for the study of architecture, the applied sciences, and the fine arts, by means of papers and discussions, classes for study, prizes, visits to public works and buildings, and excursions for sketching, &c."[27] MacLaren was elected President, with Art Club members Charles Ower and T S Robertson also serving on the committee. At the Institute's inaugural conversazione in October, MacLaren explained the new organisation's artistic interests:

"architecture is many-sided… To limit it to
everyday building would be like confining
the art of painting to portraiture, or music
to the power of speech. It is an art born of
necessity, yet it is the least imitative of any
of the arts, and offering so wide a range for

the imaginative and reasoning faculties as
to endow the lifeless material of nature with
poetic beauty".[28]

The first lecture to be organised by the Institute was on 'Architectural Art', given by Prof G Baldwin Brown on 20 November. Later in the first session, painter J G H Spindler spoke on 'Art Work in the Middle Ages'.[29] Art was also prevalent in the Institute's prize competition, held annually. The categories varied but those for the opening session included "Best Series of Five Freehand Sketches of any Building or Buildings", "Best Etching on Metals, any Subject", "Best Lithograph, any Subject". "Best Original Panel, Carved or Modelled in relief in any Material" and "Best Original Decorative Painting on Wooden Panel, in any Medium".[30]

It was architects, too, who chaired the first meetings which brought about the formation of Dundee's longest-established art society. On 29 November 1889, the city architect, William Alexander, presided at a meeting in the Committee Room of the Albert Institute of "artists resident in Dundee".[31] According to the first entry in the Minute Book of the Graphic Arts Association,

"The want of an Art Association – in such
an ardent art admiring centre as Dundee
– wide enough in its scope to embrace, not
only those practicing [sic] art professionally, but the numerous patrons and admirers
likewise, having long been felt, a movement
was initiated for the establishment of such
an association, which resulted in a general
meeting of those interested being held…"[32]

The absence of any mention of the Art Club is notable, despite many of its members being present at the meeting. Alexander laid out proposals for a new Art Association: "The idea was received with an agreeable warmth and unanimity, and it was resolved that such an Association should be organized forthwith."[33] Another architect, Charles Ower, took the lead in convening a committee to take the plan forward, joined by professional artists E S Hodgson, D Ramsay Sellars, W B Lamond and Alex Neilson, amateur painter William Seaton and curator John Maclauchlan. This committee met to deliberate on 14 January and then laid their plans before the artistic community on 28 January. At this meeting the name "Graphic Arts Association, Dundee" was agreed, a constitution was drawn up and the first Council was elected. Woodcarver James Bremner was a surprising choice as President, but the rest of the committee were all Art Club alumni – Vice-President E S Hodgson, Treasurer William Seaton, Secretary D Ramsay Sellars and Ordinary Members of Council John Duncan and Charles Ower.

As with the later years of the Art Club, it was decided to divide the Association's subscribers into Members ("Those who have been engaged in the practice of any of the graphic arts as a profession for a period of not less than five years", paying an

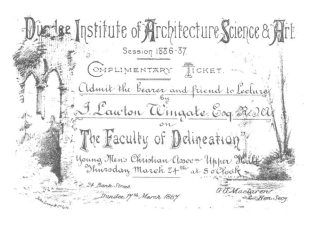

253. Unknown artist, 'Dundee Art Club Exhibition' from The *Piper o' Dundee*, 1887 *(Libraries, Leisure & Culture Dundee)*.

254. John Duncan, Invitation card for Dundee Art Club exhibition, 1888 *(Libraries, Leisure & Culture Dundee)*.

255. Ticket for a lecture by the artist J L Wingate organised by the Dundee Institute of Architecture, Science & Art, 1887 *(Libraries, Leisure & Culture Dundee)*.

annual subscription of 7s 6d) and Associates ("Those who are not eligible as Members, but who take an interest in the objects of the society" paying 5s).[34] A C Lamb and David Dawson (another antiquarian and headmaster of Brown Street Public School) were later elected as the first two Associate Members to join the Council. It was also agreed to appoint notable artists and benefactors as Honorary Members – by the time of their next meeting on 18 February John Pettie, James Archer and W D McKay had all accepted this honour, and by the end of the year they would be joined by artists Colin Hunter and John Smart, and local patrons J M Keiller, John Leng, J G Orchar, John Robertson, I J Weinberg and Ex-Provost Hunter. In a particular coup for the new Association, William McTaggart agreed to assume the role of Honorary President.

The minute of 18 February records the first members of the GAA. As well as those on the Council, these were Stewart Carmichael, Charles Duncan, Adam B Fairweather, Giuseppe Gonnella, W B Lamond, James Melvin, Alex Neilson, J F Pollock, C G L Phillips, J G H Spindler and David Smith. Although no women had yet joined, it was resolved at this meeting "that Ladies be placed under no disqualification".[35] The first female Associates soon joined, but it would be three years before the first woman was elected as a Member.

The GAA launched itself publicly on 10 June 1890 with a lecture by James Archer on 'The Art of the Present Day in its relation to the Art of the Past', chaired by McTaggart (figure 256). A large crowd gathered in the Victoria Gallery, and as the *Advertiser* reported, "Many of the audience had doubtless been brought to this lecture both by the high reputation which Mr Archer enjoys as an artist and from the fact that it was the first public appearance of the Graphic Arts Association."[36] Archer's lecture seems to have been a fairly jingoistic affair, being highly critical of French Impressionism (but praising Scotland's leading impressionist, McTaggart!) and saying that there was little point in British artists studying in Paris since the French had got all their ideas from British painters in the first place. The opinions of GAA members (many of whom had studied in Paris and were very receptive to more modern French ideas) were not recorded, but the event was considered a great success.

A key aim of the new Association was to ensure that Dundee's artists were recognised at high levels as valuable contributors to civic life. In their first annual report, the council stated: "The official recognition of the Association by the representatives of the public and the patrons of art in the district was a most gratifying item of the past year's experience."[37] Early successes in this regard included an invitation for representatives of the GAA to join the organising committee of the Home Industries Exhibition at the Albert Institute; to attend the opening of the Fine Art Exhibition of 1890; and to the Lord Provost's lunch to mark the presentation of Freedom of the City to William Gladstone.

By the end of its first year, the GAA had a total of 22 Members (including A S Edward and William Grubb) and 24 Associates (eight of whom were women, including Helen Batchelor, Leila Fleming and E M Lowdon).[38] Many of its principal activities had already been established, including various classes for study, the first of which was a Life Class. Organised initially by C G L Phillips, sixteen members joined

immediately with others to follow. The GAA awarded the Life Class a small annual sum (usually between £1 and £2), the rest of the costs (hire of models and coal to heat the room) being met by separate subscriptions from members. By the time Max Cowper took over running the class in 1892, it had 27 members. Cowper introduced "costumes of pictorial and historical interest" for the models, initially hiring these from Liverpool, including Touchstone, a Cavalier and a traditional Japanese costume.[39] In 1893 a bazaar was held to raise funds for buying costumes and backgrounds, and for hiring better premises (the large galleries in the Albert Institute being very costly to heat). The result was a studio at 48 Victoria Road which the GAA had part use of for a weekly rent of 4 shillings.[40]

The suggestion of a nude life class was first made in 1890 but does not seem to have been taken further until 1895. This provoked considerable discussion among members but propriety prevailed and it was agreed to have two classes – "male models [to] be used for the male classes & female for the female session".[41] The Draped Life Class continued at the Albert Institute (fourteen members in 1895), with the Male Nude Class (eight members) and the Female Nude Class (seven members) being held on different nights at Victoria Road. Stewart Carmichael later recalled the male class: "It is vivid to me now creeping up the long dark stairs and then lighting the stove [and] settling to study. Very good models, poorly paid I think now and they must have suffered from the cold, but the members who attended were always cheery and full of fire for their work."[42]

The nude classes later moved to the private studios of individual members, the Male Nude Class being hosted for many years by Carmichael and the Female Nude Class by Miss E M Lowdon, an amateur artist who also taught private classes in "Drawing and Painting from Life, Still Life [and] Outdoor Sketching" from her studio in Fort Street, Broughty Ferry.[43]

The GAA was always concerned with advancing the quality of art being produced by its members, and in 1897 it was "remitted to Miss Louden [sic] & Messrs Carmichael and [Frank] Laing, with powers, to superintend [the nude classes], and, if necessary, insist upon a preliminary course of study from the antique on the part of those to whom this was in their opinion necessary."[44] This may also have been intended as a way of revitalising the defunct Antique Class. Set up in 1891, the class was always under-attended. In 1893, Max Cowper reported: "If something is not done for it before long, we will, I am afraid lose access to the splendid collection of casts, for it can hardly be expected that Mr Maclauchlan will night after night, light up this large gallery for the sake of 1 or 2 students"[45]

One of the few enthusiastic attendees was Carmichael, who remembered: "The lighting was excellent, the casts were new, and we were alone with the Masters."[46] The class was ultimately abandoned in 1896, and no members of the nude classes seem to have been made to take it up again. The life classes survived longer, though continued to be restrained by ideas of what was considered socially (and morally) acceptable. In 1907, "some of the [male] students expressed a wish to introduce the semi-nude female model but the Council, after carefully considering the question, decided that it would be injudicious to permit the innovation."[47] The classes were eventually suspended in 1910, members instead being encouraged to attend life classes in the Technical College & School of Art.

The only other form of study attempted by the GAA in its early years was an Outdoor Sketching Class, also under the secretaryship of E M Lowdon. During the summer months of 1890, fourteen members went on excursions to Barnhill, Leuchars, Invergowrie and Tayport. Numbers dwindled the following year, however, "through the departure of Members during the summer months to their own favourable sketching grounds."[48] Although some improvement in numbers was reported the following year, the class seems to have ceased at that point.

Various other activities were attempted by the GAA. In 1891 J G H Spindler organised an excursion to Edinburgh to see the RSA's annual exhibition and have dinner with some of the artists from the capital who had accepted honorary membership. Spindler had arranged for a private carriage on the train and members were told to wear an ivy leaf as a badge for identification. Just days before the event the whole thing was called off, the Council blaming the North British Railway Company for having rescinded their agreed arrangements.[49]

Social activity was important to the GAA. In February 1892, a Conversazione was held in the Albert Institute, attended by around 150 people, mostly women. J G H Spindler, then President, addressed the members, advising them "not to join the ranks of the impressionists on the one hand, or the finical pre-Raphaelites on the other, but to strive to show some of the good qualities of both in all they accomplished."[50] A successful musical programme followed, with a refreshment buffet during the interval.

While one-off events like this were well attended, the numbers at regular meetings of the GAA were notably low (rarely more than a dozen including the Council). To help encourage more members, the AGM in 1894 was held in Lamb's Hotel and was more sociable in character:

> "On the conclusion of the business, the social part of the programme was entered upon and a very pleasant evening was spent in an informal fashion. Several of the ladies and gentlemen present entertained the company with vocal and instrumental music of a high order and the meeting closed about 10 pm with the singing of 'Auld Lang Syne.'"[51]

Numbers failed to rise, however, and the following year it was agreed to have a series of short talks after each meeting, critic and antiquarian A H Millar kicking off with a lecture on 'Art and Art Critics'. Most of the talks were by members, including Alec Grieve (on art as expressed in that year's exhibition), Charles S Mills (on impressionism) and Stewart Carmichael (on the relation of societies such as theirs to the public). Carmichael later claimed: "The members at that time seemed to live for art controversy. The chairman had difficulty in keeping order."[52] Though the talks prompted much discussion, they did not encourage more members to attend and soon petered out.

It was clearly apparent that the GAA's social activities were impaired by lack of suitable premises, and in 1900 they began discussions with the University Club about renting rooms in their building at 104 Nethergate, next door to the framers Thomas Murray & Son. Stewart Carmichael remembered:

> "The mood of the place was delightful. The windows of the big room looked out on an

old garden with picturesque apples and pear trees then in vigour. Below us the century old gilders had their workshops and old masters were cleaned and renovated there. Beautiful frames were made for the pictures of Edinburgh and London artists that city merchants had purchased. We envied them."[53]

An annual rent of £20 was agreed including heating, light and the use of an attendant, and the GAA moved in that September. Several of the lady members took charge of decorating the rooms and a number of periodicals were acquired for the use of members. Eventually a fairly substantial library was built up, run for many years by Mrs Carmichael. As well as familiar art publications such *The Studio*, the GAA acquired many Continental journals as well, such as *Die Kunst* and *L'Art*, which helped expose its members to a broader range of influences. In 1902 an agreement was reached with the Institute of Architecture, Science & Art to share the club rooms, and a joint programme of talks was arranged, which proved far more popular than the GAA's previous attempts.

Classes and social activities were beneficial for the members, but the GAA's principal public focus was its annual exhibition.[54] Dundee's artists had been regular contributors to the Fine Art Exhibitions since their inception and had been steadily growing in number.[55] To commemorate the opening of the 1886 exhibition, a group of Dundee's professional artists held a dinner to which several of the visiting artists were invited.[56] At the start of the 1889 exhibition, however, a letter sent to the *Courier* signed 'Amateur' complained:

> "Local artists have this time fared very badly indeed at the hands of the Hanging Committee. The truth is, they have been completely weeded out, and considerable indignation is manifested among them in consequence. …if local men do not take care they will soon find the galleries closed against them altogether. It does seem rather hard that local artists should be left out in the shade to make way for the works of needy Academicians, who have galleries of their own, but such is literally the state of affairs at the present moment. It has all along been the misfortune of our local Exhibition to depend always almost entirely for its promotion on a few antiquated gentlemen with peculiar and startling notions regarding art, whose ideas in general are full half-a-century out of date."[57]

While there may have been some truth in this last comment, the author had no grounds for complaint concerning a lack of local representation – nearly 100 of the exhibitors at that year's exhibition lived in Dundee or its immediate vicinity, a record number.

It is unsurprising, therefore, that when the decision was made not to arrange a Fine Art Exhibition in 1892-3, it was proposed (by E S Hodgson) that the GAA should promote its own exhibition instead. The use of a single gallery in the Albert Institute was agreed in April 1893, and the resulting exhibition opened in June. The GAA Council acted as the hanging committee, drafting in W B Lamond to assist them. Noted art collector I J Weinberg gave the opening address, noting that

"very great progress had been made" on previous exhibitions by local artists (referring, presumably, to those of the Dundee Art Club), but the quality of individual artworks was evidently variable: "As in a garden... [he] looked at and admired what was beautiful, and passed by other things which were not so much so, and the same thing held good in an exhibition of pictures."[58] Stewart Carmichael recalled: "To our ardent and youthful spirits the address was too condescending, for some of the pictures then exhibited have since found places in public galleries."[59] However some reviewers agreed with Weinberg – the *Wizard of the North* noted that the "pictures represent all stages of ability", some being "rather crude".[60]

In all 66 artists contributed 269 works, the principal exhibitors being A B Fairweather (twelve pictures), Stewart Carmichael and W B Lamond (eleven each), and C L Mitchell and C G L Phillips (ten each). Several women artists were also significant contributors, including E M Lowdon (nine), Mrs Mary Davids (eight) and Margaret Suttie, the GAA's first professional female artist (seven). A catalogue was produced for the exhibition (price 4d) with a cover designed by Max Cowper.

This first exhibition was sufficiently successful to warrant a second in spring 1894, and it then became an annual event. The *Piper o' Dundee* noted that "city folk will be compelled to admit that the Dundee artists are moving forward apace", while the *Wizard of the North* stated: "The art-life of Dundee is in the course of rapid development".[61] J G Orchar opened the second exhibition and (like Weinberg before him) congratulated the artists on "the steady progress you are making in art."[62]

The following year saw the start of a long tradition of inviting notable Scottish artists to open the annual exhibition. J L Wingate gave a stimulating address on 'Art Culture' to an audience of around 400, followed by an orchestral programme. The *Piper o' Dundee* included a full page of reproduction sketches of works in the exhibition, as it had formerly done for the Fine Art Exhibitions.

Unfortunately the securing of celebrated artists for this purpose was never an easy business. W D McKay had been first choice in 1895 but proved unavailable, though he did agree in 1897. In 1896, they approached James Guthrie for the first of many attempts, all to no avail. Others who declined included William Hole, George Henry, George Reid, J H Lorimer, Robert Alexander, W Y Macgregor and J Coutts Michie. In fact, not once during this period did they succeed in getting their first choice, but over the years the artists they did attract included Macauley Stevenson, James Paterson, J Campbell Noble, Alexander Roche, Pittendrigh MacGillivray, James Cadenhead, D Y Cameron and E A Walton. Several of these were renowned as members of the so-called 'Glasgow Boys', and Stewart Carmichael recalled the influence that their work had on the Dundee artists:

> "We were astonished at their opulent use of colour, their rich pictorial aspect and dignified placing of subject on canvas. As a result we keyed up our colour and forsook the low tones that had been apparent in our own work. It took time and many experiments to reap the benefits from these newly acquired discoveries. Much good canvas and good paint were wasted."[63]

Many such joint experiments were carried out in the 1890s when several Dundee artists came together to occupy the city's first shared artists' studio at 15 Castle Street (figure 257), in the former Theatre Royal building which had closed following a fire. Commercial illustrator David Clark appears to have been first on the premises in 1891, being joined over the next decade by Max Cowper, J Francis Pollock, D Ramsay Sellars, Stewart Carmichael, Alec Grieve, Helen Batchelor, Margaret Suttie, Edgar Mitchell, Robert A Kennedy, Emma Sinclair and E M Davidson.[64] "All very short of cash but most of them making a brave effort to do all good work," was how Stewart Carmichael recalled this band of artists, continuing:

> "So short were the funds one Exhibition time that we were glad to hire our model's (a shore porter's) barrow for transit of our pictures. After loading our precious burden destined for the Exhibition, Alec Grieve and myself pushed behind and Georgie the model in front guided gently the rickety barrow across the High Street up Reform Street to the impressive North door of the Institute – it wasn't style – but we got there alright."[65]

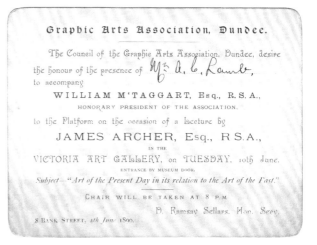

By 1897 the *Piper* was proclaiming that the GAA exhibition "has become an institution in our midst, and is an admirable index of the progress of local art."[66] An attempt had been made in 1896 to hang the exhibition in groups by artist, but this had not proved popular and had resulted in the smallest show thus far – 180 works by 51 artists. The experiment was not repeated. The principal contributors to the exhibitions were generally the same each year – Carmichael, Grieve, Mitchell and Phillips, with other artists such as Fairweather, Lamond, Spindler and Mills usually close behind. Increasingly contributions were coming in from elsewhere in the region – J W Herald from Arbroath, William Miller Frazer from Perth and Allan Ramsay from Edzell were now among the exhibiting members. In 1897 John Duncan returned from Edinburgh and became a major contributor, and David Foggie submitted his first works in the same year. George Dutch Davidson began contributing in 1898.

While the general opinion of the exhibitions was one of ever-increasing approval, the GAA's members were quick to take offence over any negative criticism. In 1900, for example, the *Piper* noted that "Wordy warfare is being waged in the newspapers over the merits and demerits of artistes [sic] and critics."[67] This protracted affair was kick-started by a review of the exhibition by A H Millar in the *Dundee Advertiser*, which condemned the Celtic and symbolist content of many of the works (see chapter three), branding them "lachrymose and lackadaisical" and tending to induce "lugubrious melancholy and despair. Art, no doubt, is multiform, but there are some kinds of it that should be taken in homeopathic dozes [sic]."[68]

This prompted a letter from 'Spectator' complaining that this "carping and contemptuous spirit … is not only unjust and ungenerous, but unintelligent."[69] Millar (writing anonymously as 'Art Critic') replied to refute the charges, concluding: "I am quite prepared to leave the matter in dispute to the judgment of the majority of Dundee artists, and to the lovers of art generally."[70] Whatever the majority may have thought,

Stewart Carmichael was not prepared to let the matter rest, complaining:

> "'Art Critic' has no care for our work, sees no merit, questions our sincerity, and boldly states his impression to the public prints. He asks for something in our work we have no desire to give, and that which we offer he rejects… To be fair to a work of art, the critic must endeavour to stand beside the artist on his platform, to see from that vantage ground… what the artist has endeavoured to express, what he has forged out of the infinite world of the beautiful."[71]

Returning to the fray, 'Spectator' went further, claiming:

"These men have for years been resolute in adhering to their own artistic methods and point of view. It has cost them much in money, in popularity, in sympathy. Is it reasonable to suppose that they would continue in this course (in spite of, for example, your art critic's annual advice) unless they felt it necessary to make a stand for the right to untrammelled individual expression, and were prepared to make sacrifices to preserve the integrity of the artistic conscience?"[72]

After a further seven letters (two from 'Pro Bono Artis' defending the artists, two from 'Black Frame' attacking them, a further response from Carmichael, one from Alec Grieve and one from C G L Phillips writing as 'Old School'), the editor decided "Enough has now been said on this subject."[73] By that time the *Wizard of the North* had published a full-page cartoon entitled 'A Bad Half Hour at the Graphic Arts Exhibition' (figure 260) and the *Piper o' Dundee* had also entered the fray: "Pictures there are that may not satisfy the crowd, but the artist has elected to speak in his own way, and those who do not comprehend are not warranted in sneering at a language they do not understand."[74]

This drew a number of responses altogether blunter than the correspondence in the *Advertiser*. 'Honorary Critic' claimed: "The Graphic Arts show is altogether too small an affair, and life is too short for time to be wasted thereon. If young ladies and gentlemen choose to trifle with art that is their affair, but I must be excused if I decide to treat their exhibitions as other kinderspiels are treated."[75]

256. Opposite page top: Invitation to join the platform party for James Archer's lecture to the Graphic Arts Association, 1890 *(Libraries, Leisure & Culture Dundee, licensor www.scran.ac.uk)*.

257. Opposite page bottom: 15 Castle Street, c.1895. Photograph from the Wilson Collection *(Libraries, Leisure & Culture Dundee)*.

258. Top left: Stewart Carmichael, cover design for the Graphic Arts Association exhibition catalogue, 1897 *(Libraries, Leisure & Culture Dundee)*.

259. Top right: Unknown artist, 'Graphic Arts Exhibition' from *The Wizard of the North*, 1899 *(Libraries, Leisure & Culture Dundee)*.

260. Above: Unknown artist, 'A Bad Half Hour at the Graphic Arts Exhibition' from *The Wizard of the North*, 1900 *(Libraries, Leisure & Culture Dundee)*.

Such criticisms at least had the effect of encouraging more people to visit the exhibitions. While the public (and collectors) of Dundee had flocked to see the big Fine Art Exhibitions, they had hitherto stayed away from the GAA's own efforts. "It was a constant wonder with us why the people of Dundee did not visit our Exhibition and buy our work," Carmichael noted, "for by this time we were having some success outside."[76] At one of their evening talks, a "violent discussion had ensued on the ignorance and apathy of the Dundee public in their own artists. One prominent artist member rose and with overwhelming scorn in his voice finished with 'the Public; the Public; the Public are a flock of sheep'."[77]

Various attempts were made to promote the exhibitions. In 1897, for example, daily adverts were placed in the local papers and 500 posters were printed and displayed around Dundee and Lochee.[78] The following year they tried paying men with sandwich boards to walk the streets throughout the duration of the exhibition.[79] Numbers attending the exhibition gradually rose, but sales remained poor. Carmichael recounted an amusing story at one of their opening nights:

> "J Campbell Noble, RSA, delivered the
> opening address and when we surrounded
> him praising his wise and stimulating lecture
> he turned quickly and said 'Now boys run
> off and sell your pictures, get hold of your
> patrons. This is the moment of the RSA
> when we sell...' Surprise came into our faces!
> Nobody buys at our Exhibition in Dundee! It
> is unheard of."[80]

The *Evening Telegraph*'s 'Here and There' columnist laid the blame for poor sales squarely at the feet of the artists themselves:

> "Time and again local art lovers have told me
> that they were kept from buying local work
> simply because the moment they evinced
> interest the local artist began to talk large
> and name a big price. There is a large and
> moneyed art-loving public in the city and
> district ready to show practical sympathy with
> the local art movement, but they are not to be
> treated as unintelligent, and are quite capable
> of forming accurate estimates of both pictures
> and prices."[81]

Mr D. R. Sellars, Secretary, Graphic Arts Association.

As early as 1892, the GAA had considered setting up its own Art Union in order to boost sales, but the idea was only agreed upon two years later. The success of the Dundee Fine Art Exhibitions' Art Union was doubtless a key influence on this, though the minutes of the time refer to "that of the Society of Scottish Artists" as the main inspiration.[82] By March 1894 a scheme had been approved by the Board of Trade and a committee empowered to run it which included such luminaries as Sheriff Campbell Smith, A C Lamb, J G Orchar, John Robertson of Elmslea, I J Weinberg, the current Lord Provost and his three predecessors. The bulk of the work was carried out by local solicitor G B Carmichael (Stewart's brother), who gradually built up a sizeable list of annual subscribers paying ten shillings each. At the exhibition in the Art Union's first year, £95/17 was awarded in prizes, yielding picture sales of £128/12/6 – "a considerable amount of patronage to local art".[83] The commission earned by the GAA on this total was £7/3/10, compared to just £1/8/7 on all other sales. The Art Union thus became, right from the outset, the main financial lifeline for exhibiting artists. Referring to the 1898 exhibition, the GAA's annual report lamented that "the financial support rendered to the Artists is so meagre. The

261. Top left: George Dutch Davidson, *The Tomb*, ink on paper, 1900. One of the works shown in the GAA's memorial exhibition in 1901 *(Dundee City Council: Dundee's Art Galleries & Museums)*.

262. Top right: Dundee Art Society council members, 1906. Left to right: Edwin J Smith, J D Mills, R J Berg, David Foggie, Edith Macintyre, Tom Ross, Charles G Soutar, C L Mitchell. Photograph from a volume of newspaper cuttings owned by Stewart Carmichael *(Dundee City Archives)*.

263. Above: Unknown artist, Portrait of David Ramsay Sellars from *The Piper o' Dundee*, 1890 *(Libraries, Leisure & Culture Dundee)*.

264. Opposite page top: Unknown artist (possibly Alec Grieve), 'The Crowning of the Old Steeple' from the *People's Journal*, 1900 *(used by kind permission of D C Thomson & Co Ltd)*.

265. Opposite page bottom: Tom Ross, 'Sketches from the Art Exhibition', featuring highlights of the Art Society's majority exhibition, from *The Wizard of the North*, 1911 *(Libraries, Leisure & Culture Dundee)*.

total amount of the catalogue prices of pictures sold was only £116, and these sales, it might be added, were entirely due to the Art Union."[84] This was in spite of repeated pleas from the local press to encourage the public to support the exhibitions. In 1901 the *Piper o' Dundee* complained of the local public's lack of interest in art: "All honour to the 'GAA' that in austere and unsympathetic times keeps the heavenly flame alight."[85]

In fact sales did slowly improve, as did the exhibition accounts generally. Having made a steady loss every year up to 1898, the following year saw the exhibition making a profit for the first time, and over the next ten years, the shows tended to alternate fairly regularly between profit and loss.

While the GAA's exhibitions were always intended as selling shows, from the start they sought to give added value by borrowing additional works from other collections. This began in the very first exhibition with the inclusion of *Return from the Fields* by Arthur Melville, loaned by Arthur Harris. The GAA wanted to include more works of this kind but the Fine Art Committee at the Victoria Galleries were anxious to avoid what they saw as competition with the main Fine Art Exhibitions, and insisted that only works by local artists could be included (Melville was allowed since, though known as one of the Glasgow Boys, he originally hailed from Angus). This restriction continued to be enforced for several years after the original run of Fine Art Exhibitions came to an end.

In 1901 the loaned works took on an altogether different significance as the GAA faced the sad duty of including in that year's exhibition a memorial display of their two recently deceased members, Dutch Davidson and C S Mills. The previous year an attempt had been made to include some work by the late artist William Yule, who had also died at a tragically young age, but Yule's father had considered the request premature and nothing was done. The shocking deaths of two such active members of the GAA so close together could not go unmarked, however – Davidson had helped to organise exhibitions and was a leading light in the decorative section, while Mills had served on the Council since 1894, latterly as Treasurer. As close friends of the artists, David Foggie and Alec Grieve were tasked with arranging matters with their families, and the ensuing exhibition featured an impressive 'In Memoriam' section decorated with wreaths supplied by one of the members of the decorative group, Annie Moon.

The result was highly praised and ironically the death of two of its most talented members seems to have given the GAA increased esteem. They finally persuaded the Victoria Galleries committee to allow non-local loan pictures, and their 1902 exhibition featured works by Gaston la Touche, George Reid and John Pettie among others. This inspired further ambition, and the following year a motion was proposed by C G L Phillips and Alec Grieve to make the next exhibition "an Exhibition of Professional Scottish Art".[86] Works by Alexander Roche, E A Hornel and others were shown in the 1903 exhibition, and by 1905 there were 41 Glasgow artists and 26 Edinburgh ones exhibiting along with many others from around the country.

Arrangements for the exhibitions did not always go according to plan. Stewart Carmichael remembered the opening of the 1908 show as particularly embarrassing:

THE CROWNING OF THE OLD STEEPLE.

Stewart Carmichael says :—" The Steeple is a human thing to me, there in the midst of a surging sea of men standing beautiful, demanding of its citizens this structural right, this diadem that would crown it as one of the stateliest of towers. There are thousands in Dundee who feel as I do, and would whlingly give their mite. I would be glad to work in the humblest capacity for such an end. I would carry mortar for a month—an artist of Dundee." Surely with such enthusiasm the thing can be easily accomplished. But artists as hod carriers—— !

Sketches from the Art Exhibition.

"…the Council of the Art Society had decided on an original and informal re-union at 9.30 at a well-known Dundee hotel… The invitations were to be word of mouth and were left to the discretion of the Council. As the function in the galleries was drawing to a close and the guests were on their way to this mysterious rendezvous some of us realised that many more invitations had been given than the Council had agreed on – and when we got down – after infinite delays – it was evident that the hotel-keeper had forgotten our coming and as we entered, waiters were hurriedly spreading tablecloths, plumping down a bottle of wine here, one of 'Johnnie Walker' there and a few rough cut sandwiches. One could see at a glance that neither drinks nor sandwiches would go round.

That was depressing enough but it reached the climax when one of the City Magistrates replying to the toast by E A Walton RSA [to] 'The Art Society' said he knew nothing about Art but he knew about water and gas and finished emphatically with the remark that the Dundee Sanitary arrangements were the best in the country."[87]

At the same time as the main annual exhibitions, the GAA was also holding smaller shows in its own rooms, including group exhibitions of black-and-white work and decorative art. In 1902, Stewart Carmichael became the first member to be awarded a complimentary solo exhibition in these rooms. Organised by Mrs Carmichael and Alec Grieve, the costs were

266. Left: Stewart Carmichael, *The Countess of Buchan 1306AD*, watercolour on paper, 1908 *(Dundee City Council: Dundee's Art Galleries & Museums, licensor www.scran.ac.uk)*.

267. Above: Charles G L Phillips, *A Highland Storm*, watercolour on paper, 1905 *(Dundee City Council: Dundee's Art Galleries & Museums)*.

268. Opposite page top: David Foggie, cover illustration for Belgian Refugees fundraising concert programme, 1915 *(Special Collections, University of St Andrews Library)*.

269. Opposite page bottom: Edwin J Smith presented with a portfolio of drawings in recognition of fifteen years as secretary of Dundee Art Society. Standing (left to right): Stewart Carmichael, James Cadzow, Mrs Carmichael, Mrs Smith, Mrs Milne, John Maclauchlan Milne, C G L Phillips. Seated: Edith Macintyre, Edwin J Smith, Florence Lee. From the *Evening Telegraph*, 1919 *(used by kind permission of D C Thomson & Co Ltd)*.

covered by the GAA in thanks for Carmichael's services to it. Its success led to a similar one being awarded to C L Mitchell a year later. Other members also arranged their own solo exhibitions, including Foggie, Grieve and J W Herald.

Throughout the GAA's first decade, membership remained roughly the same – around twenty Members and twice as many Associates. These figures doubled in the second decade following the establishment of the decorative art section (see chapter three) in 1900. Only a small proportion of these were actively involved in the running of the GAA, and some members particularly deserve special notice for their many years of service.

C G L Phillips served in multiple roles between 1893 and 1924, including Secretary, President and Vice President. At the end of the war he took on the combined role of Secretary and Treasurer.[88] In 1909 a vacancy arose on the Free Library's Museum & Art Committee (which ran the Albert Institute), and the society was instrumental in getting Phillips nominated for the post. He was unanimously elected, which meant that for the first time a professional artist was involved in the running of the

BELGIAN REFUGEES IN SCOTLAND
CONCERT - 14TH MAY 1915 - DUNDEE

museum and art galleries. In 1939 he was made an Honorary Member of the Society.

Stewart Carmichael's service was also extremely impressive. Although in the society's first two years he was twice struck from the members' roll and forced to rejoin having failed to renew his subscription, he certainly made up for this afterwards, serving in numerous roles over a 53-year period, including three separate stints as President.[89] In 1948 he was made Honorary President. Alec Grieve also served in various ways between 1894 and 1929, including two sessions as President.[90]

Many Associate Members were also active on the Council. Edwin J Smith (see figures 262 & 269) worked for export merchants MacVeigh, MacIntyre & Co Ltd but was a talented amateur artist. His distinctive illustrations appear on the covers (and many of the advertisements) for several of the annual exhibition catalogues (see figure 3). He served as Secretary from 1903 until being called up in 1918 (also taking on the role of Treasurer when the previous incumbent, C L Mitchell, left for America). He returned to the Council in various roles between 1923 and 1938, and died ten years later aged 70.[91]

Several women were actively involved with the society, including Minnie Kynoch and Edith Macintyre. Kynoch served on the Council in 1902-3 and 1913-14. She later became actively involved in public affairs, as Commissioner of Dundee Girl Guides, a member of the School Board, a Justice of the Peace and a director of Dundee Royal Infirmary. The sister of obstetrician John Campbell Kynoch, she died in 1950 leaving an estate valued at nearly £35,000.[92] Macintyre served in various roles between 1905 and 1926 (see figures 262 & 269), lastly as the first female President.[93] She had studied in Dundee under Alec Grieve as well as in London and Bournemouth. During her long career she exhibited widely, including in London and Paris, and became known for her "artistic bravado" and "unashamed...modernism".[94] During the Great War, she was a founder member and Secretary of the Steeple Club, "a centre of social and artistic activity" run by women.[95] She decorated its clubrooms in Nethergate with pastel landscapes, which she later donated to the Women Citizens' Association, who took over the rooms after the war.[96] She died in Edinburgh in 1949.[97]

Many women never served on the Council but were constantly active on the social side of the society's activities, or in running the female Life Classes. In 1900 E M Lowdon proposed expanding the GAA further by forming a separate branch in Forfar, where she was now based. She succeeded in persuading the local School Board to provide rooms for a Life Class, which was "enthusiastically begun" in 1901.[98] The branch had its own separate membership, one third of its subscriptions going to the GAA and the rest being used for its own activities. It continued successfully until the Great War robbed it of most of its members.

Most of the GAA's female members were Associates – Margaret Suttie was the only female artist to qualify as a Member until a change in the rules in 1893 allowed Associates who had been in the society for at least three years to be nominated as Members. E M Lowdon was the first to achieve this, followed by Minnie Kynoch and Leila Fleming, but the rule was rescinded in 1898.[99] After that, Associates could still apply to be Members, but had to be professional artists not amateurs, and had to submit work for approval to the Council. Some succeeded (eg David Foggie, Robert Donn, Charles Adamson, John D Revel and three female artists, Emma Sinclair, Edith Macintyre and Florence Lee[100]) but others were rejected – George Wilkie Gahan applied in 1911 but the Council concluded that "although his large picture in the Exhibition is quite up to the standard required the others are not".[101] He again tried and failed the following year, and was only finally accepted as a Member in 1939.

Running the GAA was not without its problems over the years and there were often strong disagreements between its members. David Ramsay Sellars (figure 263) was the first to fall from grace – after serving as the GAA's first Secretary he was elected President at the end of 1892, but repeatedly failed to appear at meetings. In June 1893 the Secretary minuted the "continued and persistent absence of the President".[102] A special committee was formed to deal with the matter, with the result that in November he was struck from the roll of members. It may be that his attempts at a political career (see chapter three) were the cause of this, but he continued to rent studio space at 15 Castle Street and was later assistant art master at the High School. As such he must have remained in contact with other GAA members, but he played no further part in the society's activities.

Frank Laing was another who caused problems. He joined the GAA in 1895 and first served on the Council in 1897, but resigned abruptly in March 1898. In the minutes it was "regretted that Mr Laing had seen it necessary to take this step" but no explanation was given.[103] At the end of the year, having not paid his membership subscription, Laing was struck from the roll of members, an action he then wrote to complain about, saying that he had never intended to resign. It was agreed to re-admit him without the usual payment of an entrance fee.

In 1900 Laing again caused trouble by writing to the *Dundee Advertiser*, describing himself as an "obscure, militant, and tolerated member" of the GAA and complaining about the "unqualified optimism, gratulation, and accomplished complacency" of the society's latest annual report.[104] No repercussions of this were recorded, but the following year Laing again took umbrage when a suggestion by him to divide the membership strictly into professional and lay members rather than Members and Associates was placed on the agenda to be formally proposed as a motion at a general meeting. At the meeting Laing refused to put the motion forward and promptly walked out, leaving behind a letter which explained that he had never intended it to be a formal motion with his name attached to it, and so the matter was never discussed. These kind of sudden disagreements seemed to be part of Laing's character and seem never to have spoiled his close friendships with other members. He continued to be actively involved in the society until his death in 1907, though he declined to serve as President when nominated at the end of 1903.

In 1905 a gift to the society from James Martin White proved to be the cause of some further disagreement. White had been involved with the society since lending two watercolours to the exhibition of 1902. The following year, Alec Grieve nominated him as President, but not being a member he was ineligible. Instead it was agreed to make him an honorary member and then elect him as Honorary President alongside William McTaggart. This proved to be a lucrative decision – in 1905 he agreed to make up the £16/6/3 deficit in the previous year's accounts, suggesting as a possibility that the money might be used to send a couple of the younger members to get some artistic inspiration in Paris. At a meeting on 5 June, the gift was discussed in more general terms, to be "set aside as a special fund to be used for some purpose for the fostering of art in sympathy with Mr White's intention."[105] David Foggie (clearly hoping to be one of the recipients), insisted that it should be accepted on its "original terms – viz

– that the money be used to send two young students to Paris." The matter was discussed further at the following meeting on 26 June. By this time Foggie had set his sights on getting all the money, and proposed that two members should nominate a third to go to Paris. The preferred option, however, was to award two prizes for the best set of drawings done in the Life Classes. In September the details were worked out – there would be a separate prize for Members and Associates, to be used for a trip to London or Paris. A rather complicated marking system was devised for the competition, and the society secured James Cadenhead ARSA as judge. Trouble again raised its head when George Wilkie Gahan complained that fellow press artist Tom Ross was entering as an Associate when he was eligible as a Member. Ross had in fact never attempted to become a Member, so Gahan had no fair grounds for complaint. As it turned out, Foggie won in the Members class and Ross in the Associates, so everyone was happy except Gahan (and presumably the six other un-named entrants).

Like Laing, Foggie would continue to have a somewhat fractious relationship to the society. In 1906 he resigned from Council "owing to the action of the Hanging Committee of the Black & White Exhibition in rejecting a pen study sent by him."[106] Although it was agreed that "the decision of an Exhibition Hanging Committee could not be called into question", Foggie refused to back down. He continued to be active in the society, becoming Vice President at the end of 1909 then President two years later. After moving to Edinburgh he kept in touch with the society, being honoured with a complimentary dinner in 1930 to mark his election as a Royal Scottish Academician. But in 1940 he wrote to resign from the society with a letter that was "deemed carping and critical".[107] Stewart Carmichael seems to have smoothed over any difficulties, persuading him to open the society's exhibition in 1946. When he died two years later the society held a memorial exhibition and raised £85 to buy a fine self-portrait from Foggie's widow, which is still in the society's collection today.

The various personal arguments that erupted between members were perhaps indicative of the fact that the society as a whole liked nothing better than to get into a good fight, usually with the Town Council. They campaigned regularly on various issues, including some already noted such as the position of the Queen's statue, the lack of fine art teaching at UCD or the best way to spend the Duncan of Jordanstone Bequest. Others included the design of the Carnegie Libraries in 1901-8 (both the GAA and the Institute of Architecture wanted competitions to be held, but instead the work was given directly to the Town Architect) and the proposed demolition of the Town House in 1914-5 (to which the society was vehemently opposed).

One scheme that divided opinion sharply was the proposal to add a crown spire to the Old Steeple at the City Churches. A crown had apparently been added to the building in the late fifteenth century but was destroyed by fire in 1548. Various fanciful designs were mooted over the years, including one by George Gilbert Scott shown in the 1873 Fine Art Exhibition. In December 1900 the ideas suddenly took practical form and realistic proposals were discussed in the newspapers. Stewart Carmichael was quoted in the press saying that he and other artists would gladly help with the work.[108] This led to an amusing cartoon appearing in the *People's Journal* showing members of the GAA acting as builders' labourers (figure 264).

Lengthy correspondence then ensued in the papers but the initial enthusiasm soon faded and Stewart Carmichael recalled "sharp withdrawal [of the GAA's support] when the design of a proposed ornate heavy crown appeared."[109] Nothing further happened until 1910 when William Banks came forward offering £2,500 to undertake the work. Joseph Lee's magazine the *City Echo* highlighted the renewed debate, and included short pieces by fourteen different artists including Phillips, Foggie, Grieve and press artists Tom Ross, Frank Coutts and William McMann.[110] Only two artists – Thomas Delgaty Dunn and George Wilkie Gahan – were in favour of the scheme. As it turned out, the artists need not have worried – when estimates were prepared they found that even the lowest was more than the money available, and the Ancient Monuments Commission ruled that the proposals would be structurally unsafe in any case. This plus the fact that considerable public opposition had by now built up effectively ended the whole idea.

The formation of the decorative art section of the GAA broadened considerably the kind of art that it promoted, and many felt that the name 'Graphic Arts Association' no longer reflected its wider purpose. In 1901 Frank Laing proposed changing the name to the Dundee Fine Art Society "or such other name as shall include a reference ... to these other branches of the Arts now so numerously represented in the membership".[111] After some discussion the motion was defeated by ten to four. Three years later, however, the matter was raised again. This time Stewart Carmichael proposed the adoption of the name Dundee Art Society, which was "carried by a large majority."[112]

Further changes came in 1910, when the Society was forced to moved from its premises at the University Club, the club members themselves being evicted by their landlord. Various options were looked at, including sharing premises with the Dundee & East of Scotland Photographic Association or using a room at the new Technical College & School of Art, but ultimately the Queen's Hotel agreed exclusive use of one of their rooms for £20 a year. The Society would continue to sub-let the room on certain evenings to the Institute of Architecture. A large gathering took place on 7 June to inaugurate the new premises, hosted by Lord Provost Urquhart, who had somehow been persuaded to become President of the Society for two years (though he rarely attended meetings).

That same year John Duncan was made ARSA and the Society invited him back to Dundee for a complimentary dinner. The Fine Art Exhibitions had now resumed and (having failed to persuade the organisers that the two bodies could jointly organise exhibitions), the Society was forced to make way in 1910 and 1912, holding only small exhibitions in the Queen's Hotel instead of their usual annual shows. In between these, however, the 1911 exhibition was a notable occasion, marking the Society coming into its majority after 21 years (figure 265). An impressive 331 works were included by 77 artists, all members. Deceased members were honoured, including Davidson, Mills, Frank Laing and (the most recent loss) G S Peddie. Early members such as Carmichael, Grieve and Duncan showed alongside newer ones like J Calder Smith, John D Revel and James Watson. Several honorary members also contributed works, including W D McKay, Robert McGregor and D Y Cameron. The night before the opening, a special dinner with over 70 guests was held at the

Queen's Hotel, hosted by the Lord Provost. John Duncan was present again, and gave the opening address at the exhibition, reflecting on all that had happened in the art culture of Dundee over the past 21 years. An attempt was made (without success) to get the Scottish Modern Arts Association to purchase works from the exhibition, but thanks to the influence of Dr Angus MacGillivray, a number of works were acquired for the city's permanent collection. MacGillivray was an Associate member of the Society and the first convenor of the Fine Art Association committee to be actively supportive of Dundee's artists. He persuaded a number of local gentlemen to purchase paintings from the exhibition and present them to the galleries: Martin White acquired Duncan's *Riders of the Sidhe*; A P Mathewson bought Carmichael's *The Countess of Buchan* (figure 266); William Low chose Grieve's *Pont du Cheval, Bruges* and an anonymous gentleman presented Phillips' *A Highland Storm* (figure 267). In Carmichael's words, "we had arrived."[113] MacGillivray was made an Honorary Member for his efforts, and in the annual report that year, the Society noted that its aim "should be now more than ever to bring within its influence all Art workers in the district, and to welcome every sincere endeavour for a free and personal expression."[114]

The Society was now enjoying a higher profile than ever before, which helped to attract significant new members. Perhaps the most notable was Edinburgh-based Stanley Cursiter, who later attributed part of his early success to his association with the Dundee Celtic school. He had painted a number of mythological scenes, one of which (having been signed 'SC') was mistaken for a Stewart Carmichael. "This led to some correspondence which developed into a close friendship", Cursiter later recalled.[115] Carmichael did a portrait of Mrs Cursiter in 1911, and two years later Cursiter exhibited one of his Futurist paintings, *Ribbon Counter*, at the Dundee Art Society exhibition, prompting the *Courier* to query: "whether this is to be taken seriously, or regarded as a playful skit, does not yet appear."[116]

In 1911 the Society took a lead in trying to form a larger arts organisation. David Foggie proposed that a committee be formed "to see if any cooperation were possible amongst the arts, crafts, musicians, architects & literary people in order to forms an Arts Club".[117] He and Edwin Smith met with representatives of the University Club, the Institute of Journalists, the Institute of Architecture, the Art Teachers' Association, the Orchestral Society and a number of the city's professional musicians.[118] Everyone agreed that an Arts Club was desirable, but it was realised that the only way to fund such an enterprise would be to increase considerably the subscriptions of the various affiliate societies, something few were willing to do. The matter was not discussed again.

As it turned out, the Art Society would soon be increasing its subscriptions anyway to meet the cost of new premises. The Queen's Hotel had only ever been intended as an interim solution and in May 1913 arrangements were made to take rooms at 43 Nethergate, though the cost was around double what they had been paying. Once again the Institute of Architecture moved with them.

In August 1914 preparations were well underway for the Society's next exhibition when the war began and the decision was taken to postpone the show. Instead a musical and social evening was arranged in aid of the Belgian Relief Fund (see

THE TAYPORT ARTISTS' CIRCLE.
A NORTHERN BARBIZON.

MR DAVID FOGGIE

MR STEWART CARMICHAEL

The Late MR FRANK LAING. A.R.E.

MR ALEC GRIEVE

MRS ANNA DOUGLAS

MR JAMES DOUGLAS. R.S.W

MR C. L. MITCHELL

figure 268). That year's annual report noted "a somewhat curtailed activity ... on account of the National crisis".[119] In fact, the war seems to have made relatively little impact on the Society – many of its younger members enlisted (including Edwin Smith, John Maclauchlan Milne, John Milne Purvis and Joseph Lee)[120] but exhibitions were reinstated in 1916 and became annual again until the Fine Art Exhibitions recommenced in 1920. In 1918, several of the female members of the society were also involved in an exhibition of work by women artists that Edith Macintyre organised in the Steeple Club to raise money for the Dundee Prisoners of War Fund. As well as local talent, work was lent by prominent women across the country, including Kate Cameron, Emily Paterson and Mabel Royds.[121]

When the war finally ended, the Art Society was pleased to report that "there are no fatal casualties ... among the members who were on service in the war."[122] The organisation entered the 1920s with a new record of 51 Members and 186 Associates, and with sales for its 1921 exhibition reaching almost £500.[123] This was in many ways the most progressive show it had yet staged, featuring works on loan by Van Gogh, Vuillard and the Scottish Colourist S J Peploe. The *Courier's* art critic struggled to appreciate such additions:

270. Joseph Lee, 'The Tayport Artists' Circle' from *The City Echo*, 1908 *(University of Dundee Archive Services)*.

271. Opposite page top: Members of the Tayport Artists' Circle, from the *Evening Telegraph*, 1905. Left to right: Foggie, Laing, Mitchell, Anna Douglas, Lamond, James Douglas, Grieve, Carmichael *(used by kind permission of D C Thomson & Co Ltd)*.

272. Opposite page bottom: Alec Grieve, *Street in Tayport*, oil on canvas *(Dundee City Council: Dundee's Art Galleries & Museums)*.

"The work of the French impressionists… even in their own land is not accepted without dispute, and it is not to be expected that it would make its way here without much questioning and lengthy consideration… [It] is Van Gogh's Flower studies that make most demand on our acceptance. His 'Les Glaiels' – The Gladioli – will strike most people as being hot raw colour, without any pleasing feature to redeem it… There was at one time a shibboleth – 'it's beautiful, but is it ART?' and that seems now to be paraphrased – 'If it's ugly, then it's art.'"[124]

How such significant pieces of modern art came to be shown in Dundee will be explored in chapter nine.

The Dundee Art Society was not the only artists' group in and around the city during the first two decades of the 20th century. In 1904, Alec Grieve informed the Society that "the professional artists of the neighbourhood had agreed to hold an Exhibition in the autumn of next year, & in view of this they would be unable to support the Society's Exhibition to the same extent as before."[125] This was the first indication of the formation of the Tayport Artists' Circle (figures 270 & 271), a venture which, Stewart Carmichael claimed, "created tension in the older Society."[126]

Rural artists' colonies had become a recognised trend by the end of the 19th century, particularly in Britain and France.[127] Many developed as a result of the industrial revolution, which created rapid urban development and associated social conditions that artists reacted strongly against, but also led to the expansion of the railway network, allowing artists to visit previously remote locations away from the growing cities. It seems likely that the Tayport Artists' Circle was more of a deliberate marketing ploy than a natural development – the *City Echo* described the place as "the Barbizon of the North" while the *Courier* noted: "The band of artists who have lately located themselves in Tayport have determined to emulate the founders of the Newlyn School".[128]

Unlike other artists' towns such as Barbizon, Pont-Aven, Newlyn, Straithes and Kirkcudbright, Tayport was hardly remote, directly overlooking Dundee on the opposite side of the Tay. Previously known as Ferry-Port-on-Craig, it had grown rapidly since the coming of the railway, the existing ferry terminal being expanded by a significant engineering enterprise to carry trains across the river before the construction of the Tay Bridge. Under its new name it became a burgh in 1887, and was home to increasing numbers of rich Dundonians who wanted to build their houses away from the jute factories that in most cases were the source of their wealth. It was inevitable that many of the city's artists would paint in the town, and several also chose to live there. The *City Echo* described its appeal, and its contrast to Dundee:

"It is not altogether unaccountable that some seven or eight artists, seeking congenial and inspirational environment, should gradually find themselves located in the neighbourhood of this quaint old-world Fifeshire village… Here are straggling streets, through which traffic moves with but leisurely tread. Here is the ancient harbour, with steamer fast embedded in the mud, awaiting without manifest sign of impatience the incoming of the tide. Here are the wild woodlands of Scotscraig and the sand-dunes of Tentsmuir, with the noble estuary broadening into the ocean".[129]

In fact, with the exception of Frank Laing who was born and raised in Ferry-Port-on-Craig, those artists who had resided longest in the town – Martin Anderson, David F Stuart, D Leuchars Anderson and R Smeaton Douglas – had no connection to the Artists' Circle, despite Stuart and Leuchars

Anderson both having served on the Council of the GAA. Alec Grieve was the next to settle in Tayport, moving there after his marriage in 1897 (figure 272), and he and Laing seem to have been the main instigators of the Circle. C L Mitchell followed them around 1901 and James and Anna Douglas in 1903. David Foggie had lived in Tayport prior to his marriage but had just moved to Lucklawhill a few miles away. W B Lamond lived in Tayport for no more than three or four years (c.1904-7) and Stewart Carmichael seems to have spent less than two years there (1906-7) – both soon returned to Dundee. Lastly, the sculptor Charles Adamson moved to Tayport in 1904 and remained just long enough to participate in the Circle's first exhibition before emigrating to Canada. As well as those Tayport artists not included in the Circle, another notable absentee was C G L Phillips, who certainly painted in Tayport and was on close terms with the other members.[130]

The *City Echo* claimed of the Circle: "The members take active part in the life of the community; town councillors are of their number; some time ago they saved the Common. We hear of schools for the teaching of singing and embroidery among the village children."[131] In fact only Laing served on Tayport Town Council (from 1906 until his death the following year), but he did play a leading role in securing local residents' ownership of the Common, the Council having previously used it for various purposes (including a controversial rifle range) without consultation. Laing was also an active member of the local Choral Union, but is not known to have taught embroidery![132] There is no doubt, however, that the members of the Circle enlivened the cultural life of the town. In August 1906 the *Evening Telegraph* reported: "The

273. Frank Laing,
The Yellow Girl,
watercolour on paper,
1894 *(Dundee City
Council: Dundee's Art
Galleries & Museums)*.

Tayport artists are as enterprising as they are earnest. Arriving at the establishment of a Little Bohemia in Tayport, they have succeeded in brightening the environment of the artist colony. What with open studios, picture gallery, and concerts, Tayport is winning attention in many quarters."[133]

To accompany their first exhibition, the members of the Circle held an open-air concert and lantern fête, during which Laing, Douglas and Grieve sang with Mrs Douglas accompanying them, and other performances were given by Mrs Carmichael, Mrs Mitchell, Mrs Grieve and David Foggie's sister Margaret. The *Evening Telegraph*'s 'Here and There' columnist was enraptured by the occasion: "The night was fine. The curtain was the river [stretching] from the red harbour lights of Dundee to the twinkling of lights beyond Broughty Castle. In the high vault above the stars shone around us, Japanese lamps flickered in the breeze, so that we were in the midst of remarkable feasts of light."[134]

The Circle's first exhibition opened in the Subscription School in Tayport to glowing reviews in May 1905. It featured 82 works shown in groups, "each section [of wall space] having been allocated by ballot to one member, and reserved for pictures by him... Instead of pictures incongruous in style and colour being placed together to the detriment of both, as in the ordinary miscellaneous Exhibition, the general tone of each section is harmonious".[135] This was something only rarely attempted by the Dundee Art Society, and the members of the Circle were keen to stress another key difference to the Society, namely that all of the Circle's members were professionals. That their principal aim was a commercial one was demonstrated by the fact that most future exhibitions were held in Dundee at the Albert Institute. In the catalogue for their second exhibition, they spelled out their intentions clearly:

"The Tayport Artists' Circle is a professional exhibiting body, and has been formed with the object of making a direct appeal to the public from the individual artist's point of view, and also to provide the best public means of exchange, between the buyer and the artist... The members of the Circle believe that there are many in Dundee who find great pleasure in Art, and who are seriously interested in the development of its appreciation in the city. To those they make this appeal, artistic and commercial, in the hope that this Exhibition will meet with the success that should attend every serious effort to place fine arts before the public."[136]

Not wishing to rely on individual sales, the group set up their own Art Union to help ensure financial success. Despite Grieve's threat, the members continued to submit work to the Art Society's exhibitions as well, albeit in smaller numbers than before. According to Stewart Carmichael, the members of the Circle "had no wish to break with Dundee, but had wider ambition. Exhibitions of their combined work in Glasgow, Edinburgh and Dundee were the practical outlook."[137] Three exhibitions were held in Dundee in 1905-7, and there was also one at the Scottish Gallery in Edinburgh in April 1907, featuring some 90 works which "did every credit to the members" and attracted "considerable attention among lovers of art in the capital."[138] No evidence of a Glasgow show has yet come to light, and nor have any sales figures survived to show how successful the Dundee shows were.

While for the most part the exhibitions of the Tayport Artists' Circle drew much more favourable reviews than those of the GAA had done, they were not immune from criticism. In 1906 an anonymous 'Special Correspondent' for the *Courier* penned an article about the Circle which he claimed was motivated by friendliness towards them, lamenting the fact that the public regarded the artists as "Quixotic and 'impossible'" and claiming that "the artist is likely to do better work when he is in friendly touch with his public ... than when he is rating them for not being interested in caviare, not to say cloisteral, productions."[139] The author advised them: "What you need most to do is to gag some of your own members, to sit on them heavily, and save them from bringing themselves and you into an undeserved contempt by talking 'high-falutin'" nonsense about their own work."

The catalyst for this had been a series of letters published in the *Courier* under the heading 'Beauty in Life' written by Laing, Carmichael and Foggie and followed up by a longer feature penned by all three, berating UCD for its lack of instruction in the fine arts. Following the anonymous article, the artists seem to have succeeded in gagging each other for they refrained from answering in print the points made against them, but others jumped to their defence, including George Wilkie Gahan, and a flurry of correspondence ensued, all of which ultimately aided the artists' cause.

The fourth Tayport Artists' Circle exhibition, in December 1907, featured a substantial memorial to the late Frank Laing, with 239 works by him including the vibrant watercolour *The Yellow Girl* (figure 273). The *Newport, Wormit & Tayport Annual & Directory* had proudly promoted the success of the Tayport Artists' Circle, "which has brought renown to our burgh".[140] After the death of Laing they noted that "the burgh has sustained an irreparable loss... and Tayport misses him more than words can tell."[141] Laing's death seems to have precipitated the end of the Circle as an active body – it held no further exhibitions, although the *City Echo* published a feature on the group in 1908, and the Free Library recorded the donation of some black-and-white work from them in 1913.[142] Its membership by then must have been much depleted – Adamson and Lamond had only been temporary participants; James Douglas was confined to hospital in 1908; and C L Mitchell was spending much of his time in the USA. However Tayport continued to be a popular painting spot for artists, with Alec Grieve in particular creating some fine landscapes there in later years.

The Tayport Artists' Circle had been specifically founded as a professional body, and its members (the 26-year-old David Foggie aside) were all established artists in their late 30s or 40s; the members of the Dundee Art Society had a similar average age. But a new generation of young artists was coming up behind them, also keen to combine their resources but wanting to distance themselves from their elders. Around 1900-1, a group of art students at the YMCA decided to break away from this organisation and establish their own private class, one in which social activity played a greater part. They hired a clubroom in Dock Street and formed themselves into

CHAPTER NINE

The New Art Patrons

Despite all the best efforts of Dundee's artists, a general perception existed at the start of the new century that as far as art was concerned, the city's golden age had passed. In 1901 the *Piper o' Dundee* claimed that "for some years art has not received the attention it ought to receive in a wealthy community like ours... [T]he old race of picture lovers and picture buyers, who have made Dundee's reputation as a town of artistic taste, is pretty well extinct. Where are the natural successors of Orchar, Bell and Keiller?"[1]

The rest of the country was also aware of the trend. In 1907 the *Manchester Courier* noted: "Many years ago Dundee was one of the cities foremost in the encouragement of art. At its annual exhibitions large sums of money were spent in buying pictures... Of late years financial patronage of the arts has not been so generous, partly because of the dull trade".[2] The following year, the *Scotsman* observed: "Twenty years ago Dundee was in the line of progress with its annual art exhibitions... Times became bad and the exhibitions were allowed to drop."[3] The economic excuse was frequently cited, yet the *Piper* noted that the city had made "heaps of money" during the past few years, but claimed that "nothing is being done to educate a new race of art patrons."[4]

The *Wizard of the North* had noted this problem as far back as 1894:

"To buy pictures, one must have money; and to love pictures so that they shall be a perennial source of pleasure, one must have an educated taste. Now there are a great many people who have the money, and who are willing to spend it on pictures if they can be sure that they can get their moneys' worth... The great difficulty lies in the matter of purchase. They have no confidence in their own judgment, and so they will not buy... So it is in consequence, that while all the rest of the world may be prosperous, the artist may be starving in his studio."[5]

It is no surprise that many mourned the passing of an age, as several of the city's leading art collectors and patrons died within a relatively brief period – G B Simpson and John Stewart in 1892, A B Spence in 1895, P G Walker in 1896, J C Bell and A C Lamb in 1897, J G Orchar in 1898, J M Keiller and William Robertson in 1899, William Ritchie in 1902, John Forbes White in 1904 and John Robertson of Elmslea in 1906. Of the men who had come together to organise Dundee's first major art exhibition during the BA meeting of 1867, only T S Robertson and W O Dalgleish were still alive at the beginning of the new century (Dalgleish died in 1913, Robertson ten years later).

To judge from other sources, however, Dundee was still leading the way in art patronage. In 1901 the London journal *The Year's Art* published a list of "gentlemen [who] may be mentioned as owning collections of repute" in Scotland. Of the 66 individuals named, 23 were from Dundee, nineteen from Glasgow, two from Edinburgh and one from Aberdeen.[6] In 1909 the noted art critic Edward Pinnington provided a more detailed assessment:[7]

"Taste is said to be waning, and enthusiasm for art to have dried, but the facts point rather the other way. A brief retrospect may induce measurable regret, but a wide outlook brings confident satisfaction. A few years ago – it seems but yesterday – the Forbes White pictures… were here, and now are gone. The George B Simpson's, Douglases and Chalmerses [sic] are scattered, and after them have gone the extensive acculmulation of Blair Spence, the McTaggarts and Chalmerses of John Ramsay,[8] and the rare selection of colourists at Binrock [Keiller's home]…[9] On the other hand, the Orchar of their day is an assured local fixture; the Weinberg remains intact; and the Elmslea [John Robertson's collection] has been absorbed in the city. For every dispersal, moreover, new collections are in the course of formation, and several … are attaining noteworthy rank. Even if the older idea of forming … ambitious collections is disappearing, it is giving place to one probably better, namely, the more liberal diffusion of art throughout the home atmosphere. If less concentrated in its manifestation, taste is more widespread. This is shown by the astonishing number of pictures of a high standard of artistic value gracing and enriching the residences of Dundee and district."[10]

Pinnington illustrated this trend with a series of articles for the *Dundee Advertiser* on some of these smaller collections, including those of R M Lindsay, W Brown Robertson, Rev G Elmslie Troup, the late Thomas Smieton, Charles Ower and John Simpson.[11] Few of them could remember the early years of the Fine Art Exhibitions in Dundee – the youngest was not even born then. Perhaps the most significant link to the past was broken in 1907 by the death of the Albert Institute's curator and librarian, John Maclauchlan. "Some librarians are made, but some, like Mr John Maclauchlan, Dundee, are born" was Andrew Carnegie's assessment, while the *Advertiser* claimed that "he did a work of incalculable importance in stimulating the artistic sense of the community."[12] John Duncan later recalled him as "the very heart and centre of artistic Dundee".[13] Joseph Milne had even named his son John Maclauchlan Milne after him. During his last few years, Maclauchlan had overseen a considerable expansion of activity in the Victoria Art Galleries, with more exhibitions than ever before and (from 19 November 1905) Sunday openings for the first time. These proved particularly popular – on 25 February 1906 the building recorded its highest daily attendance thus far, an astonishing 3,952 people.[14] In his report that year, Maclauchlan claimed: "there is clear and convincing proof that the Permanent, and the quickly-succeeding Loan Collections and Exhibitions of Art, are exercising a distinct refining and elevating influence on the citizens."[15]

The Free Library Committee made an astute choice in his successor. Dr A H Millar (see figure 282) took up the post in January 1908, having spent many years as literary editor (and art critic) for the *Dundee Advertiser*, and boasting "practical knowledge of museum work, obtained in Glasgow and elsewhere".[16] Millar quickly sought to make his mark, the *Scotsman* noting later the same year that "during the past few months [he] has made a notable improvement to the arrangement of the pictures in the permanent collection".[17] The lighting of the galleries was also much improved, the building being connected to the mains electrical supply in 1908, replacing the separate generator installed in 1889. Millar also changed the operational structure of the Albert Institute, creating a separate Museum & Art sub-committee, which later split again into two separate committees. These were supported by the Fine Art Association committee, also (somewhat confusingly) known as the Victoria Art Galleries committee, and formerly the Fine Art Exhibitions committee.[18]

Millar quickly sought to revive the Dundee Fine Art Exhibitions as a regular event, but this time as loan exhibitions rather than selling ones. The first opened in December 1908 and was a great success, attracting 40,000 visitors.[19] It was a smaller show than its predecessors, featuring 198 works including Leighton's *Greek Girls Playing at Ball* (loaned by J M Fraser of Invermay, who had bought it from the 1895 Fine Art Exhibition), Blommers' *Baby's Breakfast* (loaned by ex-Lord Provost McGrady) and Orchardson's portrait of I J Weinberg.[20] Contemporary Scottish art was represented largely by members of the Glasgow Boys (notably John Lavery, E A Hornel, George Henry and Joseph Crawhall), but Millar was quick to extend invitations to the city's own artists as

276. Dundee's permanent collection in the Victoria Galleries, 1906. Photograph from the Wilson Collection *(Libraries, Leisure & Culture Dundee)*.

277. Dundee Fine Art Exhibition 1910 from *The City Echo*, 1911 *(University of Dundee Archive Services)*.

well.[21] Paintings by Carmichael, Foggie, Grieve, Mitchell and Lamond were shown alongside works displayed in tribute to the late Frank Laing and William Yule.

Millar's willingness to engage with the local artists must have been partially motivated by a desire to heal the wounds of his controversial reviews of their work in the *Dundee Advertiser*, which had often led to heated exchanges in the correspondence columns. Stewart Carmichael described Millar as "an excellent antiquarian, an eminent archaeologist, a well known author ... and a most genial man in most things" but felt that he "had little use for the vital activities of the [Dundee Art] Society."[22]

Millar's views on the role of local artists formed an important part of a paper he gave at the Museums Association conference in Maidstone in 1909, where he claimed:

"The local Art Gallery, like the local Library and Museum, ought to take special notice of local matters… [T]he Art Gallery should contain examples of the work of distinguished local artists, and of landscapes of the locality, painted by eminent artists from other localities… The collecting of pictures of this kind lies peculiarly within the province of the Curator; and he should not despise either the local artist, however humble, or the local landscape, even if not the work of an artist who is alphabetically decorated. In the Art Gallery, as in the Museum, his special work should be the collection of local facts; and even a mediocre local artist is a 'fact' that should not be ignored."[23]

Putting these beliefs into practice, Millar invited three of these 'facts', Stewart Carmichael, Edwin J Smith and the architect and painter Charles G Soutar, onto the Fine Art Association committee, but it seems to have been largely a token gesture. After the 1908 exhibition, the Art Society proposed meeting with the Association and the Free Library Committee with a view to combining resources to hold annual Fine Art Exhibitions on a larger scale. Eventually on 31 May 1909 the Association agreed to receive a deputation of three artists from the Society. Carmichael later recalled:

"The meeting of the Fine Art Association was in full swing and before the deputation had been called it deliberately resolved against having anything to do with the Art Society and its scheme – this in spite of vigorous reasonings and protests from Charles Soutar, Edwin Smith and myself… Afterwards they called in the three artists of the deputation who made their speeches, unaware that the decision was unalterably against them. It was a painful mockery. I said so, nor did I choose my words too delicately. We felt our colleagues had been betrayed."[24]

Nevertheless, Carmichael and his colleagues remained on the committee for the 1910 Fine Art Exhibition (figure 277). Also present were the remaining art lovers of the previous generation: T S Robertson, W O Dalgleish and I J Weinberg – the latter for the last time (he died in 1912). But listed as either committee members or lenders are the names of many of the next generation of collectors and patrons: John Robertson, William Rettie, John Tattersall, A P Mathewson and David Galloway. All of these we shall return to later.

The 1910 exhibition was altogether more ambitious than the 1908 show, with some 426 works on display. Among the highlights were McTaggart's late work *Lobster Fishers, Machrihanish Bay* (figure 278, lent by solicitor W B Dickie), *The Knitting Lesson* by Blommers (figure 281, lent by John Robertson), the first appearance in Dundee of the Scottish Colourists (two Peploes) and also of modern French art, reflecting the changing interests of the organisers. More than

a dozen French artists were represented including Monet, Le Sidaner, Fantin-Latour, Boudin and Lépine – some on loan but most direct from the artists in Paris. According to the *People's Journal* it was "probably the best collection of pictures that has ever been brought together in Dundee".[25]

It was in 1910 that the decision was taken to host the British Association meeting in Dundee for the second time, and recalling the success of the 1867 exhibition (according to Millar), "it was thought that a similar Exhibition upon an even higher standard of excellence might be organised".[26] Once again Dundee's artists had to fight for recognition, but eventually Carmichael, Lamond and Mitchell were invited onto the committee for the 1912 exhibition. It featured 413 artworks over five (specially renovated) galleries. Among the highlights were an exceptional collection of Raeburns including *George Paterson Esq of Castle Huntly* (loaned by Charles Paterson, acquired for the city in 2006); J S Sargent's striking portrait of Lord Dalhousie (loaned by the subject); a substantial showing of the Glasgow Boys (this time also including E A Walton and Arthur Melville); Peploe's *The Gypsy*, lent by John Robertson; and further indications of Dundee's increasing interest in French painting with works by Millet and Tissot. The exhibition was accompanied by a lavishly illustrated catalogue (with photographs by J Craig Annan) and the BA handbook for the event included a history of art in Dundee written by A H Millar.[27]

The press coverage obtained by the exhibition was far more substantial than usual, and one review (in the London *Morning Post*) caused a considerable stir among the city's artists. The reviewer (probably the Arbroath-born artist and critic James Greig) spent some time praising the philanthropy of Dundee's art patrons past and present before concluding that "with all this encouragement Dundee has not produced an artist of the highest rank" and following this up with specific attacks on many of the artists in question, describing them generally as "woefully deficient in knowledge – there is no lack of feeling but it is feeble for want of direction."[28] Unsurprisingly this drew furious responses including a letter in the *Dundee Advertiser* by David Foggie, writing as President of the Art Society. His main criticism was the suggestion that the city's artists were receiving generous patronage from its art collectors, when in fact the latter's attentions were usually focused elsewhere.[29] Foggie also complained about the way that artists had been merely "co-opted" onto the BA exhibition's hanging committee.

278. Opposite page top: William McTaggart, *Lobster Fishers, Machrihanish Bay*, oil on canvas, 1901, shown in the Dundee Fine Art Exhibition 1910 (*University of Dundee Museum Services*).

279. Opposite page bottom: J Craig Annan, photographs showing the layout of the British Association exhibition, 1912. In the centre is J S Sargent's portrait of Lord Dalhousie (*Libraries, Leisure & Culture Dundee*).

THIRD GALLERY

"There are a few wealthy private 'patrons of art' in Dundee, but most of them are commercial collectors rather than genuine connoisseurs or picture-lovers, and, in each of these categories, the 'inferiority complex' is generally in full blast."[30]

This was Hugh MacDiarmid's scathing assessment of the "sterile and degenerate" artistic culture of Dundee in the early 20th century. So who were the new art patrons in the city, and was this (and Foggie's) criticism of them justified? By far the most active in promoting fine art in Dundee was John Robertson (no relation to the older John Robertson of Elmslea). Born in Aberfeldy in c.1861, Robertson grew up working as a herd boy. A picture book given to him by the local minister is said to have inspired his first interests in art, and while still a youth he came to Dundee in the hope of finding better opportunities. He took jobs in a hotel and a drapery warehouse before becoming clerical assistant to a dental surgeon. Learning the trade in his spare time, he eventually opened his own dental surgery at 27 Victoria Road.[31] Known as the Dundee Teeth Depot, it proved so successful (not least due to his "careful consideration for the feelings of lady patients") that branches were opened in Forfar, Kirriemuir and St Andrews.[32]

As his business expanded, Robertson began spending his profits buying art, which would then be displayed on the surgery walls for the appreciation of his patients. The *City Echo* noted in 1909 that "even the excruciating pangs of a toothache may be amply compensated for by a pleasure so exquisite.... We question whether elsewhere in the city there is a room so replete with valuable works of art."[33] A revised version of the same article appeared in the *People's Journal* in 1910 (both were presumably written by Joseph Lee), which noted that nothing "gives Mr Robertson more pleasure than to act as cicerone in his own delightful gallery".[34] Robertson's tastes focused on landscapes and seascapes. Like the previous generation of collectors he was a great fan of McTaggart, owning several important examples including *Crab Catchers – A June Day* (1900, now in Perth Museum & Art Gallery). McTaggart's close follower Robert Gemmell Hutchison was another favourite, the *Piper o' Dundee* noting that "his acquisitions in this direction do credit to his taste as a connoisseur."[35] Robertson owned well over a dozen Hutchisons including *The Young Yachtsman*, *The Widow's Bairns*, *The Tay Pearl* and *The Fisherman's Daughter*.

Hutchison become one of several artists with whom Robertson cultivated a close friendship, and they travelled to the Continent together on at least one occasion. A keen interest that the two men shared was in the Hague school of Dutch painters. As well as acquiring works by Israels, de Bock, de Hoog, Maris and Sluiter, he became a close friend and patron of B J Blommers, buying several works including *In the Moonlight* and *The Knitting Lesson* (see figure 281). For their silver wedding anniversary, Blommers gifted his painting *Saturday* to Mrs Robertson (who seems to be have been quite a shrewd collector herself). Robertson's interests in that part of the Continent were such that he was ultimately appointed "administrator of fine arts in Scotland to both Holland and Belgium."[36]

Robertson seems to have been the first Dundee collector to take an active interest in the Glasgow Boys, his acquisitions including Hornel's *A Butterfly*, Walton's *Joe*, Crawhall's *Rook's Nest* (c.1908, see figure 280) and Lavery's *On the Coast, Tangier*.[37] Several Dundee artists also benefited from Robertson's patronage, particularly W B Lamond, whose style was closest to that of McTaggart and Hutchison. The collection was said to be "particularly rich" in Lamond's work, including *Gathering Bait* and *Within Sounds of the Sea*.[38] A number of Charles A Sellar's landscapes and drawings by Max Cowper were also added to the collection. The Dundee-trained Henry Wright Kerr was also represented.

Robertson began to loan his paintings to the GAA exhibitions in 1903, but the first major public exposure of his collection was at the 1908 Fine Art Exhibition, where seventeen works were shown. Joining the Fine Art Association, he became increasingly involved in the organisation of the shows. He even arranged to retrieve works he'd previously sold – notably Blommers' *The Knitting Lesson*, which he twice borrowed from other owners for display before eventually buying it back.[39]

By spring 1914, planning had begun on another large-scale Fine Art Exhibition to be held the following year.[40] The outbreak of war, however, put a stop to this idea.[41] Blackout requirements meant closing the building at dusk, which "severely affected the attendance at the Galleries during the winter months."[42] In March 1915 a proposal was submitted to turn the whole of the first floor of the building into a military hospital. Elaborate plans were drawn up but eventually it was decided that the scheme would be too costly. However, the large Albert Hall within the building was used as an army

recruiting station.

It would not be until 1920, therefore, that the next major Fine Art Exhibition was held (figure 282). This time it was mostly a selling show, with just a few loans from local collectors. Robertson was not one of them, but he played an important role in the 1921 exhibition, which was held on behalf of Lord Provost Spence's Dundee Unemployment Fund. As well as donating a painting to sell in the exhibition, he was "instrumental in enlisting the sympathy of the leading Dutch and Belgian Artists and securing so many examples of their work."[43]

280. Opposite page: Joseph Lee, 'Mr John Robertson takes his Crawhall to the Exhibition' from *The City Echo*, 1910. Crawhall's *Rook's Nest* is now in the Burrell Collection, Glasgow *(University of Dundee Archive Services)*.

281. Top: B J Blommers, *The Knitting Lesson*, owned by John Robertson, reproduced in the British Association exhibition catalogue, 1912 *(Libraries, Leisure & Culture Dundee)*.

282. Above: Dundee Fine Art Exhibition 1920, committee members. Left to right: William Boyd, David Dickie, T H Smith, Alexander Duncan, W B Lamond, C G Soutar, William Rettie, A H Millar *(Libraries, Leisure & Culture Dundee)*.

A further charity exhibition followed in 1924, this time on behalf of Lord Roberts' Memorial Workshop. This time the format reverted to loans, Robertson's 28 works making him the most abundant contributor. This was despite the fact that he had sold off a substantial part of his collection at Dowell's in Edinburgh the previous year.[44] By this time Robertson had passed on the dental business to his son, and the sale was possibly a way of ensuring a decent pension that would enable him to continue purchasing after his retirement. The fine arts now became more than just a hobby to him, and in 1927 he entered a partnership with Stewart Bruce to open a Fine Art Salon on Panmure Street (later moving to Commercial Street). An extraordinary variety of exhibitions was held here, perhaps most unusually a 1938 show of original celluloid paintings from Disney's *Snow White and the Seven Dwarfs*. Robertson also took a more active role in running the Victoria Galleries, becoming Convenor of the Free Libraries Committee and the Fine Art Association. The loan exhibitions continued, and Robertson also organised major retrospectives of Philip de Laszlo (1932), Sir John Lavery (1936) and W Russell Flint (1938), all of whom had become personal friends. He died in 1943, though the firm of Robertson & Bruce continued for another decade.[45]

While Robertson was certainly the most active of the new generation of Dundee collectors, he was not the most progressive in his artistic tastes. Another group of art lovers was making far more radical purchases, which would give Dundee a reputation "for being at the forefront of artistic taste, not only in Scotland, but in Britain as a whole."[46]

The first of these was John Tattersall. Born near Glasgow in 1859, he came to Dundee as a young man and made his money first as a butcher and then as area manager for the hugely successful grocers William Low & Co. In 1902 Tattersall began buying works by the Glasgow Boys from Alexander Reid, the influential Glasgow art dealer, with whom he would briefly enter into partnership in 1916.[47] Many of Tattersall's purchases were loaned to exhibitions – three Hornels were shown at the 1903 GAA exhibition, and paintings by Henry and Walton from his collection were reproduced in the 1912 BA exhibition catalogue. At this stage, his interest was largely in Scottish painting, though he did own Lépine's *Bordeaux – Evening* and three works by Boudin including *The Jetty at Trouville* (now in the Burrell Collection); he also bought a number of Japanese prints from Reid in 1910. Although John Robertson owned at least one Peploe, Tattersall was the first Dundee collector to take a serious interest in the Scottish Colourists, buying work by all four of these artists and becoming a close friend of G L Hunter. It was either Reid or Hunter who introduced Tattersall to modern French painting. In 1919 he bought three Vuillards from Reid's exhibition of the artist's work, selling his Boudin to pay for them. All three were lent to the 1924 Fine Art Exhibition, along with nineteen other works including Peploes and Waltons (also works by McTaggart, Wingate and Fraser showing that he had not entirely abandoned the tastes of his predecessors). By that time, Tattersall had also acquired Bonnard's *Femme Rattachant sa Chemise* (lent to the Fine Art Exhibition in

1920) and a few years later he purchased Van Gogh's *View of a River with Rowing Boats* (aka *Canots Amarrés*, figure 283), shown by the Dundee Art Society in 1921 and then in the Fine Art Exhibition in 1929-30.[48] As Alexander Reid's son later recalled, this "took the place of the Boudin over Mr Tattersall's mantelpiece."[49] Tattersall continued to show works from his collection (which later included Bloomsbury modernist Duncan Grant and the Dundee colourist John Maclauchlan Milne) up until his death in 1935.

Many of Tattersall's purchases were made through Matthew Justice, managing director of the furniture and interior design business Thomas Justice & Sons (of which Tattersall became a director).[50] The firm had been started by Matthew's father in 1872 and grew rapidly. Within twenty years Thomas had "erected a pile of buildings unequalled by any similar establishment in Scotland", the Maison Justice in Whitehall Crescent comprising some 30,000 square feet of floor space. His success lay in catering "as carefully for the workman's home as for the merchant princes' mansions."[51] After buying art for himself through Alexander Reid, Matthew Justice realised that he could use his shop to display and sell paintings, and thus become an art dealer himself. In October 1919 he travelled to Paris and bought a large number of Vuillards including *Woman in Blue with Child* (c.1899, Glasgow Museums), Van Gogh's *Bouquet of Flowers* (aka *Vase with White and Red Carnations*) and works by other French painters. He evidently did well out of the ones he sold because in February 1920 he

returned to Paris to buy more (see figure 284). Like Tattersall he also struck up a close friendship with G L Hunter, becoming his official dealer in Dundee and helping to arrange a solo show for him at Thomas Murray's gallery in 1921. His personal preference, however, seems to have been for Peploe – he lent six works by the colourist to the 1924 Fine Art Exhibition, along with seven Vuillards, three Bonnards, two Marchands, a Seurat and a Hunter. This was Justice's only major showing in the Victoria Galleries, though a large number of the French paintings and Colourists lent by other collectors had been purchased from him. In 1937 he retired to Switzerland, where he died in 1942 at the age of 67.[52]

Perhaps Justice's most significant client was William Boyd, who made his money as managing director of Keiller & Son, following his father who had succeeded John Mitchell Keiller as head of the company. Boyd worked in London before taking charge of the Dundee business in 1895. With his brother R Just Boyd, he would go on to purchase a controlling interest in the company, and before his retirement in 1920 sold it to Crosse & Blackwell.[53] Boyd began collecting some time before 1912, when he first lent works for public showing at the BA exhibition. At that time his tastes followed those of Robertson and his contemporaries – mainly McTaggart and the Hague school, though he also owned works by French painters Millet and Harpignies. In 1913, along with John Tattersall, he sold parts of his collection at Dowell's in Edinburgh, and began replacing his Dutch works with French paintings

and the Scottish Colourists, though he always held on to his McTaggarts. In 1916 he lent fifteen works to the Dundee Art Society exhibition, including six Fantin-Latours, two by Harpignies and works by Bonvin, Cazin and Courbet.

Boyd retired in 1920 and was able to devote more time to his collection. The following year he renovated his home, Claremont in West Ferry, to show off his paintings (figure 285), and through Matthew Justice he began investing seriously in modern French art. As well as busts by Rodin and paintings by Sisley, Monet, Vuillard, Bonnard, Marchand and de Segonzac, Boyd's purchases included three Van Goghs, more than any other Scottish collector.[54] Two of them were first shown at the 1922 Dundee Art Society exhibition: *Le Printemps* (aka *Trees* (1890)) and *La Charrue* (aka *Field with Ploughman* (1889), now in the Museum of Fine Arts, Boston). Boyd was also the first known collector in Scotland to buy the work of Matisse, showing *Antibes* (figure 286) in the 1924 Fine Art Exhibition.

Although Boyd stopped collecting actively at the end of the 1920s, he continued to act as a patron, particularly for John Maclauchlan Milne (whose visits to France Boyd helped to finance) and the Glasgow-based Estonian sculptor Benno

Schotz. He also became a director of Dundee Royal Infirmary and chairman of the Dundee Eye Institution and the Dundee Dental Hospital & School. The latter became his most significant cause, and in 1936 he gave £17,500 to endow a chair of dentistry at University College, leading him to sell one of his Van Goghs through Robertson & Bruce (*Orchard in Blossom*, now in the Scottish National Gallery). In return the Dental Hospital presented him with a bust of himself by Benno Schotz, which he later left to the hospital along with McTaggart's *Summer Sea* (1907, presented in 1930).[55]

Why an interest in art and dentistry should so often come together in Dundee is unclear, but the Dental Hospital & School also has Benno Schotz busts of John Tattersall's son William[56] and of Mrs Annie Rettie, whose husband was the principal benefactor of the hospital, and another notable art collector. William Rettie was born in Inverurie and began work as a grocer's apprentice. He moved to Dundee around 1876 to start his own business then made the shrewd decision in 1885 to enter into a partnership with William Low, whose business was just beginning to expand into "one of the principal retail trading corporations in the kingdom."[57] Low himself would later credit Rettie for much of this success – there were also close family ties between them, Rettie having married Low's sister.[58] Low himself was an art collector and may have inspired Rettie, as might John Tattersall, the firm's area manager.[59] In 1901 the *Piper o' Dundee* noted that Rettie "has a taste for art, and is an enlightened and generous patron of latter-day

283. Opposite page: Vincent van Gogh, *Canots Amarrés*, oil on canvas, 1887, owned by John Tattersall *(private collection, image © Sotheby's Picture Library)*.

284. Top: Edouard Vuillard, *The Dressing-Room, Madame Hessel Reading at Amfréville*, oil and tempera on cardboard, 1906, bought by Matthew Justice for Alexander Duncan *(Charles H and Mary F S Worcester Collection, 1947.119, The Art Institute of Chicago)*.

artists. His collection of modern pictures is large and valuable, and gives evidence of a cultivated sense of beauty in its possessor."[60] Perhaps he enjoyed seeing beautiful smiles as well, for in 1916 he purchased a site at 2 Park Place and gifted it to the Dental Hospital, installing a stunning stained glass window in memory of his son Philip, killed in the Great War (figure 287). He also served as the first chairman of the hospital board, and the Schotz bust of Mrs Rettie was commissioned by the Hospital & School after William's death, in recognition of their generosity.[61] Like William Low, Rettie rarely lent works from his collection for public exhibition, so we have little idea of what hung on the walls of his Blackness Road mansion, Balcairn. Despite serving as chairman of the Victoria Galleries committee and being on the organising committee of at least two of the Fine Art Exhibitions, Rettie lent only one painting to them – McTaggart's *The White Sand Hills*, Machrihanish in 1910. It's also known that he commissioned David Comba Adamson to undertake portraits of himself and his wife (possibly inspired again by William Low, who also had portraits done by Adamson).[62] Rettie died in 1922 aged 70.[63]

Numerous other collectors were active in Dundee at this time, and only a brief account of the most notable is possible here. Alexander Duncan of Maulesbank, Carnoustie, ran his own boot and shoe company from c.1896 until his death in 1928 aged 61.[64] Through Tattersall he began buying work from Alexander Reid in Glasgow, and later from Matthew Justice. His particular interests were in Vuillard (see figure 284), Boudin, Bonnard and the colourists Cadell, Hunter and Peploe.[65]

Arthur P Mathewson of Vernonholme, Ninewells, ran his own company operating Grove Mills in Lower Pleasance.[66] His collection (which he first lent out for exhibition in 1910) followed similar lines to his contemporaries – Dutch painters, Fantin-Latour, several Edwin Alexanders and a fine selection of McTaggarts. He also seems to have made occasional purchases from Dundee artists, owning works by Foggie and Lamond. Japanese prints were a more unusual interest, and he amassed a collection of over 300 including work by Utamaro and Hokusai (see figure 288).[67] He died in 1913 at the age of 60 but his widow and son, Alexander, continued to loan works from his collection to later exhibitions (and the latter may have added to the collection himself).

Frederick Sharp was the son of John Sharp of Balmuir, who had made a fortune running the Miln Street jute mill. Frederick joined the family business and also served as chairman of the Alliance Trust and a director of the Caledonian Railway Company.[68] He married Martin White's sister Beatrice and in 1904 bought the Hill of Tarvit estate in Fife. To decorate the walls of his Robert Lorimer-designed mansion, he built up an impressive art collection different in many ways from those of

285. William Boyd in the music room at Claremont, c.1935, with paintings by Monet and Sisley on the walls *(private collection)*.

286. Opposite page: Henri Matisse, *Cap d'Antibes*, oil on canvas, 1922, owned by William Boyd *(Tate, © Succession Henri Matisse / DACS 2015)*.

his Dundee contemporaries – Raeburn, Ramsay, Gainsborough and Constable, as well as Dutch paintings including a number of golfing pictures that reflected another of his passions.[69] Several works from the collection were lent to the 1912 BA exhibition. Frederick died in 1932 and his son Hugh (a notable book collector) was killed in a train crash just five years later. A detailed inventory of the house was undertaken in 1938 which specified exactly where each painting was displayed, allowing the National Trust for Scotland (who were bequeathed the house in 1949) to recreate the hang.

David Galloway worked for the British Legal Assurance Company – he was Assistant Super-intendent in 1899 and by 1918 had become District Manager (by that time the company had merged with another to become British Legal & United Provident).[70] He began collecting art for his home at 4 Springfield (later moving to 11 Fort Street) around the turn of the century, his first public showing of note being the 1908 Fine Art Exhibition, when he showed works by R G Hutchison and T Austen Brown. As well as being a member of the Free Library's Museum & Art Committee, he also served on the organising committee of the 1912 exhibition, where he showed a strong selection of paintings by McTaggart, Wingate, Henry, Boudin, Fantin-Latour and others. Two years later he held a major sale of around 100 works from his collection at Dowell's in Edinburgh. The *Dundee Advertiser* reported: "Much interest was evidenced in the sale, the galleries being filled to overflowing, and many failing to gain admission. The bidding was very spirited, particularly in the Scottish section, the proceedings being frequently punctuated by loud applause."[71] The sale yielded £4,748, but Galloway seems not to have reinvested this in further collecting. In the 1924 Fine Art Exhibition (when every other collector was showing their finest treasures) his loans comprised just a few etchings.[72] He died in 1938 at the age of 77.

Andrew G Kidd (figure 289) owned a chain of bakeries which by the time of his death in 1950 comprised 34 shops in Dundee and one in Perth.[73] He had already amassed a substantial collection by the time of the 1924 exhibition, including purchases from Robertson's sale at Dowell's in 1923. These included the highest-selling picture of the sale, Blommers' *Peek-a-Bo*, bought for £1050.[74] Kidd purchased a number of Dutch paintings direct from the artists and also went for the usual Scottish names – McTaggart, Hornel and Hutchison. In 1929 the Prime Minister, Ramsay MacDonald,

chose to reproduce one of Kidd's D Y Camerons, *Morning Mists – Lochaber*, as a personal greetings card.[75] Some of Kidd's choices were more unusual – important works by A J Munnings and Frank Brangwyn, for example, and Corot's Lovers by a Lake (shown at the 1929-30 Fine Art Exhibition). He also owned a significant number of works by the Dundee newspaper artist Joseph Gray. In 1927 Kidd took out a policy with the Fine Art & General Insurance Company for his collection – the surviving document lists well over 100 works displayed in his Dalkeith Road home, his offices and a second home in London, to a total value of almost £20,000.[76]

Finally, mention should be made of solicitor John Simpson of Viewbank, Tayport; jute factory owner John N Kyd of Rosendael, West Ferry; chemist R M Lindsay of Pitkerro Road; and pharmacist Charles Young of Shamrock Street. All of these had notable collections of Scottish and Dutch paintings, at least partly acquired second-hand from the previous generation of Dundee collectors.[77]

As with the former generation, however, only a few of the collectors described here gave any lasting legacies to the city's permanent collection. These were generally the work of Scottish or English artists rather than the French painters whom many of them admired, but who were still not widely popular. John Robertson made various donations to the galleries over the years, including his own portrait by de Laszlo. He was also responsible for persuading the illustrator Frank Brangwyn to donate 67 of his paintings and drawings to the collection in 1939.

William Boyd donated works by Dundee artists John Milne Purvis (1916) and Joseph Gray (1917) and a Schotz bust of his daughter in 1934. The same year, John Tattersall gave three watercolours by E A Walton. More significant works were donated by A P Mathewson, including Noel Paton's stunning *Beati Mundo Corde* in 1910 and Carmichael's *The Countess of Buchan* in 1912; and by A G Kidd, among them Blommers' *Peek-a-Bo* and Munnings' *The Poppy Field*, both gifted in 1945. In 1914, Mathewson's widow gifted her husband's substantial collection of Japanese prints in his memory.

The most significant additions to the permanent collection came through bequests, and the one that would benefit the galleries longest was that of school teacher John Morris.

287. Top: A Ballantine & Son, memorial window for William Rettie's son Philip in Dundee Dental Hospital & School, installed 1918 *(University of Dundee Museum Services)*.

288. Above: Ando (Utagawa) Hiroshige, *Hiratsuka* from the series *The Fifty-Three Stations of the Tokaido*, print on paper, 1830s, owned by A P Mathewson *(Dundee City Council: Dundee's Art Galleries & Museums)*.

289. Opposite page: James McBey, *Andrew G Kidd*, oil on canvas, 1927 *(Dundee City Council: Dundee's Art Galleries & Museums)*.

Born in Dundee in 1819, Morris studied at St Andrews University before teaching in schools in Inverkeillor, Glamis and Mains. Retiring as a teacher in 1880, he continued to serve as Registrar for the Parish of Mains & Strathmartine until his death in 1896. The *Piper o' Dundee* described him as "a scholar of no mean repute, and an art patron of more than local fame... He took an active interest in the local art exhibitions, and was a familiar figure in the Galleries."[78] In his will, he left the residue of his estate (some £3,400) to establish the Morris Fund for the purchase of pictures for the permanent collection, being "convinced of the educative and beneficent influences of good Pictures for the people, and wishing that my native city of Dundee may possess in the future a valuable and attractive Picture Gallery".[79] A trust was set up to administer the fund, the principal trustees being W B Dickie and High School teacher Richard Scott. They were charged with selecting works in collaboration with the Fine Art Association which would be purchased for the city's collection using the interest on the fund.[80] Their first acquisitions were made in 1903: John Robertson Reid's *The Home Squadron* (figure 291, purchased from that year's RA exhibition where it had hung on the line) and Carmichael's *The Mysteries* (figure 87), which had been "greatly admired for its artistic technique and intellectual suggestiveness" at the GAA's annual exhibition.[81] As Carmichael later recalled, "It was a fine gesture of appreciation for Dundee Art."[82] Over the next few years the Trust would acquire Duddingstone Herdman's *Faggot Gatherers* (aka *Woodland Gleaners*), Hornel's *The Earth Awakening* and their most expensive purchase, Orchardson's *Voltaire* (bought for £1,200 and quickly attracting the reputation of being "Dundee's Greatest Work of Art").[83]

The Great War was represented by two important acquisitions, Lavery's *London Hospital 1915* and D Y Cameron's *Bailleul*. Significantly, Dundee artists continued to be supported, with early post-war purchases including Foggie's *Portrait of the Artist's Wife*, Duncan's *The Children of Lir* and Maclauchlan Milne's *A Fife Landscape*. The Morris Fund continued to be used for acquisitions well into the 1990s, when the remaining funds were absorbed into the museum's general acquisition budget.[84]

The next major bequest came in 1917 with the death of Mrs Elizabeth Blair of Birnam. She offered the art collection of her first husband, Archibald Anderson Watt, under the name of the Watt Bequest. Watt had died in 1883 having acquired a good number of paintings to decorate his home at Kincraig, Broughty Ferry.[85] 33 works were chosen to enter the collection, including portraits attributed to Lely and Kneller and landscapes by Sam Bough, Joseph Farquharson and W D McKay.[86]

In 1918 the architect and artist Charles Ower gifted ten works including landscapes by Carmichael, Phillips and Jane Spindler. On his death in 1921 he bequeathed half of his remaining estate to form a purchase fund for the city's collection.[87] This led to seventeen purchases in the 1930s and 40s, including works by George Morland, Laura Knight and the Scottish Colourists. The death of Ogilvy Dalgleish's widow in 1922 meant further additions, including Graham's *Moorland and Mist* and Millais' *Puss in Boots*. Four years later, the William Gibson Bequest featured works by Alexander

Fraser, W E Lockhart and Horatio McCulloch among others.

The popularity of presentation portraits continued unabated, the gallery displaying them being described as "the Valhalla of Dundee".[88] Local artists were now more frequently awarded commissions (eg Chief Constable Dewar by Mitchell (1909) and Rev Monsignor Provost Holder by Phillips (figure 292)) but for the major figures the same names continued to appear – W Q Orchardson painted Sir John Leng in 1901 and T Carlaw Martin (editor of the *Advertiser*) in 1907[89]; Tom Graham painted Rev Peter Grant in 1902 and ex-Lord Provost Mathewson in 1906; and Sir George Reid painted ex-Lord Provost Hunter in 1904. Since the employment of Herkomer and Sargent (see chapter two) there had been controversy over the use of non-Scottish artists to paint the city's civic leaders – in 1902 John Robertson wrote to the *Courier* demanding that Hunter's portrait be by a Scot, preferably a Dundee artist such as Lamond. In 1909 the English painter Solomon J Solomon was commissioned to paint ex-Lord Provost Longair, and the *Evening Telegraph* received an irate letter from "Disgusted":

> "Have we not for years been striving to establish a reputable school of art in this northern half of the island, and have we not nearly succeeded? If so, why do we send our Scottish gold set apart to art to – where? Have we not artists nearer home able and qualified to undertake the work? What about

George Henry, John Lavery, E A Walton, and H W Kerr (a son, by the way, of Dundee) – all artists of standing, who are as yet unrepresented in Dundee?"[90]

In fact, three of these four would go on to be commissioned to undertake presentation portraits, and Solomon's painting (figure 293) would prove to be one of the most distinctive examples to date, hailed by W H Blyth Martin as "excellent in likeness and colour harmonies".[91] Less popular was the next portrait by an English artist, that of Sir William Ogilvy Dalgleish by Walter Ouless (1911). The *Glasgow Evening News* dismissed the painting as "another of those Scottish commissions to English artists without distinction in style or colour which so astonish English critics here, who are well aware of the many Scottish portrait painters of superior gifts who are available."[92] The *Courier* at least praised its "serene dignity", but Blyth Martin was forced to admit that the result lacked "the poetry of an Orchardson or a Chalmers".[93] None of this prevented Ouless from being asked to paint two copies of the painting – one for Dundee Royal Infirmary (figure 294) and one for the Technical College.

It would be another twelve years before the Town Council again turned to an English artist to paint a major Dundee figure (Lord Provost Spence by Sir William Orpen), and until then it was to the leading figures of the Glasgow School that they turned instead, beginning in 1907 with a vigorous portrait

290. Opposite page: Dundee's permanent collection in the Victoria Galleries, c.1910. Photograph from the Wilson Collection *(Libraries, Leisure & Culture Dundee).*

291. Above: John Robertson Reid, *The Home Squadron*, oil on canvas, 1903, one of the first purchases of the Morris trustees *(Dundee City Council: Dundee's Art Galleries & Museums).*

292. Right: Charles G L Phillips, *The Right Reverend Monsignor Provost Holder*, oil on canvas, 1913 *(Dundee City Council: Dundee's Art Galleries & Museums).*

of ex-Lord Provost Barrie (figure 295) by Sir James Guthrie (then President of the RSA), followed by a sombre depiction of ex-Lord Provost Urquhart by John Lavery (1914) and, by contrast, a much more colourful portrait of Dundee's wartime Provost (shown in military uniform), William Don by George Henry (1920, see figure 296). Each of these paintings was greeted with great acclaim at the time, but few receive much attention today (though a selection is displayed in the City Chambers). Blyth Martin at least recognised that this concentration on portraits of the great and the good was not necessarily for the best: "It may be matter for regret that collections such as Dundee's do not grow more rapidly in landscape and figure subjects, pictures which are generally more attractive to the public".[94]

By 1926 the permanent collection was of sufficient scale to warrant the publication of an *Illustrated Catalogue of the Pictures in the Dundee Corporation Collection*, compiled by A H Millar. 450 items were listed, and in his preface Millar noted (not for the first time) that "all the Pictures in the Corporation Collection are either Donations by citizens or Loans from various quarters, and the purchase of them has not cost the ratepayers anything."[95] It would be another quarter of a century before the idea of public subsidy of art became accepted both locally and nationally – until then the development of the city's collection would continue to depend on the generosity of its wealthiest citizens.

For most of the new generation of Dundonian art enthusiasts, the 1924 Fine Art Exhibition (figure 297) provided the best opportunity to showcase the highlights of their collections. Comprising 337 works, it was held to raise funds for the Lord Roberts Memorial Workshop and was billed as "a Loan Exhibition ... which has rarely been excelled in the City."[96] John Robertson was the best represented with 28 works on show, but the most notable feature of the exhibition was Gallery Three, entirely devoted to modern Scottish and French art from the collections of William Boyd (who loaned 23 works), John Tattersall (22), Matthew Justice (twenty) and Alexander Duncan (sixteen), plus two Colourists lent by T P Fimister of Perth Road.[97] This stunning display featured Monet, Sisley, Boudin, Bonnard, Vuillard, Simon, Seurat, de Segonzac, Marchand, Friesz, Lépine, Matisse and Van Gogh, shown alongside the Scottish Colourists (including Maclauchlan Milne), William McTaggart and E A Walton. Critic Robins Millar wrote: "Such an experiment, with such famous contributors, is an event in Scotland. Art coteries will ring with the discussion it arouses. Dundee is to be congratulated on the unique nature of the exhibition... This is indeed a remarkable experience."[98]

The 1924 exhibition was not the last of its kind, but further attempts were few and on an altogether smaller level (192 works in the 1929-30 exhibition, 186 in 1934). In 1939 the BA's return was marked with an exhibition of 232 works drawn mostly from the permanent collection. By that time, however, the Victoria Art Galleries had moved towards more focused and themed exhibitions of the sort that have been held there ever since.

In 1933, an exhibition called 'A Century of Art' was held featuring works by Dundee artists held in the permanent collection. 25 artists were included, showing how far art in Dundee had come since the time of Henry Harwood. Among the names in the catalogue were new talents such as James McIntosh Patrick, who would take Dundee's artistic life forward into a new and very different era. It is no surprise that by then there was already a nostalgia for the artistic culture of a generation ago, as recalled by the *Evening Telegraph* in 1926:

"One sometimes wonders if Dundee today has anything like the... Bohemians it possessed thirty and forty years ago... [At that time] Dundee had a recognised Bohemia whose habitués maintained a daily camaraderie in quarters where they could be looked for. 'Cynicus', John Duncan, Stewart Carmichael,

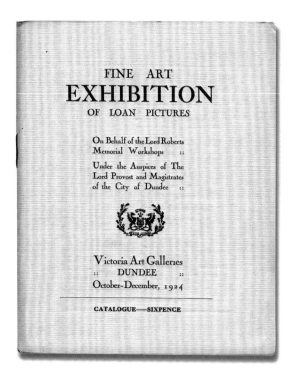

Alex [sic] Grieve, Max Cowper, and other artists could be found in the company of fledgling writers. The Bohemian atmosphere was very helpful, and the talks, walks, and smokes of those days and nights have since reacted upon some art and literature of more than local fame."[99]

293. Opposite page top: Solomon J Solomon, *Ex-Lord Provost William Longair*, oil on canvas, 1909 *(Dundee City Council: Dundee's Art Galleries & Museums)*.

294. Opposite page bottom: Walter William Ouless, *Sir William Ogilvy Dalgleish*, oil on canvas, 1911, copy by the artist made for Dundee Royal Infirmary *(University of Dundee Museum Services, Tayside Medical History Museum)*.

295. Top left: James Guthrie, *Ex-Lord Provost Charles Barrie*, oil on canvas, 1907 *(Dundee City Council: Dundee's Art Galleries & Museums)*.

296. Above: Unveiling Lord Provost Sir William Don's portrait by George Henry, from the *Dundee Courier*, 1920. Winston Churchill, who performed the ceremony, is seated second right *(used by kind permission of D C Thomson & Co Ltd)*.

297. Top right: Dundee Fine Art Exhibition 1924, catalogue *(Libraries, Leisure & Culture Dundee, licensor www.scran.ac.uk)*.

Endnotes

Introduction

1. Recent Art Movements in Dundee', *Dundee Advertiser*, 18/1/1907.

2. Dundee Art Society Annual Report 1911 (Dundee Central Library, Local History Centre).

3. Dundee Graphic Arts Association Annual Report 1890 (Dundee Central Library, Local History Centre).

4. Letter to Matthew Justice, 1923 (quoted in Bill Smith & Jill Marriner, *Hunter Revisited: The Life and Art of Leslie Hunter* (Edinburgh: Atelier Books, 2012) p115).

5. Only William Hardie's *Scottish Painting: 1837 to the Present* (Glasgow: Waverley Books, 2010) makes prolonged reference to Dundee in its section on George Dutch Davidson (Hardie had been Keeper of Art in Dundee and did much to encourage an appreciation of the city's art history). Duncan Macmillan's *Scottish Art 1460-2000* (Edinburgh: Mainstream Publishing, 2000), Murdo Macdonald's *Scottish Art* (London: Thames & Hudson, 2000) and John Morrison's *Painting the Nation* (Edinburgh University Press, 2003) make virtually no mention of art in Dundee from this period, though they all cover John Duncan's work in Edinburgh, and Macmillan and Macdonald briefly refer to Dutch Davidson. Andrew Gibbon Williams & Andrew Brown's *The Bigger Picture: A History of Scottish Art* (London: BBC Books, 1993) makes no mention even of Duncan. Of the various books written on Dundee, only Jim Tomlinson & Christopher A Whatley's *Jute No More: Transforming Dundee* (Dundee University Press, 2011) includes a chapter on art (written by myself!).

6. According to names listed in the annual Dundee Directories (held in Dundee Central Library, Local History Centre).

7. The shared studios in the former Theatre Royal building at 15 Castle Street (see chapter eight) anticipated the larger Forebank Studios founded in 1975, which became the model for today's WASPS.

8. *The Piper o' Dundee* 9/5/1900.

9. From A H Millar's review of the Graphic Arts Association's annual exhibition, *Dundee Advertiser* 20/4/1900.

10. *Dundee Advertiser* 18/2/1901.

11. Letter to *Dundee Advertiser* 24/1/1900.

12. Stewart Carmichael, 'Fifty Years of the Dundee Art Society', unpublished MS of lecture given in 1940 (Dundee of Jordanstone College Library).

13. *Dundee Courier & Advertiser* 13/4/1934.

14. Dundee Graphic Arts Association Annual Report 1900 (Dundee Central Library, Local History Centre).

15. Dundee Graphic Arts Association Annual Report 1902 (Dundee Central Library, Local History Centre).

16. Letter to Peter Carmichael 8/11/1886 (University of Dundee Archive Services, Peter Carmichael Collection).

17. Free Library Committee Report 1903 (Dundee Central Library, Local History Centre).

18. A H Millar, *Jubilee of the Albert Institute* 1867-1917 (Dundee: John Durham & Son, 1917).

Chapter One

1. T S Robertson, 'Reminiscences of Old Dundee – Its Fine Art', *Dundee Courier* 17/12/1906.

2. Catalogues for the Watt Institution exhibitions in 1842, 1843 and 1847 are held by Dundee Central Library, Local History Centre. Its history is told in James V Smith, *The Watt Institution, Dundee 1824-49* (Dundee: Abertay Historical Society, 1977).

3. Only volume one is held in Dundee Central Library Local History Centre under the title *Catalogue of Paintings by the Old Masters in the Gallery at Blackness House*. Hunter's obituary is in the *Dundee Year Book* 1882.

4. *The Wizard of the North* 30/11/1895.

5. W G Burn-Murdoch, *From Edinburgh to the Antarctic* (London: Longmans, Green & Co, 1894) p17.

6. Dundee Art Union annual report 1883 (Dundee Central Library, Local History Centre).

7. *Dundee Courier* 26/5/1864.

8. *Meeting of the British Association for the Advancement of Science in Dundee* (Dundee: Advertiser Office, 1868) p53.

9. Full details of the exhibition can be found in *Ibid*.

10. Quoted from notes for a talk on art collectors by Anna Robertson, in file held at the McManus, original reference unknown.

11. Information from their obituaries in the *Dundee Year Books* of 1892 and 1902, and from Helen Smailes, 'Dundee's forgotten Maecenas? G B Simpson and the patronage of modern Scottish art', *Journal of the Scottish Society for Art History* vol 14 (2009-10) pp29-39.

12. The letters were gifted by the executors of William McTaggart's son-in-law and biographer James L Caw and have been described by Helen Smailes as "one of the most important [collections] of its kind in any public repository in Scotland." Also of note is an album of transcriptions by Simpson of correspondence with G P Chalmers held in the RSA Archives. Smailes's work on Simpson (*op cit*) has so far been the only in-depth study of these collections and I am grateful to her for allowing me access to her research.

13. Letter to Simpson 26/3/1866 (NLS MS 6351 f40-1) and Simpson folder p70 (RSA Archives).

14. Letter to Simpson 11/1/1863 (NLS MS 6349 f127-30).

15. Smailes (*op cit*) p31.

16. The transcribed letters held in the RSA Archive were presumably for this purpose, and it is notable that Simpson refused Chalmers' first biographer Edward Pinnington's request to quote from them, presumably intending to use them himself.

17. NLS MS 6348 f174.

18. *Dundee Advertiser* 29/11/1880.

19. *Dundee Advertiser* 22/10/1902. The building is now owned by the University of Dundee and houses many of its art treasures.

20. All of the relevant sales catalogues are held in Dundee Central Library, Local History Centre.

21. *Dundee Advertiser* 16/3/1885.

22. *Dundee Advertiser* 22/10/1902.

23. Both of Ritchie's sales catalogues are held in Dundee Central Library, Local History Centre.

24. *The Wizard of the North* 30/11/1895.

25. *Dundee Advertiser* 30/8/1897.

26. *Ibid*.

27. Letter to Simpson 25/2/1861 (NLS MS 6349 f194-5).

28. *Dundee Advertiser* 30/8/1897.

29. In John Morrison's *Painting the Nation* (Edinburgh University Press, 2003) he claims that the Aberdeen (and later Dundee) collector J F White was the first in Scotland to buy modern Dutch art, purchasing Mollinger's *Drenthe* in 1862. Bell showed Mollinger's *Under the Oak* at the BA exhibition in 1867, but it is not known how much earlier he acquired it.

30. Letter from Bell among miscellaneous correspondence to McTaggart in NLS Acc.11157.

31. *Dundee Advertiser* 30/8/1897.

32. T S Robertson "Famous Scottish Artists: George Paul Chalmers", *Dundee Courier* 11/4/1904.

33. Bell's will is available on the Scotland's People website.

34. Edward Pinnington, 'Art Collections of Dundee and District. 1 – Corporation Galleries', *Dundee Advertiser* 24/4/1909.

35. *The Wizard of the North* 30/11/1895. Further accounts can be found in *Dundee Advertiser* 20/3/1877 and 30/8/1897 and *Dundee Courier* 19/3/1877.

36. *The Wizard of the North* 30/11/1895.

37. *Dundee Advertiser* 30/8/1897.

38. One of Simpson's paintings, *Bothwell Castle* by Fraser, was later donated by John Robertson of Elmslea, who had purchased it from Simpson in 1881.

39. The best general account of Orchar's life and collection can be found in David Scruton, *James Guthrie Orchar and The Orchar Collection* (St Andrews: Crawford Centre for the Arts 1988).

40. *Dundee Advertiser* 16/5/1898.

41. *Ibid*.

42. Quoted in Scruton (*op cit*) p10 and Per Kvaerne, *William McTaggart 1835-1910: Singing Songs of the Scottish Heart* (Edinburgh: Atelier Books Ltd, 2007) p108.

43. *Dundee Courier* 15/1/1885.

44. *Dundee Advertiser* 16/5/1898. Some of Orchar's anecdotes are related by T S Robertson in a *Dundee Courier* article from 26/5/1905, but as Robertson admits, "his charming style of telling them is lost for ever."

45. *The Piper o' Dundee* 18/5/1898. An interesting contrast to this was a story told by Stewart Carmichael about a fellow artist (unnamed) who said "I do not know whether it is because I am so wee or Provost Orchar so tall but every time I meet the Provost I have to be re-introduced to him." (Stewart Carmichael, 'Fifty Years of the Dundee Art Society', unpublished MS of lecture given in 1940 (Dundee of Jordanstone College Library)).

46. *Dundee Advertiser* 30/8/1897.

47. *The Piper o' Dundee* 20/3/1895.

48. T S Robertson, 'Reminiscences of Old Dundee – Its Fine Art', *Dundee Courier* 17/12/1906.

49. *The Piper o' Dundee* 20/3/1895.

50. *People's Journal* 7/12/1895.

51. His obituary of 29/5/1896 is in the newspaper obituary books held by Dundee Central Library, Local History Centre.

52. Biographical details from the online Dictionary of Scottish Architects (www.scottisharchitects.org.uk) and his obituary 5/3/1923 (newspaper obituary book, Dundee Central Library, Local History Centre).

53. T S Robertson 'Famous Scottish Artists: William McTaggart RSA', *Dundee Courier* 3/5/1904.

54. Various obituaries and tributes can be found in a cuttings book compiled by AH Millar held in the Lamb Collection, Dundee Central Library, Local History Centre.

55. Dundee Graphic Arts Association Annual Report 1890 (Dundee Central Library, Local History Centre).

56. The incident is reported in T S Robertson's article on McTaggart in the *Dundee Courier* 3/5/1904 with further details given in Kvaerne (*op cit*) p44. The latter quotes a letter from G P Chalmers to Simpson listing the guests but with no mention of Smieton. T S Robertson names David Smieton (Thomas's brother) as being there, but as Thomas was the art collector, not David, it seems more likely that Robertson is just getting his names muddled.

57. Cargill lent works by Alexander Fraser and Erskine Nicol in 1852-4, Macdonald lent a Hugh Cameron in 1866, and Smieton lent a Sam Bough in 1871. The latter was *The Vale of St John*, which Edward Pinnington described as "one of his most important, most successful, and most perfectly representative works" in an article on Smieton's collection in the *Dundee Advertiser* 5/6/1909.

58. T S Robertson, 'Reminiscences of Old Dundee – Its Fine Art', *Dundee Courier* 17/12/1906.

59. *Meeting of the British Association* (*op cit*) p xxv.

60. *The Scotsman* 2/1/1912.

61. *Belfast Telegraph* 2/1/1912.

62. A H Millar, 'The Collection of I. Julius Weinberg, Esq., Dundee', *The Art Journal* 1898 pp16-20, 84-89.

63. *Ibid*.

64. *The Scotsman* 2/1/1912.

65. Quoted from notes on Weinberg and other German Jews in Dundee compiled by C C Aronsfeld and held in the archives of the Jewish Museum, London (MS 174/1/4).

66. From an unidentified 1901 newspaper article in a cuttings book titled 'Men and Women of Mark in Modern Judea' held by the Jewish Museum, London.

67. *Dundee Advertiser* cutting included in a special edition of the *Catalogue of the Fine Art Exhibition* (Dundee 1873) held by Dundee Central Library, Local History Centre.

68. Clara Young, 'Dundee's Earliest Fine Art Exhibitions', *Journal of the Scottish Society for Art History* vol 11 2006 pp10-17.

69. *Dundee Advertiser* 2/10/1877.

70. Figures from John Maclauchlan, *The Albert Institute: its Libraries, Museums, Art Galleries and Branches* (Dundee: Winter, Duncan & Co 1908).

71. For further information on Keiller & Son, see W M Mathew, *Keiller's of Dundee: The Rise of the Marmalade Dynasty 1800-1879* (Dundee: Abertay Historical Society, 1998).

72. *Dundee Advertiser* 6/1/1899. R A M Stevenson, 'Mr Keiller's Collection in Dundee', *The Art Journal* vol 56 (1894) p56.

73. *The Piper o'Dundee* 23/12/1887.

74. Years later, Binrock House was bought by Alberto Morrocco and works of art once more lined its walls.

75. *The Mercantile Age* 30/1/1889.

76. *The Wizard of the North* 25/5/1889.

77. *Dundee Courier* 13/4/1877.

78. *The Piper o'Dundee* 15/5/1892.

79. Stewart's will is available on the Scotland's People website. His vast collection was split into various sales in December 1892.

80. T S Robertson, 'Provost Orchar of Broughty Ferry', *Dundee Courier* 26/6/1905.

81. *Ibid*.

82. *The Wizard of the North* 30/11/1883.

83. *The Wizard of the North* 28/10/1882.

84. The winners were listed in the *Courier* 2/10/1877.

85. According to the *Dundee Courier* 10/7/1880.

86. *Ibid*.

87. *Dundee Courier* 12/1/1891.

88. See the *Dundee Courier* 17/6/1879, 9/12/1885 and 11/12/1885. Further accusations of bad management were made in the *Piper o'Dundee* 21/1/1891.

89. *Dundee Courier* 21/11/1884. Using per capita GDP this is the equivalent of well over £5 million today.

90. *Dundee Advertiser* 16/5/1898. Manchester's annual exhibition also yielded more, but only because the city council spent £2,000 every year buying art from it for their permanent collection, a fact not lost on the *Dundee Courier* of 27/9/1884.

91. *Dundee Courier* 19/1/1884.

92. *Dundee Courier* 8/10/1867. Some of the works sold were listed on 14/6/1867.

93. Catalogues and other promotional material for these sales are held in the Lamb Collection, Dundee Central Library, Local History Centre.

94. Reported in *The Wizard of the North* 30/5/1891.

95. Obituaries for Robert Curr and William Dewar in the *Courier & Advertiser* 29/4/1932 and 22/2/1958 respectively. Arthur Harris's son (also named Arthur Harris) was a painter of landscape and topographical scenes who had some success in the 1890s.

96. *People's Journal* 22/11/1879.

97. Dundee Fine Art Exhibition 1880 catalogue (Dundee Central Library, Local History Centre).

98. *The Mercantile Age* 30/1/1889.

99. According to the artist in an 1884 document about the painting included in a scrapbook held by Wolverhampton Arts & Museums.

100. *The Piper o'Dundee* 9/9/1896.

101. *The Mercantile Age* 9/5/1889.

102. *The Piper o'Dundee* 6/1/1897.

103. Dundee Fine Art Exhibition 1889 catalogue (Dundee Central Library, Local History Centre).

104. *The Piper o'Dundee* 8/9/1905.

105. *Evening Telegraph* 3/11/1900.

106. Catalogue for 30th Annual Exhibition of Original Etchings (Dundee Central Library, Local History Centre). Ultimately the Great Depression killed this craze for etchings.

107. Robert Scott's obituary is in the *Courier & Advertiser* 11/2/1948.

108. Dundee Fine Art Exhibition catalogue 1910 (Dundee Central Library, Local History Centre).

109. *Dundee Courier* 21/11/1884.

110. *Dundee Courier* 12/12/1884.

111. *Dundee Courier* 15/1/1885.

112. Dundee Art Society Annual Report 1906 (Dundee Central Library, Local History Centre).

113. *Dundee Year Book* 1906.

114. The three parts of the collection are described by Edward Pinnington in articles in the *Dundee Advertiser* in 15/5/1909 and 22/5/1909. J C Robertson's obituary appears 29/2/1932 and Kydd's 3/11/1922. Both worked as chartered accountants in the firm of Moody Stuart & Robertson.

115. Figures from David Scruton, *The Victoria Galleries: Art and Enterprise in Late Nineteenth Century Dundee* (Dundee Art Galleries & Museums, 1989). John Maclauchlan gives different totals (*op cit*, 1908). A subscription document held in the Carmichael papers at the University of Dundee Archives lists Robertson & Orchar, Mrs Smieton, I J Weinberg and John Robertson as the other principal subscribers.

116. These various schemes are described in Scruton (*Ibid*).

117. City status was granted on 4 February 1889, though the official Royal Warrant confirming this was not forthcoming until 11 February 1892.

118. *Dundee Advertiser* 25/10/1889.

119. Quoted in Scruton, *op cit*.

120. *Dundee Courier* 12/1/1891.

121. See for example Jennifer Melville, 'Art and Patronage in Aberdeen 1860-1920', *Journal of the Scottish Society for Art History* vol 3 (1998) pp17-23 and Morrison, *op cit*. White's importance in the establishment of Aberdeen Art Gallery is described in Jennifer Melville, *Aberdeen Art Gallery: a History* (Aberdeen City Council, 2010).

122. *Dundee Advertiser* 21/10/1904.

123. *The Piper o'Dundee* 3/7/1889.

124. Dundee Art Society Annual Report 1904 (Dundee Central Library, Local History Centre).

125. *The Piper o'Dundee* 21/9/1892.

126. *The Piper o'Dundee* 17/11/1897.

127. *The Wizard of the North* 29/11/1890.

128. *The Piper o'Dundee* 17/2/1892.

129. *The Wizard of the North* 30/11/1892.

130. *"Old Dundee" Exhibition, Albert Institute 1892-3* (Dundee: Winter, Duncan & Co, 1892)

131. *Ibid*.

132. *The Piper o'Dundee* 8/3/1893.

133. Falconer may also have been an artist himself, if the attribution of a painting of the Royal Arch in the city's collection is to be believed, though this may be a mistake since the work looks very like the style of David Small.

134. The sales catalogue is held by Dundee Central Library, Local History Centre. The spelling of M(a)cLean's name is inconsistent, even in his own literature – I have chosen the shorter form throughout.

135. *The Piper o'Dundee* 11/1/1893.

136. This might explain why the Report of the Free Library Committee for 1893 oddly dismisses the visitor attendance as "rather indifferent".

137. *The Piper o'Dundee* 12/5/1897.

138. *The Piper o'Dundee* 16/2/1898.

139. Annotated copies of the sales catalogues (lavishly illustrated with a number of photographic reproductions) are held by Dundee Central Library, Local History Centre.

140. Quoted in Maclauchlan *op cit*, p13.

141. *Ibid*.

142. *The Piper o'Dundee* 20/11/1895.

143. Maclauchlan *op cit*, p13.

144. *The Piper o'Dundee* 26/2/1896.

145. *Dundee Courier* 6/2/1896.

146. Maclauchlan *op cit*, p13-14.

147. Obituary 21/5/1883 in the cuttings book in Dundee Central Library, Local History Centre.

148. The sales catalogue is in the Lamb Collection in Dundee Central Library, Local History Centre.

149. "Atrophy of the nervous system" was the cause stated on her death certificate. See for example Suzanne Fagence Cooper, *Effie: The Passionate Lives of Effie Gray, John Ruskin and John Everett Millais* (New York: St Martin's Press, 2011).

150. My thanks to Susan Keracher of the McManus for providing information on Caird.

151. *Dundee Advertiser* 30/8/1897.

Chapter Two

1. Dundee Courier 2/2/1874.

2. James Webster, *The Art Treasures of Scotland vol 1 – Dundee* (Edinburgh: T & A Constable, 1899)

3. Dundee Art Society Annual Report 1911 (Dundee Central Library, Local History Centre).

4. Report of the Free Library Committee 1894 (Dundee Central Library, Local History Centre).

5. Maxwell was a partner in Keiller & Son and a member of the Town Council.

6. *Old Letters* is currently with Paisley Museum & Art Gallery.

7. *Dundee Courier* 11/5/1874. Visitor numbers would continue to be impressive – over 150,000 by the end of the year and reaching half a million early in 1876. Originally turnstiles were used to count visitors, but these were soon abandoned as inaccurate, so the figures may not be correct.

8. *Dundee Courier* 7/5/1874. The report in the *Dundee Advertiser* of 8/5/1874 does not mention the Picture Gallery at all.

9. *Dundee Courier* 18/7/1874.

10. *Dundee Courier* 11/2/1882.

11. *Dundee Courier* 9/9/1892.

12. Report of the Free Library Committee 1876-7 (Dundee Central Library, Local History Centre).

13. Report of the Free Library Committee 1877-8 (Dundee Central Library, Local History Centre).

14. John Maclauchlan, *The Albert Institute: its Libraries, Museums, Art Galleries and Branches* (Dundee: Winter, Duncan & Co, 1908) p10.

15. Information on Duncan from his obituary 6/1/1878 in the cuttings books held by Dundee Central Library, Local History Centre, and from A H Millar, *Jubilee of the Albert Institute 1867-1917* (Dundee: John Durham & Son, 1917) pp65-6.

16. *Ibid*, p66.

17. Dundee Art Society Annual Report 1911 (Dundee Central Library, Local History Centre).

18. Webster, *op cit*.

19. *Dundee Courier* 14/1/1878. Ultimately, only 34 of Duncan's pictures would enter the permanent collection, the rest presumably being of too poor condition or quality.

20. *Dundee Courier* 11/2/1879.

21. *Dundee Courier* 11/1/1881.

22. Report of the Free Library Committee 1881 (Dundee Central Library, Local History Centre).

23. *Dundee Courier* 13/9/1881.

24. *Dundee Courier* 10/1/1882.

25. Orchar originally intended to gift a different John Pettie, *The Highland Outpost*, but presumably became too fond of the latter, keeping it for his own collection.

26. *Dundee Courier* 28/9/1883.

27. In 2012, for example, it was chosen as the front cover image for the Public Catalogue Foundation's *Catalogue of Oil Paintings in Public Ownership in Dundee*.

28. Webster, *op cit*.

29. Dundee Art Society Annual Report 1911 (Dundee Central Library, Local History Centre).

30. *Dundee Courier* 9/11/1886.

31. Report of the Free Library Committee 1888 (Dundee Central Library, Local History Centre).

32. *Dundee Courier* 20/1/1887.

33. Report of the Free Library Committee 1889-90 (Dundee Central Library, Local History Centre).

34. Edward Pinnington, 'Art Collections of Dundee and District. 1 – Corporation Galleries', *Dundee Advertiser* 24/4/1909.

35. Webster, *op cit*.

36. Report of the Free Library Committee 1896 (Dundee Central Library, Local History Centre).

37. Report of the Free Library Committee 1898 (Dundee Central Library, Local History Centre).

38. Webster, *op cit*. In fact, no further volumes appeared.

39. A H Millar 'The Ethics of Local Art Galleries', *Museums Journal* October 1909 pp167-8.

40. *Dundee Courier* 27/9/1872.

41. Webster, *op cit*.

42. *Dundee Courier* 10/9/1881 and Webster, *op cit*.

43. Webster, *op cit*.

44. *Dundee Courier* 15/6/1885.

45. It is now in the collection of the Tayside Medical History Museum at Ninewells Hospital.

46. *Dundee Courier* 11/6/1885.

47. Webster, *op cit*.

48. *Ibid*.

49. *Dundee Courier* 28/10/1889.

50. Report of the Free Library Committee 1893 (Dundee Central Library, Local History Centre).

51. *Dundee Courier* 24/1/1893.

52. Webster, *op cit*.

53. My thanks to Kenneth Baxter for this information.

54. *Ibid*.

55. W H Blyth Martin, 'Roll of Burgesses and Portraits' in A W Paton & A H Millar (eds), *British Association, Dundee 1912: Handbook and Guide to Dundee and District* (Dundee: David Winter & Son, 1912) p520.

56. Pinnington, *op cit*.

57. Webster, *op cit*.

58. *Ibid*.

59. Hugh MacDiarmid, *Contemporary Scottish Studies* (Manchester: Carcanet Press, 1995) p228.

60. *Dundee Advertiser* 9/10/1902.

61. Dundee Graphic Arts Association Annual Report 1900 (Dundee Central Library, Local History Centre). Several local artists had actually studied under Herkomer, including E S Hodgson and James W Herald.

62. Other portraits by Dundee painters had entered the permanent collection (such as W B Lamond's painting of the Poet McGonagall), but they were not presentation works.

63. Dundee Graphic Arts Association Annual Report 1899 (Dundee Central Library, Local History Centre).

64. Quoted by Kenneth Baxter, 'Mary Ann Baxter: Philanthropist and Founder of University College, Dundee' in Matthew Jarron *et al* (ed), *Ten Taysiders: Forgotten Figures from Dundee, Angus & Perthshire* (Dundee: Abertay Historical Society, 2010).

65. According to his speech at the inauguration of the statue, reported in the *Dundee Courier* 10/9/1863. Steell's father worked as a woodcarver in Dundee and his mother was a Gourlay, of the Dundee shipbuilding family.

66. According to Baxter, as recorded by the Special Committee and reported in the *Dundee Courier* 2/10/1862.

67. According to the *Dundee Courier* 10/9/1863, although they noted the impossibility of coming up with an accurate figure.

68. *Dundee Courier* 10/9/1863.

69. In fact a Kinloch Institute did operate for a time with a library and lecture programme starting in 1838.

70. This was not the first interdict against the proposed monument. The long and complicated story of the statue is told in the *Dundee Courier* 5/2/1872 and various early minutes and pamphlets are held in the Lamb Collection at Dundee Central Library, Local History Centre.

71. It stood where DC Thomson's headquarters were later built.

72. See for example the *Dundee Advertiser* 17/9/1869 and the *Dundee Courier* 20/9/1869.

73. *Dundee Advertiser* 17/9/1869.

74. *Dundee Advertiser* 21/9/1869.

75. *Dundee Advertiser* 17/9/1869.

76. *Dundee Courier* 5/2/1872.

77. *Ibid*.

78. *Dundee Courier* 23/10/1872.

79. *The Scotsman* 12/6/1873.

80. *Dundee Courier* 24/5/1876. Kenneth Baxter has suggested this might instead be Carmichael's son-in-law Peter.

81. *Dundee Courier* 19/6/1876.

82. *Dundee Courier* 7/2/1877.

83. *Dundee Courier* 30/8/1879.

84. *Dundee Courier* 18/10/1880.

85. *Dundee Advertiser* 18/10/1880.

86. *People's Journal* 10/4/1880.

87. *Dundee Courier* 18/10/1880.

88. Published in *Last Poetic Gems*, included in William McGonagall, *Collected Poems* (Edinburgh: Birlinn, 1992).

89. *Dundee Advertiser* 18/10/1880.

90. *Ibid*.

91. Pinnington, *op cit*.

92. The differences between the two pairs of statues are discussed by Mark Stocker in '"The head o' the Bard sweeps the Southern Sky!" Sir John Steell's

Statues of Robert Burns: From Dundee to Dunedin', *Journal of the Scottish Society for Art History* vol 11 (2006) pp18-26.

93. *Dundee Courier* 6/5/1891.

94. *Dundee Courier* 8/3/1890.

95. The development of Celtic cast collections is discussed by Sally M Foster in 'Circulating Agency – the V&A, Scotland and the multiplication of casts of "Celtic crosses"', *Journal of the History of Collections*, vol 27 no 1 (2015) pp73-96.

96. Maclauchlan (1908), *op cit*, p15.

97. Dundee Art Society Annual Report 1911 (Dundee Central Library, Local History Centre).

98. According to the Duke of Connaught's speech at the unveiling, as reported in the *Dundee Courier* 28/8/1899. Other sources give the amount as £2,500.

99. *Dundee Courier* 27/2/1897.

100. *Dundee Courier* 9/8/1897.

101. *The Piper o'Dundee* 10/3/1897.

102. *The Piper o'Dundee* 28/7/1897.

103. *Dundee Courier* 17/2/1899 and 3/3/1899.

104. *The Piper o'Dundee* 23/8/1899.

105. *Dundee Courier* 25/5/1899.

106. *Dundee Courier* 28/8/1899.

107. *Ibid.*

108. *Ibid.* The ship remained problematic, and was eventually removed, as was the branch she held in her other hand.

109. Graphic Arts Association Annual Report 1899 (Dundee Central Library, Local History Centre).

110. *Dundee Courier* 18/8/1897. A somewhat diminutive statue of Duncan did eventually appear outside St Paul's Cathedral in 1997.

111. *The Piper o'Dundee* 21/2/1894. The statue was eventually restored to the park in 2007.

Chapter Three

1. *Dundee Highland Society Year Book* 1910-11 (Dundee Central Library, Local History Centre).

2. *The Piper o'Dundee* 28/3/1888.

3. White regularly lent paintings to the Graphic Arts Association exhibitions, and his oriental collection was exhibited at the Victoria Galleries in 1899-1900. A pamphlet was produced for this entitled *Notes for the Japanese Portion of the Balruddery Collection of Oriental Art in the Victoria Galleries*, written by Mary M White.

4. Philip Boardman, *The Worlds of Patrick Geddes* (London, Henley & Boston: Routledge & Kegan Paul Ltd, 1978) p78.

5. Some of the various and complicated causes of this are discussed by Murdo Macdonald in his essay 'Patrick Geddes – Science and Art in Dundee' in Matthew Jarron (ed), *The Artist & the Thinker – John Duncan & Patrick Geddes in Dundee* (University of Dundee Museum Services, 2004) pp13-29.

6. For full bibliographic details, see Helen Meller, *Patrick Geddes: Social Evolutionist and City Planner* (London & New York: Routledge, 1990).

7. Dundee Directory 1869-70 (Dundee Central Library, Local History Centre).

8. John Kemplay, *The Paintings of John Duncan: A Scottish Symbolist* (San Francisco: Pomegranate Artbooks 1994) p59.

9. George Wilkie Gahan, *Poem "The Trials of Truth" and Smaller Poems, "God's Pathway", Art Reminiscences, etc* (Dundee: A B Duncan & Co, 1915) p366.

10. John Duncan, 'Twenty-one Years Ago', Dundee Art Society Annual Report 1911 (Dundee Central Library, Local History Centre).

11. Quoted unreferenced by Frankie Jenkins in 'John Duncan: The Art of the Ideal', *Circles* no 21 (1995) p17.

12. Nicola Ireland, '"A man of sensitive culture": A Survey of Twelve Albums by John Duncan in the Royal Scottish Academy Collection', *Journal of the Scottish Society for Art History* vol 11 (2006) pp52-8.

13. *Dundee Courier* 27/11/1885.

14. *The Piper o'Dundee* 28/10/1887.

15. *Dundee Courier* 26/10/1887.

16. *The Piper o'Dundee* 28/10/1887.

17. *Dundee Courier* 26/10/1887.

18. At the 1890 Fine Art Exhibition, Duncan showed another scene from *The Faerie Queen* called *The Idle Lake*, but as this also featured Phaedria, it may be the same painting retitled.

19. *Dundee Courier* 9/10/1888 and *The Piper o'Dundee* 10/10/1888.

20. There is some confusion over dates here, to be discussed further in chapter five. Kemplay, *op cit*, claims that Duncan was at Antwerp and Düsseldorf during the winter of 1889-90 but we know he was in Dundee in October 1889 and January 1890 so unless he was travelling back and forth his studies must surely have been the previous year.

21. John Duncan Notebook 3 (National Library of Scotland).

22. *Ibid.*

23. *Ibid.*

24. *Evening Telegraph* 30/1/1891.

25. *Ibid.*

26. *The Piper o'Dundee* 8/7/1891.

27. *The Piper o'Dundee* 10/3/1890.

28. *The Piper o'Dundee* 2/7/1890.

29. R J B Sellar, *The Scotsman* 28/11/1945.

30. *Dundee Courier* 23/12/1892.

31. Quoted unreferenced in Philip Mairet, *Pioneer of Sociology* (London: Lund Humphries, 1957) p44.

32. Meller, *op cit*, p70.

33. Boardman, *op cit*, p129.

34. Patrick Geddes, 'The Work of the Art School' an annotated manuscript by Geddes c.1893-4 in University of Strathclyde Archives, T-GED 5/1/18.

35. *Ibid.*

36. See Meller, *op cit*, p63-4.

37. Patrick Geddes, 'The Scots Renascence', *The Evergreen*, Spring 1895, p139.

38. Geddes, 'Art School' *op cit*.

39. Elizabeth Cumming, *Hand, Heart and Soul: The Arts and Crafts Movement in Scotland* (Edinburgh: Birlinn, 2006), p35-6.

40. Kemplay, *op cit*, p32. Compare this to the remarkably similar criticisms made of Geddes's teaching style in chapter seven!

41. Catalogue of the Old Edinburgh School of Art Exhibition, 1896 (University of Strathclyde Archives, T-GED 5/3/15).

42. Patrick Geddes (and possibly John Duncan), 'Aims of University Hall School of Art', undated manuscript c.1892-3 in University of Strathclyde Archives, T-GED 12/9/30.

43. Advertising notice, *op cit*.

44. Letter to Patrick Geddes, undated (University of Strathclyde Archives, T-GED 7/10/17).

45. Cumming, *op cit*, p40. Designs for these by Duncan, Hay and Nellie Baxter were exhibited at the school in 1896 along with linoleum designs by Baxter intended for a Kirkcaldy firm (University of Strathclyde Archives T-GED 5/3/15).

46. Patrick Geddes, *The Interpreter: of Seven Pictures, of Black and White* (Edinburgh: Patrick Geddes & Colleagues, 1896) p14. It is estimated that there were at least 40 murals in total by various artists (possibly as many as 80), though most have now been obscured or destroyed.

47. Patrick Geddes, *The Masque of Ancient Learning and its many meanings* (Edinburgh: Patrick Geddes & Colleagues, 1912) p49.

48. *Pan* aka *Apollo's School Days* is in Dundee's Art Galleries & Museums and *Bacchus and Silenus* is in a private collection. *The Pipes of Arcady* in *The Evergreen* was presumably derived from the same frieze.

49. The Scottish name Fingal was given in the Old Edinburgh School of Art Exhibition catalogue when the murals were exhibited to the public in 1896, but later sources give the Irish name Fionn, in keeping with the international pan-Celtic culture that the murals celebrate.

50. Contemporary accounts include *The Studio* vol 10 (1897) and *Artist* vol 21 (1898). More recent studies have included Duncan Comrie, 'Cultural Consciousness in Edinburgh: Two Visualisations of History', *History Scotland* July/August 2002, pp12-21; Francis Fowle & Belinda Thomson (eds) *Patrick Geddes: The French Connection* (Oxford: White Cockade Publishing, 2004); Clare Willsdon, 'The Ramsay Garden Murals and their links with French Mural Painting', *Journal of the Scottish Society for Art History* vol 9 (2004) pp69-78; and John Morrison, 'John Duncan, Patrick Geddes and the Celtic Revival', *Journal of Scottish Thought* vol 5 (2012) pp27-39. They also receive significant attention in Cumming, *op cit* (2006) and Duncan Macmillan, *Scottish Art 1460-2000* (Edinburgh: Mainstream Publishing, 2000).

51. Baxter may also have studied at Dundee School of Art and the evening art classes at Morgan Academy – her name appears as a prizewinner at both institutions, but this may be someone else with the same name (at least two other Nellie Baxters were pupils at the High School at this time, one of whom died in 1891).

52. Her mother Annie M Baxter had shown fine and applied art pieces in the Fine Art Exhibitions since 1884.

53. *Dundee Courier* 13/5/1892.

54. *Dundee Courier* 6/8/1891.

55. Letter to Patrick Geddes 4/11/1895 (National Library of Scotland, MS 10527).

56. Sporadic minutes survive from 1894-5 (University of Strathclyde Archives T-GED 5/1/17 and 5/3/67).

57. Some sources give James Beveridge as the commissioner but the castle was owned by Henry, who had produced textiles to Old Edinburgh School of Art designs, and it was Henry who lent the designs to the RSA exhibition in 1896.

58. See Appendix B of Megan Ferguson, 'Patrick Geddes and the Celtic Renascence of the 1890s' (PhD thesis, University of Dundee, 2011), for a list of contributors and their nationalities.

59. Robin Nicholson, 'From Fever to Fresh Air: *The Evergreen*, *The Yellow Book* and the Threat of Decadence', *Journal of the Scottish Society for Art History* vol 9, 2004, p63.

60. *The Sunday Times* 6/6/1895.

61. *Glasgow Herald* 24/5/1895.

62. Letter to Patrick Geddes 15/5/1895 (National Library of Scotland, MS 10563).

63. Quoted unreferenced in Jenkins, *op cit*, p17.

64. Nicholson, *op cit*, p66-7.

65. Duncan Macmillan, *op cit*, p298.

66. As noted by Frances Fowle in her paper '"Weakly imitative..."? Celtic sources for The Evergreen and the question of authenticity', co-presented with Heather Pulliam at the conference *The Celtic Revival in Scotland (1860-1930)*, University of Edinburgh 1-3 May 2014.

67. The price is quoted in a letter from Geddes to publisher T Fisher Unwin 28/3/1895 (National Library of Scotland, MS 10588). Ferguson (*op cit*, p129) claims that Geddes "lost a good deal of money on *The Evergreen*".

68. *The Student* 14/11/1895.

69. Megan Ferguson (*op cit*, p78) claims that the school continued to operate until 1900 when Duncan moved to Chicago – if so then he may have been travelling down from Dundee to give classes during the final three years, but he was certainly no longer in charge – the advert for his design class at UCD in 1899 describes him as "late Director". In 1900, Helen Hay exhibited at the GAA and gave her address as "Old Edinburgh School of Art", suggesting that it still existed in some form then.

70. *The Piper o'Dundee* 23/5/1900. Concerning his financial situation (and possibly his health), it is notable that Duncan did not take his own lodgings at this time but moved back in with his family in Agrabank Cottage.

71. *Dundee Courier* 15/4/1897.

72. Letter to Mrs Anna Geddes 10/2/1898 (National Library of Scotland, MS 19261).

73. *Ibid*.

74. Letter to Patrick Geddes 5/5/1898 (National Library of Scotland, MS 10530).

75. *Dundee Courier* 21/4/1898.

76. *Dundee Advertiser* 21/4/1898.

77. Fowle & Thomson (eds), *op cit*, p41. John Morrison also notes George Henry's *A Galloway Landscape* (1889, Glasgow Museums) as a possible source of inspiration (in Morrison (2012), *op cit*, p34).

78. Letter to Patrick Geddes 12/9/1898 (National Library of Scotland, MS 10531).

79. Advertising notice for a Class in Design, 14/1/1899, held by University of Dundee Archive Services.

80. The opening class was reported in the *Dundee Courier* 19/1/1899.

81. *Ibid*.

82. Technical Institute Syllabus of Science & Art Classes, 1899-1900 (Dundee Central Library, Local History Centre).

83. Technical Institute Statement of Accounts 1899-1900 (Abertay University).

84. National Museums Scotland have a beautiful quaich by local silversmith Edward Livingston gifted to the society's first president in 1816.

85. *Dundee Courier* 31/5/1872.

86. *Dundee Highland Society Year Book* 1910-11 (Dundee Central Library, Local History Centre). The various dates of the different societies are also given here, though it dates the start of the Dundee Celtic Club as 1890, evidently unaware of its earlier incarnation.

87. *Dundee Highland Society Year Book* 1910-11 (Dundee Central Library, Local History Centre).

88. Unidentified newspaper cutting from 1926 in Stewart Carmichael's cuttings book vol 3 (Dundee City Archives).

89. *Dundee Highland Society Year Book* 1910-11 (Dundee Central Library, Local History Centre).

90. Although examples of seals from the 15th to 17th century show either dragons or wyverns with tails merely crossing, the matriculation of the coat of arms in 1673 was recorded as including "two dragons, their tails being nowed [ie knotted] together underneat" (Dundee City Archives). The surviving seals from that period show tails merely overlapping, but Lamb's *Dundee* reproduces a seal from 1732 that has a distinctive Celtic knotwork pattern, which was then adopted in most later versions. My thanks to Iain Flett, Martin Allan, Carly Cooper, Jack Blair and David Bertie for their illumination of this topic.

91. Calder Jamieson, *St Salvador's Dundee 1857-1974* (booklet produced for the church in 1974 based on the author's undergraduate research for the Open University). Copies are still available in the church.

92. *Dundee Courier* 30/10/1874. It is worth noting that in September 1886 the *People's Journal* featured a large and detailed line drawing of the church's interior, which may well be the work of John Duncan (it was done at the time that he was working for Martin Anderson at the Leng press and is not signed MA as all of Anderson's larger illustrations were).

93. *Dundee Courier* 28/12/1875.

94. *Dundee Courier* 3/3/1873.

95. His obituary is in the *Dundee Courier* 17/10/1882.

96. According to *The Dilletante* 11/10/1884, but I have found no other reference to this so it seems likely that the lectures never took place.

97. All of these are still intact today.

98. *Dundee Courier* 4/2/1887.

99. *Ibid*.

100. After the demolition of the Town House the windows became part of the city museum collections.

101. *Dundee Courier* 28/8/1883.

102. *Dundee Courier* 21/12/1887. A second Industrial Exhibition was held in 1893-4.

103. Cumming, *op cit*, p52.

104. *Dundee Courier* 16/2/1891.

105. The full list of prizes is given in the *Dundee Courier* 18/3/1891.

106. *The Piper o'Dundee* 11/2/1891.

107. *Dundee Courier* 2/9/1889.

108. *The Piper o'Dundee* 4/9/1889.

109. Reid is featured in the August 1889 issue of *The Piper o'Dundee* and one of his paintings from the 1889 Fine Art exhibition is reproduced in the October issue that year. In the catalogue for the exhibition, Reid gave his address as 31 Reform Street, then the headquarters of the Dundee Art Club. Reid was also featured in two issues of *The City Echo*, February 1909 and July 1911.

110. *The Celtic Annual* 1918, p17.

111. Gahan, *op cit*, p372.

112. Technical Institute Syllabus 1889-90 (Dundee Central Library, Local History Centre).

113. Brown's help in developing the city's classical cast collection has already been noted in the previous chapter.

114. Brown's opening lectures were different at each venue, but it is presumed that the rest of the course was the same, both being advertised with the same description.

115. Technical Institute Syllabus 1889-90 (Dundee Central Library, Local History Centre).

116. Technical Institute Syllabus 1890-91 (Dundee Central Library, Local History Centre).

117. *The Studio* vol 17 (1899) p263, and vol 23 (1901) p267. Inglis was the son of local art critic James Inglis, and later taught art in Brechin, Arbroath and Clonmel, Ireland.

118. Report of the Free Library Committee 1894 (Dundee Central Library, Local History Centre).

119. *Dundee Courier* 30/3/1895.

120. *Dundee Courier* 26/5/1896.

121. Alexander Moffat & Alan Riach with Linda MacDonald-Lewis, *Arts of Resistance* (Edinburgh: Luath Press Ltd, 2008) p109.

122. *The Piper o'Dundee* 28/10/1887.

123. As with Duncan, there is some uncertainty as to the exact duration of Carmichael's stay in London. Some sources claim he went there aged 19 (ie 1886) but he was definitely exhibiting with the Art Club and winning prizes at the School of Art in the first half of 1887.

124. While there Carmichael acquired an oil study of a donkey by Herremans which he later bequeathed to the city collection.

125. Unidentified newspaper cutting, August 1890, from Stewart Carmichael Scrapbook volume one (Dundee City Archives). The painting was bought by local collector David Duncan and lent by him to the Fine Art Exhibition later that year.

126. *The Piper o'Dundee* 1/10/1890.

127. Unidentified newspaper cutting, March 1891, from Stewart Carmichael Scrapbook volume one (Dundee City Archives).

128. *Evening Telegraph* newspaper cutting, March 1891, from Stewart Carmichael Scrapbook volume one (Dundee City Archives).

129. Unidentified newspaper cutting from Stewart Carmichael Scrapbook volume one (Dundee City Archives).

130. *Dundee Advertiser* newspaper cutting, June 1893, from Stewart Carmichael Scrapbook volume one (Dundee City Archives).

131. *Ibid*.

132. *The Piper o'Dundee* 2/12/1891.

133. *Evening Telegraph* newspaper cutting, March 1891, from Stewart Carmichael Scrapbook volume one (Dundee City Archives).

134. Dundee Fine Art Exhibition Catalogue 1891 (Dundee Central Library, Local History Centre).

135. *Dundee Courier* newspaper cutting, December 1902, from Stewart Carmichael Scrapbook volume one (Dundee City Archives).

136. Various modern sources refer to him exhibiting with this society – for example Elizabeth Cumming's exhibition *Hand, Heart & Soul* – but I have found no contemporary evidence of this.

137. 1897 cutting from Stewart Carmichael's newspaper scrapbook volume one (Dundee City Archives).

138. *The Studio* vol 12 (1897) p192.

139. From the catalogue to Carmichael's memorial exhibition, possibly written by curator James Boyd (Dundee Central Library, Local History Centre).

140. Unidentified newspaper cutting, 1897, from Stewart Carmichael Scrapbook volume one (Dundee City Archives).

141. Grieve's father later became an inspector for the Water Board.

142. *Dundee Courier* 26/2/1935.

143. *The Piper o'Dundee* 10/5/1893.

144. From an unidentified newspaper cutting titled 'The Growlers' Club' c.1895 from Stewart Carmichael Scrapbook volume one (Dundee City Archives).

145. *Dundee Advertiser* newspaper cuttings, 1893 and 1895, from Stewart Carmichael Scrapbook volume one (Dundee City Archives).

146. *Dundee Courier* 21/4/1898.

147. *Evening Telegraph* newspaper cutting, 1898, from Stewart Carmichael Scrapbook volume one (Dundee City Archives).

148. Unidentified newspaper cutting from Stewart Carmichael Scrapbook volume

one (Dundee City Archives).

149. *Dundee Courier* 29/3/1899.

150. He was top of his class each year according to *George Dutch Davidson: A Memorial Volume* (Dundee: Graphic Arts Association, 1902) p1 (though did not become Dux as some sources claim).

151. *Ibid* p2.

152. In the *Memorial Volume* Foggie claims that Davidson enrolled at the start of the 1897-8 session but he is listed in the examination results for the previous session, so presumably joined midway through that. Davidson had first enrolled for other evening classes at the High School back in 1894.

153. *Memorial Volume, op cit*, p3. For further interpretation of this painting, see William Hardie, 'The Hills of Dream Revisited: George Dutch Davidson (1879-1901)', *Scottish Art Review* vol 13 no 4 (1972), p19.

154. William Hardie, 'George Dutch Davidson: "A too great perfection"', *Journal of the Scottish Society for Art History* vol 11 (2006), p29.

155. *Memorial Volume, op cit*, p2.

156. *Evening Telegraph* newspaper cutting, 1898, from Stewart Carmichael Scrapbook volume one (Dundee City Archives).

157. Stewart Carmichael, 'Fifty Years of the Dundee Art Society', unpublished MS of lecture given in 1940 (Dundee of Jordanstone College Library).

158. In a letter to Patrick Geddes dated 5 May 1898, Duncan referred to Davidson as a "very promising young artist" (National Library of Scotland, MS 10530).

159. *Memorial Volume, op cit*, p3.

160. *Ibid*, p63.

161. *Ibid*, p4.

162. Two versions of this survive, one in Dundee's Art Galleries & Museums and one owned by the family of David Foggie.

163. Letter to John Duncan 30/1/1900, quoted in the *Memorial Volume, op cit*, p49.

164. Lindsay Errington, 'Celtic Elements in Scottish Art at the turn of the century', in John Christian (ed), *The Last Romantics: the Romantic Tradition in British Art from Burne Jones to Stanley Spencer* (London: Barbican Art Gallery & Lund Humphries, 1989) p49.

165. Letter to John Duncan 18-19/1/1900, quoted in the *Memorial Volume* p26.

166. Letter to John Duncan 28/2/1900, quoted in the *Memorial Volume* p29.

167. *Evening Telegraph* newspaper cutting, 1898, from Stewart Carmichael Scrapbook volume one (Dundee City Archives).

168. *Ibid*.

169. *Dundee Advertiser* 29/3/1899.

170. *Dundee Free Press* 11/4/1899.

171. Unidentified newspaper cutting from Stewart Carmichael Scrapbook volume one (Dundee City Archives).

172. *Dundee Advertiser* 20/4/1900.

173. Letter to John Duncan 19/5/1900, quoted in the *Memorial Volume*, op cit, p36.

174. Carmichael, 'Fifty Years', *op cit*. The lecture was given in 1906.

175. *Dundee Advertiser* 20/4/1900.

176. *The Piper o' Dundee* 16/1/1901.

177. *The Piper o' Dundee* 10/4/1901.

178. Rosa Baxter was born in 1876.

179. Letter to Patrick Geddes 5/5/1898 (National Library of Scotland, MS 10530).

180. Graphic Arts Association Minute Book 5/12/1898 (held at the time of consultation by Dundee Art Society, later transferred to University of Dundee Archive Services).

181. Graphic Arts Association Annual Report 1899 (Dundee Central Library, Local History Centre).

182. *Evening Telegraph* 30/3/1899.

183. Graphic Arts Association Annual Report 1900 (Dundee Central Library, Local History Centre).

184. Westbrook's later career is worth noting. Born Jessie Ewing Duncan in 1873, she married Walter Westbrook, a senior official in the Colonial Office, and became a poet and translator. Her published works included *The Diwan Of Zeb-Un-Nissa – The First Fifty Ghazals* rendered from the Persian by Magan Lal and Jessie Duncan Westbrook (London: John Murray 1913) and *Hindustani Lyrics* rendered from the Urdu by Inayat Khan and Jessie Duncan Westbrook (London: Sufi Publishing Society 1919). My thanks to her great-grandson Sanjiva Senanayake for this information.

185. David Foggie's diary, 9/1/1901 (family collection).

186. Duncan gives Arminjon's address to Geddes in a letter 5/8/1899 (National Library of Scotland, MS 10531).

187. *Dundee Courier* 29/3/1899. Duncan would go on to show three of the designs at the Dundee Art Society exhibition in 1906. I have not been able to find images of these but it is possible that Duncan's later *Peacock and Fountain* in Dundee's Art Galleries & Museums may relate to this series.

188. The *Evening Telegraph* 1/2/1900 announced that Duncan had been given the commission, and the work was complete by March.

189. *Evening Telegraph* 28/3/1900.

190. *The Piper o' Dundee* 23/5/1900. There may have been other Dundee commissions that have not yet come to light – Duncan's obituary in the *Scotsman* 24/11/1945 claims that he undertook "the decoration of houses [plural] in

Dundee."

191. Letter to Mrs Anna Geddes 10/2/1898 (National Library of Scotland, MS 19261).

192. Letter to Patrick Geddes 5/8/1899 (National Library of Scotland, MS 10531).

193. Quoted unreferenced in Kemplay, *op cit*, p33, presumably from the Geddes papers in the National Library of Scotland.

194. Letter to John Duncan 2/4/1900 (National Library of Scotland, MS 10509).

195. Letter to Patrick Geddes 3/4/1900 (National Library of Scotland, MS 10509).

196. Letter to Patrick Geddes 5/8/1899 (National Library of Scotland, MS 10531).

197. Versions are held by Dundee's Art Galleries & Museums and National Museums Scotland, while a third came up for sale at Bonhams in 2009. The attribution of the design to Duncan was made by Clara Young in 2004 and has since become widely accepted.

198. *Dundee Courier* 21/4/1900.

199. *The Wizard of the North* 27/4/1900.

200. *Dundee Courier* 21/4/1900.

201. *Dundee Advertiser* 23/4/1900.

202. *Dundee Courier* 25/4/1900.

203. Postcard to Patrick Geddes, dated "Saturday Evening" (National Library of Scotland, MS 10531).

204. *People's Journal* 11/8/1900.

205. Graphic Arts Association Minute Book 30/4/1900 (held at the time of consultation by Dundee Art Society, later transferred to University of Dundee Archive Services).

206. William Hardie, 'George Dutch Davidson: "A too great perfection"', *Journal of the Scottish Society for Art History* vol 11 (2006), p31.

207. 'Notes on Italian Art' in the *Memorial Volume* p53.

208. 'Notes on Italian Art' in the *Memorial Volume* p56-7.

209. *Apotheosis* is now in Dundee's Art Galleries & Museums' collection (though badly in need of conservation treatment at the time of writing) but the study for *Love Retreating* (illustrated in the *Memorial Volume*) is now untraced.

210. Letter to John Duncan 8/1/1901, quoted in the *Memorial Volume* p49.

211. *Memorial Volume*, p13.

212. David Foggie's diary, 9/1/1901 (family collection).

213. David Foggie's diary, 15/1/1901 (family collection).

214. Quoted by William Hardie in 'George Dutch Davidson: "A too great perfection"', *Journal of the Scottish Society for Art History* vol 11 (2006), p27.

215. Letter to John Duncan 8/1/1901, quoted in the *Memorial Volume* p49.

216. Letters to James Bremner 17/6/1901 and 28/6/1901, and to David Ireland 28/6/1901, from Letter Book vol 2 (Abertay University).

217. *Evening Telegraph* 4/6/1901.

218. The classes are featured in the *Evening Telegraph* 14/3/1901, which also notes classes taught in the same building by Mr E M Davidson in copper and brass repoussé work.

219. Information from the Scotland's People website and the 1891 census.

220. *Evening Telegraph* 20/1/1897.

221. From an *Evening Telegraph* feature on Mrs Sinclair c.1905 under the heading 'Representative Women', from Stewart Carmichael Scrapbook volume two (Dundee City Archives).

222. *Evening Telegraph* 19/4/1907.

223. Elizabeth (aka Lily) Sinclair studied at Glasgow School of Art and in Paris, and later married the art collector and curator Duncan Macdonald (*Aberdeen Weekly Journal* 14/1/1943).

224. *Evening Telegraph* 19/1/1903.

225. *Dundee Advertiser* 13/12/1905.

226. It was exhibited in the Dundee Art Society's club rooms in December 1905. The sisters collaborated again on an embroidered cushion shown in 1908.

227. From an *Evening Telegraph* feature in May 1905 under the heading 'Representative Women', from Stewart Carmichael Scrapbook volume one (Dundee City Archives).

228. *Dundee Courier & Advertiser* 11/11/1927.

229. *Ibid*.

230. Letter from Annie Himsworth to Robert & Pat Leishman 24/6/1984 (courtesy of Pat Leishman).

231. Another notable exhibitor at this time was William Armstrong Davidson from Glasgow, who would later move to Dundee to become Head of Design in the School of Art.

232. *Dundee Advertiser* and *Dundee Courier* 13/12/1905.

233. Carmichael, 'Fifty Years', *op cit*.

234. Dundee Art Society Minute Book 3/3/1910 (held at the time of consultation by Dundee Art Society, later transferred to University of Dundee Archive Services).

235. Minute Book 21/12/1910.

236. Annette Carruthers, *The Arts and Crafts Movement in Scotland: A History* (New Haven & London: Yale University Press, 2014) p109.

237. The event was illustrated in *The Wizard of the North* July 1908.

238. See *Dundee Courier* 17/6/1908. It was presumably this that inspired Carmichael to try again with his proposed pageant in 1910.

239. *Evening Telegraph* 30/12/1904.

240. Letter to Patrick Geddes 1/1/1901 (National Library of Scotland, MS 10532).

241. Letter to Patrick Geddes 2/3/1902 (National Library of Scotland, MS 10533).

242. *Ibid.*

243. Quoted unreferenced in Kemplay, *op cit*, p44. It was Duncan that persuaded Kennedy-Fraser to travel to Eriskay and other islands to collect traditional Hebridean songs.

244. Charles Richard Cammell, *Heart of Scotland* (London: Robert Hale, 1956) p231.

245. Quoted unreferenced in Jenkins, *op cit*, p17.

246. John Duncan Notebook 2 (National Library of Scotland), transcribed by Clara Young, 2004.

247. From an unidentified newspaper cutting in April/May 1905 from Stewart Carmichael Scrapbook volume one (Dundee City Archives).

248. The publication date is uncertain but is believed to have been 1910.

249. Donald A Mackenzie, 'The Riders of the Sidhe', *Celtic Annual* 1916 p47. The 1911 exhibition catalogue gives the same names for the four symbols, but other sources describe them differently – for example as the Tree of Life or Hazel of Knowledge, the Cup of Plenty, the Glaive of Light, and the Crystal of the Will to Endure.

250. *Dundee Courier* 10/11/1911.

251. Mackenzie, *op cit.*

252. Dundee Art Society Annual Report 1911 (Dundee Central Library, Local History Centre).

253. It is also worth pointing out here the significant influence of the widely read Dundee newspaper, the *People's Journal*, which published serial fiction in abundance in both English and Scots (though not Gaelic) and in the late 19th century played a significant part in popularising the Kailyard school of literature which, however clichéd it became, was vitally important in developing a uniquely Scottish form of prose fiction.

254. A second volume, *The New Mealpoke*, was published in 1922 and again featured work by Carmichael, Grieve, Foggie and Lamond along with Joseph Lee, James Cadzow, J Maclauchlan Milne and others.

255. His claims were rejected by the Lord Lyon (my thanks to Kenneth Baxter for this information).

256. For example he gave a lecture on stained glass to the Society on 22 November 1935. A series of letters from Duncan to Bell discussing tempera painting are held in a private collection.

257. A reredos is an ornamental screen covering the wall at the back of the altar.

258. Lorimer and Duncan were also collaborating at this time on a reredos for St Andrew's Church, Aberdeen.

259. Letter to Robert Lorimer, undated but presumably January 1917 (Sir Robert Lorimer papers, University of Edinburgh Library Special Collections).

260. Letter from Col W H Fergusson to Lorimer 26/1/1917 (Sir Robert Lorimer papers, University of Edinburgh Library Special Collections).

261. *The Pictures of the Reredos in St Mary's, Broughty Ferry*, typed MS, presumably written by Duncan, c.1917 (Sir Robert Lorimer papers, University of Edinburgh Library Special Collections).

262. In 2001 the panels were restored by Sally Cheyne and Owen Davison of the Conservation Studio, Edinburgh, and a detailed account of their work (revealing fascinating details of Duncan's painting technique) can be found in *The Artist & the Thinker*, *op cit*, pp91-4.

263. See letters from Carmichael and Laing in the Geddes papers at University of Strathclyde Archives (T-GED 9/739, 9/745 and 9/746).

264. *Dundee Advertiser* 24/1/1907.

265. *Dundee Advertiser* 26/5/1896.

266. *People's Journal* 27/3/1948.

267. From an unidentified newspaper cutting c.1898-9 from Stewart Carmichael Scrapbook volume one (Dundee City Archives).

268. Possibly the painting *Suffer Little Children* now in Paisley Museum & Art Gallery.

269. From an unidentified newspaper cutting 1899 from Stewart Carmichael Scrapbook volume one (Dundee City Archives).

270. *Ibid.*

271. *Ibid.* The building has now been demolished.

272. *Evening Telegraph* 26/5/1896.

273. The redecoration was carried out by Henry Drummond, son of Alexander Drummond.

274. *Dundee Advertiser* 2/9/1904.

275. *Dundee Courier* 2/9/1904.

276. *Dundee Courier* 23/2/1903.

277. *Dundee Courier* 23/12/1901.

278. *Dundee Advertiser* 18/12/1901.

279. *The Scottish Patriot* 15/2/1902.

280. Ewen had also bought Carmichael's painting *The Old Scots Woman* and later donated it to Angus Council Museums.

281. Carmichael, 'Fifty Years', *op cit.*

282. *Dundee Advertiser* 6/8/1895.

283. *Ibid.*

284. From an unidentified newspaper cutting titled 'The Growlers' Club' c.1895 from Stewart Carmichael Scrapbook volume one (Dundee City Archives).

285. Carmichael, 'Fifty Years', *op cit.*

286. *Ibid.*

287. Letter from Carmichael to Geddes 9/1/1907 (University of Strathclyde Archives, T-GED 9/745).

288. The Growlers' Club, *op cit.*

289. *The Piper o' Dundee* 24/10/1894.

290. *The Tocsin* no 3, June 1909.

291. The bound volume of *The Tocsin* held by the University of Dundee Archives includes letters from Hardie and others. Threat of legal action may have been the cause of the magazine's swift demise (my thanks to Kenneth Baxter for this information).

292. *Forward* 11/1/1908. My thanks are due to Billy Kenefick for providing this reference.

293. *The Tocsin* no 3, June 1909.

294. Mudie spent most of the rest of his life there as, among other things, the editor of the *Sunday Times* and the author of several books on natural history which he illustrated himself.

295. Alec Grieve later created a version of it which he exhibited at the 1891 Fine Art Exhibition.

296. *The Piper o' Dundee* 18/6/1890.

297. Alan Reid, *The Bards of Angus and the Mearns* (Paisley: J & R Parlane, 1897) p557.

298. Sellars presumably campaigned in the 1891 by-election, but he is not mentioned in press coverage of the time, suggesting that he must have withdrawn some time before polling day.

299. His obituary dated 10/8/1922 is in the cuttings book in the Local History Centre, Dundee Central Library.

300. Ethel Moorhead, 'Incendiaries', *This Quarter* no 2 (1925) p247.

301. *The Celtic Annual* 1918, p17.

302. *Evening Telegraph* 14/3/1901. I have found no direct evidence of this.

303. *Dundee Advertiser* 17/4/1901.

304. From a *Dundee Advertiser* review, 1902, from Stewart Carmichael Scrapbook volume one (Dundee City Archives).

305. *Dundee Advertiser* 23/4/1902.

306. *The Piper o' Dundee* 8/5/1901.

307. My thanks to Ann Prescott for this information.

308. Full details of her various activities can be found in Leah Leneman, *Martyrs in our Midst: Dundee, Perth and the Forcible Feeding of Suffragettes* (Dundee: Abertay Historical Society, 1993).

309. In her entry for Moorhead in the Oxford Dictionary of National Biography, Leah Leneman says that it "seems certain" that Moorhead was involved in the Burns cottage incident.

310. *Dundee Courier* 6/10/1906.

311. *The Tocsin* no 3, June 1909.

312. *Dundee Advertiser* 23/4/1902.

313. According to Hugh MacDiarmid, *Contemporary Scottish Studies* (Manchester: Carcanet Press, 1995) p230. I have not found an image of the work to corroborate this or find out who else was depicted.

314. Carmichael, 'Fifty Years', *op cit.*

315. John Duncan met Taylor on Eriskay and painted her portrait in 1907 (now in Aberdeen Art Gallery).

316. Sandy Moffat claims (in *Arts of Resistance*, *op cit*, p110) that Carmichael and Wood were married, but this is of course untrue.

317. When Wood moved to Edinburgh her nationalist interests may have been further encouraged by another Dundonian, the artist David Foggie (who also made a portrait drawing of her, now in the Scottish National Portrait Gallery).

318. Carmichael's obituary in the *Dundee Courier* 6/11/1950 states that from "1926-28 he was a member of the council of the Scottish National Party." Since the SNP was formed in 1934 and its main predecessor the NPS began in 1928, the SHRA seems the most likely for Carmichael to have been actively involved in, but it's also possible that he (like Wood) was part of fellow Dundonian Lewis Spence's Scottish National Movement. Certainly Carmichael chaired at least one meeting of the Dundee branch of the National Party of Scotland (*Evening Telegraph* 17/4/1929) and spoke at a Dundee meeting of the SNP in 1938 (*Evening Telegraph* 23/2/1938).

319. MacDiarmid, *op cit*, p227.

320. *Ibid*, pp227-8.

321. *Ibid*, p231. MacDiarmid wrote an entire essay on Carmichael in 1925 which was one of a series originally published in the Scottish Educational Journal then collected in *Contemporary Scottish Studies* in 1926.

322. *Evening Telegraph* 3/12/1935.

323. Carmichael had included a *Scotsman* article from 1926 about this in his scrapbook.

324. *Dundee Advertiser* 19/2/1920.

325. *Dundee Courier* 28/9/1937.

326. From the catalogue to Carmichael's memorial exhibition, possibly written by curator James Boyd (Dundee Central Library, Local History Centre).

327. *Dundee Advertiser* 24/1/1907.

Chapter Four

1. As yet there has been no detailed history written of this period of Dundee's artistic life. Useful overviews were provided by AH Millar, 'Sketch of Art in Dundee in the Nineteenth Century', Graphic Arts Association Annual Report 1900 (Dundee Central Library, Local History Centre) and Anon, 'Dundee Artists', *Celtic Annual* 1918-9, p15-17.

2. T S Robertson, 'Reminiscences of Old Dundee – Its Fine Art', *Dundee Courier* 17/12/1906.

3. McGillivray's name is sometimes seen spelled 'MacGillivray' but the former is the more usual form.

4. *Dundee Courier* 13/4/1877.

5. The portraits of Arrott and Bell are both in the Tayside Medical History Museum at Ninewells Hospital, the former on long-term loan from Dundee's Art Galleries & Museums.

6. Details from the Dundee Directories, held by Dundee City Library Local History Centre.

7. *The Piper o' Dundee* 10/07/1889.

8. Details from Collins' obituary in the *Dundee Advertiser* 22/6/1896. Unfortunately I have been unable to find details of his birth on the Scotland's People website.

9. See *Dundee Courier* 7/10/1880, 25/1/1883 and 25/9/1886.

10. *Dundee Courier* 15/6/1875. The child is named as the son of a Mr Luke, presumably jute merchant John L Luke.

11. The first was Olnick in 1877, now in the collection of Hull Maritime Museum under the title *Eskimo throwing a Harpoon*.

12. *The Piper o' Dundee* 24/6/1896.

13. This is referred to in a letter from gallery owner William Scott to one of Collins' concerned patrons, Peter Carmichael, dated 11/11/1886, though Scott believed that "he has not taken Drink since a long time before he went over again to Edinburgh" (University of Dundee Archive Services, Peter Carmichael Collection). My thanks are to due to Kenneth Baxter for drawing this correspondence to my attention.

14. Letter from Hugh Collins to Peter Carmichael 8/11/1886 (University of Dundee Archive Services, Peter Carmichael Collection).

15. *Dundee Courier* 31/1/1896.

16. Pinnington, *op cit*.

17. Biographical details are mostly drawn from Mitchell's obituary in the *Dundee Courier* 31/5/1918.

18. The paintings of Simpson and Robertson are now in the city's collections.

19. *Dundee Courier* 12/12/1892. See also an advertising circular about the atelier in the Lamb Collection 276(11) (Dundee Central Library, Local History Centre).

20. *Dundee Courier* 18/4/1893.

21. Dundee Art Society Annual Report 1918-9 (Dundee Central Library, Local History Centre).

22. I am grateful to Dr Bill O Larson Bekkestad who now owns the Mitchell farm in Minnesota and who kindly shared his research with me.

23. Mitchell was elected Treasurer at the end of 1891 and served until 1913, his only break being his term as President in 1898-9.

24. Dundee Art Society Annual Report 1918-9 (Dundee Central Library, Local History Centre).

25. Anon, 'Dundee Artists', Celtic Annual 1918-9, p15.

26. *The Times* 25/10/1897.

27. The biographical details given here have been pieced together from various (often contradictory) sources, notably the Scotland's People website, obituaries in the *Dundee Advertiser* 21/9/1926 and Dundee Art Society Annual Report 1925-6 (Dundee Central Library, Local History Centre), and features in *The Wizard of the North* 26/12/1891 and 30/11/1894. I am also hugely grateful to Heather Jack for allowing me access to her research on Adamson.

28. Obituary of Adamson by Carmichael in the Dundee Art Society Annual Report 1925-6 (Dundee Central Library, Local History Centre).

29. *The Wizard of the North* 26/12/1891.

30. *Ibid.*

31. *The Wizard of the North* 30/11/1894.

32. *Ibid.*

33. *Dundee Advertiser* 25/10/1897.

34. *The Piper o' Dundee* 27/10/1897.

35. *The Wizard of the North* 31/5/1900.

36. Dundee Art Society Annual Report 1925-6 (Dundee Central Library, Local History Centre).

37. Allessio was, I think, Joseph's uncle, but I have not been able to determine this for certain.

38. *Dundee Courier* 23/8/1878.

39. *Dundee Courier* 7/4/1882.

40. Joseph initially announced his intention to give up the business in the

Dundee Courier of 16/2/1887 but seems to have changed his mind, eventually announcing his disposal of it to Lous and Giuseppe in the *Courier* 2/5/1889.

41. *Dundee Courier & Advertiser* 10/2/1932. Some sources give his name as Guiseppe but this is the more usual spelling.

42. Dundee Art Society Annual Report 1906 (Dundee Central Library, Local History Centre).

43. The sales notice is held in the Lamb Collection, Dundee Central Library, Local History Centre.

44. 'Dundee Artists', *op cit*, p17.

45. *Ibid.*

46. *Dundee Courier* 6/6/1895.

47. She returned to Dundee to show three flower paintings at the 1918 Dundee Art Society exhibition.

48. *Dundee Courier* 1902, unidentified cutting from Stewart Carmichael's scrapbook volume one (Dundee City Archives).

49. *Evening Telegraph* 1904, unidentified cutting from Stewart Carmichael's scrapbook volume one (Dundee City Archives).

50. *People's Journal* 27/6/1891.

51. W G Burn-Murdoch, *From Edinburgh to the Antarctic* (London: Longmans, Green & Co, 1894) p16.

52. *The Piper o' Dundee* 19/4/1899.

53. *City Echo* March 1907.

54. Dundee Art Society Annual Report 1911 (Dundee Central Library, Local History Centre).

55. *The City Echo* April 1908 (Dundee Central Library, Local History Centre).

56. The originals are both in Dundee's Art Galleries & Museums along with an earlier view of Dundee from Balgay.

57. In his obituary 29/3/1898 in the cuttings book, Dundee Central Library Local History Centre.

58. Reported in the *Dundee Courier* 1/4/1868.

59. *Dundee Advertiser* 10/9/1863/

60. *Dundee Courier* 28/9/1876.

61. Interviewed in the *Dundee Courier* 30/9/1895.

62. *Dundee Courier* 30/9/1895.

63. Much of this information comes from his obituary 12/11/1884 in the cuttings book, Dundee Central Library Local History Centre.

64. Introduction to website www.dundeecity.gov.uk/lawson/ where the collection has been digitised, though it should be noted that many of the drawings included are actually by David Small.

65. From his obituary, *Dundee Courier & Advertiser* 13/5/1927.

66. According to Michael Donnelly in his book *Scotland's Stained Glass* (Edinburgh: The Stationery Office, 1997), Small was also a successful stained glass designer before coming to Dundee, but since no other sources mention this, it seems likely this was a different David Small.

67. *Dundee Courier* 30/9/1895.

68. Born in Laurieston, Gibb lived 1839-1929.

69. *Ibid.*

70. *Evening Telegraph* 30/9/1895.

71. Quoted in *Evening Telegraph* 7/10/1895.

72. *Glasgow Herald* 7/10/1895.

73. *The Scotsman* 7/10/1895.

74. Information from a feature on Winter in the *Piper o' Dundee* 8/7/1891.

75. *Dundee Advertiser* 1/7/1891.

76. According to his obituary in the *Courier & Advertiser* 5/6/1961 he continued to attend evening classes at the Art College until shortly before his death.

77. Text by "J R" from the catalogue of an exhibition of Ross's work staged in 1980, held in the artist files of Dundee's Art Galleries & Museums.

78. *Ibid.*

79. *Dundee Courier* 16/11/1911.

80. *The Piper o' Dundee* 27/5/1896.

81. Dundee Art Society Annual Report 1911 (Dundee Central Library, Local History Centre).

82. *Dundee Courier* 7/3/1895.

83. *Ibid.*

84. Quoted in his obituary in the *Arbroath Guide* 19/10/1912.

85. *Ibid.*

86. *Dundee Advertiser* 11/12/1893.

87. 'Dundee Artists', *op cit*, p15.

88. His obituary claims 37 but this is incorrect – death certificate checked on the Scotland's People website.

89. Information from his obituary in the *Courier & Advertiser* 20/4/1937. Various sources give Dundee as his birthplace but his birth certificate found on the Scotland's People website shows this is incorrect.

90. Reviewed by the *Dundee Courier* 14/11/1888.

91. Reviewed by the *Dundee Courier* 21/6/1891.

92. *Dundee Courier* 10/10/1892.

93. *The Piper o' Dundee* 1/3/1893.

94. T S Robertson, 'Famous Scottish Artists', *Dundee Courier* 21/6/1904.

95. *Ibid*.

96. *Dundee Courier* 20/2/1871.

97. *Dundee Courier* 26/11/1885.

98. Robertson, *op cit*.

99. T S Robertson, 'Famous Scottish Artists', *Dundee Courier* 20/4/1904.

100. *Dundee Advertiser* 1/8/1906.

101. Report of the Free Library Committee 1903 (Dundee Central Library, Local History Centre).

102. Dundee Art Society Annual Report 1906 (Dundee Central Library, Local History Centre).

103. *Dundee Advertiser* 1/8/1906.

104. James is listed as "Artist" in the 1861 census.

105. First listed in the Dundee Directory in 1864-5.

106. *Dundee Courier* 12/10/1917.

107. *Evening Telegraph* 20/12/1894.

108. *The Piper o' Dundee* 8/5/1895.

109. *Dundee Courier* 24/4/1895.

110. *The Piper o' Dundee* 27/3/1895.

111. Reported in *Dundee Courier* 3/2/1896.

112. *Dundee Courier* 24/4/1895.

113. *Dundee Courier* 20/12/1899.

114. The painting is currently on long-term loan to the British Golf Museum.

115. *The Piper o' Dundee* 19/4/1899.

116. 'Dundee Artists', *op cit*, p15.

117. Stuart Fenton, "Scottish Artists and their Studios – James Douglas", *Illustrations* vol 5 (1890) p274.

118. *Dundee Advertiser* 24/7/1911.

119. This is estimated as taking place in 1883-4 in James S W Barnes, *James Douglas RSW: A Scottish Watercolourist* (Perth Museum & Art Gallery, 2002), from which publication much of the information given here about Douglas in drawn.

120. *Dundee Advertiser* 24/7/1911.

121. *The Piper o' Dundee* 10/10/1888.

122. *Ibid*.

123. *Dundee Advertiser* 24/7/1911.

124. *The Piper o' Dundee* 10/10/1888.

125. *Dundee Advertiser* 24/7/1911.

126. Barnes, *op cit*, p23.

127. *Evening Telegraph* 30/11/1905 and *Dundee Courier* 1/12/1905.

128. *Ibid*, p25.

129. *Dundee Advertiser* 24/7/1911.

130. Some sources claim Laing was born in Dundee in 1852, but his birth certificate (accessed on the Scotland's People website) proves this is incorrect.

131. He had previously taken art classes at the Dundee School of Art from the age of fourteen.

132. He also studied at the Colarossi and Delacluse academies, according to the obituary in the Dundee Art Society Annual Report 1907 (Dundee Central Library, Local History Centre).

133. Letter from David Thomson to Whistler 14/12/1892 (University of Glasgow Whistler Archive).

134. Advertising circular for Laing's etchings written by John Maclauchlan, 1896 (Dundee Central Library, Local History Centre).

135. Translated for quotation in *ibid*.

136. *Dundee Courier* 22/9/1893.

137. Joseph Milne was one of the founding members, but was only an occasional visitor to Dundee.

138. *Black Cat* December 1895.

139. Advertising circular by John Maclauchlan, *op cit*.

140. *Evening Telegraph* 22/9/1897.

141. Translated from *Gazette des Beaux Arts* series 3 vol 29 (1899) p66. My thanks to Sarah Easterby-Smith for help with this translation.

142. Translated from *Die Graphischen Künst* vol 23 (1900), p122. My thanks to Keith Williams for this translation.

143. *Magazine of Art* vol 24 (1901).

144. *Die Graphischen Künst* vol 23 (1900), p119.

145. *The Piper o' Dundee* 8/5/1901.

146. David Foggie's diary, 12/10/1900 (family collection).

147. From a tribute by "one of the 'Circle'", *Dundee Courier* 8/5/1907.

148. Report of the Free Library Committee 1902 (Dundee Central Library, Local History Centre).

149. *Dundee Advertiser*, cutting from December 1902 in Stewart Carmichael scrapbook volume one (Dundee City Archives).

150. *Dundee Advertiser* 30/1/1907.

151. *Fifth Loan Exhibition Catalogue* (Art Museum of Toronto, 1912) and Hans W Singer, *Die Moderne Graphik* (Leipzig: E A Seemann, 1920) pp317-8.

152. *Dundee Courier* 8/5/1907.

153. Lamond's father's obituary is in the *Evening Post* 24/2/1904. Information on Lamond's early life comes from obituaries in the *Advertiser* and *Courier* 4/12/1924.

154. *Dundee Courier* 4/12/1924.

155. *Dundee Advertiser* 4/12/1924.

156. *Dundee Courier* 4/12/1924.

157. He had painted at least one military portrait before, in 1888 (an unidentified *Volunteer Officer on Horseback*, now in the city's collection).

158. *Dundee Courier* 14/10/1896.

159. *Dundee Courier* 10/5/1895.

160. *Evening Telegraph* 24/12/1895.

161. *Evening Telegraph* 6/12/1898.

162. *The Piper o' Dundee* 8/5/1901.

163. *Dundee Courier* 24/4/1902.

164. *Evening Telegraph* 15/5/1902.

165. *Evening Telegraph* 5/5/1902.

166. Quoted in *Evening Telegraph* 15/5/1902.

167. *Evening Telegraph* 5/5/1902.

168. *Dundee Courier* 19/9/1904.

169. *Evening Telegraph* 5/8/1915.

170. *Dundee Courier* 4/12/1922.

171. *Dundee Advertiser* 4/12/1924.

172. *Evening Telegraph* 16/12/1925.

173. The panting is now in Dundee's Art Galleries & Museums' collection.

174. *Evening Telegraph* 28/11/1899.

175. Stewart Carmichael, 'Fifty Years of the Dundee Art Society', unpublished MS of lecture given in 1940 (Dundee of Jordanstone College Library).

176. Not Edinburgh as is often claimed.

177. *Dundee Courier* 4/10/1884.

178. *Dundee Advertiser* 29/10/1890.

179. *Dundee Courier* 21/11/1890.

180. *Dundee Courier* 13/10/1894.

181. *Evening Telegraph* 18/10/1894.

182. *Dundee Advertiser* 15/5/1909.

183. *The Scotsman* 12/1/1911.

184. *Ibid* (the same obituary also appeared in the *Evening Telegraph & Post* 12/1/1911).

185. As reported by Philip Long in the introduction to the exhibition catalogue, *The Life and Works of John Maclauchlan Milne* (London: Portland Gallery, 2010).

186. 'Dundee Artists', *op cit*, p17.

187. *Evening Telegraph* 28/3/1921.

188. *Dundee Advertiser* 25/10/1924.

189. *Dundee Courier* 5/5/1922.

190. *Dundee Courier* 31/3/1925.

191. Dundee Art Society Annual Report 1911 (Dundee Central Library, Local History Centre).

192. *Dundee Advertiser* 25/5/1896.

193. Unidentified cutting from May 1897 in Stewart Carmichael scrapbook volume one (Dundee City Archives).

194. From the foreword to *Catalogue of Exhibition of Paintings and Etchings by the late Alec Grieve* (Victoria Art Galleries, 1935).

195. *Dundee Courier & Advertiser* 28/2/1933.

196. Unidentified cutting from February 1935 in Stewart Carmichael scrapbook volume three (Dundee City Archives).

197. Much of the text for the rest of this chapter is adapted from Matthew Jarron, *David Foggie; The Painters' Painter* (University of Dundee Museum Services, 2004).

198. From the MS of a speech given by Foggie at Glasgow School of Art 1947, held by the artist's family.

199. More details of Foggie's time in Antwerp can be found in Jarron, *David Foggie*, *op cit*.

200. David Foggie's diary, 31/12/1900 (family collection).

201. David Foggie's diary, 3/1/1901.

202. David Foggie's diary, 9/1/1901.

203. David Foggie's diary, 15/1/1901.

204. David Foggie, *An Artist Abroad*, 1909 (MS for an article or lecture held by the artist's family).

205. *Evening Telegraph* 18/10/1900 and *Piper o' Dundee* 24/10/1900.

206. *Arbroath Herald & Advertiser* 19/9/1901.

207. *Dundee Courier* 14/3/1906.

208. G W Gahan, *Poem "The Trials of Truth" and Smaller Poems, "God's Pathway", Art Reminiscences, etc* (Dundee: A B Duncan & Co, 1915) p381.

209. Foggie's accounts book 1902-25 held by the artist's family.

210. *Dundee Courier* 30/9/1912.

211. *City Echo* April 1911.

212. Joseph Lee (whose portrait Foggie painted in 1911) was also an asthma sufferer, as presumably were many in such a smoke-filled industrial city.

213. The portrait was of George William Paisley of Newport, a Black Watch soldier killed in Palestine.

214. *Dundee Courier* 26/10/1921.

215. *Catalogue for an Exhibition of Oil Paintings, Water Colours and Pastels by David Foggie RSW*, 1921 (Dundee Central Library, Local History Centre).

216. Letter by David Foggie to Van Syben c.1901, copied into his diary (family collection).

217. David Foggie, 'On Looking at Pictures' (MS for an undated article held by the artist's family).

218. *Ibid.*

219. These were posthumous portraits, but Foggie had painted a version of Caird's portrait before, which Mrs Marryat lent to the Dundee Art Society's 1918 exhibition.

220. Royal Scottish Academy Annual Report 1948 (Royal Scottish Academy).

221. David Foggie's diary, 6/1/1901.

222. His oil painting of *The Young Miner* is particularly fine, and is now held by the RSA.

223. Information from the Foggie family.

224. *The Scotsman* 3/6/1948.

225. GSA speech 1947, *op cit*.

Chapter Five

1. Christopher Murray ranks it alongside London, Paris, New York and Tokyo in 'Thur's a man wi a big chin an' a dug in thon City Centre: Uncovering the Importance of Dundee Comics', *Journal of the Scottish Society for Art History* vol 11 (2006) pp75-81.

2. Parts of this chapter have appeared in a different form in my paper 'Before *The Beano* – The Prehistory of Dundee Comics', *International Journal of Comic Art* vol 10 no 1 (2008) pp9-17.

3. Staff numbers at Leng & Co do not seem to have been recorded, but some 400 attended the annual works outing to Oban according to the *Dundee Advertiser* of 26/7/1880.

4. *The Times* had attempted to illustrate Lord Nelson's coffin in 1805 but the result was so poor it was not followed up. In 1839 the *Dundee Advertiser* tried some drawings for the first time but again the technology available did not allow good quality reproduction.

5. It is worth noting that the Leng papers were a key driving force in having the bridge built.

6. *Evening Telegraph* 29/12/1879 and *Dundee Advertiser* 30/12/1879.

7. *Dundee Advertiser* 31/12/1879.

8. The story is told in *How a Newspaper is Printed* (Dundee: John Leng & Co, 1890) and *The Dundee Advertiser 1801-1901: A Centenary Memoir* (Dundee: John Leng & Co, 1901).

9. *People's Journal* 22/11/1879.

10. Elspeth Reid & Flora Davidson, *The Fortunes of Cynicus* (Dykehead: Forest Lodge, 1995) p30.

11. Anderson had been building up to this by producing cartoons in series to illustrate humorous columns (for example 'A Game of Billiards' earlier that month, featuring eight captioned panels, but will no particular narrative progression from one to the other).

12. William Donaldson recognises the significance of the *People's Journal* strips in *Popular Literature in Victorian Scotland* (Aberdeen: Aberdeen University Press, 1986) p33. Anderson was almost certainly the creator of these early strips, given that he had already introduced the form to *The Wizard of the North* – a two-picture cartoon on 29 October 1881 and a three-picture one on 30 December 1882 (which may also be the first appearance of Anderson's popular monk character).

13. Quoted from the *Dundee Advertiser* by Reid & Davidson, *op cit*, p36, who suggest that the reviewer might have been Anderson himself!

14. *People's Journal* 16/4/1932.

15. *The Piper o' Dundee* 2/2/1890.

16. *Evening Telegraph* 28/1/1890.

17. *The Wizard of the North* June 1891.

18. Quoted in Reid & Davidson (*op cit*, p110).

19. *Glasgow Evening News* 24/2/1930.

20. *Evening Telegraph* 23/8/1897.

21. Quoted by John Kemplay in *The Painting of John Duncan* (San Francisco: Pomegranate, 1994), this derives from the *Scotsman*'s obituary of Duncan 24/11/1945. Kemplay follows the *Scotsman* in claiming that Duncan spent three years in London, but since he was back in Dundee painting John L Luke in 1889 (see chapter three) having already been in Antwerp and Düsseldorf (presumably in the winter of 1888-9, though Kemplay puts it a year later), his stay in London can't have been more than two years, and may have been less.

22. This is one of three Literary Society programmes illustrated by Duncan that survive in Dundee Central Library, Local History Centre.

23. *Centenary Memoir, op cit*.

24. Not 1860 or 1872 as some sources claim.

25. G W Gahan, *Poem "The Trials of Truth" and Smaller Poems, "God's Pathway", Art Reminiscences, etc* (Dundee: A B Duncan & Co, 1915) p316.

26. *Dundee Courier* 7/5/1899. Cowper claimed in *Brown's Book-Stall* (July 1899 p407) to have been offered a cashier's position at Alex Paterson & Co with a salary of £160 a year.

27. The first newspaper illustration that can definitely be attributed to him is a cartoon bearing the monogram MC in the *Weekly News* of 10/5/1890, but his style can be detected in both individual cartoons and comic strips dating back at least as far as October 1889. Although the *Weekly News* was making increasing use of illustrations at that time, they would not appear regularly in the *Courier* until 1891.

28. While in Dundee he was also a keen cricketer, playing for the Mercantile CC.

29. A feature on Cowper in the *Dundee Courier* 23/4/1892 notes that his work had also by then appeared in the *Graphic* and *Pick-Me-Up*.

30. Quoted in *Dundee Courier* 8/6/1895.

31. This list of publications is a combination of information from *Brown's Book-Stall* (*op cit*), Simon Houfe, *The Dictionary of 19th Century British Book Illustrators and Caricaturists* (Woodbridge: Antique Collectors' Club, 1996) and http://users.ev1.net/~homeville/fictionmag

32. *The Art Record* April 1901.

33. *Ibid*.

34. For example a studio exhibition in Dundee in 1899 and his London show in 1902.

35. J G R, 'At the Sign of the Brush & Pen, Being some Notes on the Black and White Artists of to day. No 23 – Mr Max Cowper', *Brown's Book-Stall*, July 1899 p411.

36. A gouache drawing by Cowper of a Japanese field hospital was included in the exhibition *A Well-Watched War: Images from the Russo-Japanese Front 1904-1905* (Sackler Gallery, 2005).

37. Gahan, *op cit*, pp317-8.

38. A useful source of information on who published what can be found in A C Lamb, 'Bibliography of Dundee's Periodical Literature', *Scottish Notes & Queries* vol 4 (1891).

39. *Ibid*, June 1891.

40. My thanks here to Nicola Ireland, whose keen eyes spotted several drawings I had missed!

41. *The Wizard of the North* March 1910.

42. *The Wizard of the North* August 1911.

43. *People's Journal* 12/3/1904. One of the runners-up in the competition was J M Mathieson of Glasgow – probably James Muir Mathieson who had worked in Dundee for some years and would contribute regularly to the *Journal* during the Great War.

44. Dundee Art Society Annual Report 1911 (Dundee Central Library, Local History Centre).

45. *Dundee Advertiser* 27/12/1907.

46. *Evening Telegraph* 17/12/1906 and 24/7/1907. A brief biographical sketch of Pollock is provided in *The Piper o' Dundee* 24/7/1889 but I have found few other references to him prior to his death in 1923.

47. *Evening Telegraph* 14/12/1885.

48. Information from the *Courier & Advertiser* 15/5/1937.

49. Clara Young, 'In Search of John Duncan' in Matthew Jarron (ed) *The Artist & the Thinker – John Duncan & Patrick Geddes in Dundee* (University of Dundee Museum Services, 2004) p71.

50. His full name was Alexander Penrose Forbes Ritchie, presumably named after Bishop Alexander Penrose Forbes (1817-1875).

51. Ritchie later wrote an article about the Antwerp Academy for the first volume of *The Studio* (1893).

52. Information from Houfe *op cit*, Gahan *op cit* and M Bryant & S Heneage, *Dictionary of British Cartoonists & Caricaturists 1730-1980* (Aldershot: Scholar Press, 1994).

53. Anon, 'Dundee Artists' in *The Celtic Annual* 1918-9, p16.

54. *The Scotsman* 15/7/1912.

55. Information from *Evening Telegraph* 12/11/1915 and the Big Cartoon Database website at http://www.bcdb.com

56. His obituary is in the *Dundee Courier & Advertiser* 26/5/1938.

57. See Houfe *op cit* for further details. Greig (1861-1941) spent only a brief time in Dundee, but continued to send work to the GAA exhibitions for several years after his move to London. In his memoirs, Cynicus recalled Greig, claiming that "his rise to become one of the leading art critics in the country is something of a romance, for he was first of all a factory worker, and then a newspaper boy attached to the station bookstall in that town [Arbroath]." (*Glasgow Evening News* 4/3/1930). Greig evidently took umbrage at these revelations, for he wrote to the paper's editor shortly afterwards, claiming that he had never worked as a newspaper boy, and even denying the existence of a station bookstall in Arbroath! (Information from Flora Davidson, 2006). James Greig should not be confused with local landscape painter James McGavin Greig (1851-1888).

58. *The Piper o' Dundee* 18/2/1891.

59. Furniss must have been impressed with Dundee's appreciation of his talents – he made a second visit to the city in 1896 and the year before showed several original cartoons at the Fine Art Exhibition.

60. *The Piper o' Dundee* 23/3/1892.

61. *The Wasp* June 1897.

62. *The Wasp* December 1897.

63. Quoted by James Gahan in *Gahan's Diary: A Year of My Life and People I have Met* (Dundee: self-published, 1924) p207.

64. His obituary is in the *Dundee Courier & Advertiser* 24/12/1956.

65. *Dundee Courier* 15/3/1895.

66. The 1882 date comes from his obituary in the *Courier* of 16/1/1939, but as the Dundee Directories only list him from 1892, this may be a misprint. The article notes Livingstone's particular talent for illustrating sporting events, claiming he had been an enthusiastic cyclist and skater. He was found dead on a seat outside the Albert Institute at the age of 74.

67. His first signed work in the *People's Journal* appears on 9/4/1904, but a series of five unidentified cartoons illustrating a poem called 'Fiscalitis' on 19/12/1903 look like his style.

68. Unidentified newspaper cutting 5/10/1922 from the Obituary press cuttings books held by the Local History Centre at Dundee Central Library.

69. GAA Minute Book volume 1: 1890-1901 (held at the time of consultation by Dundee Art Society, later transferred to University of Dundee Archive Services).

70. The sketchbook is owned by her daughter, to whom I am most grateful for letting me see it.

71. *Aunt Kate's Fairy Tales No 4* (Dundee: Leng & Co, undated).

72. *Evening Telegraph* 25/2/1935.

73. Bryant & Heneage, *op cit*, p241.

74. For example see Denis Gifford, *Victorian Comics* (London: George Allen & Unwin 1976) p6 or Bryant & Heneage, *op cit*, pp36-7.

75. *Dundee Year Book* 1912.

76. *The City Echo* May 1912. I have been unable to identify 'VHS', though his work appears in *DTC*, the student magazine of Dundee Training College, in March 1912.

77. The story of Lee's eventful life is told in greatest detail (though not entirely accurately) in Bob Burrows, *Fighter Writer* (Derby: Breedon Books, 2004) and more recently in the introduction to Caroline Brown & Matthew Jarron (eds), *Joseph Lee: Poems from the Great War* (Dundee: Discovery Press, 2014). Part of my account of Lee's career is drawn from this, which in turn was adapted from a booklet written by myself, Caroline Brown and Michael Bolik to accompany the exhibition *Joseph Lee – War Poet & Artist* held at the University of Dundee in 2005.

78. Not the Slade, as Burrows claims.

79. While in London he is said by Burrows to have been supplying propaganda cartoons to the Tariff Reform League, a pressure group campaigning to protect Britain's trade with the colonies. If true, this certainly did not chime with the socialist ideology he later adopted, and the archive of the League held at the University of Warwick contains nothing by him.

80. Burrows claims that Lee returned to Dundee in late 1906 but as figure 183 shows he was clearly working as a press artist for DC Thomson in 1905.

81. *City Echo* March 1907.

82. R J B Sellar, 'The Poet of Dundee', *The Scots Magazine* vol 57 No 3 (1952) pp209-219.

83. Joseph Lee, *Ballads of Battle* (London: John Murray, 1916).

84. *Dundee Courier* 13/4/1916.

85. *The Scotsman* 5/12/1916.

86. *Dundee Courier* 13/4/1917.

87. Joseph Lee, *A Captive at Carlsruhe* (London: John Lane/Bodley Head, 1920) p39-40.

88. *Ibid*, p62-5.

89. To give an idea of the numbers involved, the *Dundee Courier* 29/11/1915 published a list of some 300 Dundee newspaper men serving in the war.

90. The album is owned by Ruby Scott's daughter; the cuttings are all undated.

91. Letter from Frank Coutts to Ruby Scott 31/3/1917, owned by their daughter.

92. More on Gray (and this topic generally) can be found in Matthew Jarron & Emma Halford-Forbes, 'Splendour and Sorrow – Dundee's Newspaper Artists during the Great War', *Journal of the Scottish Society for Art History* vol 20 (2015-16).

93. From text by A Harvey and F Weir on the *War Artist Joseph Gray* website at www.josephgray.co.uk/fighter-writer/. The *Evening Telegraph* 18/10/1916 claimed that he also performed this role at the Battle of Loos.

94. Reported in the *Evening Telegraph* 18/10/1916. Harvey and Weir (*ibid*) state that he came home in March 1916 but he seems already to have started work for *The Graphic* by that time, so that may have been the date of his official discharge. They put the cause down to trench fever and wounds caused by sniper fire.

95. *Dundee Courier* 27/2/1917.

96. *Dundee Courier* 19/12/1918.

97. *Evening Telegraph* 23/7/1926.

98. Letter held by the artist's family.

99. Many sources erroneously state 1962.

100. For example the *Post Sunday Special* of 29 November 1914 features French, American, Canadian and Australian cartoons.

101. The daily single-panel stories would transfer to the joint *Courier & Advertiser* in 1926 and went on to run for decades, alongside the best-selling *Billy and Bunny Books* from 1921 to 1949. Crighton (1892-1962) would go on to create Korky the Cat for *The Dandy*.

102. The two companies had actually formed a partnership in 1906; Sir John Leng's death that year allowed Thomson to take the lead role.

103. Most of this information comes from the St Andrews Preservation Trust Museum, which has an excellent collection of Patterson's work. A longer list of his magazine contributions can be found in Houfe *op cit*.

104. Some sources give his birth details as Perthshire in 1870 – the correct information comes from his birth certificate. Much of the biographical information here comes from his obituary in the *Chelmsford Chronicle* 12/4/1935.

105. *Dundee Courier* 15/1/1923.

106. Norman Wright & David Ashford, 'The men who drew Billy Bunter', *Book and Magazine Collector* 258 (2005) p29.

107. The information on the Adamson brothers presented here comes from a variety of sources, chiefly Peter J M McEwan, *The Dictionary of Scottish Art & Architecture* (Ballater: Glengarden Press, 2004), Houfe (*op cit*), obituaries in *Dundee Courier & Advertiser* 23/6/1952 and *Evening Telegraph* 20/5/1957 and http://users.ev1.net/~homeville/fictionmag, as well as those individual references given below.

108. As well as these three, there was also a fourth brother, Ewart (see n.124 below), and two sisters, Mabel and Winifred. Both sisters moved to London, the former becoming assistant manager of an art decorator's business in Kensington. In 1921 she was described as "one of the leading exponents of design and creation in lacquer work and fabric painting so much in favour with Dame Fashion" (*Dundee Courier* 10/6/1921).

109. *Dundee Courier* 22/9/1934.

110. Various drawings monogrammed SA between 1888 and 1892 are presumably his work. Adamson seems to have gone to London in 1890 but returned, hoping to make a career as a painter in Dundee. By the end of January 1891 he changed his mind and returned to London (see *Evening Telegraph* 27/11/1890 and 30/1/1891). His period of study in Edinburgh is mentioned in the *Evening Telegraph* 22/11/1900.

111. The V&A have the engraving he created for the August 1895 cover of *The Idler*; my thanks to Annemarie Bilclough for information on this.

112. *Evening Telegraph* 12/1/1909.

113. Quoted in *Evening Telegraph* 21/11/1900, which reprints an account of Adamson's adventures from *Leslie's Weekly*.

114. *Evening Telegraph* 25/8/1926.

115. Written for *Leslie's Weekly* and quoted in F A Sharf & P Harrington, *China 1900: The Eyewitnesses Speak* (London: Greenhill Books, 2000) pp128-145.

116. He is mentioned as being at the front in an advert for the first issue of the *Illustrated War News* published in *The Times* 12/8/1914, but I have found no other reference to his war work.

117. An undated self-portrait by him was sold at Christie's in 2005. In this the left side of his mouth has a notable deformation, suggesting he may have suffered a stroke. This might explain why so little is recorded of his activities in the later part of his life.

118. Letter from Mabel Adamson to Dorothy Wallace, Daywood Gallery, Virginia, USA 14/9/1964 (with thanks to Alex Kidson of National Museums Liverpool for passing this on to me).

119. *Evening Telegraph* 3/11/1900.

120. The first was painted c.1928 and is now in Gallery Oldham; the second was painted c.1931 and is in the Potteries Museum & Art Gallery, Stoke-on-Trent. Both were exhibited in Dundee (in 1931 and 1934 respectively).

121. Letter from Mabel Adamson *op cit*.

122. Stanlaws travelled initially to the USA where he worked for the *Chicago Daily News* among others. He was based in London around 1895, but was in New York by 1899 (though some sources claim that he moved there in 1901).

123. Aleister Crowley, *The Confessions of Aleister Crowley: An Autohagiography* (London: Arkana, 1989) p353.

124. Amazingly, the film was written by a fourth Adamson brother, Ewart (1881-1945), who worked as a Hollywood scriptwriter for over twenty years, mostly on low-budget shorts for the likes of the Three Stooges.

125. An illustrated catalogue of Penrhyn Stanlaws' magazine art can be found in Norman Platnick, *Signed on the Dot* (New York: Enchantment Ink, 2005).

Chapter Six

1. Stuart Macdonald, *The History and Philosophy of Art Education* (London: University of London Press, 1970).

2. *Dundee Advertiser* 6/5/1853.

3. *Ibid*.

4. *Dundee Advertiser* 23/12/1853.

5. D R Andrews has sometimes been mistaken for D A Andrews, the landscape artist described in chapter four, who (confusingly) had preceded D R in his post at the Seminaries. D A died in 1841 at the age of just 26, but since D R was listed in the 1845 Dundee Directory as "historical, landscape and portrait painter", it is possible that some of the paintings held in the city's collection attributed to D A may actually be by D R.

6. *Dundee Advertiser* 20/1/1854.

7. *Dundee Courier* 1/2/1854.

8. *Ibid*.

9. *Dundee Advertiser* 29/4/1856.

10. *Dundee Advertiser* 8/2/1856.

11. *Ibid*.

12. Quoted from Kennedy's obituary in the *Dundee Year Book* 1904.

13. *Dundee Advertiser* 12/6/1860.

14. *Dundee Courier* 9/2/1859.

15. From an address by Gordon given at the prize-giving ceremony for the Dundee Technical Institute, 23/12/1904, included in a bound volume of syllabuses and prize lists held by Abertay University.

16. Dundee City Archives holds Pupils' Registers for the School of Art from 1871-7.

17. There is some confusion about Grubb's age. His birth certificate is dated September 1849, but his death certificate in November 1903 gives his age as 52 rather than 54. His marriage certificate has him as 26 in July 1875 and the census undertaken in March 1901 has him as 51. His obituary was published in the *Dundee Advertiser* 3/11/1903.

18. Quoted from an address to the Dundee Art Society, published in their Annual Report in 1911 (Dundee Central Library, Local History Centre).

19. *Evening Telegraph* 10/11/1880.

20. Though never very successful during his lifetime, the Forfar-born Herald's watercolours have since become highly collectable. Following his study at the High School, Herald began his career in Dundee somewhat unwillingly as an apprentice house painter. Legend has it that he was sent to do some work in a house in Broughty Ferry, but on getting to the area he realised he had forgotten the address, whereupon he threw his paint and brushes into the Tay and walked all the way home to Forfar! Kerr also came to Dundee as an apprentice but soon returned to his native Edinburgh and established a successful career as a genre painter and portraitist in watercolour.

21. Dundee Art Society Annual Report 1911 (Dundee Central Library, Local History Centre).

22. *Ibid.*

23. Macdonald *op cit*, p188.

24. A complete description of the various stages can be found in Macdonald *op cit*, pp388-91.

25. *Dundee Courier* 1/4/1889.

26. Initially 3rd Grade certificates could only be taken at the National Schools in South Kensington, but this restriction was later relaxed. In Dundee schools as a whole (day and evening) in 1889, 26% of those achieving 1st Grade went on to 2nd, and only 12.3% of those went onto 3rd (*Dundee Courier* 1/4/1889).

27. Although this does not seem to have been advertised anywhere, it is clearly borne out by the Pupils' Registers of the 1870s.

28. Reported in *The Wizard of the North* 25/12/1880.

29. Recalled by John Duncan in Dundee Art Society Annual Report 1911 (Dundee Central Library, Local History Centre).

30. *People's Journal* 26/6/1880.

31. John Duncan, *op cit*.

32. Wyse's own unpublished autobiography is now available online at www.htwyse.info

33. H T Wyse, *The Brushwork Series of Second-Grade Freehand Drawing Cards* (Dundee: John Leng & Co / William Kidd, 1891).

34. H T Wyse, *Modern Methods of Art Instruction* (Edinburgh: Henry T Wyse, 1909). Wyse exhibited regularly at the Fine Art Exhibitions and those of the GAA, often showing pieces of furniture which he made in collaboration with Arbroath cabinet-maker William Middleton; some of his designs were published in *Simple Furniture* (Arbroath: Brodie & Salmond, 1900). A key member of the Scottish Guild of Handicraft, Wyse's importance to the Arts & Crafts movement in Scotland as both art educator and craftsman was recognised by Elizabeth Cumming in her exhibition *Hand, Heart & Soul* at the Edinburgh City Art Centre in 2007.

35. McIntosh Patrick's obituary of Gray was published in the *Evening Telegraph* 27/2/1957. The Duncan of Jordanstone College Collection includes a splendidly eccentric portrait of Gray by Ian Fleming.

36. Alexander studied at the School, as did William Grubb's son David. Both of them exhibited their work at the Fine Art Exhibitions.

37. High School of Dundee Prospectuses are held by Dundee Central Library, Local History Centre; they list members of staff and the South Kensington successes of the previous year's pupils.

38. Quoted from Wyse's unpublished autobiography (*op cit*).

39. Recalled by Foggie in a speech given to students at Glasgow School of Art in 1947, the text of which is held by his family. Coincidentally, his cousin Christina Foggie became Assistant Mistress at the Dundee School of Art from 1898-1903.

40. In the same speech, Foggie recalls giving lectures and teaching pupils privately. He also claims to have held a weekly class for a while in Dundee with a head model, though there is no reference to this in his surviving account book.

41. In his essay in the exhibition catalogue *The Edinburgh School* (Edinburgh: Scottish Gallery, 1993). For more on Foggie's time at Edinburgh College of Art, see Matthew Jarron, *David Foggie: The Painters' Painter* (University of Dundee Museum Services, 2004).

42. J G R, 'At the Sign of the Brush & Pen, Being some Notes on the Black and White Artists of to day. No 23 – Mr Max Cowper', *Brown's Book-Stall*, July 1899 p407.

43. *People's Journal* 2/11/1895

44. *People's Journal* 22/9/1900

45. Quoted from Grubb's obituary, *op cit*. The event was reported in the *Dundee Courier* 18/3/1901.

46. The Watt Institution had closed in 1849 but attempts were made to revive it, including a proposal in 1850 for it to host a government School of Design.

47. YMCA Dundee Annual Report 1874-5 (most of the information in this section comes from the annual reports held in Dundee Central Library, Local History Centre).

48. YMCA Dundee Annual Report 1879-80.

49. YMCA Dundee Annual Report 1883-4.

50. Some of this information comes from a feature on Ryle Smith in *The Piper o'Dundee* 30/12/1891, as well as from an undated cutting from 1945 in the Obituary Cuttings books at Dundee Central Library, Local History Centre. According to the High School Prospectuses, Smith did not earn his full Art Master's certificate from the School of Art until 1891.

51. YMCA Dundee Annual Report 1889-90.

52. Quoted from the Films of Scotland documentary *Still Life with Honesty* (1970, directed by Forsyth & Singleton).

53. Gray continued to teach science at Dundee Technical Institute from 1902. He died in 1934 aged 88. His obituary was published in the *Courier & Advertiser* 9/4/1934. One of his sons was John Gray, art master at Grove Academy (see above).

54. Jamieson died in 1950 aged 83. His obituary was published in the *Courier & Advertiser* 17/11/1950. Like Gray's, Jamieson's son (also Ninian) became a successful art teacher, working at Morgan Academy for twenty years.

55. *Dundee Courier* 11/9/1897.

56. *Dundee Courier* 1/9/1898.

57. See, for example, a front page advert for the school in the *People's Journal* 16/9/1882.

58. Senga Davidson, 'Symbolists in our midst – Stewart Carmichael and George Dutch Davidson' in Matthew Jarron (ed), *The Artist & the Thinker – John Duncan & Patrick Geddes in Dundee* (University of Dundee Museum Services, 2004), p79.

59. In 1907 he unsuccessfully applied to be art master of Harris Academy (*Dundee Courier* 15/1/1907).

60. Advert in *People's Journal* 16/9/1892.

61. Stevenson also exhibited a portrait of the late Henry Boase in 1890, indicating that he was also undertaking commissions.

62. Advertising circulars for both classes are held in the Lamb Collection 276(9-10) (Dundee Central Library Local History Centre).

63. Information from adverts in the *People's Journal* 28/8/1880 and 2/9/1905. There were numerous other private schools in Dundee at this time, each with their own or a visiting art master; these few examples must be taken as a very small selection.

64. *Dundee Courier* 7/7/1874.

65. *People's Journal* 28/8/1880

66. *Dundee Courier* 27/10/1885.

67. Technical Institute, Dundee – Syllabus of Science & Art Classes 1888-9 (held at Dundee Central Library, Local History Centre) and Hetherington Easson *et al*, *Dundee Institute of Technology – The First Hundred Years 1888-1988* (Dundee Institute of Technology 1988).

68. *Dundee Year Book* 1888.

69. The account in the *Year Book* indicated that trial classes (including Malcolm's) had been piloted the year before in University College rooms. This was confirmed by Malcolm in a letter to the *Dundee Courier* 3/4/1929 in which he recalled teaching 92 students in College Hall before the new building was ready.

70. Technical Institute Syllabus 1889-90.

71. Technical Institute Statement of Accounts 1888-1909, held by Abertay University.

72. The Brucciani orders may have included a set of casts of the Parthenon frieze, still held by the Art College today.

73. Technical Institute Syllabus 1892-3.

74. These may not have been the first day classes – according to the minute book of the Board of Studies 1888-1901 (held by Abertay University), George Malcolm asked the Board on 18 September 1889 if he could use the Art Class Rooms for private classes during the daytime. The Board agreed to the idea of Saturday classes ("that being the only day when Artisan Students could attend") but it is not clear whether or not these took place – they are certainly not listed in the syllabus.

75. Obituary in *Courier & Advertiser* 5/3/1935.

76. *People's Journal* 2/2/1895

77. *People's Journal* 12/10/1895 and Easson *et al*, *op cit*.

78. Woodhouse's obituary was published in the *Courier & Advertiser* 14/10/1933.

79. James Martin White (who served as Chairman of the Institute Committee) helped to prevent this by providing him with an additional £50 a year on top of his salary. On 16/1/1912 White wrote to Bailie Melville, "if it had not been for me, Mr Woodhouse would now be teaching in Calcutta... Thus he would have done great injury to Dundee. This I saved" (Technical Institute Letter Book vol 3, held by Abertay University).

80. Copies of all of these and many more are held in Dundee Central Library Local History Centre.

81. The figures come from the Statement of Accounts, *op cit*.

82. These figures also come from the Statement of Accounts, but do not tally with the numbers of students given in the Annual Reports of Certificates and Prizes, presumably because some of those who enrolled never paid their fees. Some of these may have received bursaries offered by the Dundee Educational Trust.

83. Both Richardson and Wyse won numerous national prizes, including a bronze medal for Richardson in 1895 for "a selection of measured drawings of old monuments in the Howff" (*Dundee Courier* 15/7/1895).

84. Thoms' importance as one of Dundee's leading Arts & Crafts architects is discussed by Elizabeth Cumming in *Hand Heart and Soul* (Edinburgh: Birlinn, 2006) and Annette Carruthers in *The Arts and Crafts Movement in Scotland* (New Haven & London: Yale University Press, 2014).

85. Macdonald, *op cit* chapter 8.

86. Technical Institute Syllabus 1895-6.

87. Annual Reports of Certificates & Prizes 1893-1902 (Dundee Central Library Local History Centre).

88. Minutes of a Meeting of the Board of Studies of the Technical Institute 24/6/1895 (Abertay University) and *People's Journal* 6/7/1895.

89. Minutes of a Meeting of the Joint Committee on Overlapping 3/2/1900 (Abertay University).

90. The Institute also rented the west wing of Dudhope Castle to provide additional teaching space – Painters & Decorators Work was the only artistic course taught there.

91. Technical Institute Syllabus 1901-2.

92. *People's Journal* 7/1/1905.

93. Copy of letter to Revel 7/3/1905 from Letter Book vol 2 (Abertay University).

94. Peter J M McEwan, *Dictionary of Scottish Art & Architecture* (Ballater: Glengarden Press, 2004).

95. Copies of letters to the SED 25/11/1902 and 3/2/1903 from Letter Book vol 2 (Abertay University).

96. Moyes left in 1912 to become art master at Aberdeen Grammar School. Paul went on to work at Belfast School of Art before undertaking further study at the Royal College of Art in London. He was described in the *Dundee Courier* 9/10/1918 as "one of the most brilliant students that have been at the Dundee School of Art" when he was killed during the Great War.

97. Copy of letter to Myles 30/6/1904 from Letter Book vol 2 (Abertay University).

98. *People's Journal* 25/3/1905.

99. *People's Journal* 22/4/1905.

100. Donn became assistant art master at the High School in 1905 and art master at Stobswell School in 1910.

101. See for example www.teara.govt.nz/1966/A/ArtsSchools/ArtSchools/en which notes that Donn "was one of the first to lift the teaching of art in schools from the doldrums into high favour". In 1931 Donn returned to Dundee to stage an exhibition of watercolours at Bain's Fine Art Gallery and give a lecture to the Art Society on 'Maori Carvings and Decorations'.

102. Technical Institute Syllabus 1905-6, 1906-7 and 1907-8.

103. For a brief history of the Training College (later Dundee College of Education) see www.dundee.ac.uk/museum/collections/education/

104. St Andrews Provincial Committee for the Training of Teachers Prospectuses (University of Dundee Archive Services).

105. *The City Echo* February 1911.

106. Taken from Delgaty Dunn's retirement speech in 1927, published in the *Evening Telegraph* 18/4/1927.

107. Though not before some embarrassing difficulties with the tendering process, reported in the *Advertiser* at various times between February and April 1907.

108. *Dundee Advertiser* 29/1/1907.

109. *Ibid.*

110. *Dundee Courier* 23/1/1907.

111. *Dundee Advertiser* 31/1/1907.

112. *Dundee Courier* 31/1/1907.

113. *Dundee Advertiser* 31/1/1907.

114. Technical Institute Syllabus 1907-8.

115. Technical Institute Syllabus 1908-9.

116. Technical Institute Letter Book vol 2, Abertay University.

117. *The City Echo* February 1911.

118. Hill and Gill had both studied at the Royal College of Art, Purvis at Glasgow School of Art and Cheyne at Gray's School of Art in Aberdeen.

119. Intriguingly, the Dundee Technical Institute's Annual Report of Certificates & Prizes for 1904-5 (Dundee Central Library, Local History Centre) lists a John M Purvis as taking art classes there, but according to the Summary of Qualifications & Testimonials in favour of John Milne Purvis, 1927 (Perth Museum & Art Gallery) Purvis was working as assistant to Murray in Perth at that time, so this is presumably just a coincidence of names.

120. It is not clear why Purvis failed to get the job, having the support of both Dunn and the Principal of the College, John S Lumsden. His other referees included Stewart Carmichael, Patrick Thoms and the art collector William Boyd (*ibid*).

121. This information comes from *John Milne Purvis 1885-1961* exhibition booklet by Robin Rodger, Perth Museum & Art Gallery, 1994.

122. Purvis's obituary appeared in the *Courier & Advertiser* 31/10/1961.

123. Richard Carr tells some amusing stories about Duncan in his unpublished history of the Art College from 1992 (copies of which are held by University of Dundee Museum Services and the Duncan of Jordanstone College Library).

124. Information from Lyon & Turnbull's catalogue of the sale of Jordanstone and its contents in 2004, following the death of the last Lady Duncan in 2003.

125. The full details of this part of the will are quoted in the *Dundee Year Book* 1909.

126. *Ibid.* This was the same site that had been considered for the proposed higher art school in 1907.

127. *Dundee Courier* 23/10/1913.

128. *Dundee Courier* 30/10/1914.

129. *Dundee Courier* 9/11/1921 and 20/11/1925.

130. A further complication worth noting is that some in the College felt that technical subjects such as weaving and dying should receive the money as they were considered closer to "industrial art" than the subjects taught by Delgaty Dunn.

131. *Evening Telegraph* 18/4/1927

132. A more detailed account of the remainder of the battle for the bequest falls outwith the scope of this book. For further information, see the exhibition catalogue by John Morrison, *The First Hundred: Dundee's Art College 1892-1992* (Dundee: McManus Galleries, 1992), part of which was revised and published as 'James Duncan of Jordanstone and the Art College in Dundee' in *Journal of the Scottish Society for Art History* vol 2 (1997) pp52-63.

133. From Lumsden's letter of reference in Purvis's Testimonials (*op cit*).

134. The diary is part of the Cynicus collection held by Fife Cultural Trust. Its writer is unidentified but mentions winning first prize for life drawing in 1910 – in the Technical College's published list of prize-winners for that year (held at Abertay University), David Graham's is the corresponding name.

135. *Dundee Advertiser* 22/12/1913.

136. Joseph Lee, *Fra Lippo Lippi* (Dundee: John Leng & Co 1913)

137. From Joseph Lee's scrapbook of cuttings and photographs relating to the play (University of Dundee Archive Services, MS 88/4).

138. Purvis's wartime career is summarised in Rodger, *op cit*.

139. Stuart Macdonald, *op cit* p296. Crane earned this reputation through his revolutionary teaching at the Royal College of Art and his influential publications on decorative art.

140. Technical College & School of Art Syllabus 1916-7 and the Scotland's People website. Hean had been a pupil at Harris Academy and the school's magazine vol 1 no 2 (1912) has a photograph of her as an art prize medallist. Milne studied at the High School and later taught art at Dollar Academy and various schools in Perthshire.

141. *The Studio* vol 72 (1917), p79.

142. *Ibid* p80.

143. Stewart Carmichael was one of the assessors employed.

144. Davidson's obituary was published in the Courier & Advertiser 11/1/1951. Some of his earlier work was featured in the exhibition *Hand, Heart & Soul* at the Edinburgh City Art Centre, 2007.

145. Now in the collections of the University of Dundee Museum Services. Hamilton also designed a memorial stained glass window for Arbirlot Parish Church in 1921.

146. Easson *et al*, *op cit*, and Statement of Accounts 1909-1934 (Abertay University).

147. *Evening Telegraph* 18/9/1928.

148. Technical College & School of Art Syllabus 1921-2. Compare this to letters written by John S Lumsden in 1904-5 in which he states that "fine art is of very secondary importance with us. Most of our students are artisans in the engineering, building and textile trades... there are practically no purely art students" (Technical Institute Letter Book vol 2, 22/11/104 and 1/1/1905, held at Abertay University).

149. *Dundee Advertiser* 4/11/1892.

150. Mackie Smith retired in 1926 and his obituary appeared in the *Courier & Advertiser* 16/7/1945.

151. *Dundee High School Magazine* vol 1 no 2 (1895).

152. His obituary is in the *Courier & Advertiser* 12/6/1941.

153. *Courier & Advertiser* 28/9/1936.

154. *Grove Academy Magazine Jubilee Number 1889-1939* (Dundee: G B Findlay, 1939). Ryle Smith retired in 1927.

155. *Courier & Advertiser* 5/3/1951.

Chapter Seven

1. 'Some Thoughts on Art by a Cosmopolitan Student', *The College* May 1889.

2. *Illustrated Catalogue of a Loan Collection of Paintings, Watercolours & Engravings in the Victoria Art Galleries, Dundee on the occasion of the British Association Meeting* (Glasgow: University Press, 1912).

3. Quoted in Donald Southgate, *University Education in Dundee: A Centenary History* (Edinburgh University Press, 1982), p31.

4. *Kirkcudbrightshire Advertiser* 27/3/1908. I am grateful to Mary Arnold and David Steel for sharing their separate researches into Jack's life and career.

5. *Dundee Courier* 9/4/1889. Ernest Boulanger taught music at the Académie des Beaux-Arts and Jules Joseph Lefebvre taught art at the Académie Julian.

6. With the possible exception of Etta Johnston, who was taken on by Patrick Geddes as an assistant during the same year.

7. UCD Calendar 1889-1890 (held at University of Dundee Archive Services). Although this is the first listing of the subject in the syllabus, the Principal's Report for the previous session makes it clear that the class had begun with seven students in the preceding summer term.

8. 'Department of Fine Arts', *The College* March 1890.

9. UCD Calendar 1889-1890 (held at University of Dundee Archive Services).

10. *Dundee Courier* 18/11/1896.

11. Quoted in the *Kirkcudbrightshire Advertiser* 27/3/1908.

12. UCD Calendar 1902-1903 (held at University of Dundee Archive Services).

13. As shown by an advert in the *People's Journal* 2/9/1905, which noted that Mitchell was assisted in his classes by Fraulein Schadewitz, formerly of the Royal Academy of Arts in Cassel.

14. *Dundee Advertiser* 31/1/1907.

15. *Ibid.*

16. Stewart Carmichael, writing in the *Dundee Advertiser* 29/1/1907.

17. Stewart Carmichael, 'Fifty Years of the Dundee Art Society', unpublished MS of lecture given in 1940 (Dundee of Jordanstone College Library).

18. The course is advertised in both the UCD Calendar 1895-1896 (held at University of Dundee Archive Services) and the Technical Institute syllabus for the same year (held at Dundee Central Library Local History Centre).

19. *The College* June 1891.

20. 'Artistic Anatomy', *The College* February 1890.

21. As with Mackay's above, the course is advertised in both the UCD Calendar and the Technical Institute syllabus for 1889-1890.

22. 'Artistic Anatomy', *op cit.*

23. A Melville Paterson, *Duval's Artistic Anatomy, Completely Revised with additional Original Illustrations* (London: Cassell & Co, 1905), p6.

24. Don's obituary is published in the *Courier & Advertiser* 20/4/1933.

25. *The Piper o' Dundee* 30/8/1899. The book in question was *A Manual of Ambulance* by J Scott Riddell (1897).

26. *Evening Telegraph* 12/7/1911. Don's obituary is in the *Evening Telegraph* 19/4/1933.

27. A Souvenir of the University College Students' Union Bazaar, 1903 (University of Dundee Archive Services).

28. Not the current school of that name on Hawkhill but the original on Blackness Road.

29. *People's Journal* 20/5/1905.

30. *Dundee Courier* 14/6/1905.

31. *People's Journal* 20/5/1905. According to H T Wyse, however, David Scott Murray had introduced plant drawing from nature at Morgan Academy in the 1890s.

32. To describe fully the artistic influence of D'Arcy Thompson's work would require a book in itself, and what I have included here draws on other material I have published, notably *A Glimpse of a Great Vision: The D'Arcy Thompson Zoology Museum Art Fund Collection* (University of Dundee Museum Services, 2014) and 'A Sketch of the Universe – D'Arcy Thompson's *On Growth and Form*', *Essays on Sculpture* vol 70 (2014) pp5-13. Thompson's own art interests were originally researched for the paper 'Sketching the Universe: D'Arcy Thompson's Growth and Form in Dundee' which I gave at the University of Oxford on 14 May 2010.

33. *The Piper o' Dundee* 7/8/1889.

34. Madge was a close friend of Thompson's star student, Mary Lily Walker, and was married to W R Valentine, a life governor of UCD.

35. *Dundee Courier* 29/12/1886.

36. Typed MS of address by D'Arcy Thompson (University of St Andrews Library Special Collections MS 45704). In 1924 Thompson was made an Honorary Member of Dundee Art Society.

37. Letter to D'Arcy Thompson 25/1/1896 (University of St Andrews Library Special Collections, MS 16359).

38. Quoted in an appreciation in the *Dundee Advertiser* 10/1/1901 – the same letter is reproduced in *George Dutch Davidson: A Memorial Volume* (Dundee: Graphic Arts Association, 1902) but with Thompson's name excised.

39. *British Association, Dundee 1912: Handbook and Guide to Dundee and District* (Dundee: David Winter & Son 1912).

40. *Illustrated Catalogue*, 1912, *op cit.*

41. The commission is noted in Foggie's accounts book (held by the artist's family).

42. From a review of the Dundee Art Society exhibition dated 20/3/1936, in volume four of Stewart Carmichael's scrapbooks (Dundee City Archives).

43. All in his papers at the University of St Andrews Library Special Collections.

44. Stephen Jay Gould in his introduction to D'Arcy Thompson, *On Growth and Form* (Cambridge University Press, Canto edition, 1992) p ix.

45. Personal communication with author, 2011. Kemp has also written about D'Arcy Thompson in *Seen | Unseen* (Oxford University Press, 2006).

46. According to Victoria Walsh in *Nigel Henderson: Parallel of Life and Art* (London: Thames & Hudson, 2001) Paolozzi discovered the book while he and Turnbull were in Paris. Paolozzi wrote to Henderson about it, who after enthusiastically reading it (in one afternoon!) shared it with Hamilton. As Moholy-Nagy's *Vision in Motion* was a key text for these artists, the discovery may have come from its mention there.

47. Pasmore had previously taught (as had Hamilton briefly) at the Central School of Arts & Crafts in London run by another D'Acy Thompson enthusiast, the Scottish painter William Johnstone.

48. John A Walker, *Learning to Paint: A British Art Student and Art School 1956-61* (published at http://fineart.ac.uk/collection/pdf/walker.pdf in 2003). See also E Crippa & B Williamson, *Basic Design* (London: Tate Britain, 2013).

49. Letter to D'Arcy Thompson, 1942 (University of St Andrews Library Special Collections, MS 19370).

50. Letter to D'Arcy Thompson, probably 1942 (University of St Andrews Library Special Collections, MS 25480).

51. Letter to Herbert Read 28/7/1946 (University of St Andrews Library Special Collections, MS 45690).

52. *The College*, vol 29, June 1932 (University of Dundee Archive Services). It is interesting to note that these are much the same criticisms that Geddes made of John Duncan's style of teaching (see chapter three).

53. *The College* December 1888.

54. Geddes's various garden schemes are described in Matthew Jarron (ed), *The Artist & the Thinker: John Duncan & Patrick Geddes in Dundee* (University of Dundee Museum Services 2004) chapters three and four.

55. D'Arcy Thompson, *Fifty Years Ago and Now*, a presidential address on the occasion of the Fiftieth Annual General Meeting of the Grey Lodge Settlement Association, formerly the Dundee Social Union and Grey Lodge Settlement, 1938 (Dundee Central Library Local History Centre). My thanks to Mary Arnold for researching Geddes's links with the Dundee Social Union for me.

56. Letter to Mrs Geddes, undated (University of Strathclyde Archives, T-GED 9/2327).

57. Patrick Geddes, *Every Man His Own Art Critic* (Edinburgh: Brown, 1888), quoted in Philip Boardman, *The Worlds of Patrick Geddes* (London, Henley & Boston: Routledge & Kegan Paul, 1978) p99.

58. Patrick Geddes, 'The Sociology of Autumn', *The Evergreen*, Autumn 1895 p28.

59. Patrick Geddes, 'The Museum and the City: a Practical Proposal', *Museums Journal* vol 16 no 5 (1908), pp371-382. Geddes's unpublished manuscript *Museums: Actual & Possible* is held at University of Strathclyde Archives, T-GED 5/1/10).

60. *Ibid*, p372.

61. For more on this and Geddes's many other museum interests, see Matthew Jarron, 'Patrick Geddes and Museum Ideas in Dundee and Beyond', *Museum Management and Curatorship* vol 21 (2006), pp88-94.

62. Memo to Marcel Hardy 14/12/1902 (University of Strathclyde Archives, T-GED 9/427).

63. In the Geddes papers at University of Strathclyde Archives. This includes a letter from Mrs Carmichael to Mrs Geddes, suggesting a close family friendship.

64. Letter to Patrick Geddes 17/6/1919 (University of Strathclyde Archives, T-GED 9/1444).

65. *Dundee Advertiser* 24/1/1907.

66. Geddes's address was reported in (among others) *The Piper o' Dundee* 27/5/1896.

67. Three articles were published, but Geddes's notes in University of Strathclyde Archives (T-GED 5/1/24) show that a fourth was drafted, concentrating on children's appreciation of art.

68. *Dundee Advertiser* 18/1/1907.

69. *Dundee Advertiser* 11/2/1907.

70. Graphic Arts Association Minute Book 4/5/1891 (held at the time of consultation by Dundee Art Society, later transferred to University of Dundee Archive Services).

71. Letter from John Maclauchlan inviting donations towards the project, 9/6/1892 (Dundee Central Library Local History Centre, Lamb Collection).

72. Graphic Arts Association Annual Report 1891 (Dundee Central Library Local History Centre).

73. Maclauchlan, *op cit.*

74. Graphic Arts Association Minute Book 14/5/1894.

75. Ironically, what has survived from Geddes's time at the Botany department are over a hundred of the commercially available botanical prints he claimed to dislike, from the Swiss Dodel-Port series and the German Kny series. They are now cared for by the University of Dundee Museum Services.

76. Riccardo Stephens, *The Cruciform Mark* (London: Chatto & Windus, 1896) p191.

77. Much of this information comes from Mary Arnold, 'Etta J Johnston: Art, Science and Social Action in Late 19th-Century Dundee', *Journal of the Scottish Society for Art History* Vol 11 (2006), pp.34-42.

78. High School of Dundee Prospectus 1884-5 (Dundee Central Library Local History Centre).

79. UCD Calendar 1889-90 (University of Dundee Archive Services).

80. Co-authored with Carnelley and published in *Proceedings of the Royal Society of London* vol 45 (1889), pp346-51.

81. Some of her various activities are referred to in the *Dundee Courier* 17/3/1914, 7/10/1915, 28/2/1921 and 11/12/1939.

82. *Dundee Advertiser* 11/2/1907.

83. For more on Bruce and Geddes, see Geoff N Swinney, 'The training of a polar scientist: Patrick Geddes and the student career of William Speirs Bruce', *Archives of Natural History* vol 29 no 3 (2002), pp287-301.

84. Quoted in G N Swinney, 'From the Arctic and Antarctic to "the back parts of Mull": The Life and Career of William Gordon Burn-Murdoch (1862-1939)', *Scottish Geographical Journal* vol 119 no 2 (2003), pp121-151.

85. *Ibid.*

86. W G Burn-Murdoch, *From Edinburgh to the Antarctic: an artist's notes and sketches during the Dundee Antarctic Expedition of 1892-93* (London: Longmans, Green & Co, 1894) p5.

87. *Ibid*, p18. Burn-Murdoch had previously shown work in the Victoria Galleries at the Fine Art Exhibitions in 1889 and 1890.

88. To put Burn-Murdoch's work into context, see D Walton & B Pearson, *White Horizons: British Art from Antarctica* (catalogue for an exhibition at the Edinburgh International Conference Centre, 2006). By contrast, artistic depictions of the Arctic date back much earlier, for example early 19th-century watercolour sketches by Dundee whaling seaman John Gowland (Dundee's Art Galleries & Museums) or those found in Alexander Smith's 1861 journal of his voyage on the Dundee whaler *Camperdown* (Dundee Central Library, Local History Centre).

89. Quoted in Swinney, *Scot. Geog. J. op cit*, p125.

90. Quoted in Swinney, *Arch. Nat. Hist. op cit*, p293.

Chapter Eight

1. *The City Echo* May 1908.

2. *Dundee Courier* 25/5/1877.

3. They were mentioned as the highlight of his collection of pictures when it was acquired by the art and antique dealer Robert Morrison (*Dundee Courier* 8/3/1886).

4. My thanks to Irene Brady of Burial Adminstration, Dundee City Council for the information on these burial lairs. Cowie's own death in 1877 may have prevented further use of the plots.

5. *People's Journal* 6/3/1880.

6. *Dundee Year Book* 1888 p110.

7. Referred to in some sources as Dundee Amateur Artists' Association.

8. 'Sketch of Art in Dundee in the Nineteenth Century', Graphic Arts Association Annual Report 1900 (Dundee Central Library, Local History Centre).

9. The original name of the Club was apparently the Dundee Fine Art Association, but this was presumably changed to avoid confusion with the organisers of the Fine Art Exhibitions, whose committee also came to be known as the Fine Art Association. The only evidence I have found of this other Fine Art Association is a set of rules in the Lamb Collection (Dundee Central Library, Local History Centre) dated 1881. I have no definite proof that this organisation is the Art Club under another name, but it has exactly the same stated aims and almost exactly the same committee. This would also explain why the name Dundee Art Club appears nowhere prior to December 1881, despite it having been founded in 1880.

10. Dundee Art Club Rules 1886 (Dundee Central Library, Local History Centre).

11. *Ibid*.

12. Stewart Carmichael, 'Fifty Years of the Dundee Art Society', unpublished MS of lecture given in 1940 (Dundee of Jordanstone College Library).

13. *The Piper o' Dundee* 2/2/1890.

14. A fine example of Fairweather's work can be seen in the Orchar Collection. He died in 1907 aged 60.

15. Quoted from Farquharson's obituary 1/5/1883 in the cuttings book at Dundee Central Library, Local History Centre.

16. *Dundee Courier* 4/6/1883.

17. *Dundee Courier* 4/5/1885.

18. *Dundee Courier* 1/5/1886.

19. Dundee Art Club Rules 1886 (Dundee Central Library, Local History Centre).

20. *Ibid*.

21. *Dundee Courier* 26/10/1887.

22. *The Piper o' Dundee* 28/10/1887.

23. *The Piper o' Dundee* 16/5/1888. The artists referred to are Giuseppe Gonnella, Alex Neilson and Martin Anderson.

24. *Dundee Courier* 9/10/1888.

25. The Dundee Directories list the Art Club up to 1890-91, though there is no other evidence that it was in operation after 1889.

26. The Dundee Directories list the Quill & Quaver Club from 1889-90 until 1892-93.

27. *Dundee Courier* 10/6/1884.

28. *Dundee Courier* 9/10/1884.

29. The full syllabus for the opening session is held by Dundee Central Library, Local History Centre.

30. *Ibid*.

31. *Dundee Courier* 30/11/1889.

32. Graphic Arts Association Minute Book volume 1: 1890-1901 (held at the time of consultation by Dundee Art Society, later transferred to University of Dundee Archive Services).

33. *Ibid*.

34. Graphic Arts Association Rules 1890 (Dundee Central Library, Local History Centre).

35. GAA Minute Book 18/2/1890.

36. *Dundee Advertiser* 11/6/1890.

37. GAA Annual Report 1890 (Dundee Central Library, Local History Centre).

38. Batchelor studied at Dundee School of Art in the 1880s and also exhibited at the Fine Art Exhibitions. Fleming and Lowdon we will return to later in the chapter.

39. GAA Minute Book 1/5/1893 and a report by Cowper on Life and Antique Classes 1892-3, included at the end of the first Minute Book.

40. GAA Minute Book 19/10/1894.

41. GAA Minute Book 4/2/1895.

42. Carmichael, 'Fifty Years', *op cit*.

43. *Dundee Courier* 12/9/1899. Her name is often written as "Lowden" but the one painting I have seen by her is signed "E M Lowdon".

44. GAA Minute Book 8/11/1897.

45. Report by Cowper on Life and Antique Classes 1892-3, included at the end of the first GAA Minute Book. Cowper's enthusiasm for using the casts is clear – in 1891 he had won a prize from the Dundee Institute of Architecture, Science & Art for "Best Sketch for Antique Subject in Dundee Art Museum of Casts", reported in the *Dundee Courier* 15/5/1891.

46. Carmichael, 'Fifty Years', *op cit*.

47. Dundee Art Society Minute Book 25/10/1907.

48. GAA Annual Report 1891 (Dundee Central Library, Local History Centre).

49. GAA Minute Book 11/4/1891.

50. *Dundee Courier* 20/2/1892.

51. GAA Minute Book 3/12/1894.

52. Carmichael, 'Fifty Years', *op cit*.

53. *Ibid*.

54. It is worth noting that the Society was unusual in the breadth of its activities. When James Cadenhead opened the annual exhibition in 1906, he noted with envy the Society's classes and club rooms, claiming that nothing of the sort was held by the Aberdeen Artists Society, the Glasgow Institute, the SSA or the RSW.

55. Twenty artists give Dundee addresses in the 1877 catalogue, compared to around 70 by 1880.

56. *Dundee Courier* 4/10/1886.

57. *Dundee Courier* 25/10/1889.

58. *Dundee Courier* 8/6/1893.

59. Carmichael, 'Fifty Years', *op cit*.

60. *The Wizard of the North* 30/6/1893.

61. *The Piper o' Dundee* 14/3/1894 and *The Wizard of the North* 30/11/1894..

62. *Dundee Courier* 29/3/1894.

63. Carmichael, 'Fifty Years', *op cit*.

64. It's possible that either Cowper or Pollock may have beaten Clark to it – although Clark is the first to be listed there in the Dundee Directory, on 15 July 1891 the *Piper o' Dundee* reported that Cowper had moved to a "natty studio" in Castle Street, making no mention of Clark. Pollock is not listed in the 1891 Directory but gives 15 Castle Street as his address in the Fine Art Exhibition catalogue later that year.

65. Carmichael, 'Fifty Years', *op cit*.

66. *The Piper o' Dundee* 20/1/1897.

67. *The Piper o' Dundee* 2/5/1900.

68. *Dundee Advertiser* 20/4/1900.

69. *Dundee Advertiser* 21/4/1900.

70. *Dundee Advertiser* 25/4/1900.

71. *Dundee Advertiser* 27/4/1900.

72. *Ibid*.

73. *Dundee Advertiser* 7/5/1900, the other letters appearing 30/4/1900, 2/5/1900 and 4/5/1900.

74. *The Piper o' Dundee* 2/5/1900.

75. *The Piper o' Dundee* 9/5/1900.

76. Carmichael, 'Fifty Years', *op cit*.

77. *Ibid*.

78. GAA Minute Book 25/1/1897.

79. GAA Minute Book 13/5/1898.

80. Carmichael, 'Fifty Years', *op cit*. The opening referred to was in 1900.

81. *Evening Telegraph* 23/4/1896.

82. GAA Minute Book 8/1/1894.

83. GAA Annual Report 1894 (Dundee Central Library, Local History Centre).

84. GAA Annual Report 1898 (Dundee Central Library, Local History Centre).

85. *The Piper o' Dundee* 20/3/1901.

86. GAA Minute Book 9/11/1903.

87. Carmichael, 'Fifty Years', *op cit*.

88. Phillips became Secretary at the end of 1893, then an ordinary member of Council in 1903, then President 1904-5. After a year off he was back as ordinary member of Council until 1908, then again at the end of 1909 for a further two years, then once more in 1917. He became Secretary and Treasurer in 1918, remaining as such until becoming Vice President in 1923-4.

89. Carmichael started as an ordinary member at the end of 1893, also serving as Vice President 1894-5 and 1925-6, and President 1900-1, 1915-6 and 1927-8

90. Grieve was Vice President 1898-9 and President 1902-3 and 1917-8.

91. Smith was an ordinary member of Council 1923 and 1932-4, then Vice President in 1938.

92. *Evening Telegraph* 23/6/1950.

93. Macintyre served as Council member in 1905-6 and 1911-2, then Vice President 1915-6 and President 1925-6.

94. *Evening Telegraph* 15/4/1930.

95. *Dundee Courier* 9/8/1918.

96. *Dundee Courier* 9/2/1934.

97. *Dundee Courier* 31/12/1949.

98. GAA Minute Book 2/12/1901.

99. Fleming was educated at Constitution House and UCD. She exhibited at the Fine Art Exhibition in 1895, the *Courier* noting that she "stands out distinctly among the local women amateur workers" (21/11/1895) but I have found no further trace of her.

100. Florence Lee (see figure 269) taught art at Morgan Academy (*Evening Telegraph* 12/9/1910).

101. Dundee Art Society Minute Book 23/11/1911.

102. GAA Minute Book 27/6/1893.

103. GAA Minute Book 7/3/1898.

104. *Dundee Advertiser* 24/1/1900.

105. Dundee Art Society Minute Book 5/6/1905.

106. Dundee Art Society Minute Book 17/12/1906.

107. Dundee Art Society Minute Book 24/4/1940.

108. *People's Journal* 22/12/1900.

109. Carmichael, 'Fifty Years', *op cit*.

110. *The City Echo* August 1910.

111. GAA Minute Book 4/3/1901.

112. GAA / Dundee Art Society Minute Book 8/1/1904.

113. Carmichael, 'Fifty Years', *op cit*.

114. Dundee Art Society Annual Report 1911 (Dundee Central Library, Local History Centre).

115. In a letter to William Hardie 18/11/1973, now in the National Library of Scotland.

116. *Dundee Courier* 31/10/1913.

117. Dundee Art Society Minute Book 17/2/1911.

118. Dundee Art Society Minute Book 12/5/1911.

119. Dundee Art Society Annual Report 1914 (Dundee Central Library, Local History Centre).

120. Lee was actually nominated for Council the day after Armistice Day, despite still being in a POW camp at the time!

121. *Dundee Courier* 9/8/1918.

122. Dundee Art Society Annual Report 1919 (Dundee Central Library, Local History Centre).

123. Dundee Art Society Annual Report 1921 (Dundee Central Library, Local History Centre).

124. *Dundee Courier* 1/4/1921.

125. Dundee Art Society Minute Book 25/11/1904.

126. Carmichael, 'Fifty Years', *op cit*. I am grateful to James S W Barnes and Senga Davidson for sharing with me their separate researches into the history of the Circle.

127. See Nina Lubbren, *Rural Artists' Colonies in Europe 1870-1910* (Manchester University Press, 2001) and Laura Newton (ed), *Painting at the Edge: British Coastal Art Colonies 1880-1930* (Bristol: Sansom & Co, 2005), though neither mentions the Tayport colony.

128. *The City Echo* April 1908 and *Dundee Courier* 3/5/1905.

129. *The City Echo* April 1908 (Dundee Central Library, Local History Centre).

130. One other professional artist, James Webster, was resident in Tayport at the time of the Circle's exhibitions, but also took no part in them. Later residents included William Macdonald (1883-1960), a painter known for his Spanish scenes.

131. *The City Echo* April 1908.

132. Information from the *Newport, Wormit & Tayport Annual & Directory* 1907 and 1908 (Dundee Central Library, Local History Centre). The embroidery school was started by the Baxter sisters and Elizabeth Burt (see chapter three), but it is possible that members of the Circle (most likely Anna Douglas) were involved as well.

133. *Evening Telegraph* 22/8/1905.

134. *Evening Telegraph* 24/8/1905.

135. *Dundee Advertiser* 3/5/1905.

136. Tayport Artists' Circle Second Exhibition Catalogue (Dundee Central Library, Local History Centre).

137. Carmichael, 'Fifty Years', *op cit*.

138. *Newport, Wormit & Tayport Annual & Directory* 1908 (Dundee Central Library, Local History Centre) and *Dundee Courier* 18/4/1907.

139. *Dundee Courier* 21/5/1906. In his newspaper scrapbook volume two (Dundee City Archives), Stewart Carmichael attributes the piece to "Rev Dr Woods", possibly William Wood, Pastor of Newport Congregational Church (my thanks to Kenneth Baxter for this suggestion).

140. *Newport, Wormit & Tayport Annual & Directory* 1907 (Dundee Central Library, Local History Centre).

141. *Ibid*, 1908.

142. *The City Echo* April 1908 and Report of the Free Library Committee 1913 (Dundee Central Library, Local History Centre).

143. Its origins are reported in the *Evening Telegraph* 12/10/1903.

144. No catalogue is known to survive but nineteen artists are mentioned by name in the *Dundee Advertiser*'s review of 14/10/1903.

145. *Dundee Advertiser* 15/10/1903.

146. *Ibid*.

147. Diary in the Cynicus collection held by Fife Cultural Trust.

148. Technical College & School of Art Syllabus 1921-22 (Dundee Central Library, Local History Centre).

149. According to Wyse's own unpublished autobiography at www.htwyse.info

150. *Dundee Courier* 28/2/1898.

151. *Dundee Courier* 7/9/1903.

152. Quoted from a speech given to students at Glasgow School of Art in 1947, the text of which is held by his family.

153. Henry Wright Kerr, also Dundee-trained but Edinburgh-based, became ARSA in 1893 and RSA in 1909.

154. My thanks to Nicola Ireland (formerly Royal Scottish Academy) for this information.

155. Letter from Douglas Bliss to Foggie's widow following his death, 1948 (family's collection).

156. 1897 cutting from Stewart Carmichael's newspaper scrapbook volume one (Dundee City Archives).

Chapter Nine

1. *The Piper o' Dundee* 20/3/1901 and 16/1/1901.

2. *Manchester Courier & Lancashire General Advertiser* 19/11/1907.

3. *The Scotsman* 15/12/1908.

4. *The Piper o' Dundee* 16/1/1901.

5. *The Wizard of the North*, 30/11/1894.

6. *The Year's Art* vol 22 (1901) p217.

7. Based in Montrose, Pinnington was said to be "among the foremost of Scottish art critics" (*Aberdeen Weekly Journal* 5/3/1900). A regular contributor to the *Art Journal*, he was the author of *The Life of George Paul Chalmers* (1894) and *Sir David Wilkie and the Scots School of Painting* (1900).

8. John Ramsay was a Tayport collector whose large assortment of McTaggarts had just been sold by Aitken Dott in Edinburgh in March 1909 – a sale which Frances Fowle describes as an important turning point in the commercial popularity of McTaggart's work (Frances Fowle, *Van Gogh's Twin: The Scottish Art Dealer Alexander Reid 1854-1928* (Edinburgh: National Galleries of Scotland, 2010) p111).

9. The colourists referred to here are members of the Scott Lauder group, not the later Scottish Colourists.

10. Edward Pinnington, 'Art Collections of Dundee and District. V – Elmslea', *Dundee Advertiser* 22/5/1909.

11. The articles were part of a series published in the *Dundee Advertiser* every Saturday from 24/4/1909 to 12/6/1909.

12. *Dundee Advertiser* 2/10/1907.

13. Dundee Art Society Annual Report 1911 (Dundee Central Library, Local History Centre).

14. *Dundee Courier* 26/2/1906.

15. Free Library Committee Report 1906 (Dundee Central Library, Local History Centre).

16. *The Wizard of the North*, 30/1/1908.

17. *The Scotsman* 15/12/1908.

18. This confusing state of affairs came to a head in 1921 when the Free Library Committee and the Victoria Art Galleries Committee clashed over who was responsible for running the galleries – see *Dundee Courier* 30/9/1921.

19. Reported in the Free Library Committee Report 1908 (Dundee Central Library, Local History Centre).

20. Details from *The Scotsman* 15/12/1908 and from the Loan Exhibition of Pictures 1908-9 catalogue (Dundee Central Library, Local History Centre). *Greek Girls Playing at Ball* is now in the Dick Institute, Kilmarnock. When McGrady's collection was sold after his death, *Baby's Breakfast* was described as a copy (the catalogue for the auction by James A McLean & Sons is in the Lamb Collection, Dundee Central Library, Local History Centre).

21. This was the largest showing for the Glasgow Boys thus far in Dundee, though the Dundee Art Society had shown Hornel's work in their 1903 exhibition; Melville and Lavery had been showing in the Fine Art Exhibitions since the 1880s, and Walton and Henry since the 1890s.

22. Stewart Carmichael, 'Fifty Years of the Dundee Art Society', unpublished MS of lecture given in 1940 (Dundee of Jordanstone College Library).

23. A H Millar, 'The Ethics of Local Art Galleries', *Museums Journal* October 1909 pp165-171.

24. Carmichael, 'Fifty Years', *op cit*.

25. *People's Journal* 15/10/1910.

26. A H Millar (ed), *Illustrated Catalogue of a Loan Collection of Paintings, Water Colours and Engravings in the Victoria Art Galleries, Dundee on the occasion of the British Association Meeting* (Glasgow: University Press, 1912), p5.

27. A W Paton & A H Millar (eds), *British Association, Dundee 1912: Handbook and Guide to Dundee and District* (Dundee: David Winter & Son, 1912) pp665-671. Millar's essay is based on one he had originally written for the

Graphic Arts Association's Annual Report in 1900.

28. *Morning Post* 2/9/1912, included in the Newspaper Record of the BA event (Dundee Central Library, Local History Centre).

29. *Dundee Advertiser* 4/9/1912, in Newspaper Record (*ibid*).

30. Hugh MacDiarmid, *Contemporary Scottish Studies* (Manchester: Carcanet Press, 1995) p228.

31. Information from his obituary in the *Dundee Courier* 1/7/1943.

32. 'A Successful Dundee Teeth Specialist', *The Wasp* Christmas Number 1901.

33. 'The Collection of a Local Connoisseur', *The City Echo* February 1909.

34. 'The Fine Art of Art Collecting – Notable Local Gallery', *People's Journal* 19/2/1910.

35. 'Modern Scottish Art – Notable Dundee Collection', *The Piper o`Dundee* 22/12/1905.

36. *Dundee Courier* 1/7/1943. I am not entirely sure what this role involved, but it seems to have been part of a scheme funded by the governments of those countries to encourage foreign loans of work by their artists.

37. Rev G Elmslie Troup, minister of West Church, Broughty Ferry, was another keen follower of the Glasgow Boys at this time, owning works by Guthrie, Crawhall, Walton, Henry and Millie Dow.

38. *The Piper o`Dundee* 22/12/1905.

39. In 1912 it was lent by R H Brechin of Glasgow and in 1924 by Mrs David Wallace of Broughty Ferry. Robertson had bought it back by the time of the 1939 BA exhibition.

40. It is mentioned, for example, in the *Evening Telegraph* 4/5/1914.

41. Curiously, the Free Library Committee Report 1914 (Dundee Central Library, Local History Centre) mentions that a loan exhibition of pictures from local collectors was held November 1914 – January 1915, but I have found no press notices at all for this.

42. Free Library Committee Report 1916 (Dundee Central Library, Local History Centre).

43. Fine Art Exhibition catalogue 1921 (Dundee Central Library, Local History Centre).

44. Robertson seems to have insisted on anonymity for this sale – his collection was combined with that of the late Samuel Low of Monifieth and advertised as "Two very valuable cabinets of modern paintings, including that belonging to the late S M Low, Esq" (*The Scotsman* 6/1/1923).

45. It is last listed in the Dundee Directories in 1954-5.

46. Frances Fowle, 'Pioneers of Taste: Collecting in Dundee in the 1920s', *Journal of the Scottish Society for Art History* vol 11 (2006), p.59. Fowle's chapter (pp59-65) gives a far more detailed account of Tattersall, Justice and Boyd than I am able to do here.

47. Martin Bailey & Frances Fowle, *Van Gogh and Britain: Pioneer Collectors* (Edinburgh: National Galleries of Scotland, 2006) p.72 and Fowle, Frances, *Van Gogh's Twin, op cit* p.117. In Fowle's otherwise excellent book on Alexander Reid, Tattersall's profession is mistakenly given as dentist.

48. The painting was bought in 1935 by a later Dundee collector, Royan Middleton.

49. Transcript of a lecture by A J McNeill Reid to the Dundee Art Society (undated), held in the Scottish National Gallery of Modern Art archive.

50. The two were actually neighbours in Minto Place, Justice at no 2 and Tattersall at no 5.

51. *The Piper o`Dundee* 1/6/1892.

52. His brief obituary appears in the *Courier* 1/6/1942.

53. Details from Boyd's obituary in the *Courier* 28/7/1941.

54. Boyd's significance as a collector of Van Gogh and French Impressionism has been highlighted by the National Galleries of Scotland (thanks to research by Frances Fowle) in the exhibitions *Van Gogh and Britain* (2006) and *Impressionism and Scotland* (2008), along with their associated publications.

55. He also gifted McIntosh Patrick's portrait of Prof H Gordon Campbell, commissioned by Boyd in 1939. All are now in the University of Dundee Museum Collections.

56. The first graduate of the school, William Tattersall later lectured there and became president of the British Dental Association.

57. *The Piper o`Dundee* 19/1/1898.

58. Rettie's importance to the success of the business is borne out by Stewart Howe in *William Low & Co: A Family Business History* (Dundee: Abertay Historical Society, 2000).

59. Low rarely lent works to public exhibitions so we know little of what his collection comprised, though the *Piper* (*op cit*) claimed that it "would be considered noteworthy even in the cabinets of much older and more experienced collectors."

60. *The Piper o`Dundee* 2/1/1901.

61. Mrs Rettie also gifted three pieces of Monart glass for display in the hospital.

62. *The Wizard of the North* 31/3/1899 describes the portrait of Mrs Rettie – she is not named, but is described as the wife of "one of our leading citizens".

63. His obituary is in the *Courier* 21/3/1922.

64. Information from the Dundee Directories and the Scotland's People website.

65. Fowle's *Van Gogh's Twin* (*op cit*) describes some of Duncan's dealing with Alexander Reid.

66. The Dundee Directories list Barclay, Osborne & Mathewson in 1880-1 then A P Mathewson & Co from 1882-3 until 1913-4.

67. My thanks to Susan Keracher of the McManus for information on his Japanese print collection.

68. His obituary is in the *Courier* 15/8/1932.

69. Hilary Horrocks (ed), *Hill of Tarvit: 100 Years* (Edinburgh: National Trust for Scotland, 2006).

70. Details from the Dundee Directories, which suggest that he retired c.1920.

71. *Dundee Advertiser* 9/3/1914.

72. Galloway's collection of etchings was singled out by A J McNeill Reid as possibly the best in Dundee in the transcript of his Dundee Art Society talk (*op cit*).

73. His obituary is in the *Courier* 12/4/1950.

74. *The Scotsman* 5/2/1923.

75. A letter to this effect is one of a number of documents about Kidd's collection now owned by journalist Norman Watson. I am very grateful to him for giving me access to these documents.

76. This document is also now owned by Watson. Using per capita GDP, this sum is the equivalent of nearly £5 million today.

77. Simpson is listed at that address in the Dundee Directories from 1886-7 until 1923-4. Young appears from 1869-70 until 1956-7, but this presumably represents two different generations. Kyd's obituary appears in the *Courier* 2/1/1931 and Lindsay's 9/1/1925. Lindsay and Simpson's collections are discussed in articles by Edward Pinnington in the *Advertiser* 8/5/1909 and 12/6/1909.

78. *The Piper o`Dundee* 26/2/1896.

79. Morris's will is available on the Scotland's People website.

80. It's not clear who made the choices of which works to acquire – Morris only specified that the trustees should choose "three gentlemen known as Judges of Pictures".

81. Undated cutting (probably *Evening Telegraph* 19/8/1903) from the first volume of Stewart Carmichael's scrapbooks p125 (Dundee City Archives).

82. Carmichael, 'Fifty Years', *op cit*.

83. *Dundee Courier* 8/11/1907.

84. Information from A H Millar, *Jubilee of the Albert Institute 1867-1917* (Dundee: John Durham & Son, 1917); *Dundee City Art Gallery Catalogue of the Permanent Collection of Paintings, Drawings and Sculpture* (Dundee: Corporation of Dundee Museums & Art Galleries Department, 1973) and Anna Robertson and Clara Young's introduction to *Consider the Lilies: Scottish Painting 1910-1980 from the Collection of the City of Dundee* (Dundee: Dundee City Council Leisure & Communties Department, 2006).

85. Millar (*ibid*).

86. The Lely and Kneller are now catalogued as "studio of" and "follower of" respectively.

87. My thanks to Susan Keracher of the McManus for showing me the relevant parts of Ower's will.

88. Free Library Committee Report 1913 (Dundee Central Library, Local History Centre). The description had been used before, for example in the *Evening Telegraph* 20/10/1909.

89. The Leng commission was deemed of sufficient importance to be mentioned in the Court Circular in *The Times* 12/8/1901.

90. *Evening Telegraph* 25/3/1909.

91. W H Blyth Martin, 'Roll of Burgesses and Portraits' in Paton & Millar, *BA Handbook, op cit*, p521.

92. Quoted in *The City Echo* May 1911.

93. *Dundee Courier* 4/3/1911 and *BA Handbook, op cit*, p521.

94. *BA Handbook, op cit*, p520. Blyth Martin would be honoured with his own presentation portrait (by Henry Wright Kerr) in 1924.

95. A H Millar, *Illustrated Catalogue of the Pictures in the Dundee Corporation Collection* (Dundee: Corporation Art Galleries, 1926).

96. Fine Art Exhibition catalogue 1924 (Dundee Central Library, Local History Centre).

97. Fimister ran a large plumbing and heating engineering business based in South Tay Street.

98. Unidentified cutting (possibly *Glasgow Evening News*) in the newspaper cuttings book 1924 held in Dundee Central Library, Local History Centre.

99. *Evening Telegraph* 25/8/1926.

INDEX

Aberdeen 27, 29, 41, 42, 44-45, 89, 94, 111, 115-116, 131, 163, 192, 208, 214, 220, 222
Académie Colarossi 67, 216
Académie Delacluse 216
Académie Julian 109-110, 139, 141, 220
Adam, Patrick William 20
Adams, William 93
Adamson, Alexander 99
Adamson, Charles 98-99, 183, 187, 189
Adamson, David Comba 95-96, 129, 200
Adamson, Ernest Stanley – see Stanlaws, Penhryn
Adamson, Ewart 218
Adamson, Howard – see Somerville, Howard
Adamson, James 139
Adamson, Mabel 140, 218
Adamson, Sydney 139-140, 143
Adamson, Winifred 218
Adventure 141
Albert Institute (see also Victoria Art Galleries) 5-10, 13, 16, 18-19, 26-28, 32, 36-38, 42-47, 60, 79, 109, 111, 116, 167, 170-171, 173-177, 182, 189, 192-193, 197, 218
Alexander, Edwin 200
Alexander, Robert 31, 177
Alexander, William 27, 174
Allan, Robert T M 147, 159
Allan-Fraser, Patrick 16
Anderson, David 144
Anderson, D Leuchars 187
Anderson, Martin 5, 7, 30, 42, 49, 61, 97, 101, 110, 125-128, 130, 132, 157, 173-174, 187, 206, 212, 217, 222
Anderson, Robert Rowand 74, 153
Andrews, David Angelo 98, 100, 110, 115, 218
Andrews, D R 142, 218
Angelico, Fra 71
Annan, James Craig 194, 195
Antwerp Academy 51, 63, 69, 71, 95, 120-122, 127, 131, 159, 211, 216, 217
Arbroath 16, 75, 82, 100, 104, 107, 121, 131, 145, 178, 190, 194, 212, 217, 219,
Archer, James 12, 31, 38, 39, 175, 178,
Ariel 127
Armitstead, George 39
Arrott, James 92
Art, L' 177
Artistic Supply Company 140
Art Journal, The 17, 19, 223
Art Record, The 129
Art Union (Fine Art Exhibitions) – see Dundee Art Union
Art Union (Graphic Arts Association) 180-181
Auchmithie 112-113, 115, 129
Auld, Walter 137

Baird, George 147
Balfour Street School 112, 147
Ballingall, Hugh 36, 44, 60
Banks, William 185
Barclay, William 106-108
Barnhill 137, 176
Barns-Graham, Wilhelmina 145, 165
Barrie, Charles 96, 205, 207

Batchelor, Helen 175, 178, 222
Bates, Harry 45-47
Baxter, Annie M 211
Baxter, David 15, 40-41, 47, 147, 155
Baxter, Ellen 40-41
Baxter, George 161
Baxter, John Boyd 38, 160,
Baxter, Mary Ann 40-41, 44, 160, 161
Baxter, Nell (Nellie) 54-55, 57, 73-74, 76-78, 211, 223
Baxter, Rose (Rosa) 72-73, 75-79, 213, 223
Beardsley, Aubrey 55, 72
Beatts, John M 23
Beggarstaff Brothers 140
Bell, Alexander 92
Bell, James Torrington 83
Bell, John Charles 10, 12-13, 16, 31, 100, 192, 208
Bell, John Zephaniah 9, 92
Berwick-upon-Tweed 12
Beveridge, Henry 53-54, 211
Bibliothèque Nationale, Paris 111
Billy and Bunny 139, 218
Billy Bunter 139
Binrock House 19, 192, 209
Black & White 114, 129
Blackness House 9
Black Watch, The 133, 136-138, 158, 217
Blair, Elizabeth 202
Blair, J T R 79
Blair, William 112, 114
Blair, W R 145
Blairgowrie 15, 108, 109
Blommers, Bernardus Johannes 23, 193-194, 196-197, 201
Bodley, George Frederick 58-60
Bonnard, Pierre 197-200, 206
Bonvin, François 199
Botticelli, Sandro 51
Boudin, Eugène 194, 197-198, 200, 201, 206
Bouguereau, William-Adolphe 95
Bough, Sam 11, 13, 16-17, 19, 30, 100, 202, 209
Bowie, John 165
Boyd, R Just 198
Boyd, William 118, 197-201, 206, 220, 224
Brancusi, Constantin 89
Brangwyn, Frank 201
Brechin 97, 145, 212
Bremner, James 61-62, 73, 77, 113, 149-150, 174
British Association for the Advancement of Science 4, 9-11, 15-16, 23, 39, 43, 117, 160, 164, 192, 194, 197-198, 201, 206, 208
Brodie, William 42, 44
Broughty Ferry 9-10, 12-13, 14, 59-61, 81, 83, 92, 94, 100-101, 146-147, 161, 202, 219, 224
Brown, Alex C 137
Brown, David Millar 121
Brown, Gerard Baldwin 44, 62, 148, 161, 174
Brown, James Michael 27, 95, 130
Brown, Thomas Austen 201
Browne, Gordon 82
Browne, Hablot K (aka Phiz) 30
Browne, Tom 134
Brownlee, William 40, 42-44

Bruce, Stewart 197
Bruce, William Speirs 171
Bruegel, Pieter 10, 16
Brussels 22, 63, 66
Bryson, William 27
Buik, Thomas 93
Buist, Alexander Jefferson 37
Burnett, Thomas 36
Burne-Jones, Edward 58-60, 83
Burn-Murdoch, William Gordon 9, 52-53, 95, 99, 170-171, 221
Burns, Robert (artist) 55, 57, 61
Burns, Robert (poet) 42-44, 84, 89, 97
Burns & Harris 131
Burt, Elizabeth 72-78, 223
Burton, Mary Hill 54
Bystander, The 139

Cadell, Francis Campbell Boileau 118, 200
Cadenhead, James 55, 82, 177, 184, 222
Cadzow, James 157, 159, 183, 214
Caird, James Key 30-31, 105, 123, 217
Caird Hall 91, 123
Cairns, John 12, 100
Cairns, Robert D 144-145
Cameron, David Young 177, 185, 201, 202
Cameron, Duncan 102, 106
Cameron, Hugh 12, 14, 16-17, 20, 27, 34, 209
Cameron, Kate 186
Campbell, Alexander 96
Camperdown, Earl of 9
Cappon, Jane 95
Cappon, Thomas Martin 95-96, 143, 153, 173
Caracciolo, Giovanni Battista (Battistello) 36
Cargill, Thomas 16, 209
Carmichael, George B 180
Carmichael, James 41, 43
Carmichael, Marion 79, 91, 177, 182, 189, 221
Carmichael, Peter 208, 215
Carmichael, Stewart 4-7, 47, 63-69, 71-73, 76-79, 82-85, 87, 89-91, 94-99, 109-111, 116, 118, 120-121, 143, 147, 152-153, 160-162, 168, 173, 175-187, 189, 191, 193-194, 201-202, 206, 208, 212, 214, 220, 222
Carnegie, Andrew 95, 98, 113, 184, 192
Carnelley, Thomas 97, 167, 169, 170
Carnoustie 16, 51-52, 107, 130, 170, 200
Carracci, Annibale 15
Carrie, James 135, 190
Cassell's Magazine 129
Cassie, James 11, 107-108
Castle Street studios 4, 67, 78, 98, 172, 178, 184, 208, 222
Caw, James Lewis 208
Cazin, Jean Charles 199
Celtic Annual, The 62, 82-83, 88, 95, 98, 107, 109, 117, 131,
Central Fine Art Gallery 75, 109, 115,
Central Reading Rooms, Barrack Street 45, 82, 98
Central School of Art 63, 147,
Chalmers, George Paul 11, 13-14, 16, 29, 32, 192, 204, 208, 223
Chapman & Son 12
Chateau du Donjon 74
Cheyne, Edith 155, 157, 220

Chicago 36, 74-75, 79, 97, 111, 218
Christie, James 61
Christie, James Elder 84
Chums 129
Churchill, Winston 88, 134, 135, 207
Cimabue 71
City Assembly Rooms 113
City Echo, The 6, 82, 87, 99, 100, 121, 135-136, 149, 152, 155, 172, 185-187, 189, 190, 193, 196, 212
Claesz, Pieter 33
Clark, David 20, 26, 130-131, 178
Clarke, John G 148
Clepington Parish Church 59
Cole, Henry 142, 143
Coleridge, Gilbert 165
Collins, Hugh 6, 37, 92-94, 215
Collins, Janet (Jennett) 94
Congleton, M Hart 73
Connaught, Duke of 47
Constable, John 19, 23, 103, 201
Constant, Benjamin 95
Constitution House Institution 147, 223
Cook, Theodore 165
Cooper, Francis 156
Cope, Arthur Stockdale 39
Corot, Jean-Baptiste Camille 29, 162, 201
Coupar, Nellie 135,157, 158
Courbet, Gustave 199
Coutts, Frank 52, 134, 137, 143, 157, 158, 185, 190
Cowie, Robert 108, 142, 172, 222
Cowper, Max 30, 62, 128-129, 131, 140, 145, 174, 176-178, 196, 207, 217, 222
Cox, Edward (of Cardean) 30,
Cox, James 32, 43
Cox, J D 34
Crabbe, John C 15, 23, 117
Crane, Walter 85, 158, 220
Crawford, Edmund Thornton 12, 15, 100
Crawford, Hugh Adam 156
Crawhall, Joseph 193, 196, 224
Crichton, John 9
Crighton, James 139, 218
Crone, Robert 32-33
Croome, Mr 142
Crowley, Aleister 141
Crowquill – see Lee, Joseph
Cruickshank, George 50
Cumming, Gershom Gourlay 100-101
Cunningham, Margaret 73, 75, 76
Curr, Robert 23, 209
Curr & Dewar 23
Cursiter, Stanley 165, 185
Cynicus – see Anderson, Martin

Dalgleish, William Ogilvy 15-16, 27, 34, 38-39, 98, 100, 155, 192, 194, 202, 206
Dalhousie, 13th Earl of 16, 18, 39, 43
Dalhousie, 14th Earl of 194, 195
Dali, Salvador 165
Davids, Mary 177
Davidson, Edward M 178, 213
Davidson, George Dutch 4-7, 68-78, 95, 121-122, 143, 164, 178, 180, 181, 185, 208, 213, 220

Davidson, William Armstrong 158, 213
Davidson, T M 52, 82
Dawson, David (jute merchant) 110
Dawson, David (teacher) 175
D C Thomson & Co Ltd 125, 128, 129, 132-134, 136, 137, 139, 141, 157, 210, 218
de Bock, Théophile 196
de Chavannes, Puvis 51
de Hondecoeter, Gillis 33
de Hondecoeter, Melchior 33
de Hoog, Bernard 196
de Laszlo, Philip 197, 201
del Piombo, Sebastiano 15
de Segonzac, André Dunoyer 199, 206
Dempster, George 37
Dewar, David 94, 204
Dewar, William 23, 209
Dickie, William Bruce 121, 194, 202
Dilettante, The 130
Dollar 147, 220
Don, Alexander 162-163
Don, William 205, 207
Donn, Robert 73, 151, 183, 191
Douglas, Anna 110, 186-187, 223
Douglas, James 24, 109-110, 127, 153, 186-187, 189
Douglas, R Smeaton 187
Douglas, William Fettes 11-12, 21, 36, 192
Dow, Thomas Millie 224
Dowell's Ltd 12, 13, 30, 197-198, 201
Doyle, Arthur Conan 139
Drummond, Alexander 43, 60, 107, 214
Drummond, Henry 214
Dudhope Castle 220
Dudhope Museum 116
du Maurier, George 132
Dunbar, Arthur A 153
Duncan, Alexander, 197, 199-200, 206, 224
Duncan, Charles 175
Duncan, David 212
Duncan, George 33-34, 210
Duncan, Admiral Viscount (of Camperdown) 47, 211
Duncan, James (of Jordanstone) 5, 142, 154-156, 163, 184, 220
Duncan, John 1, 4, 7, 23, 32, 34, 36, 45, 47-58, 61-64, 66-69, 71-83, 85, 90, 99, 103, 105-106, 118, 120, 122-123, 126-127, 130-131, 143-145, 147, 149, 164, 168, 173-175, 178, 185, 191-192, 202, 206, 208, 211-214, 217, 221
Duncan, Marjorie 103
Dundee Advertiser, The (artists working on) 88, 101, 125, 127-128, 130, 131, 133, 135, 137, 139
Dundee Amateur Art Association 129, 172
Dundee & East of Scotland Photographic Association 185
Dundee Antarctic Expedition 170-171
Dundee Art Club 4, 7, 15, 50-51, 61, 63, 67, 87, 97, 103, 107-108, 115, 127-128, 133, 171-175, 177, 212, 222
Dundee Art Society (see also Graphic Arts Association) 5, 18, 29, 45, 48, 72, 78-79, 81-83, 85, 89, 91, 95, 97-98, 105, 108, 110, 116-118, 121-122, 130, 134, 136, 143, 145, 155, 159, 163-164, 180-187, 189-190, 193-194, 198-199, 213, 215, 217, 220
Dundee Art Students' Club (see also Dundee

School of Art Club) 190
Dundee Art Union 16, 21-22, 26-27, 31-32, 180
Dundee Auction Rooms 12, 31, 109, 110, 117
Dundee Burns Club 43
Dundee Celtic Club 59, 212
Dundee Chamber of Commerce 15, 17, 29, 149
Dundee Courier, The (artists working on) 125, 128-129, 133-134, 137, 139
Dundee Dental Hospital & School 199-200, 202
Dundee Educational Trust 220
Dundee Exhibitions of Industry 60-61, 97, 212
Dundee Fine Art Exhibitions 4-7, 12, 14-24, 26-34, 36, 38, 44, 50-51, 54, 60-61, 63, 66-67, 81, 87, 93-95, 97-98, 100-101, 103, 106-108, 110-111, 115-116, 118, 128-131, 133, 139, 143-147, 155, 157, 160, 171, 173, 175, 177, 180-181, 184-186, 192-201, 206-207, 211-212, 214, 217, 219
Dundee Free Press 71
Dundee from the Tramcars 136
Dundee Gaelic Musical Association 59, 67, 91
Dundee Graphic Arts Association – see Graphic Arts Association
Dundee Highland Society 59, 82, 87, 90-91
Dundee Institute of Architecture, Science & Art 54, 174-175, 177, 185, 222
Dundee Institution 147
Dundee Liberal Association 84
Dundee Master Painters Association 150
Dundee Naturalists' Society 48
Dundee Orchestral Society 185
Dundee Public Baths 83, 101
Dundee Rep Theatre 155
Dundee Royal Infirmary 9, 15-17, 19, 34, 38, 82, 123, 163, 167, 183, 199, 204, 206
Dundee School Board 86, 145, 147, 151, 153, 183
Dundee School of Art (High School) 7, 9, 21, 49, 61, 63, 68, 73, 87, 103, 106-107, 120, 134, 139, 142-147, 149-150, 163-164, 170, 211-212, 216, 219, 222
Dundee School of Art Club 157-158, 190-191
Dundee Social Union 86, 167, 170, 221
Dundee Technical Institute / Technical College & School of Art 5, 15, 48, 58, 62-63, 73, 76-77, 97, 105, 134, 135, 140, 146-159, 161-163, 167, 176, 185, 190-191, 204
Dundee Town Council 6, 16, 19, 26-27, 32-33, 37-38, 42, 44, 46-47, 60, 78, 87, 105, 110, 120, 142, 153, 184, 204, 210,
Dundee Training College 151, 156, 158, 163, 190, 218, 220
Dunfermline 53, 112, 159
Dunn, Thomas Delgaty 62-63, 76, 82, 145, 148-153, 155-156, 158-159, 162-163, 166-167, 185, 190-191, 220
Dürer, Albrecht 165
Düsseldorf 51, 57, 127, 211

East of Scotland Institution 147
Eaton, Robert C 73
Ecole des Beaux Arts 95
Edinburgh 4, 12-15, 19, 22, 30, 36-37, 41-45, 48, 51-55, 57-58, 61-62, 74-75, 78-80, 82-83, 85, 89, 92, 94-95, 97, 99, 102, 106-111, 114, 116-117, 121-123, 129-130, 139, 145, 148-149, 155, 159, 161, 164, 167, 170-171, 176-178, 181, 183-185, 189, 191-192, 197, 199, 201, 214, 216, 218-219, 223
Edinburgh College of Art 123, 145, 159, 219

Edinburgh Social Union 52, 167
Edward, Alfred Sanderson 36, 103, 106-107, 173, 175, 191
Edwards, David 97
Edzell 107, 17
Elmslea 12, 26, 192
English Illustrated Magazine 127
Eureka 131
Evening Telegraph, The (artists working on) 125-126, 133
Everard, P L 22
Evergreen, The 54-55, 57, 62, 72, 78, 82-83, 164, 166, 170-171, 211-212
Ewart, David Shanks 164-165
Ewen, John Taylor 78, 84, 214
Ewing, James Alfred 167

Faed, John 160
Faed, Thomas 160
Fairweather, Adam Barnet 173, 175, 177-178, 222
Fairweather, Alexander 171
Falconer, James 30-31, 209
Fantin-Latour, Henri 194, 199-201
Farquharson, David 12-13, 20-21, 37, 100
Farquharson, Joseph 202
Farquharson, Robert C 130, 173
Feathers, Peter 148
Fenwick, James 26
Fergusson, Henry Balfour 32, 38-40
Fergusson, John Duncan 118
Fergusson, William Henry 83
Fernbrae 17
Ferrier, D H 46-47
Ferry-Port-on-Craig – see Tayport
Fimister, T P 206, 224
Findlay, Andrew B 150
Findlay, David 100
Fine Art Association 83, 185, 193-194, 196, 197, 202, 222
Fleming, Leila 175, 183, 222, 223
Flint, William Russell 197
Focosi, Alessandro 17
Foggie, Christina 219
Foggie, David 4, 7, 26, 30, 47, 68-69, 73-74, 76, 79, 82, 87, 105, 111, 118, 120-124, 143, 145, 152-153, 165, 168, 178, 180-187, 191, 193-194, 196, 200, 202, 213-214, 216-217, 219
Foggie, James 120
Foggie, James K 26, 121-122
Foggie, Margaret 121-123
Forfar 79, 84, 96, 101, 107, 183, 196, 219
Forrest, Alfred 165
Fra Lippo Lippi 157-158, 190
Fraser, Alex 23, 173
Fraser, Alexander 11-13, 15, 17, 20, 34, 197, 204, 208-209
Fraser, James 133
Fraser, John M (of Invermay) 193
Fraser, John Simpson 31, 104, 107
Fraser, Simon G 115-116
Fraser's Art Saloon 173
Frazer, William Miller 178
Free Library Committees 14, 27, 32-34, 36-37, 39, 105, 108, 116, 182, 189, 193-194, 201, 223

Freeth, Hubert 165
Friarton Grove 73-74
Friesz, Achille-Émile Othon 206
Fulton, Angus 146
Fun 129, 139
Furniss, Harry 30, 132, 217
Fyfe, William 75, 113, 115

Gabo, Naum 165
Gahan, George Wilkie 49, 62, 121, 128-129, 132-133, 183-185, 189
Gahan, James 132
Gainsborough, Thomas 132, 201
Galloway, David 194, 201, 224
Gardiner, Marion 134
Garrido, Eduardo 17-18
Gear, William 145
Geddes, Patrick 4, 7, 48-49, 51-55, 57-58, 61-64, 68, 73-75, 78-80, 82-85, 91, 99, 122, 127, 163-164, 166-168, 170-171, 191, 211-212, 220-222
Gibb, William 101-103, 215
Gibson, James S 146-147
Gibson, Robert 146, 150, 153, 155
Gibson, William 202
Gilfillan, George 92, 97, 112, 114
Gill, Ernest 155, 157-158, 220
Gillies, William 145-147
Giotto 9
Gladstone, William 21-22, 84, 175
Glasgow 4, 19, 27, 29, 31, 45, 53, 57, 62-63, 68, 69, 76, 79, 87, 95, 98, 101, 109, 111-112, 115, 117, 125-126, 138, 140, 144, 155, 158, 161, 177, 181, 189-194, 196-197, 199-200, 205, 213, 217
Glasgow School of Art 53, 62, 95, 125, 145, 151, 153, 155, 161, 190, 213, 216, 219, 220, 222-224
Gonnella, Allesio 97
Gonnella, Giuseppe 51, 97, 150, 173-175, 222
Gonnella, Joseph 97
Gonnella, Louis 97
Goodchild, Jason 31
Goodfellow, Miss 147
Gordon, James 142
Gordon, John Watson 33-34
Gowland, John 222
Graham, David 157, 190, 220
Graham, James 52
Graham, Peter 15, 202
Graham, Tom 31, 36
Grammar Fairies, The 51-52, 120
Granny's Gossip 133
Grant, Duncan 198
Grant, Francis 16
Graphic, The 128, 134, 137, 139, 217-218
Graphic Arts Association 4-5, 7, 40, 47, 49, 51, 57, 61-64, 66-69, 71-73, 75-77, 83-89, 96-98, 102-103, 105, 107-108, 110-112, 114-117, 120-121, 127-131, 133, 139, 145, 147, 151, 155, 168, 170, 172, 174-185, 187, 189-190, 196-197, 202, 217, 219
Graphischen Künst, Die 111
Gray, David 147
Gray, David Burns 130
Gray, Effie 31
Gray, John 145, 219
Gray, John Y 147-148, 150, 219

Gray, Joseph 137-138, 201, 218
Gray, Sophy 31
Great War 89, 99, 114, 116-118, 122, 131, 136-140, 151, 158, 168, 182-183, 185-186, 190, 196, 200, 202, 217-218, 220
Greig, David Middleton 98
Greig, James 113, 131-132, 194, 217-218
Greig, James McGavin 217
Grieve, Alec 4, 7, 47, 67-69, 71-72, 74, 76, 79, 82, 85-87, 89-90, 98, 114, 116, 118, 120, 143, 153, 168, 174, 176, 178-179, 181-187, 189, 191, 193, 207, 212, 214, 222
Grieve, Christopher Murray – see MacDiarmid, Hugh
Grieve, Emma 79, 189
Grove Academy 10, 145, 159, 219
Grubb, Alexander 145, 219
Grubb, David, 219
Grubb, William Mortimer 143-147, 149-151, 159, 162-163, 170, 175, 190, 219
Guthrie, James 109, 177, 205, 207, 224

Haden, Seymour 111
Hals, Frans 23
Hamilton, Edith 73
Hamilton, James Steedman 158, 220
Hamilton, Richard 166, 221
H & F Thomson 82
Hardie, Keir 85, 87
Hardy, Marcel 167
Harmsworth London Magazine 129
Harper's Magazine 140
Harpignies, Henri-Joseph 198
Harris, Arthur 23, 181, 209
Harris & Curr / Harris & Fairweather 22-24, 31
Harris, William 38
Harris Academy 38, 48, 54, 68, 147, 151, 159, 163, 219-220
Harwood, Henry 9, 31, 36, 87, 92, 130, 172, 206
Haw Wull 138-139
Hay, George 16
Hay, Helen 53-55, 75, 211-212
Hean, Winifred E 157-158, 220
Hearst's 141
Heatherley's School of Art 135, 139
Henderson, Frank 34, 44
Henderson, Keith 165
Henderson, Nigel 166, 221
Henderson, William 153, 155
Henry, George 101, 177, 193, 197, 201, 204-205, 207, 212, 223
Hepworth, Barbara 165
Herald, James Watterston 60, 82, 143, 147, 178, 182, 210, 219
Herdman, Robert 15, 17, 38
Herdman, Robert Duddingstone 202
Herkomer's School (see also von Herkomer, Hubert) 107, 160, 210
Herremans, Lieven 63, 212
High School of Dundee (see also Dundee School of Art) 7, 15-16, 46, 52, 67, 87, 95, 97, 142, 144-147, 150-151, 153, 155, 159, 162, 184, 202, 211, 213, 219-220
Hill, David Octavius 34
Hill, Perry 152, 155, 158, 220
Hill of Tarvit 200-201
Hodgson, Edward Smith 105, 107, 116, 139,

173-174, 177, 210
Hodgson, John Evan 36
Hokusai, Katsushika 200
Holbein, Hans 10, 16
Holder, Joseph 99, 116, 204-205
Hole, William 4, 177
Holl, Frank 36
Home Industries Exhibition 61, 97, 115, 175,
Hood, George 43
Hornel, Edward Atkinson 55, 57, 95, 181, 193, 196-197, 201-202, 223
Hospitalfield House 16, 43
Hotel des Artistes 141
Hunt, William Holman 48, 50
Hunter, Colin 36, 175
Hunter, David (of Blackness) 9
Hunter, George Leslie 4, 118, 197-198, 200
Hunter, William 39, 60, 175, 204
Hunter, Mrs (of Hilton) 50-51
Husband, Agnes 85-87
Hutchison, John 36, 41, 43-44
Hutchison, Robert Gemmell 196, 201
Hutton, David 142
Hutton, James 63

Idler, The 127, 139-140, 218
Illustrated Bits 129
Illustrated London News, The 40, 128-129, 140
Imandt, Marie 98, 109
Imperial Hotel 64
Imprints 82, 121
Independent Labour Party 85-87, 122
Indiapolis 27
Industrial Exhibitions – see Dundee Exhibitions of Industry
Inglis, Allan 61-62, 212
Inglis, James 212
Invergowrie 59, 114, 159, 176
Ireland, David 77, 149-150
Irvine, James 94
Israels, Jozef 196

Jack, Margaret – see Foggie, Margaret
Jack, Martha (Patti) 160-161, 170
Jamieson, Ninian R 147, 150, 219
Jerome, Jerome Klapka 140,
Jerome, John P 172
J Gonnella & Co 97, 148, 164
John Leng & Co 7, 125-129, 131, 133-136, 138-139, 157, 212, 217
Johnston, Etta 48, 162, 168-171, 173, 220-221
Johnstone, William 221
Jones, John 173
Justice, Matthew 118, 198-200, 206, 208, 224
Justice, Thomas (see also Thomas Justice & Sons) 121, 198

Kandinsky, Wassily 69
Kay, Archibald 98
Keiller, Alexander 118
Keiller, John Mitchell 19-20, 26, 36, 173, 175, 192, 198
Keiller & Son 19, 131, 198, 209-210
Kelvin, Lord 27
Kennedy, John 21, 34, 142-144, 146

Kennedy, Robert A 178
Kennedy-Fraser, Marjory 80, 91, 214
Kerr, Christopher 37, 92
Kerr, Henry Wright 143, 196, 204, 219, 223, 224
Kidd, Andrew G 201, 203, 224
Kidd, William 129, 219
Kilgour, John 112
Kinloch, George 41-43, 93
Kinnaird, George, 9th Lord 9-10, 16, 43, 92
Kinnaird, Arthur, 10th Lord 38, 44
Kinnaird Hall 30, 59, 79, 137
Kinnear, James 116
Kippen, Helen – see Baxter, Nell
Kirkcaldy 7, 130, 211
Kirsty at the Cooncil 133
Klee, Paul 165
Kneller, Godfrey 202
Knight, Laura 165, 202
Kunst, Die 177
Kyd, John N 201
Kydd, William R 27
Kyle, Thomas 173
Kynoch, John Campbell 183
Kynoch, Minnie 183

Labour Leader, The 85, 127
Lady's Realm 129
Laing, Elizabeth 79
Laing, Frank 4-5, 76, 82-83, 89, 109-112, 143, 152-153, 165, 176, 184-189, 191, 193, 216
Lamb, Alexander Crawford 7, 30, 43, 101-103, 105, 112, 175, 180, 192
Lamb's Hotel 23, 30, 116, 172, 174, 176
Lamond, Margaret 156
Lamond, William Bradley 4, 82, 99, 112-115, 129, 139, 160, 174-175, 177-178, 186-187, 190-191, 193-194, 196-197, 200, 204, 210, 214
Landseer, Edwin 19, 27
Langlands, James 143, 153
la Touche, Gaston
Lauder, Harry 114
Lauder, Peter D 63, 147
Lauder, Robert Scott 34, 37, 107, 161, 223
Laurens, Jean-Paul 110
Lavery, John 101, 193, 196-197, 202, 204-205, 223
Lawrence, George 114
Lawson, Alexander 101
Lawson, Charles S 100-102
Lee, Arthur 99-101
Lee, Florence 79, 183, 223
Lee, Joseph 6-7, 81-82, 87-89, 99, 121, 133, 135-137, 146, 149, 152, 155, 157-158, 163, 168, 185-186, 190, 196, 214, 217-218, 223
Lees, Mrs J G 73
Lefebvre, Jules Joseph 220
Leighton, Frederic 14, 17, 193
Lely, Peter 16, 202
Leng, John 10, 41, 87, 99, 125, 175, 204, 218
Leonardo da Vinci 10, 167
Lépine, Stanislas 194, 197, 206
Le Sidaner, Henri 194
Leslie, James 157-158, 190
Leslie-Jamieson, George 44

Leslie, Ower & Allan 134
Leslie's Weekly 140
Lesser, Wolfe 22, 24
Lewis, Wyndham 89
Liddle, Grindlay 23-24, 103, 107, 157
Life 140
Lindsay, James Bowman 44
Lindsay, R M 192, 201
Lindsay, William 92
Lindsay & Scott 60
Lindsay Street Hall 172
Littlejohn, Mrs E 127, 133
Liverpool 7, 22, 75, 163, 176
Livingstone, Tom 132-133, 218
Lochee 31, 61, 115, 128, 136, 147, 180
Lochee Science & Art School 115, 147, 150
Lockhart, William Ewart 19, 36, 204
London 4, 7, 10, 12, 19-20, 22-23, 27, 36, 39-40, 44-45, 51-52, 55, 59, 61, 63-64, 66-67, 69, 75, 78, 85, 87, 89, 92, 94-96, 98, 103, 106-107, 110, 113-114, 117, 121, 125, 127-132, 135, 137-141, 143-144, 148, 151, 166-167, 174, 177, 183-184, 191-192, 198, 201-202, 218, 220-221
Longair, William 79, 204, 206
Longair, Mrs 79
Longbow, The 129, 139
Longforgan Parish Church 61
Lorimer, John Henry 177
Lorimer, Robert 83, 200, 214
Lorne, Marquis of 27, 60
Low, H G 7, 135
Low, James F 17
Low, Samuel M 224
Low, William 84, 96, 185, 199-200
Lowdon, E M 175-177, 183, 222
Lowson, Leonard 134-135, 143
Lowson, Miss 147
Ludgate Monthly, The 131
Luke, John L 51, 215, 217
Lumsden, John S 150-151, 153, 157, 220

'Mac' 132
McCallum, Duncan 132
McCulloch, Horatio 15, 20, 37, 204
MacDiarmid, Hugh 40, 89-90, 196, 214
Macdonald, Duncan (Bailie) 40, 145
Macdonald, Duncan (curator) 213
Macdonald, Henry 16-17, 209
MacDonald, Ramsay 127, 201
Macdonald, William 223
Macdougald, George 98, 174
McElwee, Bessie 79
McEwan's Art Saloon 108
McFarland, William 93, 97
MacGillivray, Angus 83, 90, 185
McGillivray, George 36, 92, 100-101, 215
MacGillivray, James Pittendrigh 177
McGonagall, William 44, 112, 130, 210
McGrady, Henry 23, 39-40, 44-45, 51, 193, 223
McGregor, Robert 185
Macgregor, William York 177
McInroy, John 144
Macintyre, Edith 180, 183, 186, 222
Mackay, J Abrach 59

Makay, John Yule 161-162

Mackay, R Fenton 174

Mackay, Robert F 50, 103, 127

McKay, William Darling 4, 13, 31, 175, 177, 185, 202

Mackenzie, David (architect) 16

Mackenzie, David (artist) 32

Mackie, Anne 54-55

Mackie, Charles 13, 52-55, 82

Mackintosh, Charles Rennie 158

McLaren, David 150

MacLaren, James 42, 174

Maclauchlan, John 13, 18, 22, 26, 30-31, 33, 37, 44-45, 84, 107, 111-112, 116, 170, 174, 176, 192, 209

McLean, James A 23, 30, 223

McLeod, Dan 137

Macleod, Fiona – see Sharp, William

MacLeod, Malcolm C 81-82, 87

McMann, William 133, 138, 185

Macnee, Daniel 21, 38

Macrae, Mary 48

MacTaggart, William 145

McTaggart, William 11-17, 27, 34, 36, 39-40, 112, 175, 184, 192, 194-201, 206, 208, 223

MacWhirter, John 15-17, 34

Magazine of Art, The 111, 127

Magnet, The 139

Malcolm, George 146, 148-150, 155, 159, 219

Malloch, James 163, 167

Manchester 30, 41, 96, 162, 192, 209

Marchand, Jean 198-199, 206

Maris, James 13, 196

Marryat, Emma 123, 217

Martin, Thomas Carlaw 204

Martin, William Henry Blyth 39, 40, 204-205, 224

Mason, Marion 54

Mathers' Hotel 172

Mathew, James P 129-130, 132

Mathewson, Alexander 95, 175, 204

Mathewson, Arthur P 185, 194, 200-201, 224

Mathieson, James Muir 217

Matisse, Henri 7, 199, 201, 206

Matthew, Barbara 73

Maxwell, Charles Chalmers 32-33, 94, 107, 210

Maxwell, John 145

Meal-Poke, The 68, 82, 95, 166

Meek, Jane F 75

Meisonier, Ernest 17

Melville, Arthur 159, 181, 194, 223

Melvin, James 175

Methven & Simpson 51, 60

Metropolitan 141

Michie, James Coutts 177

Middleton, Royan 224

Middleton, William 219

Millais, John Everett 14-15, 19, 31, 36-37, 202

Millar, Alexander Hastie 6, 17, 33, 37, 71-72, 84, 96, 101, 167, 176, 178, 193-194, 197, 206, 208, 224

Millar, Robins 118, 206

Millet, Jean François 194, 198

Mills, Charles S 5, 76, 174, 176, 178, 181, 185

Mills, J D 180

Miln, Thomas Weston 33

Milne, John Maclauchlan 105, 116-120, 183, 186, 192, 198-199, 202, 206, 214

Milne, Joseph 24, 116-117, 119, 19-192, 216

Milne, Louise R 157-158, 220

Milne, William Watt 117

Mitchell, Charles Louis 39-40, 94-95, 147, 153, 160-161, 177-178, 180, 182-183, 186-187, 189, 193-194, 204, 215, 221

Mitchell, Edgar 178

Mitchell, Hutton 139

Mitchell, Meta 134, 190

Moderne Graphik, Die 112

Moholy-Nagy, Laszlo 165

Mollinger, Gerrit Alexander 13, 29, 208

Moncur, Alexander Hay 38

Monet, Claude 194, 199-200, 206

Montgomery, George 133, 136

Moon, Annie 73, 75, 77, 181

Moon, Mrs 76

Moore, Henry 165

Moorhead, Ethel 88-89, 214

More, Jacob 32

Morgan, John 93

Morgan Academy 115, 145, 147, 151, 159, 190, 211, 219, 221, 223

Morland, George 202

Morris, John 201-202, 224

Morris, Phil 34

Morris, William 52, 57-60, 83, 85, 127

Morrocco. Alberto 209

Morton, Alfred Elijah 132, 138-139

Moyes, John McQueen 151-152, 155, 220

Mucha, Alfons 88

Mudie, Robert 87, 214

Munch, Edvard 69

Munnings, Alfred James 201

Murray, David 18, 36-37

Murray, David Scott 144-145, 155, 159, 162, 190-191, 220-221

Murray, Thomas (see also Thomas Murray & Son) 26, 93

My Weekly 134

Napier-Brown, Meta G 79

Nasmyth, Alexander 9, 15, 100

National Art Training Schools – see South Kensington

National Competition – see South Kensington

National Portrait Society 140

Neilson, Alexander 61, 97, 173-175, 222

Newbery, Fra 53, 57, 62

Newcastle 132, 166

Newport 78, 96, 118, 161, 171, 189, 217, 223

Newtyle 112

Nicholson, Ben 166

Nicol, Erskine 13, 15, 209

Nicoll, Agnes 134, 190

Nicoll, Annie 157-158

Nicoll, James 52

Nicoll, Thomas 94

Noble, James Campbell 75, 109, 177, 180

North, Marianne 170

North East of Scotland Art Teachers' Association 155, 185, 190

Norwell, William 61, 73, 84

Ogilvie, George 150

Ogilvie, James 23

Ogilvy, John 38, 93

Old Dundee Exhibition 29-30, 92, 94, 100-103

Old Edinburgh School of Art 53-54, 57-58, 80, 211-212

Oliphant, Helen 88

Olnick 215

Orchar, James Guthrie 10, 13-17, 19, 21-22, 26-27, 31-32, 34-36, 39, 43, 45, 111, 116, 170, 173, 175, 177, 180, 192, 208, 210

Orchar Gallery 13, 118, 222

Orchardson, William Quiller 11-12, 14, 18-20, 27, 30, 37, 38-40, 193, 202, 204

Orpen, William 204

Ouless, Walter William 204, 206

Our Special Artist 21, 44, 129

Ower, Charles 110, 116, 153, 173-174, 192, 202

Paisley, George William 122, 217

Pall Mall Budget 127, 131

Pall Mall Magazine 129, 140

Paolozzi, Eduardo 166, 221

Paris 4, 14, 20, 50-51, 61, 67, 75, 86, 88-89, 92, 95-96, 109-112, 118-119, 121, 139-141, 160, 165, 175, 183-184, 194, 198, 213

Parker, Francis Wayland 74, 79-80

Pasmore, Victor 166, 221

Paterson, Andrew Melville 162-163, 170

Paterson, Charles 194

Paterson, Emily 186

Paterson, James (Broughty Ferry artist) 101

Paterson, James (Glasgow artist) 177

Paton, Joseph Noel 12-13, 24, 30, 109, 201

Patrick, James McIntosh 145, 206, 219, 224

Patterson, George Malcolm 139, 218

Paul, George Brodie 74, 96

Paul, Philip Reid 151, 220

Peacock, W Lawson 23

Pearson's Magazine 140

Peddie, George Salmond 48, 130, 157, 185

Penny Illustrated Paper 131

Penny Pictorial Magazine 129, 139

People's Journal, The (artists working on) 88, 125-126, 130, 133-138, 181, 184, 196, 212

Peploe, Samuel John 118, 186, 194, 197, 200

Perigal, Arthur 100

Perth 18-19, 48, 78, 88, 91, 113, 145, 147, 155, 178, 201, 220

Peterson, William 44

Petrie, Tom 150, 157

Pettie, John 4, 12, 14, 16, 31, 35-36, 38, 139, 175, 181, 210

Peyton, William W 60

Phillip, John 9, 15, 17, 19-20

Phillips, Charles Gustav Louis 61, 84, 103, 105, 115-116, 127, 143-144, 147, 160, 173, 175, 177-179, 181-183, 185, 187, 190, 202, 205, 222

Picabia, Francis 89

Picasso, Pablo 166

Pick-Me-Up 129, 131, 139, 217

Pinnington, Edward 13, 37, 40, 44, 94, 117, 192, 208-209, 223-224

Piper o' Dundee, The (artists working on) 7, 15,

20-21, 26, 29, 73-74, 95, 128-132, 134-135, 139-140, 172, 175, 177, 179-180, 212
Pitreavie Castle 54
Plenderleith, Robert J 159, 191
Pollock, Jackson 166
Pollock, John Francis 130, 175, 178, 217, 222
Post Sunday Special, The 139
Poussin-Dughet, Gaspard 33
Private Smiler 138
Pryde, Thomas 73, 77, 150
Public Seminaries – see High School of Dundee
Punch 129-130, 132, 134, 139-140
Purvis, John Milne 105, 152-153, 155, 157-159, 186, 190, 201, 220

Queen's Hotel 14, 79, 81, 185
Queen Victoria 19, 24, 26-27, 36, 45-47, 60, 107, 127
Queen Victoria Print & Picture Shop – see Robert Scott's Fine Art Saloon
Quill & Quaver Club 174, 222
Quiver, The 129

Raeburn, Henry 9, 19, 94, 132, 194, 201
Rambler, The 129
Ramsay, Allan (Edinburgh painter) 201
Ramsay, Allan (Edzell painter) 24, 60, 104, 107, 143, 173, 178
Ramsay, James 74-75
Ramsay, John 192, 223
Ramsay Garden, Edinburgh 53-54, 56-57
Raphael 9, 51
Read, Herbert 165-166
Read, Katherine 92
Redgrave, Richard 143
Red Letter, The 134
Red Magazine, The 140
Reid, Alexander 197-198, 200
Reid, Edward Waymouth 163
Reid, George 27, 29, 38, 154, 177, 181, 204
Reid, George Ogilvy 15
Reid, James Eadie 61, 131, 163, 212
Reid, John Robertson 202, 205
Reid, Robert Peyton 38
Rembrandt van Rijn 9, 111, 162
Rettie, Annie 199, 224
Rettie, William 96, 194, 197, 199-200, 202, 224
Revel, John Daniel 105, 151, 183, 185, 190
Revue Moderne, La 105
Reynolds, Joshua 16
Rhind, John 97
Ribera, Jusepe 36
Richards, Frank 139
Richardson, Alex 148-149, 219
Richmond, William Blake 61
Ritchie, Alexander Penrose Forbes 131, 143, 217
Ritchie, William 10, 12-13, 16, 26, 43, 192, 217
Rivers, Elizabeth 165
Roberts, David 9
Robert Scott's Fine Art Galleries 24-26, 57, 96, 110-112, 129, 137, 140
Robertson, James 150
Robertson, J C 27

Robertson, John Murray 62, 148
Robertson, John 20, 194, 196-198, 201, 204, 206, 224
Robertson, John (of Elmslea) 26-27, 34, 36, 45, 84, 94, 175, 180, 192, 208, 209
Robertson, Thomas S 9-10, 13, 15-16, 20-21, 27, 32, 92, 107-108, 111, 173-174, 192, 194, 208
Robertson, W Brown 36, 192
Robertson, William 9, 13-14, 16, 21, 36, 38, 192, 209
Robertson & Bruce 197, 199
Roche, Alexander 98, 177, 181
Rodin, Auguste 199
Rollo, Jean C 134-135, 157
Rombouts, Salomon 33
Romney, George 16
Rosebank Parish Church 15, 82, 84
Ross, Tom 88, 105, 133, 135, 150, 157, 180, 184-185, 190
Rossetti, Dante Gabriel 68, 72
Rothenstein, William 165
Rough, George 38
Rover, The 141
Royal Academy 19, 27, 36, 39, 45, 50, 67, 93, 95, 98, 107-109, 113, 116, 140, 143, 155, 159-160, 202
Royal College of Art 146, 151, 220
Royal Scottish Academy 11-12, 14, 16, 21, 31, 34, 38, 50, 57, 68, 75, 81, 87-88, 91-92, 105, 107-110, 112, 114-118, 121, 123, 125, 129-130, 140, 143, 149, 151, 155, 159-160, 173, 176, 180, 184-185, 191, 205, 211, 223
Royal Scottish Society of Painters in Watercolour 31, 110, 121, 145, 155, 191, 222
Royal Society of British Artists 107, 114, 191
Royal Society of Painter-Etchers 111
Royal Society of Portrait Painters 140
Royds, Mabel 186
Rubens, Peter Paul 9-10, 16, 51
Rushworth, George 137
Ruskin, John 31, 60, 96
Russell, James 95-96, 129-130, 135, 141, 172

St Andrews 54, 78-79, 109, 125, 139, 150, 160, 165, 196, 202
St Andrew's Roman Catholic Chapel (later Cathedral) 60
St John's Cross Church 82
St John's Free Church 61
St John the Baptist Episcopal Church 61, 155
St Joseph's Roman Catholic Church 61
St Luke's Free Church, Broughty Ferry 60-61
St Luke's Parish Church, Lochee 61
St Mary's (Dundee Parish) Church 60
St Mary's Episcopal Church, Broughty Ferry 81, 83
St Paul's Episcopal Church (later Cathedral) 59
St Paul's Magazine 131
St Rule's Parish Church, Monifieth 60
St Salvador's Episcopal Church 58-59
St Stephen's Church, Broughty Ferry 58, 60
Sargent, John Singer 40, 194-195, 204
Saturday Evening Post, The 141
Saunders, Margaret 42
Schotz, Benno 199-201
Science & Art Department – see South Kensington

Scott, George Gilbert 9, 16, 59, 184
Scott, Mrs John C 51
Scott, Patrick 92
Scott, Richard 202
Scott, Robert (see also Robert Scott's Fine Art Saloon) 24, 26, 85, 110, 116, 148
Scott, Ruby 134, 137, 157, 190
Scott, Tom 109
Scott, Walter 41, 43-44, 52, 54
Scott, William A (see also William A Scott's Fine Art Gallery) 23-24, 215
Scott's Stationery Warehouse 109
Scottish Art Teachers' Association 152, 155, 159, 190
Scottish Colourists 4, 81, 118, 187, 194, 197, 199, 202, 206
Scottish Education Department 144, 150-151, 153, 155, 158-159, 161, 190
Scottish Gallery 189
Scottish Guild of Handicraft 219
Scottish Home Arts & Industries Association 61
Scottish Home Rule Association 89
Scottish Modern Arts Association 185
Scottish National Pageant 79
Scottish National Party – see National Party of Scotland
Scottish Patriot, The 63, 84
Scottish Society of Art Workers 57
Scrymgeour, George 130, 132, 141
Seafield House 10-11
Seaton, William 174
Sellar, Charles A 196
Sellar, Mrs 52
Sellar, R J B 135
Sellars, David Ramsay 87, 143, 174, 178, 180, 184, 214
Sérusier, Paul 55
Seurat, Georges 198, 206
Sharp, Beatrice
Sharp, Frederick 200-201
Sharp, Hugh 200
Sharp, John 43, 201
Sharp, William 54-55, 69, 74
Shoodlue 93
Simon, Lucien 206
Simpson, George Buchan 10-13, 15-17, 19, 22, 34, 94, 100, 192, 208
Simpson, John 12, 192, 201, 224
Simson, David 92
Simson, George 92
Simson, William 92
Sinclair, Emma 76-78, 81, 178, 183
Sinclair, Lily 78, 213
Sisley, Alfred 199-200, 206
Sketchy Bits 131
Slade School of Fine Art 137, 166, 218
Slezer, John 100
Sluitor, Willy 196
Small, David 100-102, 135, 209, 215
Smart, John 12, 36, 175
Smieton, Mrs 209
Smieton, David 209
Smieton, John More 52
Smieton, Thomas 16, 192, 209
Smith, Alexander 222

Smith, David 175

Smith, Edwin J 5, 180, 183, 185-186, 194, 222

Smith, Harry 150

Smith, James Mackie 159, 190, 220

Smith, John Campbell 39-40, 94, 180

Smith, Joseph 150

Smith, Joseph Calder 105, 120, 185, 190

Smith, William Ryle 146-147, 150, 153, 155, 159, 190, 219-220

Snell, James Herbert 18, 36

Society of Illustrators 140

Society of Portrait Painters 95

Society of Scottish Artists 36, 111, 117, 121, 155, 180, 191

Solomon, Solomon Joseph 157, 204, 206

Somerville, Howard 139-140

Soutar, Charles G 180, 194, 197

South Kensington 9, 16, 44, 63, 78, 140, 142-151, 158, 160, 190, 219

Spence, Alexander 197, 204

Spence, Alexander Blair 10, 14-15, 20-22, 32, 94, 192

Spence, Lewis 214

Spencer, Stanley 137

Spindler, James Gustavus H 106, 108-109, 147, 153, 173-176, 178

Spindler, Jane 106, 108-109, 172-173, 202

Stanlaws, Penrhyn 139-141, 218

Steell, Gourlay 15

Steell, John 40-44, 173, 210

Steeple Club 183, 186

Steggall, John Edward Aloysius 58, 153, 163, 167

Stevens, Robert 26

Stevenson, Andrew 142

Stevenson, Rea 147, 219

Stevenson, Robert Macauley 69, 177

Stewart, David 149

Stewart, John (artist) 9, 92

Stewart, John (collector) 19-20, 32, 36, 92, 97, 192

Stewart, John Anderson 92

Stirton, Robert 86

Strand, The 129

Strathmore, Countess of 27

Strathmore, Earl of 19, 43

Stuart, David F 187

Studio, The 61-62, 66, 147, 150, 158, 177

Sturrock, James 42-44

Suttie, Margaret 98, 177-178, 183

Tatler, The 139

Tattersall, John 118, 194, 197-201, 206, 224

Taylor, J Edward 132

Taylor, Rachael Annand 89, 214

Tayport 5, 7, 12, 68, 78, 89, 94, 105, 110-112, 115-116, 118, 120-121, 125, 127, 157, 161, 187, 189-190, 201, 223

Tayport Artists' Circle 5, 89, 110, 112, 114, 116, 120-121, 168, 186-189, 223

Thomas Justice & Sons 78, 198

Thomas Murray & Son 26, 51, 67-68, 84, 107, 114, 118, 121-122, 125, 176, 198

Thompson, D'Arcy Wentworth 7, 48, 61, 97, 163-167, 221

Thoms, William

Thoms, Patrick (Provost) 44

Thoms, Patrick (architect) 76, 149, 153, 220

Thomson, David Couper 125, 134, 139, 173, 218

Thomson, Isabella Lauder 161

Thornycroft, William 45

Thornton, Thomas 39, 46-47

Tissot, James 194

Titian 9

Tocsin, The 87, 135, 214

To-Day 128, 140

Town House 42, 59, 105, 115-116, 185, 212

Traquair, Phoebe Anna 57

T Richardson & Co 23

Troup, George Elmslie 192, 224

Turnbull, William 166, 221

Turner, Joseph Mallord William 14, 19

University Club 176, 185

University College, Dundee 4, 7, 15-17, 29, 44, 48-49, 52, 57, 61-62, 79, 82-83, 94, 97, 146-148, 152-153, 155-157, 159-170, 189, 199, 212, 219, 223

Urquhart, James 105, 165, 185, 205

Utamaro, Kitagawa 200

Valentine, Madge 164, 221

Valentine & Sons 8, 60, 82, 114

Valentine's Saloon 51

Vallance, William Fleming 12, 16, 34

van Berchem, Nicolaes 33

Van Dyck, Anthony 9

Van Gogh, Vincent 7, 51, 186, 198-199, 206

Vanity Fair 131

Vasari, Giorgio 51

Velasquez, Diego 9

Verlat, Charles 51, 63

'VHS' 135, 218

Victoria & Albert Museum – see South Kensington

Victoria Art Galleries (see also Albert Institute) 27-29, 36, 39, 44, 51, 59-60, 63, 81, 83, 87, 90, 96, 110, 112, 114, 116, 118, 120, 145, 160-161, 163, 165, 167, 175, 181, 190, 192-193, 197-198, 200, 204, 206, 222, 223

Victoria Road School 147, 151

Vine, The 33

Volunteer Drill Hall 10, 16

von Herkomer, Hubert (see also Herkomer's School) 39-40, 107, 204, 210

Vuillard, Edouard 186, 197-200, 206

Walker, Mary Lily 167, 221

Walker, Peter G 10, 16, 192

Wallace, Mrs David 224

Walton, Edward Arthur 98, 177, 182, 194, 196-197, 201, 204, 206, 223

W & D C Thomson – see D C Thomson & Co Ltd

Ward Chapel Mission Hall 82-83

Ward Road Baptist Church 84, 116

Wasp, The 132-133, 138

Watson, May 76, 79

Watson, Archibald 39

Watson, James 159, 185, 190

Watt, Archibald Anderson 202

Watt Institution 9, 15-16, 146, 219

Watts, George Frederic 48

Webster, George 44

Webster, James (artist) 223

Webster, James (critic) 32, 34, 36-40

Weekly News, The 115, 125, 128, 137, 217

Weekly Welcome, The 134

Weinberg, Isaac Julius 17-19, 36-37, 45, 173, 175, 177, 180, 192-194, 209

Weizenberg, August 36

Westbrook, Jessie 73, 75, 213

West End Academy 139

Whistler, James Abbott McNeill 4, 14, 24, 31, 88, 107, 110-111, 118, 132

White, Dyke 138

White, J B 133

White, James Martin 48, 63, 68, 82, 111, 170, 184-185, 200, 211, 219

White, John Forbes 27, 29, 190, 192, 208-209

Whyte, Miss 147

Wilkie, David 34, 92, 223

William A Scott's Fine Art Gallery 23-24

William Low & Co 197, 200

Willis, Emma – see Grieve, Emma

Willis, Marion – see Carmichael, Marion

Willis, Susan 79

Willison, George 37, 92

Willison Free Church 61

Wilson, A Ure 79

Wilson, David 134

Wilson, George 150

Wilson, Richard 32

Wingate, James Lawton 13, 27, 112, 175, 177, 197, 201

Winter, Richard Davidson 1, 50, 75, 102-103, 105, 115, 143, 173

Winter, William 50, 52

Wintour, John Crawford 15

Wizard, The 141

Wizard of the North, The (artists working on) 5, 21, 23, 29, 48-49, 88, 126, 129-133, 135, 138, 173, 179, 181, 217

Women Citizens' Association 183

Women's Freedom League 89

Women's Social & Political Union 88

Wood, Wendy 89, 214

Woodhouse, Thomas 149, 159, 219

Woodman and the Elves, The 80, 82

Woodville, R Caton 24

Wright, John 42,

Wyse, Henry Taylor 75, 82, 144-145, 167, 190, 219, 221

Wyse, James 62, 149, 219

Yeaman, James 38, 43, 92

Year's Art, The 192

Yeats, William Butler 77

Yellow Book, The 55, 140

Young, Charles 201

Young, Frank W 149-150

Young Men's Christian Association 48, 57, 61, 78, 135, 145-147, 150, 153, 155, 189

Yule, William 95, 110, 181, 193

Publications of the Abertay Historical Society

Currently in print

No 37   Michael St John, The Demands of the People, Dundee Radicalism 1850-1870. (1997)
ISBN 978 0 900019 33 3

No 39   Lorraine Walsh, Patrons, Poverty & Profit: Organised Charity in Nineteenth Century
Dundee. (2000) ISBN 978 0 900019 35 7

No 41   Ian McCraw, Victorian Dundee at Worship. (2002) ISBN 978 0 900019 37 9

No 42   Andrew Murray Scott, Dundee's Literary Lives vol 1: Fifteenth to Nineteenth Century.
(2003) ISBN 978 0 900019 38 7

No 43   Andrew Murray Scott, Dundee's Literary Lives vol 2: Twentieth Century. (2004) ISBN
978 0 900019 39 5

No 45   Annette M. Smith, The Guildry of Dundee. (2005) ISBN 978 0 900019 42 5

No 46   Mary Verschuur, A Noble and Potent Lady: Katherine Campbell, Countess of Crawford.
(2006) ISBN 978 0 900019 43 2

No 47   Kenneth Cameron, The Schoolmaster Engineer: Adam Anderson of Perth and St Andrews
1780-1846. (2007) ISBN 978 0 900019 44 9

No 48   Sarah F. Browne, Making the Vote Count: The Arbroath Womens' Citizens Association,
1931 945. (2007) ISBN 978 0 900019 45 6

No 49   Ann Petrie, The 1915 Rent Strikes: An East Coast Perspective. (2008) ISBN 978 0
900019 46 3

No 51   Matthew Jarron et al (editors), Ten Taysiders: Forgotten Figures from Dundee, Angus and
Perthshire. (2011) ISBN 978 0 900019 48 7

No 52   Susan Keracher, Dundee's Two Intrepid Ladies: A Tour Round the World by D.C.
Thomson's Female Journalists in 1894. (2012) ISBN 978 0 900019 49 4

No 54   Julie S Danskin, A City at War: The 4th Black Watch, Dundee's Own. (2013)
ISBN 978 0 900019 51 7

No 55   Catherine Rice, "All their Good Friends and Neighbours": The story of a vanished hamlet in
Angus. (2014) ISBN 978 0 900019 54 8

All publications may be obtained through booksellers, the society's website or by post from Catherine
Smith, Sales Secretary, Abertay Historical Society, Alder Archaeology, 55 South Methven Street,
Perth, PH1 5NX (e-mail: csmith@alderarchaeology.co.uk)

John Duncan respectfully invites
Henry Wyse Esq and Party
to view in his Studio, 3 Sea Wynd
Nethergate, a number of Italian
and other sketches, which together
with a collection of Richard D Winter's
etchings, will be exhibited there
for a few days   27/6/91.

"Independent & Individualist"
ART IN DUNDEE
1867-1924

Matthew Jarron

NUMBER 56
DUNDEE 2015